Y0-CCR-691

GUIDANCE PRACTICES AND RESULTS

EXPLORATION SERIES IN EDUCATION

Under the Advisory Editorship

of

JOHN GUY FOWLKES

Guidance Practices and Results

JOHN W. M. ROTHNEY
Professor of Education
University of Wisconsin

WITH THE ASSISTANCE OF

CAROL CARLSON, PAUL DANIELSON, PAUL DYBVAD, ROBERT HEIMANN, ROBERT JACKSON, HENRY KACZKOWSKI, ROBERT KEYES, ALBERT KRUEGER, PETER MERENDA, JOHN PUTMAN, ROBERT REMSTAD, PERRY ROCKWELL, JOHN SCHMIDT, LOUIS SCHMIDT, MARVIN THOSTENSON, DAVID SCHREIBER, PAUL THOMPSON

HARPER & BROTHERS, PUBLISHERS, NEW YORK

GUIDANCE PRACTICES AND RESULTS

Printed in the United States of America

D-H

Library of Congress catalog card number: 58-6136

It would not be too much to say that on the success or failure of our guidance program hangs, in all probability, the success or failure of our system of public education.

JAMES B. CONANT

CONTENTS

LIST OF TABLES

Chapter I

Chapter II

Chapter III

Chapter IV

Chapter V

Chapter VI

Chapter VII

EDITOR'S INTRODUCTION

Land to be beneficially productive must be fertilized and cultivated. Land left fallow harbors weeds, thistles, and thorns which plague the welfare of man. Effective fertilization of land demands an inventory of the nature of the soil revealing its chemical strengths and deficiencies as a guide for adding nitrogen or phosphate. Essential moisture, sunshine, fertilization, and cultivation together with soil conservation and rotation of crops provide an environment which makes land the source of life for both man and beast.

If this be true of land, how much more urgent and imperative it is that human beings be cultivated—developed. Ancestry, home, church, school, and opportunity to work are major factors in the optimum environment for the maximum development of men and women as well as of boys and girls. Full advantage can be taken of an optimum environment only if, as nearly as possible, a complete inventory of the capacities, strengths, and weaknesses of human beings is at hand as a basis for making what seem to be the best decisions and choices concerning study, work, and play.

Although in the last analysis each individual must work out his own salvation, i.e., decide for himself, intuitively a person at any age seeks the reaction, judgment, advice, suggestion, or recommendation concerning an important decision or action. Consequently, during recent years, an increasingly large number of counseling services has been made available from not only the school but also from professional commercial agencies.

The faith that not only high school students but at times even more so their parents put in these counseling services imposes an inspiring and frightening responsibility on those who counsel. This circumstance demands that counselors both exert every effort toward the development of the highest possible sensitive skill in their work and evaluate the results of their labors.

The work herein presented is an artful portrayal of what are generally accepted as the best practices in counseling. Further, it is a report of an attempt to discover the effect of counseling on students throughout high school as it is revealed in their lives during the five-year period immediately following graduation.

The author of this volume has long been recognized not only as an eminent scholar in the theory and techniques of counseling but, more importantly, as a generous, understanding, and effective counselor. Many years of pleasant and profitable association with Dr. Rothney as a friend and professional colleague make it an unusual pleasure to present this distinguished contribution to the professional counselor and to all those concerned with the fullest development of our high school students.

JOHN GUY FOWLKES

January, 1958

PREFACE

Counselors who are in preparation for work in schools get most of their professional preparation in courses that concentrate on various aspects of the guidance process separately. They take courses on principles, organization of guidance, testing, interviewing, observational techniques, and perhaps others on case studies and evaluation. The chief limitation in the offering of such separate courses is that the counselor-in-training may have some difficulty in seeing the guidance process as a whole. Study of the materials in this volume should assist students to avoid this limitation by seeing the processes as they have been applied longitudinally in secondary schools. In their reading of this book they will see the common and unique problems and concerns of high school students, techniques for collecting data about them, methods of putting the data to use in helping youth to help themselves to solve their problems, and procedures for evaluating the whole process by collection of follow-up data. They will see how the techniques, methods, and procedures described in this volume were actually tried out in what has come to be known as the Wisconsin Counseling Study.

The study was designed to set up a guidance program similar to those commonly provided in public secondary schools and to appraise its effectiveness. Evaluation was done by securing evidence about the development of all the individuals who were counseled at the end of their school careers and three times within the five-year period after they had obtained their high school diplomas.

It should be noted that guidance workers, since they are members of an educational team, must work for ultimate objectives similar to those of other educators, even though their procedures may suggest temporary variation from them. In appraisal of the postschool outcomes of high school guidance services, then, the results must be stated as they are in this book, in terms of the extent to which guidance has helped to meet the objectives of the American secondary school. In order to do so, a determined effort was made to create circumstances typical of those in which counselors are placed and to use methods commonly employed by secondary school counselors. The situations and methods were modified as they are in any good counseling situation by some new procedures, which are described. It is believed, however, that the situations in which the investigators worked were typical and that the methods employed may be used by conscientious counselors in secondary schools.

Particular emphasis has been placed on the follow-up procedure for evaluation, because guidance is the fastest growing of all services currently offered by public schools. When such growth in any educational practice occurs, the time must come for appraisal of its effects lest size be mistaken for value and claims be confused with results.

Many suggestions of methods for appraisal of guidance services have been offered but most fail to recognize that, since guidance is concerned with development of persons, appraisal procedures must attempt to determine whether development of individuals under guidance has occurred. And, since guidance is largely concerned with choices that individuals make among present and future actions, appraisal must deal with counselors' current and future performances.

The study covered a period of eight years. During that time the writer has become indebted to so many persons that it would be impossible to name them. Dr. John Guy Fowlkes, formerly Dean of the School of Education at the University of Wisconsin, made it possible for the author to arrange his schedule so that he could do the field work for the study, and Dean Lindley J. Stiles made similar arrangements so that the follow-up studies could be completed. All the subjects, counseled and uncounseled, have helped to set a new record for returns on follow-up questionnaires, and the 50 who permitted tape recording of follow-up interviews five years after completion of high school have been especially helpful.

Members of the faculties of the schools were particularly coöperative throughout the whole eight-year period.

Many graduate students have done much work on the study. Dr. Paul Danielson and Dr. Louis Schmidt, who assisted the writer in the counseling, deserve special mention. Some of the assistants who worked for longer periods than others are named on the title page. Dr. Paul Trump assisted in the process of getting post-high school data. Appreciation to them and to Mrs. Kathleen Rockwell for typing services are hereby expressed.

Financial assistance for the field work was provided by the Social Science Research Committee and the School of Education of the University of Wisconsin. Funds for the completion of the study were provided by the Public Health Service of the U.S. Department of Health, Education, and Welfare. The computing services provided by the Numerical Analysis Laboratory of the University of Wisconsin were particularly helpful.

Those who know about longitudinal research, regardless of their appraisal of its merits, will appreciate that many hours have gone into the planning, execution, and reporting of the study published in this volume. Many of those hours have been taken from those commonly reserved for family activities. To my wife and sons I express my appreciation for (as many of the subjects of this study would put it) "sweating out" the eight years that this longitudinal study has required.

JOHN W. M. ROTHNEY

Madison, Wisconsin
January, 1958

GUIDANCE PRACTICES AND RESULTS

CHAPTER I

Introduction to Guidance Problems

This is a report of an attempt to counsel students and to determine its effectiveness. Eight hundred and seventy students in all the sophomore classes in four representative high schools were distributed randomly into control and experimental groups. No counseling was provided for the members of the control group but the experimental subjects were counseled throughout their remaining years in high school. In order to determine the effectiveness of the counseling and to learn about the problems that youth and young adults meet in the process of coming of age, all of the 690 students who remained to graduate were followed up six months, two and one-half years, and five years after they completed their high school careers.

In this volume the practices used in the counseling and in appraising its effects are spelled out so that readers may see how they can be used, with local modifications, in their own situations. Since this is the first study in which intensive investigation of the practice and evaluation of counseling has been carried over a long period of time with such a large population, it is possible that more questions are raised than answered, but workers in counseling and related fields need to consider such questions if they are to accomplish the goals which they set up and which others expect them to meet.

In all the many definitions and descriptions of counseling it is implied that workers in the field must help youth to help themselves to solve their problems. Those problems may be classified as adjustment, social, personal, vocational, and educational, or they may be placed under any of many other headings. Regardless of the labels used, however, most writers about counseling imply that progress in the solution of young persons' problems may be made if youth are encouraged to discuss them with a counselor. There is little evidence that classification of problems actually aids in their solution or indeed that the process of counseling itself can be justified. Faith and hope rather than evidence of accomplishment are offered as justification for the offering of most counseling services.

In the hurried pace at which educators currently feel required to work, the practice of securing evidence about youths' problems by means of check lists, inventories, and questionnaires has become common. The instruments usually contain items that are thought to represent concerns of youth and they are categorized so that the figures derived from them can be manipulated quickly. The scores, profiles, or other numerical indices obtained from the instruments are then compiled and christened as the problems of youth that should be of concern to counselors.

There is, of course, a certain plausibility in the results that are obtained by such processes. Regardless of the many limitations of check list, questionnaire, and inventory methods they do disclose certain fairly general and partially valid categories of youths' problems. It is always found, for example, that there is a category on the family, another on health, still another on sex, and certainly one on choice of postschool training or career. It is this too general categorization, however, which has created chaos in the guidance field. It has resulted, for example, in the belief that the problems that have been classified can be solved by having youth discuss them in group meetings, in special weekly home room sessions, or in multiple counseling programs. The grouping of problems into categories has led to the notion that they are the same, or at least so markedly similar for each youth, that procedures that may help in the solution of one will necessarily assist in another. It has encouraged some educators to believe that formulas for solving them can be derived and used with all youth of the same general age and school level. It has also led many educators to think of guidance as a group rather than a personalized process and to reduce the number of opportunities for youth to discuss their *personal* problems individually with someone who has the qualifications and the time to work with them.

In the process of carrying out the study reported in this volume the writer and his assistants became very familiar with problems and plans that concerned each of the 347 high school youth who formed the experimental group. They learned about many of the situations that produced or aggravated their problems and about the various factors that prevented or limited the accomplishment of their plans. The problems, plans, and situations could be classified into broad categories but they seemed to be unique to each youth in the way that each had developed, the particular manner in which circumstance influenced him, and the way in which he reacted to them. In the following presentation of problems, for example, the heading of *family relations* is just a convenient label for a category. The items in it have in common only the fact that they seemed to stem directly (but uniquely for each youth) from his family circumstances. The reader will be aware that although the problems arose initially from the family situation, they did influence and were influenced by other circumstances.

The use of the words "problem" or "difficulty" in the following sections of this chapter may connote to the reader something that the writer does not intend. *The words as they appear here do not imply extremely serious, rare, or emergency situations that require single, drastic, and hasty treatment.* The samples given in the following pages are common and almost "normal" developments in the process of growing up. Their universality and similarity do suggest, of course, that opportunities to consider them should be provided in regular high school classes. Their individuality within the greater universality, their irregularity of occurrence in time, and their variability in intensity suggest, however, that *personalized* assistance must be provided.

VOCATIONAL PROBLEMS AND CHOICES

The thinking of the subjects of this study about vocational choices ranged from that of counselees who had "no idea of what I want to do after high school" to those who had made choices before entering high school, persisted in them throughout the high school period, and actually entered the occupation after they had been graduated. The range of interest in occupational choice extended from subjects who suggested apathetically that, "something will turn up" to almost neurotic anxiety about "choosing the right thing right now." Without forcing the issue or implying that a specific choice was desirable, the counselors raised questions at almost every interview about what the student planned to do after high school. This was done to remind the counselees that a choice based on self-analysis and study of available opportunities would probably be better than a hurried unconsidered one at the time of graduation.

In some cases where general post-high school training (as in a liberal arts course at college) seemed assured and suitable it was recognized that postponement of choice by some counselees until they had explored vocations further was highly desirable. In most cases, however, the selection of a first job or a place of training where he could start preparation for it was essential before graduation from high school. Although the multipotentiality of the counselees for achievement in many different kinds and levels of jobs or training was recognized, and the desirability of considering broad areas rather than specific jobs was acknowledged, it was essential that each counselee choose one in which to start. Thus a boy who wanted to enter the mechanical field was informed about many kinds of mechanical positions, but the time came when he had to find *one* specific opening in which he could begin work.

Samples of the kinds of activities that the counselors shared with their counselees, and illustrations of some of the problems they met are presented in the following paragraphs.

1. *Counselees were informed and encouraged to inform themselves about the advantages and disadvantages of occupational opportunities they had chosen, were considering, or should con-*

sider. The naïveté of high school students about occupations, even those well represented in their own communities, presented a real problem. Sometimes they knew very little about even their fathers' occupations.

2. *Counselees were encouraged to talk about their reasons for making the choices they had made.* As discussion of those reasons continued it was possible to recognize the influence of such factors as: ignorance of occupations, glorification of unusual vocations with high-sounding names, attractiveness of the remote, admiration of persons whom they liked but whom they were not like, pressures of ill-informed persons, lack of realism in considering themselves and opportunities, too high ambitions, morbid fear of failure, and many other factors.

3. *Opportunities for work experience, visits to places of business or training, and conferences with persons who could inform them about opportunities were discussed with the counselees.* Many took advantage of the opportunities, and the implications for each person were considered in detail.

4. *Attempts were made to broaden counselees' outlook about vocational opportunities other than those available in their particular communities.* Mere proximity of particular kinds of factories, foundries, and similar places of business caused some students to narrow their choices of occupations and to exclude consideration of opportunities not represented in their home towns.

5. *The counselors provided information and suggested methods for securing further information about training for advancement in an occupation.* Opportunities in short courses for youth who planned to farm, and vocational or adult school offerings for those who planned to enter trades and business were discussed with the counselees.

6. *Discussions about the advantages and disadvantages of apprenticeship training were held with many subjects.* The impatience of youth to be free and independent of adult supervision, and the desire to take a job that provided higher initial pay meant that the student often rejected the long-time benefits of apprenticeship so that he could take immediate advantages of the current

high rates of pay for unskilled labor. The fact that a particular occupation offered a good retirement or pension plan was of little concern to many youth. Retirement seemed so far off that they tended to ignore it as a factor in occupational choice.

7. *The implications of current economic conditions always needed consideration in vocational planning.* In 1950 and 1951, high prices for agricultural products made farming seem particularly attractive. At that time, too, jobs were plentiful and pay was so high that employment immediately after completion of high school seemed much more attractive to youth than several years in training with its consequent delay in drawing a pay check and getting an automobile.

8. *Many of the girls wanted only temporary jobs.* They were engaged to men who were serving in the armed forces and they wanted to work only until their fiancés were released from service. The occupations chosen, and entered immediately after graduation were stopgaps for which they had previously shown neither interest nor fitness.

9. *Required service in the armed forces affected the planning of many youth.* It was necessary for boys to weigh the possible effects of volunteering immediately, beginning a job and waiting for the military draft, or requesting that they be drafted as soon as they became of age. The pros and cons of each of these actions were discussed at some length with the counselees. The choices of girls who planned to marry boys who were so affected showed the influence of their indecision.

10. *Students who did not have enough financial resources to begin college developed plans for working their way through.* They needed to make decisions as to whether they should work a year before starting college, whether they could raise the funds by part-time and summer work while in training, or whether they should plan to work and study in alternate years. The advantages and disadvantages of such plans were discussed with each youth.

11. *Combinations of such factors as those mentioned above produced serious conflicts for many youth.* One boy reported in his senior year that he wanted to postpone or avoid military service, would like to go to college, and wished to marry soon after

graduation. His father wanted him to remain on the farm and, if he did so, he could be assured of early marriage and a good income. He might also get an agricultural deferment from military service. If he went on to college it might mean delay in marriage and probably postponement of military service. Since his father and fiancée were trying to influence his choice, and since many of his teachers were urging him to attend college, he wanted to talk over his dilemma with someone who could consider his problem without personal prejudice.

Such factors as those listed above seem to have produced the variability in vocational choices described in later chapters of this volume.

EDUCATIONAL PROBLEMS AND PLANS

Complete elaboration of all the educational problems that were met and the issues that were raised by the experimental subjects of this study is not possible here. A list of some of the general problems is given below with occasional elaboration. Reading of the latter will show that the grouping of problems under general headings does outline an area of concern, but does not indicate the nuances and subtleties involved, nor the real complexity of the problems that particular individuals faced.

Although there has been much discussion of educational guidance, it has never been made quite clear as to just what should be subsumed under that heading. Reports about educational guidance of high school students usually reveal that counselors are concerned primarily with helping them to decide whether or not they should elect college preparatory courses. And if the student does not propose to go to college, his choice among electives is often governed by what a counselor *thinks* may be a wise choice. If the counselee chooses cabinetmaking as a vocation, it is usually suggested that he elect woodworking, and if he chooses to go into mechanical work, the election of shop courses is encouraged. Actually the requirement for entrance into many such vocations is only a high school diploma without specification of high school courses. When a counselor suggests the election of specific courses, then, he is usually doing so on the basis of his *belief* rather than knowledge that the courses are *required* for particular occupations.

If a student has chosen the college preparatory course the selection of electives is rarely a difficult matter. Unless he wishes to enter one of the increasingly fewer colleges that require long lists of specific courses for matriculation, there is little restriction on students' choices.[1] If, for example, the student has definitely made up his mind that he will enter a certain college of engineering, the counselor must point out to him that specific sequences in mathematics are required. It is only in such relatively rare cases, however, that educational guidance, in the sense of selection of courses, can be specifically based upon stated requirements.

With the above statements in mind the reader may now look at a *sample* of problems in educational guidance that the counselors discussed with the members of the experimental group of this study.

1. *Selection among various broad curricular groupings offered by the schools.* Choice of one program from the college preparatory, business, trade, or general groups involved consideration of such matters as a student's post-high school training plans and the greater prestige value for parents and students of college preparatory courses.

2. *Selection among electives within or without broad curriculum groupings.* Here consideration was given to such matters as possible vocational and avocational values of courses. It was sometimes necessary to secure special permission to elect subjects generally limited to a curriculum group as in the case of a boy in the college preparatory program who wanted to take a machine shop course. It was also necessary to get permission for college-going students to take typewriting and to make special arrangements for the election of certain science courses that might be useful in armed forces experiences. Parents' insistence on certain kinds of training needed consideration. One farmer, for example, insisted that his son take only academic work in school since he

[1] A. E. Traxler and Agatha Townsend, *Improving Transition from School to College,* New York, Harper & Brothers, 1953.

thought he could teach him the practical aspects of agriculture and machine work at home.

3. *Arrangement for taking university correspondence courses that the school did not offer to meet specified requirements or to provide for a student's interests.* In the smaller schools where curricular offerings were limited, students were advised that they could take correspondence courses and get full credit toward graduation.

4. *Consideration of students' course loads.* Such factors as health, desire to finish school in less than the usual time, enrichment, opportunity to work for pay, correlation of work in the local vocational school, and participation in work experience programs were given consideration.

5. *Selection of courses designed particularly to prepare for marriage.* Several of the girls were engaged to be married soon after graduation and they wanted to elect combinations of courses that would prepare for homemaking as well as for the work they planned to do outside the home.

6. *Provision of special help with study habits or with difficulties in particular courses.* Occasionally the counselors helped students to work out study schedules and gave assistance with study technique as time permitted. Some counselees were referred to the services provided by the schools. In other cases conferences were held with the students' teachers.

7. *Arrangement of special summer courses or experiences.* These provided enrichment, permitted make-up work, or offered special preparation for a planned experience.

8. *Interpretation of educational data.* When data about test scores and educational records or requirements seemed necessary the counselors provided and interpreted them.

9. *Information was given about availability and methods of obtaining scholarships and other aids for post-high school training.*

Many of the problems that the students met seemed to be caused by the rigid, narrow, and antiquated curricular requirements common to American secondary schools. Such requirements are not likely to be changed for many years. Counselors who may not approve of them and who may be working hard to get them revised must still face the realities of their existence in working with counselees.

PERSONAL-SOCIAL ADJUSTMENTS

Solution of problems in the areas described above required the subjects to make adjustments, and hence it would seem almost unnecessary to add another category devoted to them. There are, however, some special problems that do not fit into those areas and that are commonly discussed under the heading of personal-social adjustments. In general they deal with youths' problems in getting along with other persons, particularly their peers. These do not fall into neat categories. If they are forced into such classifications for statistical manipulation, the categories cover up the fact that similarity of behavior does not mean equivalency. The following *samples* indicate some of the problems in adjustment that the counselors saw when they worked with the cross section of high school students that formed the population of this study.

1. *Some youth were extremely shy, reserved, and withdrawn.* They found it difficult to mix with other youth, to volunteer in class, or to offer their services for school activities. Many of them were unhappy, others seemed to be unconcerned, and still others were definitely worried about their lack of status in their peer groups. Some eagerly sought help in solving their problems, some tried out procedures planned coöperatively with the counselor, and still others rejected all invitations to discuss their problems.

2. *Some youth seemed excessively anxious to participate in groups.* One girl had so scheduled her time that she was free for only a few hours per week, "and then when I knit in those free hours I'm planning something else."

3. *Problems of grooming and related problems of presenting an acceptable appearance troubled many youth.* When this problem was considered with a boy the counselors used good grooming charts as a basis for discussion of the condition. The general procedure in the case of girls was to refer them to women teachers who were known to be interested in such matters.

4. *Development of strong interests and enthusiasms produced changes in usual behavior.* Some youth who had participated in many group activities withdrew to pursue new interests and sometimes the reverse of that situation developed. When the counselors discussed such enthusiasms and the possible outcomes of their pursuit a few students seemed to develop new personal insights.

5. *Some rural youth seemed never to become assimilated to city high schools.* Limited in opportunities to participate in extracurricular activities by having to meet bus and commuting schedules, they had few chances to make friends. For some of them school was not a particularly friendly place and they seemed to appreciate the opportunity to talk things over with persons who were interested in them. Plans for improving their situations were sometimes worked out during interviews.

6. *Violent temper tantrums resulted in difficulties for some students.* Momentary lapses that resulted in swearing at a teacher, refusing to follow instructions, criticizing school personnel publicly, and "walking out" on teachers seemed, at times, to bring consequences out of proportion to the behavior. Discussion of such events with counselors sometimes seemed to help the student.

7. *Outstanding performances in athletics, dramatics, music, and other activities brought special problems to some students.* The hero of the football team was seasonally in so much demand that his marks dropped but his ego-satisfactions were raised high. The leading lady in the school play enjoyed a brief period of high prestige. At times the letdown after a large buildup raised serious problems of adjustment. Occasionally jealousies that developed during competition produced very unhappy consequences. Many of the students who met such problems seemed to appreciate the opportunity to discuss them with the counselors.

8. *Some brighter students who could achieve high academic records did not want to earn reputations of being "greasy grinds."* In order to avoid them some tried to pose as regular fellows, and, in trying to do so, their behavior showed considerable variability.

9. *Physical development with consequent increase in masculinity and femininity produced problems for many of the subjects.* Although most of the counselees took their development in stride,

marked differences in behavior could be seen. Rejection of the feminine role by some girls and failure to develop masculinity by some boys produced reactions of their peers that ranged from indifference to rejection, and, in some cases, even to ridicule. Extremes in expression of the sexual role resulted in similar reactions by peers but occasionally it produced temporary periods of great popularity. Problems of sex were seldom raised by the counselees but there could be little doubt that they were present.

FAMILY RELATIONSHIPS

The items listed below are *samples* of problems raised by family circumstances that needed special consideration in counseling of the students and their parents. In some cases they presented difficulties that could be overcome by application of various techniques, but in others they seemed insuperable. Whether or not they were overcome, their effects on the attitudes of each of the youth were considerable.

INFLUENCE OF THE FINANCIAL STATUS OF PARENTS

1. *Some youth were required to contribute to the support of their families.* Their activities, performances, and plans were seriously affected by this situation. One boy, for example, was faced with the alternative of holding two part-time jobs or withdrawing from school to take a full-time job.
2. *Some families could not provide any financial support for post-high school training.* The youth who wanted to continue their education were forced to give up their ambitions or find a way to raise the money that was needed.
3. *Both parents in some families were employed outside the home.* Their children were forced to perform so many household tasks that recreational pursuits and academic achievements were seriously curtailed.
4. *Some rural parents kept students out of school for long periods to help with farm work.* The academic records of those students were low simply because they were absent frequently during planting and harvesting seasons.

5. *Some fathers held two jobs to support large families.* In some cases this situation placed heavy home responsibilities on their high school age sons and limited their educational and recreational pursuits.

6. *Stepparents refused to accept financial responsibility for their stepchildren.* One boy who found himself in this situation was required to pay for his room and board from the earnings of his part-time job.

7. *Some parents chose to spend limited financial resources for their own benefit.* One boy was deprived of the financial support that he had been promised for post-high school training when the parents bought a new automobile.

8. *Occasionally parents offered money rewards for their children's school accomplishments.* By doing so they encouraged students to get high marks by *any* means.

9. *A few parents gave their children too much money.* One boy who received generous allowances yielded to temptations to buy liquor and to engage in other nonacceptable activities.

10. *In some cases significant changes in the family financial circumstances seriously affected the students' plans.* One home that had been rated very high in socioeconomic status was reduced to poverty when the father defaulted on his financial obligations. The son, who had enjoyed considerable prestige, and who had made elaborate plans for training that required much financial support, found that the family was now in disgrace and his own plans impossible of realization. One student suffered because his father lost income as a result of a prolonged strike. Another was required to change his plans when the coming of a new baby required the use of money that had been saved for him. One student met new problems when his father entered bankruptcy proceedings and still another's attitudes were seriously altered when the family received a substantial inheritance.

11. *Irregularity in family income created uncertainties in the planning of some youth.* One girl was not sure that there would be enough money retained in September to send her to college, although there had been enough in the spring.

INFLUENCE OF HEALTH STATUS OF MEMBERS OF A FAMILY

1. *Prolonged illnesses of parents presented difficulties for several youth.* Some students were required to drop out of school, others' activities and performances were curtailed, and still others were required to change plans that had seemed to be sound at the time they were made.

2. *Alcoholism of one or both parents brought problems that were difficult for some students to cope with or understand.* They tended to think of their parents' alcoholism as disgraceful behavior rather than as a symptom of illness. They rejected their parents and sought to escape from unhappy situations by behavior that was disruptive rather than adjustive.

3. *Mental illness of parents brought feelings of shame to some students.* They did not understand its causes and they worried that they too might have inherited tendencies to mental imbalance.

4. *The illness of a father sometimes meant that the mother must work.* This condition sometimes brought serious disturbance of normal family routine and activities.

5. *Death of a parent usually meant the changing of a student's plans and the development of many new problems.* Plans that had seemed sound and fully capable of accomplishment needed revision. Sometimes it was necessary to abandon plans that had seemed to be very satisfactory.

INFLUENCE OF SOCIAL AND RELIGIOUS ATTITUDES OF THE FAMILY

1. *Some parents insisted that their children take their post-high school training in sectarian schools and colleges.* Despite the youth's preferences, the lack of particular curricula that he wanted, and even despite the cost, parental pressure to attend a sectarian college was sometimes so strong that the youth was forced to give up what had seemed to be well-conceived plans.

2. *Parents sometimes interfered actively with courtship and plans for the marriage of a son or daughter to persons of different religious beliefs.*

3. *Parents who had been financially successful wanted their children to reflect their own achievements.* They insisted that the child become socially prominent, attend the "right" college, and marry well. They interfered with their children's activities and attempted to regulate their choices. Sometimes they sought to achieve the goals they had set for their children by application of extreme sanctions. Extreme pressure by parents for their children's participation in certain social institutions and activities resulted in reactions ranging from attitudes of apathetic submission to violent rebellion. Some of these attitudes tended to become generalized toward all other organizations.

4. *Some parents made it very clear to their children that they did not trust them.* By constant surveillance of their activities, including even extreme invasion of privacy, they developed attitudes of suspicion, raised doubts in the youths' minds about their own competence, and unwittingly encouraged the development of deceitful practices.

5. *Sometimes two parents disagreed on disciplinary or regulatory practices that were to be used.* Caught in the conflict of parents' opinions, some youth felt insecure and resentful. Occasionally they rejected all parental counsel or control.

6. *Occasionally an "only" girl in a farm family was expected to do the work that a son might have been required to do.* In at least one case the girl resented the coercion and indicated her displeasure at home and at school.

INFLUENCE OF PARENTS' ATTITUDES TOWARD YOUTH

1. *One or both parents were sometimes oversolicitous about their child's progress.* Their strenuous efforts to assure high performance and acceptable behavior often produced embarrassment and conflict.

2. *Some parents neglected their offspring.* Seemingly unconcerned about their child's progress they provided little supervision, encouragement, or assistance. They became concerned only when the youth got involved in academic or disciplinary difficulties. Even in those circumstances the action they took was

just enough to clear up the current difficulty. When it was settled they reverted to their previous apathetic behavior.

3. *Some parents participated in the recreational, academic, or vocational interests of their children.* The range of participation extended from those who shared interests with their children and abetted their development to those who tended to discourage or prohibit any development of interests. One parent burned a manuscript of a story that her daughter had written. Another provided large sums of money for the development of a collection that interested his son. Still others studied about the subject of their children's interests so that they might participate jointly in it.

INFLUENCE OF PARENTS' ATTITUDES TOWARD VOCATIONS

1. *Some fathers were determined that their sons would enter their occupations and some mothers insisted that their daughters follow the vocations in which they had been employed before marriage.* When sons or daughters rejected the occupations chosen for them by either or both parents they were often subjected to pressures that made them depressed, confused, or apathetic.

2. *Some parents attempted to dissuade their children from entering their occupations.* In such circumstances they attempted to put obstacles in the way of a student so that he could not make his own choices.

3. *Mothers and fathers sometimes disagreed about the wisdom of a youth's choice of vocation.* The result was usually confusion and conflict at home. One boy wanted to be an actor, the father was determined that he should enter his plumbing business, the mother applied pressures to have him enter church work and the counselors thought that none of these three was a suitable choice. The mother's will finally prevailed.

4. *Some fathers provided special incentives to encourage their sons to enter into their occupations as partners.* By expanding their business enterprises, tendering tempting financial offers, and encouraging participation in the occupation while the youth was

in school (even at the expense of school attendance and performance), they induced the youth to become partners in their work.

5. *Strong father-son relationships sometimes brought subtle pressures on the son to enter the father's vocation.* Under such circumstances a son might resist all efforts to have him consider opportunities in, or fitness for, other vocations. Subtle pressures included such things as taking the boy on frequent hunting and fishing trips, to tournaments, and to conventions of members of an occupation. These were sometimes offered to the youth despite the fact that they required long absences from school.

INFLUENCE OF PARENTS' ATTITUDES TOWARD EDUCATION

1. *Some parents were willing to provide financial support for the post-high school education of their sons but not for their daughters.* One girl could not get a scholarship that she sought because it was awarded on the basis of merit *and* need. Since her family had considerable financial resources she could not qualify under the need criterion. Because her family did not approve of college for girls she was faced with the choice of giving up plans to go to college or earning enough to pay her expenses.

2. *Some parents were unwilling to provide support for the education of their children because they did not have enough faith in the value of education.* In some cases the parents encouraged their sons to leave school before graduation because they could not even see any value in obtaining a high school diploma.

3. *In some cases the parents had decided that at least one of their children, usually the youngest, must go on to higher education.* The one who was singled out was subject to strong pressures to comply, regardless of his own desires and interests.

4. *Some parents insisted that their child should undertake the same kind of training that they had undergone at the same institution.* The pressures they exerted to get the child to conform to their wishes sometimes resulted in serious disturbances for him. In some cases the student was willing and the parents' enthusiastic support was helpful.

5. *Some parents insisted that their child should not undertake the kind of training they had experienced.* The insistence resulted at times in rebellion, in reluctant acceptance of the parents' decisions, or in serious discord at home.

6. *Some mothers and fathers disagreed seriously about the kind of education their child should undertake in high school or after graduation.* The resulting conflicts produced some real problems for the students.

7. *Some parents applied punishments or rewards in attempts to get their children to do well at school.* At times their anxiety about school achievements brought serious problems to the student.

8. *A few parents went to ridiculous and even embarrassing lengths to assure their child's success in school.* Some parents plagued school personnel for special permissions and additional homework. Others attempted to curry favor or use their influence to raise their children's marks. At times their efforts produced effects quite different from those that had been anticipated.

9. *Some parents publicly criticized school practice and personnel.* Such behavior sometimes resulted in acceptance by the students of their parents' attitude toward education and they did not put forth their best efforts.

INFLUENCE OF LOCATION AND MOBILITY OF HOMES

1. *Some homes were attached to places of business.* In at least three cases the fact that the home was above or adjacent to certain buildings created irresistible diversions, temptations, and distractions for the student.

2. *Location of family homes seemed to influence some youths' choice of activities, occupations, and training.* A neighbor who was very successful, and who flaunted his success, influenced one boy to choose that occupation though it seemed to be particularly unsuitable and very unlikely of accomplishment. The availability of a small college campus within a block of his home made it seem particularly attractive to one youth, though it seemed that he might have profited more from going elsewhere.

3. *Families that moved frequently created some problems for their children.* Changes in commuting arrangements, the loss of part-time jobs, and changes in availability of companions resulted in alterations of behavior or performance.

4. *Some farm homes were located far from the high school.* Youth from such homes were required to spend as much as two hours per day on a school bus, and the lost time limited their activities. In some cases the distance from the school prevented participation in many late afternoon and evening activities sponsored by the schools.

INFLUENCE OF SIBLINGS

1. *A youth's plans were often influenced by his older siblings' experiences in employment, training, the armed forces, or in marriage.* These were often related at great length and with much feeling. Since they were of long duration and highly personalized, a sibling's experience often influenced the youth's planning more than any other factor.

2. *The presence of an older sibling in the home sometimes affected the future of a youth.* The eldest farm boy was usually expected to take over the family farm and a younger son was expected to seek employment elsewhere. Since farming was a venture that required large capital expenditures, some younger boys were required to reject agriculture as a career although they would have preferred not to do so.

3. *Illness of a sibling sometimes influenced a youth's plans.* The illness required such large expenditure of family funds that it was impossible for some youth to get financial support to implement their plans.

4. *The presence of accelerated or retarded siblings in the same grade and in the same classes occasionally affected achievements and behavior.* In some cases extreme competitiveness resulted and, in one situation, it produced such violent resentment that a youth dropped out of school.

5. *The behavior and performance of younger siblings were sometimes appreciated more than those of older children.* At

times this resulted in jealousy, resentment, and the feeling that the older one's merits were not appreciated. Occasionally satisfaction with the younger child's performance resulted in desirable reduction of pressure on an older child.

MISCELLANEOUS INFLUENCES OF FAMILY SITUATIONS

1. *The occupation of a parent sometimes made students unusually concerned about "correct" behavior.* In some cases it resulted in the feeling that the student could "get by" because of his preferred status.

2. *Some children of former teachers felt that their parents were overconcerned about school performances and behavior.* At other times, parents' knowledge of school practices and educational opportunities was particularly helpful in planning.

3. *Some youth whose parents were convicted of criminal activities met real problems in maintaining "face."* Increased sensitivity created by attitudes of others, and embarrassment from unfavorable publicity raised knotty problems for some youth.

4. *Some parents failed to challenge their children.* Occasionally a son knew that he would always be well received as the prodigal son and that the family would take good care of him regardless of misbehavior or failure. Having a "cushion" to rely on, he saw no need of striving to accomplish at a high level or of behaving in an acceptable manner.

5. *Family names sometimes caused embarrassment.* Unfortunate family names such as Backhouse or Harlot (these are synonyms of the names of two of our subjects) resulted in much teasing or ridicule by other students.

6. *Difficulties at the home sometimes made youth reject their parents.* One boy resented his father's immoral behavior so much that he decided to abandon his last name. He actually sent in his application to a university under another name.

HEALTH AND PHYSICAL HANDICAPS

The influences of family situations on the behavior and performances of youth have been spelled out in considerable (but not complete) detail to illustrate how they operate. If each of them had been operating independently and they could have been isolated and recognized, they would have been difficult enough for a counselor to cope with, even if he had unlimited time to work with his counselees. But problems seldom came singly. They were usually associated with other problems that arose at home or in school. Nothing short of complete case histories can ever portray the hazards that youth meet in the process of coming of age. *Samples* of the hazards that family situations produce have been given in the previous section. When one turns to the area of health he finds additional problems.

Descriptions of the health status of the experimental subjects of the study described in this volume were obtained from records kept in the schools and from interviews with the counselees, their parents, and their teachers. A summary of the health problems, made by tabulating the entries on the cumulative records, is presented in Table 1. Some of the subjects had several of the handicaps or problems, and very few of the total group reported that they did not have any. The categories used in the table do not always represent common medical classifications. The ones used here are descriptive of health problems as a nonmedically trained counselor must meet and deal with them. An appendix operation, for example, may mean only a short period of absence from school, but if it comes at a critical time it may loom up as a very important factor in the decisions a youth must make. A visual defect that can be corrected by the wearing of glasses is quite a different problem for the counselee than a pronounced squint. A persistent case of acne may be a matter of great concern to a girl who plans to be a waitress, but the common adolescent case of acne that clears up at the usual time may present only a temporary period of distress to the youth who has begun dating.

In addition to the health difficulties diagnosed and reported by competent medical personnel, the counselor must take into consideration health problems,[2] real or imagined, that students report. One boy, for example, claimed that he suffered greatly in cold weather. He wanted to sit near a radiator while he was in

TABLE 1. Numbers and Percentages of 344 High School Students Reporting One or More Health Problems and Physical Handicaps

Problem or Handicap	Number	Percent [a]
Wearing glasses	102	29.6
Serious skin blemishes (acne, boils, warts, scars, eczema)	34	9.9
Short-term diseases, injuries, operations (appendicitis, broken bones, chicken pox, mastoids, mumps, muscle strains, throat troubles, tumors)	33	9.6
Extended illnesses and injuries (anemia, diabetes, female troubles, hearing handicaps, hemophilia, kidney trouble, polio, ruptures, thyroid malfunction, tuberculosis)	28	8.2
Allergies (asthma, food allergies, hay fever)		
Physical difficulties	19	5.5
Severe dental problems	14	4.1
Back, ankle and joint difficulties	14	4.1
Minor ear troubles	13	3.8
Visual handicaps (not correctable by glasses)	12	3.5
Serious speech handicaps	9	2.6
Recurring headaches	6	1.7
(other than associated with other health conditions and including one migraine case)	6	1.7
Unclassified (car sickness, epilepsy, easily fatigued, posture problems, very unusual height or weight)	9	2.6

[a] Percentages do not total 100 because some of the subjects reported more than one of the conditions.

school and he felt that, since he wanted to do outside work, he would have to move to a warmer climate after he had finished high school. A girl who exhibited such violent temper tantrums at the beginning of each menstrual period that she had to be ex-

[2] See, for example, the cases of Nancy and Jim in J. W. M. Rothney, *The High School Student,* New York, The Dryden Press, Inc., 1954, pp. 160–178.

cluded from classes needed special counseling even though the medical report on her was negative. A student who wanted to enter training for the nursing profession but who had special food allergies needed more than the usual help in her vocational planning, and the girl with epilepsy who wanted to become a teacher required special consideration. In dealing with some counselees who had health or physical handicaps there was the special problem of use of their handicaps as alibis for not doing as well as they might. In other cases special treatment was required for those who were spurred on to extreme overcompensatory behavior.

The counselors were not specialists in the field of health but, as noted above, they were forced to be concerned with health problems during counseling. They referred cases to medical personnel or suggested to counselees that they seek professional advice. They informed teachers about some of the less obvious health difficulties of their students and considered procedures for making adjustments in their classes. They discussed the educational and vocational implications of health handicaps with counselees and others concerned.

PRINCIPLES GOVERNING COUNSELING PROCEDURES USED IN THIS STUDY

Now that the reader has seen representative samples of youths' problems, he may turn to consideration of some of the guiding principles that governed the actions of the counselors in helping the students to solve their current problems and developing methods of attack on those that might arise in the near future. Specific details about how these principles were implemented are given in Chapter III.

COUNSELING IS AN INDIVIDUAL MATTER

The foundation of counseling lies in the fact that there are *personal* problems to be considered; thus counseling must be concerned with one person at a time. It seemed that someone with well-defined qualifications and with a dispassionate but kindly interest would have to find time to help each youth to find his way in the forests of his own desires and the superimposed geography of social opportunities, rewards—and road blocks. It was felt that someone must be available to help each youth untie the psychological knots or release the tensions that came inevitably in the process of coming of age in America. The presence of a trained counselor was needed when important choices were to be considered so that the counselee might be helped to see the personal and social implications of his choices. And if there were hidden personal reasons that made it impossible for a youth to mediate between his personal performances and interests on the one hand, and the ramifications of social need on the other, someone was needed to bring out the issues so that they could be analyzed. One of the basic hypotheses of the study reported in this volume was that these things could be done by counselors who had time, patience, a reasonable measure of wisdom, adequate preparation for their work and who cared.[3] The counselors attempted to be wise friends who helped in the analysis of personal situations.

COUNSELING REQUIRES COÖPERATION OF MANY PERSONS

Actual counseling was done in interviews, but many persons contributed to the guidance process. As practiced in this study it began with an interview with a subject before any other data were obtained. This procedure was used so that the counselor would not prejudge the subject or be tempted to apply to the individual any generalizations that had been derived from group data.

As soon as the first interview was completed, however, data about the subject was sought from many persons and various sources. Teachers who had sufficient opportunity to observe a subject were frequently asked to describe (*not* rate) his behavior in their classes. Parents' descriptions of their children's behavior were sought and persons who were familiar with the subjects'

[3] One of the subjects of the study expressed this well in a follow-up report. She wrote, without prompting, the following statement: "I certainly appreciated the counseling I received. I love to talk to people and not have them *half interested* in me or laugh at my ideas but be *genuinely interested* in my future."

health status were consulted. Students' classmates volunteered information and occasionally other persons provided valuable data about the subjects.

The information was put to use in interviews with the subjects and in conferences with their parents or teachers. Without the coöperation of such persons in providing data and putting the results of the conferences into service of the student, much counseling seemed to be ineffective. Teachers who observed well, studied the data when it was pooled, and then did something about them helped many of the youth with their problems and plans. Parents who shared in the collection and interpretation of information about their children made possible the implementation of plans that could not otherwise have been carried out. For these reasons, then, the counseling that was offered can be described as a coöperative process. This designation does not imply that the core of it—the interview with the youth—could have been neglected, reduced, or its importance underemphasized.

COUNSELING IS A COMPLEX PROCESS

The originators of the guidance movement were primarily concerned with vocational guidance and, in its early stages, the concept of "putting the square peg in the square hole" was commonly accepted. Little consideration was given to the shaping of the peg or the hole. As the movement has grown it has been continually restructured as a result of the discovery of the depth and range of individual differences in all the characteristics of youth. Increased knowledge about occupations and methods of preparing for them, and acceptance by counselors of responsibility for assisting counselees with emotional and adjustment problems have brought increased demands on guidance workers. As restructuring proceeds, the counselor's task becomes much more difficult.

The problems that youth meet are seldom simple. Usually a number of circumstances, situations, personal factors, and particular pressures by grownups add complexities to what has seemed to some adults to be relatively simple matters. One boy, for example, seemed to be faced only with the problem of choosing between going to college or staying on the farm after high school graduation. Involved in his decision, however, were the following considerations.

1. He did like to study and was so successful in academic work that success in post-high school education seemed likely.
2. His parents were very domineering and when they insisted that he remain on the family farm after high school graduation he was afraid to protest.
3. He wanted to marry as soon as possible but thought he could not afford to do so if he were to go on to college.
4. He disliked the thought of military service and wanted to avoid it. If he stayed on the farm there was some possibility of an agricultural deferment from military draft and if he went to college an educational deferment seemed likely.
5. He considered going to the draft board to ask that he be drafted as soon as he came of age. In that way he thought he might complete his military requirement in minimum time and get support for his education under the G.I. Bill.
6. If he were to go to college contrary to his parents' wishes he could not expect their financial support, but military service might provide funds for a college education.

All these problems, and others, were involved in making his choice of a post-high school activity. A solution might have been achieved by concentrating on the choice with the hope that, once it had been made, his timid, hesitant and indecisive behavior would be corrected. The issues might also have been resolved by treatment of the personality difficulties in the hope that when they were cleared the vocational choice problem would be solved. In either case the counseling would be an involved and delicate process.

If the depth and strength of youths' problems are not fully investigated, they may seem puny to adults. And those who do not appreciate their complexity often propose that helping students with their problems is something that can be done by teachers while they are carrying out their other duties. The effectiveness of such methods has not been determined. It seemed to the counselors in this study that the problems of our subjects were so complex that their solution by accidental and incidental means was unlikely.

COUNSELING IS A CONTINUING PROCESS

Too often when persons think of counseling they think of dealing with emergency situations in which a problem has become so involved that the student comes voluntarily for help or is sent to a counselor by someone who recognizes that an acute problem exists. Good counselors do not wait until problems reach the acute stage. They are concerned with the *development* of youth and they are aware that, in the process, many problems must arise. They try to help youth to anticipate problems and to plan ahead so that they can be avoided or adroitly met.

In the study reported in this volume *all* the subjects were called in for introductory interviews. Although counseling should be a voluntary process, it was deemed advisable to make it clear to the students that counselors were available to help them to help themselves. Discussions in all the interviews dealt with current problems but they were also designed to encourage counselees to think about their choices of post-high school activities. All the experimental students were told that the counselors would be available for consultation during the next three years and they were invited to drop in to see them at any time. They were also told that, whether or not they chose to do so, they would be called in occasionally. In no sense, however, was counseling thrust upon them. If, when they were called in, they chose not to discuss their problems, they simply indicated that fact and the interview was terminated. This situation occured occasionally during the first, but never in the last year of the study.

At each session previous discussions and decisions were recalled and the student's cumulative record was considered. The continuity indicated in this practice made it clear to students and their parents that counseling was not to be a "one-shot" affair, that all decisions did not have to be made on the spur of the moment, and that solutions to current problems would depend in part on previous experiences and further developments.

Basic to the continuing procedure was the belief that significant changes in the counselee and in his opportunities might occur as he matured. In the interviews his record was considered as evidence of his development *up to that time* and his opportunities were considered *as they now appeared.* Possibilities of change in him and his situation were always given consideration.

COUNSELING SHOULD BE OFFERED TO ALL YOUTH

At various times and in various ways it has been suggested that counseling is something that should be offered to youth only under such conditions as these:

1. He is having academic difficulties.
2. He is at the point of transferring from one school to another or from school to a job.
3. He is likely to drop out of school.
4. He has become involved in violations of the law or of the regulations of an institution.
5. He has become a senior and must make a choice.

When counseling is provided only to students in the above situations, it must fail to meet the needs of all the children of all the people and must serve inadequately the few whom it attempts to serve. Those who grudgingly give a place to the counselor as a specialist in the schools usually suggest that he will be concerned primarily with deviant pupils. This view of a counselor's duties has been held by some persons for a long time and it has recently appeared again in the 1955 *Yearbook* of the Association for Supervision and Curriculum Development. On page 8 of the yearbook the following statement appeared.

> Some aspects of guidance must be separated from instruction for the reason that teachers are not especially trained or do not have the time to deal with them. The committee recognizes that there will probably always be some *deviate pupils* whose problems require the direct service of specialists of various sorts—problems with which teachers can deal unaided only at certain risk of being accused of operating as "quacks." It also recognizes that a considerable number of pupils have certain problems such as serious speech and reading

disabilities with which only specialized personnel are competent to deal. In the application of technical therapeutic techniques, the yearbook committee is confident that the undertaking should be in the hands of a person trained especially in psychology, guidance, and therapeutic work.

This restatement of the old concept that a youth should get help from a person trained in psychology and guidance only if he is sufficiently deviant reminds one of the old saw about locking the barn door after the horse is stolen. Preventive help is not to be given, the chance to talk one's problems over is to be denied until he is "deviant" or his difficulties are rather obvious as in the case of "speech" or "reading disabilities."

The counselors in this study believed that *every* student should have the opportunity to discuss his problems with persons who were trained in psychology and guidance. With the provision of that service it was hoped that many pupils might avoid later deviant behavior or serious difficulties. Furthermore, they did not attempt treatment of speech and reading disabilities because such duties seem to lie in the province of specialists in those fields.

Basic to the idea of counseling as it is considered in this study is the belief that to every youth there comes a time when he wants to talk things over at some length with someone who is neither a teacher, preacher, principal, nor parent. He wants to be heard by someone who is not by definition and title primarily a subject matter specialist, a moralizer, a boss, or a person on whom he has long been dependent. And he wants to talk things over even though he has not exhibited deviant behavior or suffered from serious difficulties. He wants to discuss his plans with someone who understands what is involved in youth's planning and who can, with as little bias as possible, consider the problems without time restrictions.

COUNSELING IS AN ECLECTIC PROCESS

At the present time there is no incontrovertible evidence that one method of counseling representative samples of American youth is better than any other. Claims have been made by many persons about the efficacy of certain methods of counseling, but they are based largely on faith rather than on demonstrated effectiveness. Many new practices have been introduced and accepted without adequate evaluation of the old and without adequate evidence of their superiority over methods previously used.

The use of an eclectic approach to counseling in this study was suggested by the lack of evidence about the effectiveness of any one method of counseling and by appreciation of the complexity, uniqueness, and variability of behavior within the individual and among groups. Thus, in the attempt to be eclectic the counselors listened until a youth who wanted to talk had finished. Sometimes he was encouraged to rephrase and reconsider what he had said. At other times, as when a youth seemed likely to fail to achieve something he sorely wanted (a scholarship, job, or elective position) because of rather obvious shortcomings on his part, direct approaches were employed.

When important issues were to be resolved the youth was usually encouraged to report the pros and cons of the issue as he saw them. The counselor often suggested additional considerations and, after they had all been brought together, the youth was left with the responsibility of making his own decision. When he found it difficult to do so the arguments were reviewed again and he was instructed about further sources of information or new approaches to his problem. When a decision was made, the counselor usually suggested that the counselee review the considerations to see if all factors had been considered. Many of the youth and their parents wanted to be assured that they had made the "right" decision. It was not possible, of course, to give such assurance but the excellence of their planning, or the lack of it, was subject to comment.

It should be noted that these youth were minors for whose actions the parents were legally responsible. They were also members of schools and communities and were subject to their rules and regulations. The youths' criticism of the actions of school personnel and parents were heard, but direct action that resulted in violation of school regulations or proposed illegal acts could not be condoned. The youth who chafed under regulations and restrictions was told why such regulations existed and was informed of the possible consequences if he should violate them. In some cases, he was definitely advised not to go ahead with plans that would certainly lead to trouble. Usually a substitute plan could be worked out with him.

A review of the counselors' notes on counselees' cumulative records at the end of the three-year period of the study revealed that the verbs listed below had been used freely.

interpreted	arranged	assisted	administered
discussed	demonstrated	complimented	listened
referred	encouraged	informed	suggested

These verbs were most commonly used in connection with the following nouns:

performances	electives	avocations	tests
requirements	health	sources	school-leaving
opportunities	vocations	appearance	records
			agencies

Examination of the words reveals the eclectic approach that the counselors used in their work with the youth. It became clear as the study progressed that the wide ranges of youths' behaviors, performances, adjustments, interests, and opportunities precluded the use of any single method. Even the development of rapport required the use of such diverse procedures as challenging the counselee directly, employment of homemade projective devices, counselor-centered sessions, and just listening until the counselee had talked himself out. The actual process of helping students to help themselves required almost as many approaches or variations of a single approach as there were individuals. The counseling in this study provided for no set number of interviews for each client and no specified number of minutes per interview. No attempt was made to hold to a consistent ratio of counselor-client participation or to any other application of any procedure to every case.

SUMMARY

In this chapter a *sampling* of the problems of a large representative group of youth in senior high schools has been presented. The description of problems has preceded a statement of six general principles that guided the counselors who tried to help the youth to help themselves to solve their problems. Before the reader goes on to examine details about the students themselves, the settings in which they were found, and the activities of the counselors, it would be well to review this chapter.

In his review the reader should keep in mind the fact that the listing of the several samples of problems separately does not indicate that they occurred that way. Few of the problems fitted into just one of the categories that have been employed. Family situations influenced educational performances, vocational choices and personal-social adjustability. Vocational choices created family problems where none had existed before and social maladjustments influenced educational performances. Relationships among such factors may be recognized by thorough study of some of the case studies that appear later in this volume.

The reader should keep in mind, too, that youths' problems and difficulties are not usually discreet events that appear suddenly and are solved quickly. Some are of long duration.[4] They have their roots in events that occurred many years previously and they continue for many years despite the best efforts of counselors who try to help students to solve them, to mitigate their effects, or to compensate when neither solution nor mitigation is possible. It is in recognition of the depth and complexity of the problems, and in awareness of the timing of changes in their influence on the behavior of specific individuals that the counselors can find clues for effective work with each client.

As our subjects increased in age, their problems frequently changed and increased in number.[5] Occasionally the solution of

[4] See C. V. Millard and John W. M. Rothney, *The Elementary School Child—A Book of Cases,* New York, The Dryden Press, Inc., 1957.

[5] This paragraph is taken from J. W. M. Rothney and B. A. Roens, *Guidance of American Youth,* Cambridge, Harvard University Press, 1950. Although this was written many years ago it applies as well now as it did at that time.

one problem brought others to solve. The student who, as the result of efforts by the counselors and teachers, had found that school work could be challenging was now faced with the problem of securing financial support for higher education—something which had not caused him any concern up to that time. The youth who had withdrawn from other students, and who had responded to the counselors' efforts to help him to overcome his fear of others, met a new problem when his enthusiasm for group activities resulted in neglect of school assignments. Changes in home situations such as those caused by the failure of a father's business, changes in health conditions, development of a new interest, and countless other factors, brought new problems so frequently that a case could never be closed. Finally, of course, there was the problem of the decision that all the subjects were required to make regardless of their original status—the decision concerning the choice of vocation, or the making of a plan for further education.

In the following pages an experiment in providing *personalized* assistance to help youth to help themselves in solving their problems is described. Since the kind of personalized service that could be offered was a function of the characteristics of the subjects and the circumstances in which they were found, the following chapter is devoted to descriptions of the youth and the locale of the experiment.

CHAPTER II

The Setting and Subjects of the Study

Selection of the high schools in which the study was to be made was influenced by the factors of geographic location, representativeness of Wisconsin schools, and willingness of the school authorities to participate in the study. Location was a determining factor because travel funds were limited and because the investigators were required to return frequently to the University to carry on their teaching duties. Representativeness in Wisconsin made it seem desirable to include two small town and two small city high schools, since these are common in this part of the country and because they yielded the size of population that the investigators could handle in the time available. Several schools met these first two criteria. Letters were addressed to their superintendents containing brief descriptions of the proposed research and requests that the writer be permitted to carry it out in their schools. All the superintendents were willing to coöperate and the schools that were most representative, and at the same time permitted the most economical travel arrangements, were selected.

LOCALE

The four communities in which the high schools are located are described below.

Community *W*, with a population of some 21,000, is situated in southeastern Wisconsin. It is an industrial city located near a large metropolitan area. Its chief products are gasoline motors, metal castings, aluminum steel sashes, air-conditioning equipment, beer, malted milk, and dairy products. Several health resorts are located within or near the city. Only 9 percent of the 1600 pupils in the high school came from rural areas. A small private college is located within the city limits. The city is known as one with a great deal of community spirit and one in which more than the usual cultural advantages and concern for youth are evident.

Community *X* in south-central Wisconsin, the largest of the four, has a population of some 30,000. It has 70 industries that produce chiefly machine tools, leather goods, burial caskets, refrigerators, canvas products, infant hosiery, and auto parts. Retail establishments depend heavily on the trade of those who reside outside the city. The community is reputed to be conservative in spirit, and city expenditures are kept to a minimum. Many parochial schools draw off large numbers of youth from the public schools.

Community *Y* is a town of some 5000 population near the capital city of the state. It is the center of a rich agricultural area, but its small industrial activity is centered around a foundry, a trailer fabricating company, a textile printing firm and several vegetable canning plants. The population, largely of Scandinavian ancestry, increased only 1 percent during the period between the census of 1940 and that of 1950. It is a town of many churches and it contains so many social, fraternal, and recreational organizations that it has frequently been described as "overorganized." Thirty-eight percent of the students in the high school commuted from farm homes.

Community *Z,* the smallest of the four, has a population of 3000 persons, predominantly of German origin. Located some ten miles from community *Y,* it is the center of a rich agricultural area in which the chief crop is tobacco. The storage of inner leaf cigar tobacco, the fabrication of trailers, and the making of shoes are the chief industries. The residents are active in social, civic, and community affairs, and the community offers more to its population than most towns of its size in this area. Approximately 40 percent of the high school youth came from farms.

A rather thorough comparison of these four communities in terms of the occupational levels of their residents in comparison with Wisconsin and the United States was done by Schmidt,[1] who used the population of this experiment in his study of realism of vocational choice. He used the data of occupational listings in the 1940 United States Census, which are divided into ten job categories in approximate descending order of average socioeconomic status of the workers.

To reduce the United States Census occupational categories into equal units for comparative purposes, Schmidt used a procedure devised by Kelley.[2] The values assigned by this procedure to each occupational category for the United States as a whole, the state of Wisconsin, and the four cities from which the subjects of this study were drawn are found in Table 2.

TABLE 2. Normalized Values for Occupational Categories for United States, Wisconsin, and the Four Cities of the Study (After Schmidt and Kelley)

	United States "a" values	Wisconsin "a" values	City *W* "a" values	City *X* "a" values	City *Y* "a" values	City *Z* "a" values
Professional and semiprofessional	1.98	2.06	2.06	1.99	2.26	2.27
Farmers and farm laborers	.98	.89	1.33	1.26	.84	.98
Proprietor, managerial, and official	.44	.24	.90	.83	.09	.33
Clerical and sales	.14	–.01	.54	.46	–.13	.14
Craftsmen and foremen	–.21	–.33	.01	–.02	–.36	–.22
Operatives	–.65	–.76	–.56	–.57	–.63	–.71
Domestic service	–.97	–1.05	—	—	—	—
Protective service	–1.10	–1.13	–.84	–.92	–.72	—
Service	–1.20	–1.28	–.93	–.99	–.77	–.97
Laborers	–1.80	–1.86	–1.52	–1.55	–1.37	–1.52
Mean "a" values	—	—	.11	.05	–.09	.04

[1] Louis Schmidt, *Primary Mental Abilities and Vocational Choice,* unpublished Ph.D. thesis, University of Wisconsin, 1949.

[2] T. L. Kelley, *Statistical Method,* New York, The Macmillan Company, 1924.

The averages of the "*a*" values are regarded as comparative scores descriptive of the general socioeconomic level of each group described. The mean score for city *W* was a plus .11, for city *X* a plus .05, for city *Y* a minus .09, and for city *Z* a plus .04. In this method of comparison a plus score indicates general superiority of the group compared to the United States as a whole and to the state of Wisconsin. It can be observed that three of the four cities of the study are slightly above the average in occupational classification level. The fourth, city *Y*, has a minus score of .09 which indicates that it is slightly below the occupational level of the United States and the state of Wisconsin.

In addition to the above indices of the general socioeconomic level of the cities of the study, an inference as to the socioeconomic level of the homes of our subjects can be made from examination of the occupation of their fathers. The percentages of workers in each of the occupational categories of the Census Bureau found in the United States at large, in the state of Wisconsin, and in the population of the study are listed in Table 3.

TABLE 3. Percentages of Fathers of the Subjects of the Wisconsin Counseling Study in Each of Ten Occupational Categories and the Percentages of Workers in Each Category in Wisconsin, and in the United States (Census of 1940)

Occupational Category	Percent of Population of United States	Percent of Population of Wisconsin	Percent of Fathers of Subjects of This Study
Professional and semiprofessional	.06	.05	.05
Farmers and farm laborers	.22	.31	.15
Proprietor, managerial, and official	.10	.09	.10
Clerical and sales	.13	.11	.12
Craftsmen and foremen	.14	.14	.23
Operatives	.18	.15	.15
Domestic service	.01	.01	—
Protective service	.02	.02	.01
Service	.05	.04	.03
Laborers	.09	.08	.16

These figures show that the subjects of this study come from a group that is fairly representative of both the state and the country in regard to their fathers' occupational classification.

In Table 4, the occupational classifications of the fathers of the

TABLE 4. Percentages of Fathers of the Subjects of the Study in Each of Ten Occupational Categories by Cities

Occupational Categories	City *W*	City *X*	City *Y*	City *Z*
Professional and semi-professional	.05	.06	.03	.03
Farmers and farm laborers	.09	.09	.38	.30
Proprietor, managerial, and official	.09	.11	.11	.08
Clerical and sales	.13	.13	.06	.07
Craftsmen and foremen	.27	.23	.13	.21
Operatives	.16	.19	.05	.14
Domestic service	—	—	—	—
Protective service	.02	.02	.01	—
Service	.03	.02	.02	.01
Laborers	.16	.15	.21	.16

members of the study from each community are presented. From these data it can be seen that the occupations of the fathers of the groups from city *W* and *X* are largely industrial, while those from cities *Y* and *Z* tend to be agricultural. The differences in overall comparisons of the socioeconomic levels of the members of the study and the levels of Wisconsin and the United States as a whole are not so great that the four communities can be deemed atypical of the United States and Wisconsin. Excepting those from large agricultural areas and exclusively metropolitan areas, the subjects of this study can be said to be representative of Wisconsin and much of the United States.

SOCIOECONOMIC STATUS

Indications of the socioeconomic level of the subjects were obtained by rating their homes. The method employed was proposed by Hollingshead,[3] who used it to rate the socioeconomic status of the subjects of his study of youth in a Midwestern city. It was possible to get an approximation of Hollingshead's data that permitted use of his rating method for our subjects. In his scale five classes of socioeconomic level are used to distinguish between the idle rich, wealthy professionals, average wage earners, poor but honest hard workers, and the downtrodden. A condensed but substantial description of these classes with a comparison of percentages of homes of our population and those in Hollingshead's study is presented below.

	Percent Wisconsin Counseling Study	Percent Hollingshead Study
Class I Inherited wealth. Accumulated invested wealth is typical. Owners of two or three cars. Leisure is dignified. Not more than two or three children per family. Church membership. Divorce is condemned. Social codes are strictly observed. Personal publicity is avoided. Education is highly regarded.	0.0	1.0
Class II Wealthy but wealth earned rather than inherited. Own the newest car. Country club membership. Two children per family. Active in church work. Both sexes active in civic organizations. Education is highly respected.	5.6	7.9

[3] A. B. Hollingshead, *Elmtown's Youth,* New York, John Wiley & Sons, Inc., 1949.

	Wisconsin (*Continued*)	Hollingshead (*Continued*)
Class III		
Half of men are self-employed or work for salary or wages. Women may work to supplement family income. Own their homes. Put up a "good front." Three to four children per family. Join many groups. Women are active in welfare organizations. Seek publicity. Not as well educated as those persons in Classes I and II.	29.6	37.5
Class IV		
Wage earners. Poor but honest. Hard workers. Earlier marriage, more children and less family stability than in top three classes. Not active in church or joiners of community organizations but men may be active in labor groups. Few are high school graduates. Likely to be skeptical of value of education.	62.5	46.9
Class V		
Meager income. Laborers. Sometimes irregular in employment. Live in slum areas and are often considered to be "scum" by members of other classes. They have many children. Religious ties are weak or nonexistent. They do not participate in community activities. Have frequent scrapes with the law. Families are unstable. Education is usually limited to the elementary school.	2.3	6.7

It will be observed that there are some differences in the percentages of homes in each of the categories but the comparison is not particularly important here. The figures show that none of the subjects came from the first class of homes and that less than 3 percent came from the kinds of homes that are typical of slum areas. Almost two-thirds came from homes of the third class, which is composed of what Hollingshead has described as wage-earning, poor but honest, hard-working people. Extremes of wealth and poverty were very rare.

MENTAL ABILITY TEST SCORES

Further evidence of the extent to which the subjects of this study were representative of students in Wisconsin high schools was obtained from comparison of the means and standard deviations of mental test scores of the subjects with those achieved by other students in the state. For many years the Henmon-Nelson Test of Mental Ability was administered in the tenth and twelfth grades to all the students in more than 95 percent of the public high schools in Wisconsin. In 1949 the procedure was changed so that the tests were administered in the freshman and junior years. The subjects of this study were among the groups who were given the tests during the changeover period, so they were taken in the tenth and eleventh grades. They were administered by the school personnel in the usual manner and according to the directions sent to all the schools that participated in the testing program. In Table 5 the comparison of our subjects' scores with those of more than 27,000 public high school students is presented. Examination

TABLE 5. Comparison of Means and Standard Deviations of Raw Scores on the Henmon-Nelson Test of Mental Ability of Students in Wisconsin High Schools and Students in This Study

Group	Year	Number	Mean	Standard Deviation
State of Wisconsin	1949	27,924	49.22	12.57
Wisconsin Counseling Study	1949	860	49.02	12.79
State of Wisconsin	1950	29,368	57.27	11.53
Wisconsin Counseling Study	1950	805	56.92	12.05

of the figures in the table indicates that the means and distributions of our subjects are very similar to those made by students in public high schools in Wisconsin.

THE HIGH SCHOOLS

The population of our study consisted originally of *all* the sophomores (tenth graders) who were enrolled in four high schools. In communities *W*, *Y*, and *Z*, grades 10, 11, and 12 were in buildings separated from the junior high, although some teachers taught classes in both the senior and junior high schools. In city *X* the junior and senior high schools were in different parts of the city, and since there was no overlapping of school personnel, entrance to senior high meant a complete change for the students in teachers and school facilities. The separation in the latter case also meant that the students encountered marked differences in the outlook on education held by members of the junior and senior high school faculties. Adjustment to senior high school presented more problems to students in community *X* than in the other cities.

Study of the curricular offerings of the schools presented in Table 6 indicates that they are representative of the schools in their area. The larger schools offered so many electives that the students were required to give more consideration to choice of courses. The absence of any core curriculum or of any experimental courses is noticeable. Schools *W*, *X*, and *Y* grouped their courses into the general areas of college preparatory, business, agriculture, trade, and general. Certain restrictions in electives were demanded for students who majored in those areas. Similar restrictions were in effect in school *Z*, although they were not stated so explicitly or so regularly enforced. The only subjects required of every student in the four schools during the senior high school period were two years of English, one year of United States history and three years of physical education. Biology in the tenth grade and a course in American or social problems during the senior year were the next most commonly required courses.

TABLE 6. Curricular Offerings of the Four Schools

	City *W*	City *X* [a]	City *Y*	City *Z*
Required courses:				
Grade 10:	English	English	English	English
		Geometry or arithmetic		World history
	Biology		Biology	Biology or algebra
	Physical education	Physical education	Physical education	Physical education
Grade 11:	English	English	English	English
	U.S. history		U.S. history	U.S. history
	Physical education	Physical education	Physical education	Physical education
Grade 12:	American problems		Social problems	English
	Physical education	Physical education	Physical education	Economics and social problems
		U.S. history		Physical education
Electives:				
	Commercial English	English	English IV	Creative writing
	Speech	Speech	English survey	
	Dramatics	World literature		
	Journalism			
	Debate			
	Latin	Latin	Latin	Latin
	Spanish	Spanish	Spanish	Spanish
	German	German		
	Science of aviation	Biology		Biology
	Physics	Physics	Physics	Physics
	Chemistry	Chemistry	Chemistry	Chemistry
	Arithmetic	Arithmetic	General mathematics	
	Algebra	Algebra	Algebra	Algebra
	Geometry	Geometry	Geometry	Geometry
	Trigonometry	Trigonometry		Advanced mathematics
	Solid geometry	Solid geometry		
	Senior mathematics	Advanced algebra		

TABLE 6 (*Continued*)

	City *W*	City *X* [a]	City *Y*	City *Z*
Electives:				
	Mechanical drawing	Drafting	Printing	Industrial arts
	Machine shop	Machine shop	Machine shop	
	Woodworking	Woodworking	Woodworking	
	General metals	Auto metals		
	Architectural drawing			
	Cabinetmaking			
	Blueprint reading		Home management	
	Home economics	Home economics	Home economics	Home economics
	Agriculture	Agriculture	Agriculture	Agriculture
	Art	Art	Art	Art
	Band	Band	Band	Music
	Chorus	Choir chorus	Choir	
	Orchestra	Orchestra		
	A capella choir		A capella	
		Music appreciation		
	World history	World history		
	Geography	Geography	Geography	
		Economics		Psychology
			Modern history	
	Typewriting	Typewriting	Typewriting	Typewriting
	Shorthand	Shorthand	Shorthand	Stenography
	Bookkeeping	Bookkeeping	Bookkeeping	Bookkeeping
	Clerical practice		Advanced stenography	
	Commercial law		Business practice	
	General business			
	Salesmanship			
	Business workshop			

[a] In school *X* students were required to carry two academic subjects each year.

To illustrate the choices offered to a student the program of studies from one of the schools is reproduced below. From it he was to choose his program for the following year. Since the subjects had made their choices for the tenth grade before the study was begun, and since two courses in the junior year and one in the senior year were required, our subjects were usually permitted to elect only five courses during the last two years of senior high school. In many cases, they had been told that college entrance requirements reduced the number of choices open to them. In certain programs, such as the commercial course, there was seldom more than one or two free choices left for the student, even though the list of electives seemed to be long and varied. In general the student was permitted to change from one broad area to another (from college preparatory to commercial, for example) but it was sometimes difficult for him to pick up the basic courses he had missed. Such difficulties often resulted in a student's decision to remain in an area despite his desire to change.

A mere listing of curricular offerings cannot portray a school. Many additional factors, such as adequacy of buildings and supplies, teacher competencies and attitudes, size of classes, community support for the schools, and general morale of teachers and students, must be considered. Since the writer, in the course of this study, spent three days per week for three years in the schools, it was possible to observe some of these factors. The following brief combination of statistical data and subjective comments is designed to give a general picture of the settings in which subjects of the study were found.

One of the schools had a staff of 14 full-time teachers supplemented by subject-field specialists who devoted part of their time to the junior high and elementary schools in the town. Although several teachers had been in the town for many years, there was a rapid turnover because many left to take positions in larger cities at increased salaries. A six-period school day with an additional supervised and very effective activity period following a hot lunch program presented splendid opportunities for the development of hobbies and skills in clubs or other informal groups. Students were generally, but not rigorously, classified into "ability" groups

TABLE 7. Program of Studies

Grade 10	Grade 11	Grade 12
English (required)	English (required)	English
Debate	Journalism	Commercial English
	Speech	Debate
	Debate	
Geometry	Advanced algebra [a]	College algebra [a]
(Algebra, if not taken in 9th grade)	Solid geometry [a]	Trigonometry [a]
	(Geometry, if not taken in 10th grade)	Senior mathematics
World history	U.S. history (required)	American problems (required)
Biology (required)	Chemistry	Physics
	Geography	Science of aviation
		Geography
Latin (Caesar)	Cicero or Virgil	Virgil or Cicero
(Beginning languages, if not begun in 9th grade)	German	German
	French	French
	Spanish	Spanish
Agriculture	Agriculture	Agriculture
Bookkeeping	Advanced bookkeeping	Office practice
	Typewriting	Typewriting
	Personal typewriting	Personal typewriting
	Shorthand	Shorthand
		Commercial law
		Business administration
		Salesmanship [a]
		Commercial workshop
Woodwork	Woodwork	Woodwork
Drafting	Drafting	Drafting
Machine shop	Machine shop	Machine shop
Blueprint reading		
Home economics	Home economics	Home economics
Vocational homemaking		
Band	Band	Band
Orchestra	Orchestra	Orchestra
Vocal music	Vocal music	Vocal music
Art	Art	Art

[a] One-semester courses.

based on scores achieved on a reading test administered in the ninth grade. The high school published an annual yearbook that was outstanding for a school of its size, but it did not have a school newspaper. A small ten-page mimeographed handbook about school regulations and curricular offerings was given to each student. Almost two-fifths of the students came from farm homes and the fine relationship between town and farm students reflected the generally good coöperation of their parents. Specialist guidance services had been directed by a person who taught or carried on other duties for half of each day and devoted the other half to guidance work throughout all levels of the whole school system. A remedial teacher served pupils at all levels and occasional use was made of psychiatric services available at the county seat. Observation of, and discussions with, teachers, administrators, and students indicated that general school morale was high.

One of the schools had a staff of 44 teachers who devoted full time to senior high school teaching. Several parochial schools attracted so many students that class size was small and teaching loads were light. The school had a six-period day composed, for most students, of four classes, one study hall, and one period of physical education. Students reported to an "advisor" for five minutes at the beginning of both morning and afternoon sessions. The time was used for checking attendance and making announcements. This session was sometimes called a home room meeting, but the five-minute period did not permit home room advisory activities. Many student clubs were listed, but they were generally inadequately sponsored and poorly attended. The Junior Girls Social Club, for example, met only once each year and the meeting was attended by less than one-fifth of the junior girls, although all were listed as members. The school yearbook and newspaper were significantly lower in quality than those produced by much smaller schools. A very brief mimeographed statement of curricular offerings was the only guide given to students as an introduction to school policies and practices. The hot lunch program was discontinued and students from rural areas or outlying districts were not supervised or offered any activities during the lunch period of one and one-half hours. Specialist guidance services were offered by two deans who had two periods each day to devote to guidance *and other activities*. No attempt was made to give any group guidance other than a career day whose program emphasized college attendance and entry into the professions. A minimum testing program was carried out but no use was made of professional, remedial, psychological, or psychiatric services. The faculty was composed largely of elderly persons who had remained in their positions for many years despite their lower-than-average salary schedule. Low morale was indicated by their frequent complaints, feuds, and unwillingness to continue professional training. The faculty did not meet regularly. Emphasis in the school was placed on college preparation, and those boys and girls who did not plan to continue education beyond the high school level were given scant attention. The course failure rate was high, the drop-out rate was disturbing, and the morale of the students significantly below that of the other schools. It was almost impossible, in a part of the state where enthusiasm for high school athletics was very high, to get out enough students at the games to make up a cheering section.

In a third school a staff of 15 full-time teachers was supplemented by some who devoted part of their time to the junior high school. There was a six-period day. A 20 minute home room period was supposedly given over to group guidance, but it was actually used for a study hall, for making routine announcements, collecting funds, or completing other housekeeping duties. Mimeographed sheets containing curricular offerings and statements of school policy were given to the students annually. A highly organized and vigorously supported club program was offered and only a rare student avoided involvement in one or more of the activities. The school annual and newspaper were considerably better than those commonly produced in schools of this size. The hot lunch and noon activity programs were well supervised and much appreciated by the rural students who composed almost half of the student body. The teacher turnover rate was high because many of them moved up to cities where salaries and other opportunities were greater. They participated freely in faculty meetings and school or community projects. Their morale seemed to be high despite the fact that the school building was crowded and obsolete and the low per capita wealth of the town population provided only minimum supplies and equipment. An excellent ninth grade group and individual orientation program made the tenth grade students more aware than those in the other schools of educational and vocational guidance problems. Specialized guidance services were provided by a "director of guidance" who had two periods a day free from teaching to carry on guidance throughout all levels of the school system and such other duties as attendance officer and general assistant to the principal. Some use was made of persons trained in remedial or psychological work and of the county psychiatric services.

Many members of the staff of 89 teachers in the fourth school taught at least one course in the junior high school adjacent to the senior high. They commonly taught five classes per day, supervised a study hall or a student activity for one period, and had one hour free. Classes were large, and crowded conditions limited the activities of the teachers, but they and the students cheerfully made the most of an unfortunate situation in the belief that a new building would soon bring relief. A 50-page handbook describing policies and practices of the school was revised frequently enough to keep it up to date and useful to new faculty members. The staff consisted of a corps of teachers with many years of experience, but there was enough turnover each year to provide new stimulation. There was very little experimentation within the curriculum, but the trial of a work-experience program and some experiments in student-faculty planning of school affairs by the use of student commissions indicated that attempts at progress were being made. Many student activities were encouraged and the excellent school newspaper, annual, literary magazine, dramatic offerings, musical performances, displays of art and industrial arts projects, and other products of the students' activities attested to the vigor with which they were pursued. The morale in this school was unusually high.

The guidance program in this school had received much attention but the personnel to whom the duties had been delegated had never been given enough time to carry them out effectively. The following description of it, taken from the handbook for teachers, is presented to indicate the intention of the school.

Director of Guidance and Placement

The title of Director of Guidance has been officially established and one man placed in that position. He has five periods per day to devote to this position. A strong committee will work with him to carry on the widespread work of guidance. This committee, under his leadership, has the opportunity of becoming of ever increasing importance to the school administration. It is to be understood that the responsibilities given to the Guidance Department will be accompanied by corresponding authority to carry out the necessary plans.

1. *Specific duties and powers*

   a. To plan and execute the work of Educational and Vocational Guidance.

   (I) Meet with Guidance Committee appointed from the staff, special field counselors, class advisors, home room teachers and a student guidance commission as is necessary to help plan the entire guidance program. Some of the activities to include orientation, Theme of Guidance per grade, testing, subject elections, counseling, etc.

   (II) Supervise the functioning of the class advisers in securing the pupils' election of subjects and of revisions made necessary because of changes due to any cause.

   (III) Encourage the development of group guidance in the heads of all departments in incorporating guidance material into classrooms. Heads of departments may call upon the director and his committee to help find suitable material for class group use.

   (IV) To help the entire faculty through bulletins, pamphlets, or teachers' meeting to incorporate guidance techniques into the classroom.

   (V) To develop a plan for individual counseling. The director will hold his own conferences and is empowered to send individuals to other staff members to counsel. All members should have much to contribute and do contribute much good advice to students. The director may investigate the special abilities of staff members with the idea of making the individual contributions more significant.

(VI) To study maladjustments of students. All maladjustments and disciplinary problems are to be reported to the class adviser or the director at once. The guidance workers are not to enter the disciplinary field, but may be able to advise with the disciplinary agents and the pupil because of their misunderstanding of that pupil. They may help in preventing a growth of trouble.

(VII) Assign the Guidance Committee a regular meeting date and hour.

b. To plan and carry through follow-up studies as they seem necessary or desirable. The committee should then make recommendations as to curricular changes that seem advisable in the light of continued findings.

c. To plan and carry through placement of high school students and graduates in job positions.

It was most unfortunate that time was not given for school personnel to carry out the program. Interest in guidance was high in both the school and the community and the annual senior career night was one of the outstanding events in the city.

THE SUBJECTS OF THE STUDY

It was from the schools described above that the subjects of the study were chosen. *All* of the 870 sophomores in them were subjects of the study. They were split up into an experimental group whose members were counseled and a control group who were not given any counseling.

In a previous publication [4] this investigator has discussed the problem of securing adequate control groups for experimentation in the study of human beings and particularly in the field of guidance. It was pointed out that experimenters are usually ex-

[4] J. W. M Rothney and B. A. Roens, *Guidance of American Youth,* Cambridge, Harvard University Press, 1950, pp. 111–119.

pected to have a control group if they are to get under the panoply of scientific respectability. The common practice is to set up control groups by matching individuals or groups on the basis of a very few factors such as age, school grade, and intelligence test score and to assume that similar groups have thus been obtained. In the study of growing human beings such an assumption is simply naïve. There is much evidence from studies of human behavior that indicates that early experience influences subsequent behavior, but the evidence is usually overlooked when control groups are set up. Christie[5] has shown that neglect of the influences of preëxperimental experience of animals is one of the reasons for the frequent inability of experimenters to obtain comparable results in similar experiments with rats. And the problem is very much more complex with growing human beings than with rats because of the greater diversity of human experience. Examination of Table 8 indicates that there are no important differences between the subjects of our control and experimental groups in terms of chronological age and test scores. Examination of the conditions under which our subjects were living and had lived as they are outlined briefly in Chapter I, and in the appended case histories, suggest that one cannot be safe in assuming that they are really comparable groups except in socioeconomic status, schools attended, chronological age, and the performances sampled by the tests.

The factors that influence the behavior of an adolescent are legion and, in a sense, the patterns of factors are unique for each individual. No two of our subjects had the same home conditions. Even those who came from the same home had different environmental experiences since the older one of the pair had a younger sibling and the younger one an older brother or sister. No two of them had the same problems in school, in the choice of education, or in selection of a vocation. No two could have had the same experiences out of school or was likely to profit from them to an equal extent. No two had the same facility in dealing with academic materials either in classes or on tests, regardless of the fact

[5] R. Christie, "Experimental Naïveté and Experimental Naïveté," *Psychological Bulletin, 48*:327–339, 1951.

that they happened to make the same total scores on the sampling of performances obtained. Even the same chronological ages of two persons do not guarantee any similarity in any other characteristic.

In setting up control groups the experimenter usually employs controls on several obvious and readily available variables and then assumes (or perhaps just hopes) that he has obtained some comparability in his groups. The too ready carry-over of the controlled study technique from the laboratory, the agriculturist, and the animal psychologist seems not to give enough consideration to the complexity of human beings.

A study of the kind described in this report could not be as controlled as a tight laboratory experiment simply because the behavior of the subjects was not subject to any regulation outside of the counseling sessions. Actual school hours constituted less than 25 percent of these subjects' waking hours, and many forces beyond the school were operating during the out-of-school hours. Even within the time spent at school, diverse factors were affecting behavior. When all the factors that can influence behavior are considered, it seems presumptuous to believe that a few hours of counseling, spread over a three-year period, could have any effect on an adolescent's behavior. It certainly cannot be compared to the influence that an animal psychologist can exert upon the behavior of his subjects by use of cages, arrangement of feeding schedules, and even 24 hours per day of manipulation and observation. Nor can counseling be compared to the work of the psychologist in the laboratory who is working on, say, the conditioning of an eye-blink. Although these differences cannot be denied by anyone who has thought about them, there is a tendency to neglect them and to fail to distinguish between laboratory experiments and field studies carried out in normal situations. The choice between an artificial laboratory type of study and an experiment in a natural setting can be made by an investigator. When he makes the decision to do the latter, he should not be expected to meet the standards that are suitable only for the former. Field studies of human beings can never use control group methods as rigorously as they can be used in the laboratory.

Interpretation of results obtained by control group methods must always be tempered by awareness of this limitation.

Despite all the limitations of control group studies noted above it seemed desirable to use experimental and control groups to see whether those who were given counseling would differ from those who were not with respect to the criteria described in the reports on follow-up studies presented in Chapters V and VI. In making the decision it was accepted that we would not be dealing with groups that were equivalent except in the sense that the averages and distributions of their scores and ratings were as nearly identical as possible. The control and experimental subjects of this study are *similar* in socioeconomic level, attend *similar* schools at the same grade level, and are of *approximately* the same average age. The basic question that the study attempts to answer is simply whether a group of such students who are given additional counseling of the kind described in the next chapter will behave differently with respect to the specified criteria from a *similar* group who did not receive such counseling. It is recognized, of course, that the subjects of both groups received much counseling from parents, teachers, and peers. *The difference here is that the experimental subjects received counseling over and above that which persons in the control group could have obtained.*

Before the actual experimental and control groups could be set up, a few of the original group of 900 sophomores had transferred from or dropped out of school. Examination of the school records indicated that some of the students who were listed as sophomores had accumulated enough credits so that they could almost be classified as juniors, and they were dropped from the list of subjects for the study. At the time the experimental and control groups were set up there were 870 beginning sophomores in the four schools.

Various methods might have been used to distribute the 870 subjects into a control group whose members were not to be counseled and an experimental group whose members were to get counseling. The classical method for comparison studies in educational and psychological research involves the use of "matched pairs." This method had been used previously by the investigator in a study of counseling.[6] It required manipulation of such variables as intelligence test scores, measures of socioeconomic status, and previous school marks until pairs of subjects were matched. It was found that pairs so "matched" were quite different simply because the process of matching subjects in eight factors could not cope with the complexity, dissimilarity, and instability of human beings. It was also noted that the method tended to ignore inner thought processes, the use of language in other than test situations, and countless other influences that might operate to make individuals significantly different despite their seeming likeness. These limitations of the "matched pair" method seemed to be so serious that the method was rejected for the current study.

It would have been possible to use a "fishbowl" technique to distribute the subjects into control and experimental groups. This procedure is similar to the one used in selecting draftees under the first peacetime draft law of 1940. At that time numbers assigned to possible draftees were put in steel capsules, which were placed in a giant bowl. The capsules were mixed and impartial blindfolded persons drew them out. All possible precautions were taken to obtain a chance selection, but as Parten [7] has pointed out, the mixing was not as thorough as it might have been, and the failure to secure randomness was evident in the published lists of numbers drawn. To avoid the possibility of this error, and because there seemed to be a better way, the fishbowl technique was rejected for this study.

The table of random numbers procedure might have been used but it has its limitations. Kendall [8] and Babington-Smith [9] have demonstrated by checking published tables of random numbers against mathematical tests of randomness that the tables do not

[6] J. W. M. Rothney and B. A. Roens, *Guidance of American Youth,* Cambridge, Harvard University Press, 1950.

[7] M. B. Parten, *Surveys, Polls, and Samples,* New York, Harper & Brothers, 1950.

[8] M. G. Kendall and B. Babington-Smith, "Randomness and Random Sampling Numbers," *Journal of the Royal Statistical Society, 101*:147–166, 1938.

[9] M. G. Kendall and B. Babington-Smith, "Second Paper on Random Sampling Numbers," *Journal of the Royal Statistical Society,* 6:51–61, 1939.

meet the tests. Tippetts' Table of Random Numbers,[10] perhaps the most widely used of all tables, does not pass all the known tests for randomness. And there is always the possibility that any *single* set of random numbers may not produce a random sample.

If all the proper precautions had been taken, however, it might have been possible to use any one of the methods noted above to get two samples and thus have met the condition of randomness, "that every individual in the population would have the same probability of being chosen." Both were rejected simply because, though each might have guaranteed randomness in the selection of our groups, neither would guarantee the selection of two samples representative of each other.

Some researchers have recognized the limitations of so-called "pure" random sampling and have devised techniques that give more assurance of obtaining both randomness and representativeness in their samples. It has been noted that, in some cases, depending on the arrangement of the source list from which the cases are to be drawn, the drawing of alternate names gives a better sample than lottery drawing. It precludes the chance of drawing a poor random sample, which is unlikely to (but can) occur with the lottery technique. If the names of the subjects are listed alphabetically, and there is no known or even suspected direct or indirect relationship between the names and the problem to be studied, the sample that is obtained by drawing every other name may be considered a random sample of a population.

In selecting our groups we drew up master lists of all the sophomores in each of the communities by alphabetical arrangement of their last names. The first name on the list of subjects was put in the control group and second name was placed in the experimental group. This process was repeated until each subject was in either the control group or the experimental group for *his community.* The decision as to whether the first name on the list would be put in the experimental or control group was determined by the flip of a coin. Since the first name in the first town was put in the control group, that practice was followed in the

[10] L. H. Tippetts, *Random Sampling Numbers Tracts for Computers,* No. XV, ed. Karl Pearson.

other three communities. The only exception to the strict placing alternatively in control and experimental groups occurred when twins or siblings were in the sophomore classes of the schools. In such cases both were put in the same group because it was felt that a counseled twin or sibling might influence the other and the work that was done with the parent of one twin might affect what the parents would do with the other.

The results of the process of distributing the subjects into control and experimental groups will be seen in Table 8. The distribution indicates that the girls exceeded the boys by 14 and that

TABLE 8. Distribution of Subjects by School, Group, and Sex

	Experimental Group		Control Group		Total	Total	
	Boys	Girls	Boys	Girls	Boys	Girls	Total
City *Z*	21	13	17	15	38	28	66
City *Y*	33	22	30	29	63	51	114
City *X*	73	75	78	72	151	147	298
City *W*	88	111	88	105	176	216	392
Total	215	221	213	221	428	442	890

two more cases fell into the experimental than in the control group. The slightly greater number of girls agrees closely with the national distribution for ages 15 to 19 according to the United States Census of 1940, which shows that there are more girls of those ages despite the birth rate of 105 boys to every 100 girls. The difference of two cases in the size of the experimental and control groups is attributed to the twin and sibling distribution noted above.

As suggested above, any procedure for setting up control and experimental groups in a study of this kind has some limitations. It would stretch the laws of probability to assume, with only 870 subjects, that *all* the factors that influence behavior of a group of adolescents would, in effect, cancel out so that the groups were equivalent. It is possible, however, to show that they are similar with respect to age and to such short, simple, and highly structured samples of behavior as one can get from standardized tests.

In Table 9 the means and standard deviations of the scores of the control and experimental subjects on chronological age and six test scores are presented. No attempt has been made to estimate the significance of the differences reported in the table because the

TABLE 9. Chronological Ages and Test Scores of the Experimental and Control Groups at the Beginning of the Study

Measurement	Group	Number [a]	Means	Differences in Means (E-C)	Standard Deviations	Differences in S D (E-C)
Chronological age (months)	Experimental	432	184.23	–1.17	7.26	–1.09
	Control	428	185.40		8.35	
Raw scores on Henmon-Nelson Test of Mental Ability	Experimental	432	49.66	1.32	11.98	–0.58
	Control	428	48.34		12.56	
Primary mental abilities (raw scores)						
Verbal	Experimental	430	23.99	1.31	8.28	–0.33
	Control	431	22.68		8.61	
Space	Experimental	432	18.89	–0.60	11.73	–0.42
	Control	431	19.49		12.15	
Reasoning	Experimental	432	15.88	0.40	5.70	–0.28
	Control	429	15.48		5.98	
Number	Experimental	432	19.87	1.04	8.24	0.58
	Control	430	18.83		7.66	
Word fluency	Experimental	432	35.75	1.25	12.28	0.52
	Control	432	34.50		11.76	

[a] Differences in numbers are the result of exclusion of some cases whose birth dates had not been verified at the time of testing and to some test papers so badly marked that they could not be scored.

groups were drawn from the same sample and they are not independent. For those who insist on tests of significance, however, the following figures are given. The differences between means of chronological age, standard deviations of the Henmon-Nelson test scores, and the PMA scores are significant at the 5 percent level. The difference between standard deviations of chronological age was significant at the 1 percent level. All other differences are insignificant. The differences in means of test scores are all less than 1.5, and five out of six are positive. All differences in standard deviations are less than 0.6 and two out of six are positive. With differences of this size on tests of this kind it appears that our groups are similar enough for the purposes of this study. It would be difficult to maintain, in view of what is known about the relationships of test scores to vocational choices, educational performances, and social adjustments, that the small differences in test scores indicate any important advantages of one group over the other.

The average difference of one month in age of the control and experimental subjects is also unimportant. Decisions about educational, vocational, and social problems are not, at this level, a function of differences in one month of chronological age. All four of the differences in the table seem to be of the chance kind that can occur when large numbers of cases such as we have here are distributed on bases other than the measurements used in Table 8. For the purposes of this study, then, we may say that we have *similar* groups with respect to chronological age and particular standardized test scores. It is not claimed, for the reasons previously given, that these experimental and control groups are identical in any respect. It just seems, in view of the methods used, that they are likely to be similar with respect to the problems that would be met in their counseling. Claims for identity of human beings presume too much and lean too heavily on the long arm of coincidence.

Some additional indications of the similarity of the control and experimental groups were obtained from some tabulations required in carrying out one of the incidental researches on the girls in the study. In Table 10 distributions of the family circumstances of the girls in the study who remained to graduate are presented. It is obvious that there are no important differences between the groups with respect to the parents, stepparents, or relatives with whom our subjects were living.

The educational levels of the parents or stepparents of the *girls* in the study are indicated in Table 11. Examination of the figures

TABLE 10. Family Circumstances of the Girls in the Wisconsin Counseling Study

Family Circumstances	Number Experimental	Number Control
Living with both parents	145	142
Father deceased, living with mother	9	7
Mother deceased, living with father	3	5
Father deceased, living with remarried mother	7	10
Mother deceased, living with remarried father	5	7
Parents divorced, living with one parent	8	7
Parents separated, living with one parent	3	2
Living with relatives	3	3
Total	183	183

presented there reveal no really important differences. The greater number of high school graduates among the parents of the experimental group seems to have been compensated for, in part, by the number of parents of the control group who had some college training. In both groups it should be noted that more than half of the parents were not high school graduates.

TABLE 11. Education of Parents of the Girls of the Wisconsin Counseling Study

Educational Level	Mother's Education Number		Father's Education Number	
	Experimental	Control	Experimental	Control
Elementary school	64	60	79	77
Junior high school	12	3	6	7
Some high school	33	49	28	40
High school graduate	27	8	27	7
Special school training	9	8	8	7
Some college	12	21	10	17
College graduate	13	12	7	5
Advanced degree	1	0	2	1
Total [a]	171	161	167	161

[a] For 34 mothers and 38 fathers it was not possible to get accurate information. In some cases their education had been obtained in foreign countries and it was difficult to assess American equivalents. In others, queries brought such vague answers that classification could only be very uncertain.

From the figures in the two tables above it is clear that neither the control nor the experimental group was superior to the other in terms of the marital status of the parents or the levels of education they had achieved.

At times throughout this report on the study, and particularly when the results are examined, all the subjects in the control or experimental groups are placed together regardless of the city in which they lived. Heimann [11] explored the clustering effect of the intraschool homogeneity as it might affect the between-school differences in a random sampling of the whole group while he was making a study of individual consistency of the subjects of this study. By use of procedures developed by Marks [12] he found that there was no violation of the effects of intergroup differences when the test scores of the subjects in the four different schools were treated as if they had come from one. His investigation indicated that it would be appropriate to combine the subjects from the four schools for the purposes of, and in the manner in which such combinations have been used, in the study.

It will be observed from the description of the methods used in setting up the two main groups that control and experimental subjects attended the same school in the same city and it will be inferred that there would be some "contamination" of one group by the other. Evidence of it was not difficult to find by interviews and observation. A counseled boy who was pleased with the process brought in his control-group friend to get the same attention and it took considerable tact to avoid counseling him and, at the same time, to keep enough rapport with him so that he would respond to follow-up requests after completion of high school. But he *had* been "contaminated" by his friend. The investigator even observed an experimental boy with his arm around a control-group girl while off on an evening's excursion and it was assumed that some "contamination" might have resulted. Counseled parents probably contaminated some of their bridge-playing cronies and

[11] Robert A. Heimann, *Intra-Individual Consistency of Performance in Relation to the Counseling Process,* unpublished Ph.D. thesis, University of Wisconsin, 1952.

[12] Eli Marks, "Sampling in the Revision of the Stanford-Binet Scale," *Psychological Bulletin, 44*:413–434, 1947.

contaminated teachers may have done occasional counseling of control-group cases.

The only way in which such contamination might have been avoided other than by use of the animal psychologists' technique of 24-hour surveillance would have been to choose the control and experimental subjects from widely separated communities. That, however, would have required that the communities, and particularly the schools in them, be enough alike to warrant the assumption that similar factors had in the past and were currently influencing the subjects of the study. When the dangers of matching communities and their schools were arrayed against the dangers of the kind of contamination noted above, it appeared that the latter was the least perilous of two dangerous alternatives.

SUMMARY

In this chapter descriptions of the original subjects of the study have been presented and the communities and schools in which they were found have been described. Procedures for setting up the control and experimental groups have been outlined. It has been suggested that the subjects were representative of the students who attend public high schools in Wisconsin and in parts of the United States other than in large cities. It has been indicated that half of the subjects were to be counseled, that a similar half were not to be given any special counseling, and that the subjects would be followed up into their post-high school careers so that the differences between them could be assessed. In the following chapter the procedures used in the study are described.

CHAPTER III

Methods and Procedures

In this chapter the techniques for collecting data about the subjects of the study are presented in considerable detail. It will be observed that many methods were used, that not all of them were employed for each of the experimental subjects, and that the frequency and intensity with which a procedure was used varied from individual to individual. It becomes apparent immediately that this study is not a single-variable experiment in which the treatment of the experimental subjects is given to the same extent and in the same way to all the subjects. The single-variable procedure was not employed because the investigator believed that counselors must recognize individual differences and attempt to adapt and modify procedures to fit the person. If this premise is accepted it cannot be concluded that any set of data-gathering devices or treatment will be used uniformly in counseling. And this premise did direct the procedures used in this study. If the reader prefers not to accept it he will not approve the methods employed and may choose not to read further. The writer and the reader may come to the parting of the ways at this point with the reader perhaps insisting that the scientific method has been violated.

If the scientific method requires automaticity in dealing with humans and denies freedom to the experimenter to adapt to individual differences that persons exhibit, express, and reveal, the method must be rejected or adapted. In this study, use of an aspect of the scientific method *has* been made in the setting up of control and experimental groups, but general similarity rather than equality is claimed. Further application of the scientific method in a study of counseling in the form of automatic application of identical procedures to every individual, regardless of his characteristics and problems, could not be condoned.

GENERAL DISCUSSION OF PROCEDURES

The procedures described in the following pages reflect the point of view held by the investigator. The difficulty one meets in stating a point of view on counseling has been well described by Arbuckle.[1] The semantic confusion that occurs when persons attempt to define counseling as shown in these words: "despite a certain rapprochement, counselors still tend to think of counseling all the way from the broad, all-inclusive omnibus definition which makes counseling and guidance practically synonymous, to the much narrower concept of counseling as being synonymous with psychotherapy." But the difference does not stop there. Some persons have made counseling a group affair, others suggest that it can be a catch-as-catch-can procedure that teachers carry on in their spare moments, and still others consider it something that must be done only with subjects who have serious problems.

The writer has indicated the point of view that lies behind this study several times in different contexts. While the study was in progress he wrote that, "In the process of coming of age in America there are times when every youth wants to 'talk things over' with someone who is neither parent, preacher, principal, nor teacher." [2] At the same time and in the same place he said that, "mass procedures, no matter how well intentioned, must fail to accomplish the objectives of education unless they are supplemented by adequate attention to the individual." Later he indicated that, "In a country in which the individual is considered to be so important, surely some time in his school career can be used

[1] D. S. Arbuckle, "Our Semantic Wonderland in Counseling Theory," *Personnel and Guidance Journal, 32*:160–162, November, 1953.

[2] J. W. M. Rothney and B. A. Roens, *Counseling the Individual Student,* New York, The Dryden Press, Inc., 1949.

to give him personal attention." [3] In such statements, and in the discussion surrounding them, the writer was trying to suggest that counseling should not be limited to problem children or to those with serious disabilities, and that it should not be just an incidental part of a teacher's duties. Counseling by a specialist, he suggested, should be provided for every student. He indicated that provision for it would still be necessary even when the educational millennium came and all teachers were well trained, vitally interested in their pupils, and had small enough classes so that they could know their students well.

The arguments in support of this view are many even though the research evidence is scant. All students have problems even though they may not be aware of them, and one of the tasks of the counselor is to raise questions that the youth, because of his lack of experience, may not have thought of asking of himself. Many students reveal during counseling a lack of knowledge about themselves or about educational, vocational, and social opportunities. As students increase in age their problems and questions frequently change or increase in number, and when the answer to one of their queries is obtained it may raise new questions. And, regardless of whether the secondary school student has questions or problems implicit or hidden, there must always be need of consideration and reconsideration of problems in selection of occupations or post-high school training. These are some of the basic reasons why it appears that adequate counseling should be provided for all students. They are the reasons, too, why all the experimental subjects of this study were called in and given an opportunity to talk about their problems and plans. Counseling was not thrust upon them but they were informed that it was available.

It is frequently implied that teachers can assume responsibility for the counseling in addition to, or associated with, their other duties if the student shows no serious problems or disabilities.[4]

[3] J. W. M. Rothney, *The High School Student: A Book of Cases,* New York, The Dryden Press, Inc., 1954.

[4] See, for example, *Guidance in the Curriculum,* Association for Supervision and Curriculum Development *Yearbook,* 1955.

Apart from the common objection that teachers are not well enough prepared to counsel, there is the further objection that a youth may be literally torn apart by his many teachers who are all well-intentioned but who collectively confound his confusion. Teachers will not usually bring to the student, as counselors can, a comprehensive view of the educational scene (because they are specialists), its vocational outcomes and possibilities (because of the necessary limitation on learning about other vocations while in teacher training or in teaching), a large view of the social and domestic circumstances of each case (because they have so many pupils to meet), and the time (because they have many other duties) to put these things together so that the student and his parents may make suitable choices.

It is sometimes said that, if counselors are available, teachers may feel free from responsibility for meeting student needs. The implication of such a statement is, of course, that the effectiveness of teachers will be reduced if students are given additional help by a counselor. Such a statement, besides condemning the members of the profession by implying that they will take the easiest way, fails to recognize what good counselors do in addition to the interviewing of problem pupils. Counselors are aware that an antiquated narrow or rigid school program and a teaching staff that fails to do its job can make much of their work futile. In their efforts to help students to help themselves, counselors will be continuously working with teachers in devising programs that attempt to meet student needs. By discovering needs that were not known to exist and by bringing them to the attention of teachers in a broader and more personalized context (since he has used his skills and time to clarify them in terms of particular pupils) the counselor may bring a better concept of needs of students to their teachers and in a way that is likely to result in action. The fact that these things can be done has already been demonstrated in an experimental study.[5]

That counseling should be provided for *all* students by a specialist who has had time and skill to bring together an assembly

[5] J. W. M. Rothney and B. A. Roens, *Guidance of American Youth,* Cambridge, Harvard University Press, 1950.

of marks, scores, and observations about each student and to interpret it to him and to others was the basic point of view of the writer when this study was begun. It should be noted that it was his *belief*. Although there appeared to be little evidence to support it, there seemed to be none to refute it. The effectiveness of providing counseling for all students of the kind and in the situations described in the previous chapter had never been adequately evaluated, and one of the major purposes of this study was to make such an evaluation.

Although the methods used in the study were determined in large part by the concept of counseling held by the investigator, they were supplemented from other concepts derived from previous research by others. They suggested that it would be unwise, in view of the evidence about the complexity of human beings, to adopt only one method for exclusive use. They also suggested that the eclectic method might be most useful, since it made use of as varied a methodology as seemed to be needed to collect the data about each of the individuals and to put them to use in helping them to help themselves with their problems and plans.

In making decisions about methods of collecting data, certain criteria to govern the process were used.[6] They had been described previously by the investigator. These criteria, with a brief statement about them, are presented below.

Criterion 1. *Any datum about an individual that assists in the understanding of his behavior must be given due consideration.* The emphasis in this criterion is on the use of the word *any*. An investigator using this criterion will seek his data in many different places and by various methods. He may set up minimum lists of data that he wants to get on every subject, but beyond that minimum there are no restrictions. *He will be looking for what seems important to the particular individual he is studying even though it may be of no concern to any other member of the group.* After certain basic information about all the subjects has been obtained, the process of collecting data will become an individual affair. The effect of the application of this criterion may be observed throughout the study.

[6] Rothney, *Counseling, op. cit.,* pp. 48–65.

Criterion 2. *The culture in which the individual is reared must be thoroughly examined.* In this study it was not always possible to make as thorough an examination of the cultural settings as the investigator would have liked, but consideration of the counselee as an "individual in a situation" was always attempted. Recognition of the mores, economic circumstances, and social pressures influencing the counselees was attempted in every case. Much of the work with school personnel, parents, and community members was directed toward that end.

Criterion 3. *Longitudinal data must be used in the study of the individual.* The period of time devoted to this investigation did not permit the collection of enough longitudinal data to permit the development of a completely adequate pattern of behavior for each counselee. It was long enough, however, to permit the discovery of the usual behavior and level of performance of many individuals. Data on school performance for four years were obtained and supplemented by three-year records of test performances, participation in activities, choices of careers or training, health, and as many other factors as could be obtained. The longitudinal data made possible various studies of the consistency and variability of our subjects with respect to several important characteristics.

Criterion 4. *Conceptualization must be continuous as each separately evaluated datum is added in the study of the individual.* Those who heed this criterion will avoid the error of generalizing about a subject too soon on the basis of incomplete data. The classification of the subjects of this study on information obtained in its early stages was studiously avoided. At the end of each of the first two years the investigator went over the cumulative folders of the experimental subjects and made some very tentative judgments about them and their plans, but as new data were added, the tentative judgments were often revised. The collection of additional information by various means provided new insights into what had originally seemed to be difficult problems. New conceptualizations sometimes required that the subjects be counseled in a manner quite different from what the previously obtained data had suggested.

Criterion 5. *Any datum about an individual that is to be used in his counseling must be appraised in terms of its accuracy and economy.* Acceptance of this criterion fully would mean that evidence about the reliability and validity of every data-gathering device would be required and that the selected devices would be those that provided the most dependable data at least cost. Unfortunately the validity and reliability of some of the instruments described later in this section cannot be determined. The usual methods for assessing reliability, for example, cannot be applied to interviews or personal documents. And sometimes an invalid instrument may still provide useful data for counseling. (An autobiography, for example, may be written to deceive the reader, but the fact that deception was attempted is a valuable piece of information.) It was not always possible, therefore, to assess the validity and reliability of all the sources of information used in the study, and the investigators weighed the lack of evidence on these factors in using the data.

The problem of economy was raised many times during the investigation. It will be noted later that *all* the subjects were interviewed during the first year. It would certainly have taken less time to administer a questionnaire to all of them. But could the same rapport, the same understanding of the subject, the same information about the outstanding characteristics of the students, and the same statements of the students' problems and plans have been obtained? The investigators were faced with the problem of trying to get much information either by time-consuming interviews or by mass-questionnaire methods. They chose the former after weighing the probable outcomes of both methods in terms of amount of time required to get them.

As far as possible, the procedures in the collection of data were determined by the five criteria described above. It is recognized that other investigators might set up and be guided by different or additional criteria or even make different decisions about the use of certain techniques, while accepting these criteria. Since, however, these five are the ones that guided the investigators in this study, they should be kept in mind while reading descriptions of the methods used and the results obtained.

THE WORKING CONDITIONS

In addition to a description of the methods used in the study the reader should know about certain conditions under which the work with the students was carried out. The conditions which presented limitations, and in some cases produced strengths, are described below.

The investigators were free from teaching duties only three days of each week and their time had to be apportioned to the four schools in approximate proportion to the size of their populations. The fact that the investigators were itinerant proved to be a disadvantage in that they were not always in the right place at the right time for their counselees. Returning to a school after a week's absence they found sometimes that an event of importance to a counselee had occurred and action had been taken without the counsel that *might* have resulted in a different course of action. At times this may have been beneficial to the student. At others it may not. It is for this reason, for example, that no conclusions are drawn in this study about the relationship between counseling and drop-out rate. It seemed that more dropouts might have remained in school if the counselors had been present at the time that a student made his decision to leave, but there is no evidence to that effect. Since the counselors were itinerants, their opportunities to know the subjects, their parents, teachers, schools, and communities were not as great as they would have liked. This lack of complete familiarity must be considered in the interpretation of the results of the study.

The fact that the investigators came from the state university may have compensated in part for their itinerant status. One of the investigators bore the title of Doctor and there was no doubt that the title had an initial prestige value greater than that held by faculty members of the high schools. Maintenance of the prestige depended, however, on performance rather than title. The assistants in the study were known to have advanced status in the field of guidance and this, too, had prestige value with high school students and their parents. Whether this prestige compensated for the counselors' absences at times when important decisions were made could not be determined, but both must be considered in the appraisal of the conclusions.

Since, by the design of the study, the counseling was done by the investigators, questions must be raised about the extent to which they could do the kind of counseling and data-collecting that high school counselors can and do carry out. It has been indicated that one of the investigators held a doctor's degree. The assistants had completed their masters' degrees in guidance and had studied beyond that level. It might be inferred that they would be better informed and more capable of carrying on counseling activities than those who usually counsel in high schools. The only statement that applies here is that the investigators *tried* to do what they believed good high school counselors would do under similar circumstances. The belief was based on reading about counseling and on their observations of it. They may have occasionally exceeded the level at which they aimed, or fell below it, but it seems unlikely that they departed significantly from the fluctuations in performance that any counselor might undergo.

The investigators attempted to become regular staff members of the schools. They attended faculty meetings when they were in the school, led some meetings in discussions of guidance or curricular problems, attended the usual school assemblies and social functions, and even participated in faculty decisions on school policies. Although they were frequently called upon as consultants to school personnel on such problems as the selection of tests and the use of cumulative records, they were probably not called upon more than a regular counselor in a school would be. The fact that they did not have unusually high status in the schools was attested to by the fact that some of their recommendations were rejected.

Since none of the schools had a satisfactory collection of materials about occupations and training opportunities, the investigators were required to carry a collection of references and pamphlets with them. Some of the schools began to prepare similar materials, and as time passed it was possible to introduce a student to some references and to suggest that he continue their study in the files of the school. Testing and other equipment, such as the homemade projective devices described later in this chapter, completed the investigators' traveling kits. Additions to them were made as circumstances required.

Since the investigators were very much concerned about getting complete follow-up returns after the subjects had completed high school, many attempts were made to publicize the idea that there would be checks on the students' post-high school performances. The investigators accepted and even sought invitations to speak to parent-teacher groups, service clubs, and other community gatherings. At such meetings some of the basic problems in guidance were raised, the procedures employed in the study described, and the intent to follow up the students was emphasized. Arrangements were made to have pictures of the investigators inserted in the school newspapers and annuals. Statements of their intention to follow up the subjects for at least five years were repeated frequently. The effectiveness of these procedures is evident in the responses to follow-up studies.

It has been suggested that the working conditions for the investigators were very similar to those that high school counselors commonly meet, except for the fact that the investigators were itinerant. The procedures employed were the kind that are commonly recommended for use by such counselors, and the usual feelings of having insufficient time to do a thorough job were present. In general, the application of the procedures seemed to be near the level that one would expect from high school counselors.

With this background of procedures and working conditions the reader may now turn to examination of the following specific year-by-year reports of the counselors' activities.

ACTIVITIES OF THE FIRST YEAR

As soon as registration was completed and school routines had been established, the writer and an assistant [7] began their work in the schools. They planned to see each of the 870 sophomores

[7] Dr. Louis Schmidt, then a graduate student in guidance and now Associate Professor of Education at the University of Indiana.

during the first year of the study and, until the control and experimental groups were set up, they called in students in alphabetical sequence for interviews. Since it was not known which of these pupils would become control or experimental subjects, the interviews were exploratory and very brief. The student was informed of the purpose of the study and of the plans of the investigators when he was given the following mimeographed statement.

To Pupils in the Guidance Study

The tests and interviews which you are going to take, will help us to help you to find out the things that you can do best. Because of the competition which exists in the world of work today, it is important for you to find what your abilities are in order to develop them to your best possible advantage. As a result of all these tests and interviews we hope to be able to advise you about various kinds of work and study. It is also our purpose to aid you in learning more about your own strong points and to help you to make the best of your opportunities.

We hope that you will do your best on the tests which are given to you. Remember that they have nothing to do with your school marks. You may now ask any questions about the work.

The following statement appeared on the reverse side of the statement above. The subjects were asked to read it and to take it home to their parents.

To Parents of Students in the Guidance Study
(To be taken home by the student)

The purpose of this study is to help you and your children find out the things that they can do best, and to encourage their development along those lines to the fullest extent possible. This is done by a careful study of each individual over a period of years and by administering the best tests available. These tests have no bearing or influence on school marks. The testing and examining which is provided in this study would cost approximately $50.00 annually if given by a private guidance clinic.

All pupils in the 10th grade will be assisted in this study. The request of any parent to have his son or daughter withdrawn will be given immediate consideration. Parents' wishes are always considered first.

The work is being done by staff members of the University of Wisconsin with the close coöperation of all school personnel and no important decisions concerning any pupil are made without consulting and without the approval of school authorities and parents. The Staff members are Dr. John W. M. Rothney, Professor of Education, and Louis Schmidt, third year graduate student in guidance.

After the student had read the statement he was asked if he had any questions about the plan and those that he had were answered. This initial contact was intended to develop rapport with all the 870 subjects and to try to impress them with the fact that the counselors planned to follow their progress after they had completed high school. Some of the students who later became members of the control group were not interviewed again during the three years that they were in senior high school, but they responded to follow-up questionnaires long after they finished high school. Apparently the initial interview with all the students, when combined with the other procedures designed to increase follow-up returns, was effective and the amount of time that it required seemed to be justified.

Notes about observations of outstanding characteristics of the subjects were made during the first interview and they were added to his cumulative record. Since it was not known whether the subject would become an experimental or control at the time of the first interview no student received particular attention. The subjects were never informed about their experimental or control group status, but it became clear to many of the experimental subjects in the last two years of high school that they were getting more attention than some of their fellow students.

As soon as all the subjects had been interviewed the control and experimental groups were set up in the manner described in the previous chapter. During the remainder of the first year the experimental subjects were called in for interviews. They were reminded of the purpose of the study and the process of counseling was begun.

The first interviews were introductory and exploratory in nature. The following guide sheet was used, but *if the subject preferred to enlarge on any of his answers or wanted to talk about some other matter, the sheet was discarded completely,* and the information required to complete it was obtained at a later session.

Interview Guide Sheet

Are you living at home with your father and mother?

What is your father's occupation?

How much education did he have?

Does your mother work? How much education did she have?

Did your mother work before she was married?

(Boy) Does your father want you to go on to the same kind of work he did?

(Girl) Does your mother expect you to do the same kind of work she did?

How many brothers and sisters do you have? How do you get along with them?

Is there anything special about the members of your family?

Have you ever discussed your school program with your parents?

Do you plan to stay in school until you graduate?

What plans for education or training do you have after you leave high school?

Have you made up your mind as to what occupation you are going to enter? What others are you considering?

Do both of your parents agree with your plans? If not, what do they suggest?

If you could do just as you pleased, what would you like to be doing five years from now?

If you could spend all of your time on one subject, which would it be?

If any subject could be dropped out of your high school program, which one would you like to see dropped?

What part-time or school vacation jobs have you had? How long?

What activities, other than school work, are you active in?

What do you do at home when you haven't any school work to do?

Is there anything about your health that keeps you from doing the things you like to do?

How do you get along with the other students in school? In your neighborhood?

Do you think that the new draft law will affect your educational or vocational plans?

The questions were spaced on the sheet so that the interviewers could write out the students' responses. The subjects were told that the interviewer was making notes because he could not remember their answers without reminders and because anything that the student said might be helpful in the choices he was to make. The counselor sat at the left side of the student so that he could read the counselor's notes if he chose to do so. Occasionally when a student seemed to be inhibited because notes were taken, the interviewer discarded the guide sheet and relied on his memory. Such situations were rare in the first year and by the end of the third year none of the students seemed to be concerned about note taking by the interviewer. At the end of each day of counseling the notes were transferred to the subjects' cumulative records. Frequent discussion of methods and of the whole interviewing processes brought a high level of agreement between the two counselors in interview methods and in the recording of data on cumulative folders.

At the end of the first year all the control group subjects had been seen once. All the experimental subjects had been seen twice, or had had at least one interview of greater length than those held with members of the control group. Entries had been made for each of the 870 students on the Cumulative Record for Junior and Senior High Schools.[8] They consisted of names, addresses, birth dates, ninth and tenth grade marks of the students copied from the records of the school, scores on the S.R.A. Test of Primary Mental Abilities given by the experimenters and other tests given by the schools, interview notes on the experimental subjects, and brief notes of outstanding characteristics of control group subjects.

During the first year excellent rapport had been developed with all the subjects and with most of the administrative and teaching personnel of the school. The purposes of the study seemed to be

[8] Published by the American Council on Education, 1785 Massachusetts Ave. N.W., Washington 6, D.C.

clear to students and teachers and to many parents of the subjects. The experimenters, because they became regular members of the school staff as far as their itinerant status permitted, were free to carry on their interviews even to the extent of taking students out of regular classes if they could not be seen at other times. The achievement of the first year indicated that the objectives had been reached and that those for the second year of study seemed likely of accomplishment.

ACTIVITIES OF THE SECOND YEAR

Plans for the second year required that intensive counseling of the experimental subjects would be carried on and rapport with members of the control group maintained. During the counseling process it was necessary to collect additional information about each subject, to interpret it to him, to his parents, or to school personnel, and to record it so that it could be useful in current procedures and later evaluation. Since 180 of the 870 original subjects were lost by dropouts, transfers, and family moves during the last two years of the study, more time could be given to the remaining subjects. A new counselor [9] took over the duties of assistant to the writer and remained with the study for two years.

THE TESTING PROGRAM

During the second year, while the students were in the eleventh grade, the test data previously collected were supplemented by the administration of selected parts of the Differential Aptitude Tests to all the subjects of the study.[10] It seemed unwise in view of the kinds of information already obtained about the students, and in view of budget limitations, to administer all the parts of the test to all the subjects. It seemed obvious that some of our horny-handed sons of the soil were not likely to be interested in clerical work as a career and the administration of a clerical test to them would neither have helped the individuals nor increased

[9] Dr. Paul J. Danielson, at that time a graduate student in guidance and currently an Associate Professor of Education at the University of Arizona.

[10] Published by the Psychological Corporation, 522 Fifth Avenue, New York.

rapport with them. Similarly it seemed to be a waste of time and money to give the mechanical reasoning tests to those girls who were enthusiastic about, and skillful in, typing and shorthand but who shunned all kinds of machines.

To avoid the seeming waste and probable loss of rapport, the following procedure was used. All the records of each of the subjects was studied. On the basis of that study each subject was put into one of three groups. If it seemed likely that he might go on to college training, he was given the Verbal Reasoning, Numerical Ability, and Language Usage sections of the Differential Aptitude Tests. If commercial or clerical work seemed likely, the Clerical, Language Usage, and Numerical Ability parts of the test were used. And if agricultural or mechanical choices seemed likely, a subject was given the Mechanical Reasoning, Space Relations, and Number Ability sections of the test. It will be noted that all the subjects took the Numerical Ability test. The scores were recorded on the cumulative record and interpreted to the student in the manner described later in this chapter. If further testing seemed to be indicated for a particular student at any time during the study it was provided for by administering additional sections of the Differential Aptitude Tests or by giving all or selected parts of other tests.

Since, except under the rare situations cited immediately above, no further testing was done, a summary picture of the tests available for counseling purposes is presented below. Some of the tests had been administered routinely in the schools and others were given by the investigators.[11]

During the spring of their sophomore year in high school, all the students were given the S.R.A. Primary Mental Abilities Test.[12] The test had received much attention *at that time* (1948) because, as the following abstracts from the manual indicate, it seemed to hold promise as a counseling aid.

[11] The Kuder Preference Record, which was administered to some of our subjects by school personnel, is not considered to be a test but simply a preference record. Its use will be discussed later.

[12] This material on the tests has been published previously in *The High School Student* by John W. M. Rothney, published by The Dryden Press, Inc.

The S.R.A. Primary Mental Abilities Test

Authors: L. L. and T. G. Thurstone
Publishers: Science Research Associates, Chicago, Ill.

According to the manual, the test is designed to measure five basic intellectual abilities: Verbal-meaning, Space, Reasoning, Number and Word Fluency. Again according to the manual, these terms are defined as follows:

Verbal-Meaning (V) is said to be the ability to understand ideas expressed in words. It is needed in activities where one gets information by reading or listening. High ability in V is especially useful in such school courses as English, foreign languages, shorthand, history, and science. V is needed for success in such careers as secretary, teacher, scientist, librarian, and executive.
Fifty problems similar to the one below are presented to measure V:

Ancient: A. Dry B. Long C. Happy D. Old

The word meaning the same as the first word is to be marked. Time for this test is 4 minutes.

Space (S) is said to be the ability to think about objects in two or three dimensions. Blueprint reading, for example, requires this ability. The designer, electrician, machinist, pilot, engineer, and carpenter are typical workers who need ability to visualize objects in space. S is helpful in geometry, mechanical drawing, art, manual training, physics, and geography classes. Twenty problems similar to the one below are given in the test for S:

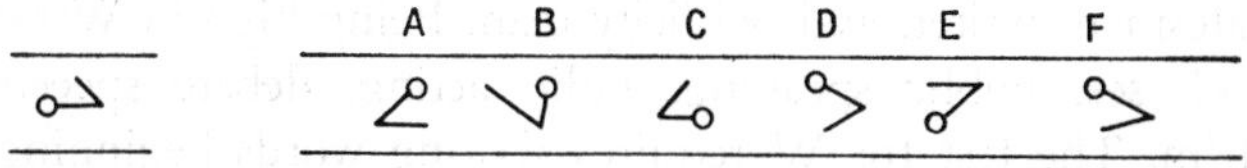

A B C D E F

Every figure which is like the first figure is to be marked. Time, 5 minutes.

Reasoning (R) is described as the ability to solve logical problems—to foresee and plan. It is the ability that helps to make inventors, doctors, teachers, executives, statesmen, scientists, and supervisors outstanding. The higher a student goes in school, the more R he needs for success. Understanding science and mathematics takes a lot of R. Recent research has shown that R is really two separate abilities: inductive reasoning, the ability to reason from specific cases to a general rule; and deductive reasoning, the ability to reason from stated premises to a logical conclusion. The present test is a composite measure of both abilities. Thirty problems of the type below are presented in the R test:

a b x c d x e f x g h x h i j k x y

The box containing the next letter in the series is to be marked. Time, 6 minutes.

Number (N) is said to be the ability to work with figures—to handle simple quantitative problems rapidly and accurately. Accountants, cashiers, comptometer operators, bookkeepers, bank tellers, sales clerks, and inventory clerks are usually high in N. Number ability is useful for school success in business arithmetic, accounting, bookkeeping, and statistics. Seventy problems similar to the one below are included in the N test:

```
 17
 84    R    W
 29
---
140
```

The answer given is to be indicated as right or wrong. Time, 6 minutes.

Word Fluency (W) is described as the ability to write and talk easily. People to whom words come rapidly and fluently are high in W. Careers requiring W include: actor, stewardess, reporter, comedian, salesman, writer, and publicity man. Being high in W helps in drama classes, public speaking, radio acting, debate speech, and journalism. The test for W requires writing words beginning with the letter "S." Time, 5 minutes.

The reader is cautioned that no evidence is presented in the test manual to indicate that people who score high in verbal meaning (V), for example, do succeed in the careers or courses indicated. He may learn, by study of this test, that it is desirable to look at test items rather than merely test titles. Without the label, would not the test for V be called a vocabulary test and the N test be simply an achievement test in addition? And he should ask whether series recognition and extension may properly be labeled with the term "reasoning." In use of the test for the study of the cases in this volume, it may be well to avoid the labels of Primary Mental Abilities and to describe the five processes in these terms:

(V) Recognition of the one out of four words that comes nearest in definition of a key word.

(S) Recognition of simple designs when they have been turned in different directions.

(R) Recognition of the series in which items appear, and extension of that series.

(N) Recognition of correct answers to simple addition problems.

(W) Speed in writing words beginning with a given letter.

All the schools used the Henmon-Nelson Test of Mental Ability in the tenth and eleventh grades. It is described briefly below.

The Henmon-Nelson Test of Mental Ability

Authors: V. A. C. Henmon and M. J. Nelson
Publishers: Houghton Mifflin Company, Boston, Mass.

This test consists of 90 multiple-choice items arranged in order of increasing difficulty. A wide variety of items is used, including common vocabulary types, analogies, and series. It is designed to measure the mental ability of students in junior and senior high schools. It is said to be useful as a partial guide in: (1) dividing students into sections on the basis of general ability; (2) advising students as to courses or subjects they should pursue; (3) vocational guidance; and (4) determining students' capacity for higher education. The user of the test is reminded that in all such situations all other pertinent data, such as the student's interests, emotional characteristics, and mechanical aptitude should also be considered. The test is currently given to freshmen and juniors in more than 90 percent of Wisconsin high schools.

Other tests used by some of the schools and mentioned occasionally in this volume are listed below.

The Coöperative Test of Reading Comprehension

Authors: F. B. Davis and others
Publishers: Educational Testing Service, Princeton, N.J.

Scores are provided for vocabulary, speed of comprehension, level of comprehension, and total score. It is designed for use in the identification of the relative strengths and weaknesses of a class, placement, measurement of growth, and guidance. It may also be used for administrative surveys and curriculum study.

This test has the usual multiple-choice type of vocabulary items similar to those used to measure (V) or Verbal Meaning in the Primary Mental Abilities tests but this one is labeled a reading rather than a verbal-ability test. It also has the usual paragraph to be read by the student and the common multiple-choice type of items covering materials of the paragraph. No suggestions are made about what is to be done with the student who is speedy in misunderstanding what he reads.

The Progressive Reading Test

Authors: E. W. Tiegs and W. W. Clark
Publishers: California Test Bureau, Los Angeles, Calif.

This test contains 200 multiple-choice vocabulary items from mathematics, science, social sciences, and general literature. There are also sections under the heading Reading Comprehension which purport to measure students' skills in following directions, familiarity with references, and understanding of ideas expressed in paragraphs.

Otis Quick Scoring Mental Ability Tests

Author: Arthur A. Otis
Publishers: World Book Company, Yonkers, N.Y.

Minnesota Paper Form Board (Revised form)

Authors: Rensis Likert and William Quasha
Publishers: Science Research Associates, Chicago, Ill.

At the time that the tests were administered, each student was told why they were to be taken and the uses to which the scores would be put. The following statement was given in mimeographed form to each student before he began work on the tests. Many of the statements were taken home to parents.

During the past two years we have talked with each of you and have given you tests to help you to find out the kind of work or training for which you are best suited and to help you to get a good start when you finish high school. We will want to see you again next year and several times in the five years after you finish high school to see how you are getting along.

Today we are going to take more tests that will help to show whether you can do some of the things you have told us you want to do. We can't give all of you exactly the tests you want to take at this time, but if you want to try others, come in to see your counselors and we will arrange special tests for you.

Most of you have been called in and told about the scores you made on the tests which you took last year. Since we see each of you separately, it takes much time and we have not yet been able to see all of you this year. We will do so as soon as we find time. If you want to learn about your scores before we call you, come in to see us and we will set a special time for you.

The test results, along with the other information you have given us, should help us to help you make a good choice of work or training after you leave high school, so do your best. No one is expected to get every question right and you will probably do better on some of the tests than on others. These test scores will have nothing to do with school marks or class work.

Most of the students responded well to the challenge of the tests and generally good effort on their part was noted.

As soon as the test scores were obtained, they were converted into percentiles for ease of interpretation to students, teachers, parents, and principals.[13] Each experimental student was then called in for an interview and his test score interpreted.

Interpretation was done individually. During an interview the tests were shown to each counselee to remind him of their titles and form. He was then shown his scores, and interpretation was done in terms of percentiles. Thus the interviewer would say: "This is a test of numerical ability (or any other test title) and

[13] J. W. M. Rothney, "Interpretation of Test Scores to Counselors," *Occupations, The Vocational Guidance Magazine,* February, 1952, pp. 320–322.

you have scored at the sixtieth percentile. That means that, on this test, you have done as well as or better than 60 percent of the students of your grade in Wisconsin high schools." To check on the students' understanding of what had been said, the interviewer followed up by asking: "Then what percent of Wisconsin students in your grade made higher scores than you did?" If the student did not answer correctly the explanation was repeated. The implications of the test scores were then considered during the counseling.

As soon as the interview was completed the counselors wrote notes concerning the reaction of the subjects to the scores and interpretations that had been given. An exact scale was not used, to avoid too early formalization of the reactions and the potential danger of premature lumping into categories. At the end of the experimental period 811 reactions of 340 students to interpretation of their test scores were available. A summary of these reactions with samples of students' comments and counselors' observations is presented in Table 12.

Interpretations of the data in the table will vary with the point of view of the reader. In general they seem to indicate that the reaction of these students was favorable or positive. If one combines items numbered 1, 2, 4, 6, and 9, the percentage of positive or favorable reactions is 60.4. A combination of items 7, 8, 11, 12, and 14, representing those items in which neither positive nor negative reactions are clearly indicated, comprises 31 percent of the total. Items 3, 5, 10, and 13, which may be interpreted as negative responses, constitute only 8.6 percent. A check on individual records indicated that only 5.2 percent of the students produced these negative reactions.

Readers of the table may wish to make combinations other than those given above, but one would be hard put to find evidence that telling students their test scores results in significantly large numbers of negative reactions on the part of counselees. In only 3 percent of the cases did the counselors note obvious disappointment. Of course serious disappointment that resulted in severe emotional disturbance in even one case would be a matter of concern to a counselor, but no such disturbances were observed.

TABLE 12. Reactions of Counselees When Told Their Test Scores

Reaction	Number	Percent
1. Seemed to feel that expectations were confirmed Samples: "I knew I had done well on that test." "I knew I could be at the top in math."	215	26.5
2. Seemed surprised that scores were higher than expected Samples: "I'm not that smart!" "I just can't believe I made that score."	27	3.3
3. Seemed surprised that scores were lower than expected Samples: "I usually do better than that in mechanics." "I thought I did better on the reasoning test."	12	1.5
4. Seemed pleased with test results Samples: She was obviously happy with her scores. "I'm glad to get these scores. Usually we never know what we have done."	174	21.5
5. Seemed disappointed at test results Samples: "I'm disappointed at that low number score." "I think I should have done better than that."	24	3.0
6. Showed considerable interest in scores Samples: He asked many questions about the tests. He asked if he could copy them to show his parents.	55	6.8
7. Seemed unconcerned about test scores Samples: "My plans are all set. Those scores don't mean much to me." "School tests don't affect me."	83	10.2
8. Did not show any noticeable reaction Samples: Counselor could not see that she was affected. It was not possible to tell whether or not the interpretation had any effect on her.	33	4.1
9. Test scores seemed to encourage current plans Samples: "Now I feel that I can go to college." "Guess I can go ahead with my plans now."	19	2.3
10. Test scores seemed to discourage current plans	7	0.9

TABLE 12 (*Continued*)

Reaction	Number	Percent
Samples: "My scores and low grades rule out college." "I'll have to think of something else I can do in case I can't make premed."		
11. Test scores did not seem to influence current plans	35	4.3
Samples: "I know what I want and test scores don't make any difference." He simply ignored test scores in planning.		
12. Commented about test situation	86	10.6
Samples: "I didn't feel well that day." "I went too fast in that mechanical test." "I didn't understand directions on space test."		
13. Seemed to be skeptical of value of tests	26	3.2
Samples: Said number score couldn't be right because she finds arithmetic an easy subject. She questioned the value of timed tests.		
14. Did not seem to understand explanation of scores	15	1.8
Samples: She could not grasp interpretations even when time was taken to repeat them. He seemed not to understand what was meant.		
Total	811	100.0

Since these data were obtained in a longitudinal study during which the subjects were studied intensively by the counselors over the three-year period, it is unlikely that serious disturbances resulting from telling students their test scores would have escaped detection. For the same reason it is not likely that inner reactions without surface manifestations could have gone unnoticed.

The tentative conclusion was simply that telling sophomore, junior, and senior high school students their test scores and interpreting these scores to them during counseling interviews seemed not to cause significant negative or disturbing reactions.

The enthusiasm of most of the students about the counseling process, in which interpretation of test scores played a prominent part, suggests that they want to know about their performances. The counselors, though wishing they had better tests to use in the process, believe that the interpretation of test scores to counselees after good rapport has been established over a period of time is a valuable procedure in the counseling of high school youth.

Since the manuals of the tests contain reports about validity, reliability, and norms it is not necessary to repeat them here. Heimann,[14] who had previously examined the effects of cluster sampling in the group, computed the means, medians, standard deviations, and skewness of the distributions of the test scores on 28 subsections of all the tests that were used. Kaczkowski [15] computed the intercorrelation between many of the subtest scores. The evidence from the computations by these two researchers indicated that: (1) the distributions of the scores were nearly normal; (2) the intertest correlation coefficients, as noted in Table 13, were generally low; (3) the content of the tests was

TABLE 13. Intercorrelation Coefficients Between Test Scores of 324 Experimental Subjects

	1. H.N. Soph. Year	2. H.N. Junior Year	Primary Mental Abilities 3. Verbal	4. Space	5. Reason	6. Number	7. Word Fluency
2. Henmon-Nelson Junior Year	.897						
3. Pma Verbal	.628	.681					
4. Pma Space	.181	.212	.160				
5. Pma Reasoning	.564	.548	.492	.292			
6. Pma Number	.346	.341	.339	.201	.410		
7. Pma W-Fluency	.474	.442	.417	.055	.376	.217	
8. Differential Aptitude Test (number)	.607	.638	.426	.249	.506	.404	.218

[14] Robert A. Heimann, *Intra-Individual Consistency of Performance in Relation to the Counseling Process,* unpublished Ph.D. thesis, University of Wisconsin, 1952.
[15] Henry R. Kaczkowski, *Discrimination Among Eight Groups of High School Students,* unpublished Ph.D. thesis, University of Wisconsin, 1954.

homogeneous in that they measured some aspect of performance of an intellectual nature; (4) the population of this study as described by test scores was large, heterogeneous, and representative of an important group.

Some problems in the use of tests arose during the study, and they are noted here in the hope that others may profit from recognizing them. The variability in performances from the first to the second administration of the Henmon-Nelson Test of Mental Ability, for example, presented some difficulties in interpretation. The extent of variation in percentiles of subjects from the tenth to the eleventh grade may be observed in Table 14. Although the

TABLE 14. Comparison of Percentiles on the Henmon-Nelson Tests of Mental Ability Achieved by 731 Subjects in Their Sophomore and Junior Years

Junior Year Percentile	Percentile Achieved During Sophomore Year										
	0–10	11–20	21–30	31–40	41–50	51–60	61–70	71–80	81–90	91–100	Total
91–100						2	2	2	24	53	83
81–90					3	4	11	12	26	21	77
71–80		1			3	6	17	15	21	11	74
61–70			3	7	6	14	17	9	9	1	66
51–60		1	2	11	9	10	12	11	5		61
41–50	1	1	11	16	11	15	16	8			79
31–40	6	10	10	11	21	14	16	1			89
21–30	4	9	9	10	8	5	3	3		1	52
11–20	17	21	14	12	3	2	1	1			71
0–10	49	14	8	3	1	3			1		79
Total	77	57	57	70	65	75	95	62	86	87	731

agreement is generally high, there are enough changes from one year to the next to make interpretation to the student a difficult process. Differences in the middle of the range could be minimized in view of the nature of percentiles, but decreases and increases as great as some of those indicated in Table 14 were difficult to interpret to counselees or their parents. The difficulties illustrate the need for more data about the stability of test scores than is indicated by a high reliability coefficient obtained by split-half or immediate retest methods if the test is to be used in longitudinal studies.

Another serious problem was caused by the titles on the tests. When, for example, some students were shown their low scores on the number section of the Primary Mental Abilities Test they became skeptical of the test because they had achieved high marks in their mathematics courses. They pointed out that there was more to "number" than rapid addition of columns of figures, and when they saw disparities between test scores and marks, they tended to reject the former in favor of the latter as indicators of what they might achieve at later times. Sometimes this situation resulted in the students' rejection of all test scores.

Still another problem arose from what might be called lack of face validity of the test that contained pictures and diagrams. It was difficult to convince the boys who were interested in farm, auto, or airplane mechanics that Mechanical Reasoning could be measured by the section of the Differential Aptitude Tests that consists of pictures of swings, race tracks, and billiard tables. They would not believe that test scores obtained from it might have any relationship to success in what they proposed to do. The brighter boys could grasp the explanation, but many who were successful in their shopwork or part-time mechanical jobs rejected as unimportant the scores they achieved on any pencil or paper "mechanical" tests.

In general, it appeared that the students did not consider test scores useful in helping them to make academic and vocational choices. So many factors other than test performances seemed, to them, to be of much more significance in their planning for the future. Parental occupations or attitudes, geographic location, availability of opportunity, length of time of training, financial support for post-high school education, health, plans for marriage and countless other factors seemed to them to be much more important than test scores in making their plans. And the haste of many of the subjects to get out of school and into any job that would pay enough so that they could put a down payment on a used car caused them to reject evidence that might have suggested different lines of action. Observation of the problems of counseling in this study suggested that tests are of considerably less value than publishers of tests would have us believe.

INTERVIEWS

Intensive interviewing of the experimental subjects really began during the year that they were in the eleventh grade. Procedures somewhat similar to those used during the first year were employed, but some differences in emphasis during the second year are described below. At the beginning of the year alphabetical rosters of all the experimental subjects were drawn up and the subjects were called in for interviews in order of their last names. As time went on, variation from the alphabetical arrangements occurred because some subjects asked to come in, some teachers referred students, and because the usual arrangement of taking students out of study halls for interviews was not always satisfactory. At times, students had to be seen at hours convenient to them. The alphabetical arrangement, then, was just a device to get things started, and after the program was well under way convenience of counselors or students and requests by the subjects themselves determined the order in which they were seen. The students came to know that they could come in to talk to counselors at any time, and many of them became regular visitors. Care was taken, however, to arrange that all the experimental subjects were seen during the second year. The range was from a minimum of one interview for a very few cases to as many as 20 or more for those who were eager.

At each preliminary session the student was given the following mimeographed statement.

To Pupils in the Guidance Study

When you were in the tenth grade you were interviewed and tested by counselors who discussed with you your plans for work or education after you finished high school. This year and next we will continue the interviews and tests started at that time. The additional tests and interviews which you are going to have will *help us to help you* to find out the things that you can do best. You have probably realized by this time that it is important for you to find your own strong points.

You may remember that the counselors told you that the interviews and tests have nothing to do with your school marks.

We want you to understand fully what we are trying to do. If it is not clear, the counselors will answer any questions.

On the reverse side of the sheet the following statement appeared.

To Parents of Students in the Guidance Study
(To be taken home by the student)

The purpose of this study, begun last year when your son or daughter was in tenth grade, is to help you and your children to find out the kinds of work and study that they can do best, and to encourage development along those lines to the fullest possible extent. To accomplish this purpose, a careful study of each individual is made over the three-year period of senior high school by administering the best tests available and by interviews with the student. The tests have no bearing or influence on school marks. They will be used to measure fitness for certain occupations or educational opportunities. Services provided to each individual in this study would cost approximately $50.00 a year if given by a private guidance agency.

The counseling is being done by Professor John Rothney and Mr. Paul Danielson of the University of Wisconsin with the close cooperation of all school personnel. No important decisions concerning any pupil are made without approval of school authorities and parents.

Parents are encouraged to consult with the counselors at any time. We would like to have a least one interview with the parents of each student this year so that plans for the future can be given full consideration at this time. Appointments may be made by phoning the secretary of the high school, or students may make the arrangements after their interview with the counselor.

At the beginning of the interview the subject was asked to read the statements and ask any questions he might have about the work. Requests for interviews by parents suggested that most of the sheets were being taken home and that parental interest in counseling had been aroused. The information helped to allay any fears that parents may have had about the interviewing. As in many high schools, the calling in of a student for an interview had usually meant that he was in trouble.

Again during the second year a guide sheet was used for the interview, but *it was not followed if the counselee preferred to discuss some other subject or wanted to spend all the time elaborating on one of the topics raised by a question.* The guide sheet for the second year is presented below.

Is there any change in your family situation from what you told us last year?

If you could spend all your time on one of your present subjects, which one would it be? Why?

Which one would you like to drop? Why?

Do you plan to stay in school until you graduate?

What occupation have you decided to enter?

Do both your parents agree with your plans? If not, what do they suggest?

What are your plans for training after you leave school?

What job(s) did you have during the summer vacation?

Do you have a part-time job at present? What do you actually do?

Do you plan to look for a part-time job? What sort of job would you like? Why?

What school activities do you take part in?

Are there any school activities you would like to take part in but can't for some reason? Why choose them?

Why not participate?

Is there anything about your health that keeps you from doing what you'd like to do?

If you were to ask your friends what kind of person you are, how do you think they would describe you?

Who are some of your closest friends?

What do you do when you haven't any school work to do?

What problems do you have about your education? Choice of vocation? Getting along with other people?

If things worked out just as you wanted, what would you like to be doing five years from the time you leave school?

Comments about the concepts and principles that lay behind the interviewing procedures are presented in the section headed General Discussion of Procedures in this chapter. It must be emphasized that the questions were only *guides*. Only *in very rare instances did the interviewers start with the first question and go through to the end.* The presentation of the list of questions given above suggests more stereotyping than was intended and it tends to present a picture of rigidity in interviewing that was neither planned nor practiced.

RESPONSE TO COUNSELING

After each interview the counselors made a notation on the cumulative record or interview guide sheet about the implied or stated response of each subject to the counseling situation. Study of the highly subjective notations indicated that the counselees' reactions could be classified into several fairly discreet categories. An attempt to place each of the subjects' reactions into them produced the totals and the differences between girls and boys that appear in Table 15.

TABLE 15. Percentages of Experimental Subjects Classified by Their Reactions to Counseling

Reactions	Exper. Girls (N=181)	Exper. Boys (N=162)
Enthusiastic response. Sought more than usual opportunities for counseling.	34.8	25.3
Accepted counselor. Participated freely but did not seek more than usual opportunities.	52.5	40.7
Indicated during interviews that they did not need assistance by the counselor.	3.9	18.5
Indifferent or passive during interviews. Seemed unaffected by counseling.	8.8	13.6
Changeable. In more than one of above categories at some time.	0.0	1.9
Total	100.0	100.0

It is apparent immediately that the general response was favorable. Approximately one-third of the girls and a quarter of the boys were very enthusiastic. They were the subjects who were waiting for the counselors when they arrived in the morning and who came in for special sessions after school. More than half of the girls and two-fifths of the boys were not quite so eager but they indicated that they appreciated the efforts of the counselor. Almost five times as many boys as girls indicated that their plans were all set and that they had no problems in which the counselor could be helpful. Most of the 3.9 percent of the girls in this category had plans for early marriage and many of the boys in this group were planning to go back to the family farm or had arranged to work in business with their fathers. Many of the subjects in this group, both male and female, were good students from good homes who had worked out good plans. More boys than girls were indifferent or passive in the counseling situation. They talked and listened but there seemed to be no noticeable effect. To them it seemed to be another one of the school routines in which they showed little concern. Perhaps these could be described as cases in which rapport was not well established.

The difference between girls and boys is reflected in the chi-square for the first four categories of 25.16, which is significant at greater than the .001 level. (The zero figure in the fifth category precludes the use of chi-square.) Whether this difference means that the counselors developed greater rapport with girls or whether girls generally are more receptive to male counselors cannot be determined at this time, but it is clear that, under the conditions of this study, the girls were more responsive in the counseling situation.

ADDITIONAL SOURCES OF DATA

Time and varying conditions within the schools did not permit the procuring of the same kinds of data for all the 870 subjects. In some schools the practices carried on routinely for all students furnished usable information, in others certain practices were introduced at the suggestion of the counselors, and in still others changes in school policy and practice resulted in the use of techniques that produced usable information about students.

BEHAVIOR DESCRIPTIONS

In one school the personality rating scale that had been used was discarded and a revision of the Behavior Description Method developed in the Eight Year Study of the Progressive Education Association was utilized.

The practice was to have each teacher fill out one such form for each student in her classes each year in senior high school. The counselors obtained the descriptions and entered them on the cumulative record. Information thus obtained provided valuable insights about the students of one of the schools and it seemed unfortunate that the other schools did not collect data of this kind. A study of consistency in behavior in which the Behavior Description was used is reported by Heimann.[16]

A sample of the descriptions obtained by this method follows.

AUTOBIOGRAPHIES

At all times during the study the investigators were looking for dependable information about the experimental subjects from any available sources. Samples of students' work in classes, studios, shops, clubs, at home, or at play were obtained whenever possible. Some information about such performances was obtained for many subjects and examples of written materials of some kind for each subject were procured. Among them were students' performances on assignments given by teachers, writing submitted to newspapers, the school literary magazine in one city, and high school annuals.

The best source seemed to be the autobiographies, which were usually written for English teachers when the students were in their junior year. In one city all members of the junior class were split into two groups regardless of their experimental or control

[16] R. A. Heimann, *Intra-Individual Consistency of Performance in Relation to the Counseling Process,* unpublished Ph.D. thesis, University of Wisconsin, 1952.

Name of Student JESSIE Teacher SMITH

City WESTOWNE Grade 11 Subject ENGLISH

Please describe this student by checking the statements which best characterize him. Write additional comments if you think they will help us to understand him.

RESPONSIBILITY

_____Does even more than he is required to do in assignments.

_____Does without prodding what he is told to do but no more.

_____Needs prodding except on special assignments.
Which ones? _____

✓ Needs some prodding on all assignments.

_____Needs constant prodding to get anything done.

_____Doesn't do his assignments even when he is prodded.

INFLUENCE

_____Habitually controls the activities of other students.

_____A leader but will accept group decisions.

_____Doesn't control but does strongly influence the activities of others.

✓ In certain groups he influences others. Which groups? _____

_____Is carried along by nearest or strongest influence.

ADJUSTABILITY

✓ Appears to feel secure in group situations.

_____Seems anxious about his standing in groups, but others accept him.

_____Other students reject him. Why? _____

_____He withdraws from the group.

CONCERN FOR OTHERS

_____Shows balance in considering the welfare of himself and others.

_____Certain problems of group welfare seem to interest him. Which? _____

✓ Is not interested about welfare of others unless what they do affects him.

_____Talks about welfare of others but does nothing about it.

_____Shows no concern for welfare of others.

Comments: JESSIE IS NOT TOO RELIABLE WHEN ASSIGNMENTS ARE EXPECTED TO BE IN ON TIME. SHE IS ABSENT A GOOD DEAL BECAUSE OF TRIPS, COLDS, ETC.

group status for the purpose of conducting an investigation of the use of the autobiography in counseling. One group wrote from relatively unstructured directions while the others followed a highly structured outline. The directions given to the group who were to write *without* detailed instructions were given the following guide.

Instructions for Writing Your Autobiography

The purpose of this assignment is to make you aware of the variety of things that influence us in our "growing up" and in developing plans for our future. Besides being an assignment in writing about a very interesting person, YOU, the autobiography will help you to decide "What kind of person am I?" "How did I get that way?" and "What do I hope to become?"

Keep these three questions in mind and write freely about yourself. Include anything that you feel helped make you what you are. You will not be asked to read your autobiography in class nor will your teacher discuss it.

You may begin writing during this period and then may complete the autobiography at home or in study periods, as you wish. The papers will be due two weeks from today.

Those who were to write from a *structured* outline were given the following guide.

Instructions for Writing Your Autobiography

The purpose of this assignment is to make you aware of the variety of things that influence us in our "growing up" and in developing plans for our future. Besides being an assignment in writing about a very interesting person, YOU, the autobiography will help you decide "What kind of person am I?" "How did I get that way?" and "What do I hope to become?"

The purpose of the questions listed below is to give you some ideas that will help you describe what makes YOU a person different from everyone else. Read them over carefully before you begin writing and keep them in mind as you write. Refer to them from time to time if necessary. DO NOT ANSWER THE QUESTIONS DIRECTLY BUT WEAVE THE IDEAS THEY GIVE YOU INTO THE PATTERN OF YOUR LIFE.

I. The Present—"What kind of person am I?"

1. How would you describe yourself to someone whom you have never seen? Would your friends describe you the same way? Are you the same person to your parents, to your teachers, to your friends, or at home, in class, on the sports field?
2. Is there anything about your physical appearance or health that makes you different than other people? In what way?
3. What are your likes and dislikes? What special interests do you have? Do you have any special moods, such as quietness or daydreaming, sudden spurts of energy or ambition? Does having to do some types of things, such as housework, school work, an interesting activity, affect you differently?
4. What are your social activities? Do you prefer to spend your time with one or two close friends, or with many others? Do you change friends frequently? If so, why?
5. Do you have any faults or handicaps that might contribute to making you the person you are? Are there any things at which you are better than other people you know? What things?

II. The Past—"How did I get that way?"

1. What things in your "family history" have influenced you? Consider such things as family interests, economic status, family friends, relatives, occupations of parents, brothers, sisters, attitudes of parents, religious connections, discipline, special family events, places you have lived, etc.
2. What kind of people have you had as friends? Why did you choose them? How have they influenced you? Have you led or followed them in your activities? Do any people stand out in your memory, such as "favorite uncles" or other members of your family, teachers, or famous people, as having special influence on your actions or behavior?
3. Have you always had things pretty much your own way? If so, how has that affected you? How about the effect if the reverse is true? Have you been permitted to make your own decisions in matters that were really important to you?
4. Have your parents and teachers as well as other people in your life always understood you and what you were trying to do? Have they given you the attention you thought you should have? Has this made any difference to you?
5. What particular experiences have stuck with you for a long

time? Can you imagine why? Have they influenced you in any way? What things have you done that have given you great satisfaction? Are there any experiences that have had the opposite effect? Why?

6. What activities, social or otherwise, in school or out, have you especially enjoyed? What influences have these activities had on you? Are there any activities which have not been enjoyable? What and why? Are there any activities in which you would have liked to participate that you could not get into? What and why?
7. Has school been an enjoyable experience for you? Why or why not? Do you remember anything that happened in school that might have had a special influence on you, such as an embarrassing moment, special school honors or recognition, or perhaps, just the opposite?
8. Have you had any job experiences that have been especially important to you? In what way? How have you spent your spare time? Has reading or a hobby influenced you in some way?
9. Has there been anything about your health that has had some effect on you? In what way?

III. The Future—"What do I hope to become?"

1. Do you have fairly definite plans as to the type of occupation you will enter and the type of training you hope to get after leaving high school? If so, what are they? Has anyone helped you make these plans? What kind of opposition, if any, are you meeting in your plans for the future?
2. If you do not have definite plans, do you see any problems in this regard? Are there things you would like to do in the future that seem impossible now? What and why?
3. Have you changed your plans frequently regarding an occupation? What are some of the occupations you have considered and why have you changed your mind? Has failure or low grades in particular subjects made any difference? High grades?
4. Have you had enough confidence in yourself in the past to go ahead with plans even though it was difficult to do so? Is that still the case?
5. Have you ever wanted to do something you thought too foolish

to mention to others? Did you forget about it or go ahead? Is there anything about yourself that you would like to change? Would you like to be more like someone else you know? Who and why?

6. How do your ideas of what you are now match with what you "hope to be"?

Keep the above questions in mind as you write and include anything additional you feel is necessary in describing yourself. YOU WILL NOT BE ASKED TO READ YOUR AUTOBIOGRAPHY IN CLASS NOR WILL YOUR TEACHER DISCUSS IT. You may begin writing during this period and then may complete the autobiography at home or in study periods, as you wish. The papers will be due two weeks from today.

Danielson and Rothney[17] described their study of the use of structured and unstructured autobiographies in a journal article. The methods and results are described in the following paragraphs taken from that article.

In this study we have considered the autobiography as a device for obtaining hints or clues of student problems and have sought answers to the two following questions: (1) Is there any difference between the number and types of statements of student problems elicited through structured and unstructured forms of the autobiography? and (2) Are there any specific kinds of student problems recognizable in reading the autobiographies that are peculiar to one or the other of the approaches?

METHOD

The subjects of this investigation were two groups, each composed of 78 juniors who were members of 12 sections of English in a representative Wisconsin high school. The two groups were compared on factors of intelligence, as measured twice by the Henmon-Nelson Test of Mental Ability, age, and rank in class. No statistically significant differences between these factors were noted.

[17] Paul J. Danielson and John W. M. Rothney, "The Student Autobiography: Structured or Unstructured?" *Personnel and Guidance Journal,* 33:30–33.

The subjects were asked to write autobiographies as an assignment in English, and two weeks were allowed to complete the work. One group, consisting of six sections of English, was asked to write an unstructured autobiography with no suggestions as to content beyond that of writing about "What kind of person am I?" "How did I get that way?" and "What do I hope to become?" The members of this group, and the second one, were told that they would not have to read their autobiographies in class nor would the teacher discuss them.

The members of the second group composed of students in six sections of English were asked to write structured autobiographies. This group was given the detailed two-page outline of questions described above as a guide in writing.

Upon completion of the assignment, the autobiographies were read by the investigator and by three other experienced counselors or counselors-in-training. A frame of reference for reading was provided to standardize the approach as far as possible. The readers were asked to note from context or direct statement what seemed to them to be clues to possible student problems, and to indicate the material in the autobiography that prompted them to make the observation. With the exception of the writer, the readers were not aware that the autobiographies they were reading were obtained by different methods.

The problems noted in each autobiography were taken from the readers' reports and placed on cards, along with a notation as to the form of autobiography from which it was elicited. Any problem that one or more readers thought was suggested in the autobiography was included in the tabulation. A total of 701 suggested or tentative problems was noted in 156 autobiographies of both forms. The cards containing the problems were separated first by major problem area—"Financial," "Socioemotional-Personal," "Vocational," "Personal Appearance-Physical Health," "Education," and "Family Relationship" without regard to the form of the autobiography from which they were elicited. In the same manner, the cards in each major area were further separated in terms of specific problems noted within each major area. Finally, tabulation of specific problems from the structured and unstructured autobiographies was made. Comparisons were then made of the differences in problems recognized in each form of the autobiography in terms of specific problems and in terms of total problems found in each major problem area.

The range of specific problems noted by readers falling within major areas was greater than anticipated. The very small numbers involved in the samples obtained precluded, therefore, any useful statistical treatment or differences between percentages of specific problems noted in each form. Analysis by inspection suggested, however, that, with the possible exception of specific problems falling under the heading of "Family Relationship" (e.g., "Excessive work at home," "Strict family discipline"), neither the structured nor unstructured approach appeared to be superior in bringing out cues or hints about the individual that would be helpful to the counselor.

When specific problems were disregarded and comparisons between the structured and unstructured forms were made in terms of all problems found in the major problem areas, some differences emerged. The results of such comparisons are presented in Table 16.

TABLE 16. Comparison of Frequencies of Problems Appearing in 78 Structured and 78 Unstructured Autobiographies

	Structured		Unstructured	
Problem Areas	Number of Problems	%	Number of Problems	%
Finance	22	6	18	6
Personal appearance—physical health	33	8	20	7
Family relationships	35	9	48	16
Education	73	18	39	13
Vocation	87	21	62	21
Social-emotional-personal	152	38	112	37
Total problems elicited	402		299	

Inspection of this table reveals that, for all practical purposes, there is no difference between the two forms of autobiography used in this study in terms of the percentages of problems elicited from four of the major problem areas. In the cases of the "Education" and "Family Relationship" problems elicited from the autobiographies, however, it is evident that greater numbers of problems appear in the structured and unstructured forms, respectively. A comparison made between the two forms of the autobiography in terms of total problems elicited from each revealed that the structured form produced a significantly greater number of problems.

In working with an individual student, the counselor needs to be aware of problems as they arise and as they might affect the counselee in meeting his current and future needs. One of the tasks, in this regard, is to bring these problems "out in the open" so that they can be approached more readily by both the counselee and the counselor. In identifying and isolating problems, the counselor relies on data obtained from many techniques, one of which is the autobiography. The problems suggested to the counselor, as he reads the autobiographies written by his counselees, must be regarded as tentative hypotheses to be substantiated or discarded in the light of other data. This, of course, is true of the interpretation of data obtained from any other single source.

With the student autobiography, as with other techniques, there is the problem of choice among different approaches. In the case of the technique discussed here, the question was essentially, "Will students react differently when asked to respond to one of two methods of writing an autobiography?" Within the framework of the approach described herein, the answer would appear to be a qualified "yes." The irreversibility of the individual precludes the possibility of trying two approaches with the same individual under identical conditions, hence we have the experimental limitations of the matched-groups design.

The results indicate that the structured form of the autobiography suggests more tentative problems than the unstructured. This probably should not be surprising because the outline provides the student autobiographer with many leads and suggestions. In any event, if the counselor's interest is essentially "volume," without particular emphasis on specific problems or problem areas, he will risk overlooking problems to a lesser degree if he uses the structured form. Similarly, if it is problems in the area of "Education" that the counselor wishes to elicit for further investigation, the structured form is likely to prove most profitable. This finding tends to substantiate the opinion of others. It suggests, too, that the counselor may further increase his data in the area of "Education" by refining the structured approach and by designing a topical outline for the area similar to the one suggested by Rothney and Roens.[18] Should the counselor desire to elicit problems concerning "Family Relationship," the unstructured form is likely to prove more profitable. This may have implications for the counselor who wishes particularly to supplement "Family" data obtained from other sources when there is a suspicion that the student is having difficulties in this area. There appears to be no particular advantage in either form in eliciting problems in the major areas of "Financial," "Social-Emotional-Personal," "Vocational," or "Personal Appearance—Physical Health." These findings, of course, are limited to the broad inclusive form of the autobiography as contrasted with the topical form, which might be designed to elicit problems in a single, defined problem area such as a vocational autobiography.

The study described here was designed to determine the differential value of high school students' structured and unstructured autobiographies for counseling purposes, in terms of the degree to which each form suggested students' problems. Two matched groups, each of 78 junior class students, were asked to write autobiographies, one group structured, the other unstructured. The autobiographies were read by counselors who noted problems as suggested by context or direct statement. The problems were categorized, totaled, percentage comparisons were made, and the significance of the differences determined. The results suggest that the counselor is likely to elicit a significantly greater number of statements of students' problems when the structured form is used; that the structured form suggests a significantly greater number of problems falling under the major area of "Education";

[18] J. W. M. Rothney and B. A. Roens, *op. cit.*, pp. 108–109.

and that the unstructured form appears to elicit a significantly greater number of problems falling under the major area of "Family." These findings appear to have implications for the counselor when choosing the form of autobiography to be used as a tool in the counseling process.

Copies of the autobiographies obtained may be found in a previous publication by the writer, but a sample of one and the suggestions of problems of a student that it revealed are presented below.[19] It is edited only to prevent identification. All original constructions and spelling have been retained.

Autobiography of Christine

I was born on January 21, 1933 in Rosemont Community Hospital, which is located on the southside of Cincinatti.

Since my earlier life is quite vague, I'll begin about ten years ago in my second home which was Gary, Indiana.

Chicken pox, I suppose every one gets them in their childhood. Well I did, and how they itched. But that didn't bother me to much as I had the boy next door as a play-mate. He had had them and he'd come over and we'd make mud pies. We used floury dough, mud and coloring and then put them in the ice box. Well, one afternoon my mother looked in the icebox and feasted her eyes on these green moldy pies. Now I guess you might say that ended everything and well, you'd be right.

Later on that summer I broke a few windows, my foot, and a garage door. This ended with the arrival of my favorite uncle. I don't know exactly why but even to this day I have looked up to him.

Sometime later, December 7, 1941, to be exact, my father enlisted in the Navy, which made a very abrupt change in my life. My mother and I move to his mother-in-law's in Milwaukee. There we stayed for about four years. During the course of this time I became somewhat of a spoiled child.

When my father came back in 1945, we searched for a home. Finally we decided to build one. We moved into our new home which also was in Milwaukee about a year after we started to build. I made friends fast and usually kept them. I went with a crowd of boys and girls and we did everything together. This, I think, in itself is one

[19] J. W. M. Rothney, *The High School Student: A Book of Cases,* New York, The Dryden Press, Inc., 1954.

reason why I dislike to limit myself to one or two friends. I feel that a group is much more fun and interesting. Although I do feel this way, I did have one particular friend, but she wasn't the limit of my friends. She was more or less someone to confide in and talk to.

My other friends were of a good nature but I don't feel I can judge people, in that all my friends weren't nice. Although they all didn't come up to my standards I wasn't to easily influenced by them as I am quite stubborn in my ways. I usually got my way due to this fact, but here lately I have learned to see the other person's point of view and agree with them (sometimes).

About ten months later in 1948 my Dad took a new job in Milwaukee. That meant we must move again. So move we did, to ____________. There I was put up a grade (which made me like the ____________ way.)

Unlike before when I had made my friends so quickly, I now found the students were cold. They weren't unfriendly but more or less unwilling to accept me as I came from Chicago. This changed me quite a bit and I made little effort to make friends. Finally I broke into the general swing of things and went with many very nice kids. Finally I met Ann and Mickey. They're two of the nicest friends a person could have even if we do get angry at each other once in a while.

Ann and Mickey are swell but as I said before I dislike to limit myself to one or two people. But I'm afraid to break away from them because if I did I wouldn't know who to go with. I also like dancing, ice skating, tennis and other activities, none of which they care for.

I hate to sit around, it makes me nervous. Usually I have plenty to keep me busy. I collect records and raise collies to keep me busy. In addition homework has its share of my time. My collies, Lady and Heather, sure give me excitement. Lady is the oldest and the mother of Heather. I bought her when she was two weeks old with money I had saved over a three year period. She's a pure bred and my favorite possession, mostly because she's something I worked for.

I guess some of the things I have said sound like I don't like life, or people, but I do. I've had fun especially this past summer. This was when I met Jim, He took me to the state fair which was the biggest thrill to me because I've never been to one. We went to the auto races too (something else I'd never seen). He was a very close friend and I respected him more than any other person of my age. His influence on me changed my way of thinking somewhat to my advantage.

Now to the question of what kind of a person I *hope* to be.

The medical field has always fascinated me for some reason although I once wanted to become a math teacher, but some marks in English were quite low so I have given up the idea. My marks in science and math have always been high which is one reason I chose this field. I'd like to be some kind of a medical technician in a laboratory.

My plans for a medical career may be postponed for awhile, since I intend on working my way through college and training school. In a way I'm glad I have to work before I enter college. It may make me appreciate the education I will receive.

As to foolish notions, I've had many and they have gotten me into trouble. I've learned but my foolish emotions still try to rule me. This and other factors may change my future entirely.

From the autobiographies the counselors often drew up lists of tentative problems that served as a basis for discussion in the interview. From the autobiography presented above the following leads and their sources were noted:

Problem	Notation
1. Realizes a "stubbornness" that isn't yet altogether under control	". . . as I am quite stubborn in my ways. I usually got my way due to this fact, but here lately I have learned to see the other person's point of view and agree with them (sometimes)"
2. Need for social adjustments	"Ann and Mickey are swell but as I said before I dislike to limit myself to one or two people. But I'm afraid to break away from them because if I did I wouldn't know who to go with."
3. Needs to be busy all the time	"I hate to sit around, it makes me nervous. Usually I have plenty to keep me busy."
4. Financial need	"My plans of a medical career may be postponed for awhile, since I intend on working my way through college and training school. In a way I'm glad I have

	to work before I enter college. It may make me appreciate the education I will receive."
5. Concern over lack of emotional control	"As to foolish notions I've had many and they have gotten me into trouble. I've learned but my foolish emotions still try to rule me. This and other factors may change my future entirely."

An abstract from one autobiography in which an experimental subject described herself is given below. It has not been edited in any way.

As for my likes and dislikes I can best describe them in this manner—

I like:
Short hair, bangs, clothes styles today,
Reading and eating, watching a play.

Hon-Hon my cat, autumn and snow,
Television, antiques, Perry Como.

Riding a horse, our dogs Major and Mike,
Chemistry, boating, taking a hike.

Dancing by night, fishing by day,
The season of summer, harvesting hay.

Fingernail polish, jewelry, perfumes,
Movies, Bing Crosby, big living rooms.

Cozy homes, be-bop, and school,
Football and boys, the piano and pool.

I hate:
Too much make-up, Shakespeare, and peas,
Concieted people, ironing, and "D's".

Short fingernails, worms, and work,
Polka-dots with plaids, and a snobby sales clerk.

Writing a letter, setting my hair,
History and show-offs, people who stare.

Braggers, strong winds, socks with heels,
Dirty field jackets, eating apple peels.

Vaughan Monroe's singing, Lightning, and cliques,
Historical novels, and clocks with loud ticks.

Saddle shoes with stockings, homework, and pugs,
Cowboy music, tight people, and bugs.

Although there may have been some loss in accuracy of self-description to get the rhymes in her poem she had raised some interesting points for discussion. And that was the primary purpose for which the student autobiography was used in this study.

OTHER PERSONAL DOCUMENTS

Occasionally an assignment by teachers resulted in the production of documents that provided many clues, hints, and suggestions about the subjects or suggested topics that could be discussed in interviews. In one school the teachers of English in the junior year required the students in her classes to write letters of introduction in which they were to comment about their current status and future plans. A sample of one of the letters follows.

I am not quite sure yet as to what my future plans are. I know that my strength (if I may call it that) lies in the drama. At least that is the particular type of literature I enjoy doing the most. I have many weaknesses in English, but my most serious weakness is in grammar. I have very little confidence in myself when I attempt work in grammar. I feel that I've given up before I try. Yet in spite of that feeling, I know that I have accomplished much in the field of grammar. At the beginning of the first semester, I knew absolutely nothing about the parts of a sentence, And now I feel that I know a little something about it.

At this moment, as far as I know, I plan on going on to the University of Wisconsin, and majoring in the fields of Geography and History. I would like to become a teacher of these fields if it is possible. The situation at the present is indefinite, because of the Korean War. One of my brothers is already in the army and the other is awaiting his draft notice. And since my father is not living, I have to depend on their help for my college education. Therefore, I am very uncertain of my future.

Still another source was the literary magazine published annually by one of the schools. The following poem by a boy who was known to prefer to take life casually but who was harassed by ambitious parents might suggest some projection of his difficulties.

Just a Little Longer

When school nights are here,
And Mother reminds me that bed time is growing near,
I say, "Just a little longer."

When I finally go to bed,
And the next morning comes—oh the dread—
I say, "Just a little longer."

And when the day is done,
And all the children go home to play and run,
Teachers says, "Stay—just a little longer."

One girl who was later to choose a major in English and become a teacher of that subject won honorable mention with the following poem.

Signs of Spring

Green grass, stately trees,
Swooping butterflies, buzzing bees,
They're all signs of spring, that's what they are!
Each has a secret, "Spring's not far."
It's a message of gladness, of joy, and of cheer,
It means a new hope, for spring is near.

One subject, who was later to become a brilliant university student, broke into print in the literary annual of the school during her sophomore year with the following poem.

Sensations

I look through my open window
And what do I see?

A well kept lawn, some evergreen trees
An oak and two elms clothed in fresh summer garments of green.
And I see a road beyond the trees
And beyond the road, a field with hay for some farmer.

I look through my open window
And what do I hear?
The sound of the wind, and the rustle of leaves,
And faintly, the steady hum of the rain
Falling gently, oh so gently
On the thirsty earth.

I look through my open window
And what do I smell?
The perfume of the blossoms of the locust trees
That border the lawn,
And the freshness of the air
That makes one's nostrils quiver with delight.

I look through my open window
And what do I feel?
The cooling touch of the playful breezes
And a delicate spray of rain on my face
And in my mind I feel secure
And at peace with the world.

Not all the personal documents were literary gems. In school newspapers the articles, editorials, reports, and letters to the editor often revealed a good deal about the problems and the thinking of some of our subjects. In the following signed letter to the editor, one of our subjects presented forcefully, if not always grammatically, a situation that was causing him considerable concern.

A new problem has come about. Today we are living in a world of many rules and laws. I would like to discuss a problem that has come up in our high school rules and laws. The problem I have been referring to is tardiness.

The law at the school is three tardinesses per semester. That is fine for kids that don't have to work until all hours of the night. But there is a small percent that does need to work. What about them? Is there any special arrangement made for them? Certainly not.

I, for example, work nights and have been tardy four times. This in turn, has caused a riot with certain faculty members of school. Why? Because of their rules. What I am driving at is that there should be special arrangements made for those special ones that need to work nights.

I don't think that school will be out any if they would break down and give those less fortunates who need to work nights a good deal.

It doesn't matter to anybody what your excuse is, because after you use your quota of tardy passes you get one hour for any over. But they ask you to fill in an excuse. I think this is unjust and is unfair to the student body.

Shall we see what can be done about it?

Another subject who willingly accepted many responsibilities around the school, who graduated first in her class, and who was a leader in student council affairs wrote the following editorial to the school paper.

Lost: A red billfold containing stamp book, lunch ticket and pictures, Will the finder please return it to the office?

A notice similar to this appears at least once a week in our daily announcements. Many more times than not, the rightful owner of the billfold or what have you, never sees the lost item again.

It all boils down to one fault; someone has little or no regard for property. This goes for the careless loser as well as the sly stealer. The loser often leaves books in desks only to forget about them, and takes no precautions to avoid having things taken by leaving his locker unlocked. When he has lost something he sometimes fails to recognize or claim it, as is proven by the over-crowded board of things found in the office. A motive can be seen for stealing sums of money, but the individual who takes insignificant little articles just to steal, is the really low-down person.

The reputation of a school is built on the morals it stands up for. Stealing has been stated as "an offense against morality or welfare." Supposedly, we are all here for one reason: to get an education. And we can't even turn our backs and trust our fellow students.

The documents presented above are just samples of the materials that were available to the counselor at no cost of time or money. Sometimes they simply elaborated what was well known about the subjects, but at other times they provided excellent clues and hints about their problems and behavior. Although it is not possible to reproduce them here, it should be noted that additional information about our subjects was obtained from such sources as the pictures they painted, the cartoons they drew, the products of their efforts in woodworking or metal shops, their performances in dramatic or musical offerings, and the displays they produced for special occasions. All of them became part of the record of the student and many of them were useful in the counseling process.

PROJECTIVE TECHNIQUES

No use was made of any formal or standardized projective methods, since reviews of their effectiveness and consideration of the time required in their administration suggested that the results would not be worth the expenditure.[20] The projective device as an aid to interviewing was not abandoned, however. The counselors carried in their kits a set of ambiguous pictures of individuals and social situations taken from illustrated magazines and a set of photographs depicting certain common occupations. If a subject was hesitant in talking about himself during the interviews the counselors sometimes resorted to the ambiguous pictures to see if, in responding to them, the subject might inadvertently reveal problems that he would not disclose under direct questioning or in free discussion. Some pictures depicting men and women at work in certain occupations were used occasionally when subjects indicated that they had no idea of the kind of work that they wanted to do. In such cases the counselors showed the counselee one picture at a time and waited for comments or other responses that might indicate his reactions to the kind of work suggested by the pictures. No scoring of reactions was done and no recordings of verbatim response were made. Since no experimentation was done with students' responses and since the projective devices were used on very few subjects there will be no further discussion

[20] John W. M. Rothney and Robert A. Heimann, "Development and Application of Projective Tests of Personality," *Review of Educational Research, 23*:70–84 and *26*:56–71.

of the method other than to indicate that, in a few cases and under rather unusual circumstances, the homemade projective devices seemed to be helpful in the counseling process.

CONFERENCES WITH PARENTS

As noted above in the description of interviewing procedures, each student was given at each year's preliminary interview a mimeographed statement about the study to be taken home to his parents. In it the parents were invited to come to the school to examine their child's record and to consider his problems and plans. Approximately half of the parents of the experimental subjects responded to the invitation singly or in pairs. They were shown the cumulative record and a discussion of educational and vocational choices of their children followed.

Many of the parents found that the leisurely conference with a counselor about their children of high school age was a new experience. They had become used to the idea that a parental conference consisted of a few words with a teacher while other parents waited for their turn on a school visiting night. Longer conferences had usually been held only when their children were "in trouble." In this new experience they generally seemed not to know what to think or say. Some of the conferences were difficult because statements made by the counselors as suggestions for consideration were likely to be taken as recommendations. Many parents admitted complete ignorance of educational and vocational opportunities for their sons or daughters and asked for definite advice on what should be done. Others, of course, were seeking for approval of decisions they had already made, and still others sought to get the counselors to ally themselves with the parents in order to coerce the student to do what they wished. Examination of the family problems described in Chapter I will indicate the subjects of discussion during conferences with parents. The general impression of the counselors was that the parents appreciated the opportunity to talk about the problems and plans of their children. In many cases there was evidence that the discussions had resulted in improvement of attitudes and increased understanding.

WORK WITH SCHOOL PERSONNEL

In a previous study by the writer, one of the aims had been the instruction of teachers, principals, and other school personnel so that they might assist students in recognition of their limitations and development of their possibilities.[21] That study had indicated that it could be done successfully. In view of that finding and the limitations of time in the current study, the instruction of school personnel was not stated as one of its objectives. In making the decision to leave it out of the objectives, however, it was recognized that a great deal of it needed to be, and would be, done.

Interviews with teachers were held for many purposes, under widely varying conditions, and by diverse methods. Sometimes they were of the chance meeting-in-the-hall type at which either teacher or counselor raised questions about students. At times they were conferences by appointment, at which both teachers and counselors brought together the information each had about the student and, after comparing notes, decided on some course of action. At other times counselors and teachers worked together on the Behavior Description procedure, described earlier in this chapter. At all times there was free interchange of information among teachers, counselors, and other school personnel in the interest of securing valid information about the students and putting it to use in their service.

The reader must be cautioned against a too ready acceptance of teachers' statements about their students. It has been demonstrated many times that the marks that teachers give tend to be unreliable, and it is questionable whether the comments they make about their students are always valid. Among the factors that militated against complete reliability and validity were: (1) insufficient opportunity to observe individuals, because of large classes; (2) inadequate recording of observations over a period of time so that important trends in behavior were forgotten; (3) the potent influence of recency in determining what comments would be made about a student at a specific time; and (4) the

[21] John W. M. Rothney and B. A. Roens, *Guidance of American Youth,* Cambridge, Harvard University Press, 1950.

effect of the teacher's basic points of view about youth on the selection and interpretation of what she reported. Particularly important in the factor was the failure of middle-class teachers to understand the problems of the student from higher or lower socioeconomic levels.[22]

In addition to the conferences, teachers and other school personnel participated to a limited extent in the study. Teachers were invited to sit in during one interview so that they might learn what was being done. Many of them responded to the invitation. The counselor's records were kept in the school file, and faculty members were free to consult them whenever they chose to do so. And despite the fear that has often been expressed about the danger that such information might be mishandled, there was no evidence that this ever occurred. Occasionally the counselors were asked to confer with the principal about a particular subject, and if he was a member of the experimental group, the invitation was accepted. Advice was often sought from the counselors about guidance practices in the schools and, whenever it was possible to do so, it was freely given, since improvements in those practices were likely to affect experimental and control groups to approximately the same extent.

In this brief description of work with school personnel it must not be assumed by the reader that such work is not a very important part of the work of a counselor. When time is limited an experimenter must make some choices concerning the use of available time. The decision to spend most of the time of this study with the students themselves reflects only the fact that, since it had been demonstrated that intensive counselor work with a faculty could bring results, these counselors were concerned particularly in the current study with what could be done with the actual counseling process in the amount of time available to them.

MISCELLANEOUS SOURCES OF INFORMATION

In this section brief statements are made about the way in which the counselors obtained data on the subjects by using materials that are available in almost any school and which require

[22] See the study by Heimann and Schenck in Chapter VII.

only common observation and some clerical time. Among such sources are the following.

1. *Reports in school and community newspapers.* The following description by a school newspaper reporter of an experimental subject who was chosen as "senior of the week" brought additional information to supplement what was known about her. The validity of the data must be questioned in view of their source, but when added to the others already obtained, they could be used in interviews with the subject.

> Many honors—many activities—that's what we connect with the name of our outstanding senior girl of the week. She's Betty, Editor-In-Chief of the school newspaper, a member of the literary annual editorial board, vice president of the Honor Society, a member of the Social Commission, Mask'n' Wig, Quill and Scroll, National Forensic League, a past president of the Y-Teens, and a member of the NHSPA.
>
> Long brown hair tops her five foot four height. Seventeen year old Betty has unusual eyes (so she says!!). They vary between hazel, green and brown. (Only person we've ever known with three!)
>
> Betty is, of course pretty wrapped up in journalism since she spends the majority of her time in the newspaper office helping cub reporters, advising editors and presiding over staff meetings. After graduation she plans on going to the University of Wisconsin to study journalism. Betty's secret ambition is to have something of her's published. At the present time she's getting writing experience in college prep English which rates high on her list of class favorites.
>
> In her spare time when Betty's not with Carla, she reads, sews, dabbles in painting, swims and she often writes something, rewrites it and throws it away. Betty appreciates good music, good radio programs and movies.
>
> She thinks "our high school is a grand school because of the wonderful people who run it and because of the wide range of subjects and activities." But Betty would like it better if students were not limited to the number of activities to which they might belong.

Occasionally news reports such as the following were important. The boy mentioned in the paragraph below wanted to go to college but had very limited financial resources. He thought that he might win a scholarship if he could continue to improve his swimming performances to the point where he would be an All-State choice. The newspaper clipping reported that he was making progress toward reaching the goal that he had set, and the plans that were to be discussed further during interviews.

> Swimming his best race this year Albert breaststroked to first place and broke the previous record held by Joe also of this city. His time was 1:07 flat. With this time Albert has a good chance of being an All-State choice.

2. *Questionnaires used by others.* Some teachers felt that they could obtain valuable information about their students by having them fill out short questionnaires about themselves. Despite the limitations of this method, the counselors sometimes found them to be valuable sources of information. In one city the questionnaires filled out by our subjects in response to a group that was studying community recreation facilities provided a check on what the counselors knew about the nonschool activities of many of the subjects.

3. *Membership lists.* At certain times all the schools made up lists of members of various clubs, organizations, and extracurricular activity groups. These, with their lists of officers, provided further evidence of the subjects' activities within the school. Reports of participation in church and community activities were observed in local newspapers.

ACTIVITIES DURING THE THIRD YEAR

The subjects of the experiment became high school seniors during the school year 1950–1951. During this year processes begun earlier and described previously in this chapter were continued and intensified. The data collecting process became more selective, however, as efforts were made to provide more interview time for each member of the experimental group.

Very little testing was done during the last year because, except in rare cases, it seemed that the most important data that test scores could provide had already been obtained. If, however, after the record had been studied and it seemed that further testing would be helpful, a student was given tests and the scores were interpreted to him. And if a subject asked for tests they were provided.

The Kuder Preference Record [23] was given to the seniors in two schools by members of the faculties. They had taken the same Record in the ninth grade and the two sets of scores made possible a study of the consistency of preferences over the high school period. Studies of the relationship between scores on the Kuder Preference Record and entry into occupations are presented in Chapter VII. Occasionally the subjects requested interpretations of their Preference Record scores and this was done as well as the manual of the Record permitted. Examination of that manual revealed, however, that the purpose of the Preference Record was simply to indicate occupational areas in which further exploration by the subject was recommended. It did not permit interpretation of scores in terms of subjects' fitness for particular occupations or training experiences and the students were carefully reminded of that limitation. The reader who has noted the caution with which this instrument was used may want to examine the article [24] on interest inventories written by two of the counselors. The article drew in part on their experiences in trying to use one inventory in this study.

INTERVIEWS

Most of the time of the counselors during the third year was used for interviews with the experimental subjects. Procedures similar to those described previously in this chapter were continued. At each interview the students were given the following mimeographed statement.

To the Seniors

We have called you in again to talk with you about your plans for work or training after you graduate this year. It is during this year

[23] Published by Science Research Associates, 228 S. Wabash Avenue, Chicago 4, Ill.

[24] John W. M. Rothney and Louis Schmidt, "Some Limitations of Interest Inventories," *Personnel and Guidance Journal, 33*:199–200.

that you must make one of the most important choices of your life—the choice of a job or a school to attend next year.

We will call in *all* the seniors from time to time this year, but if you want to talk more about your plans before you are called in again do not wait until we send for you. Come in at any time before classes, between classes, or after school and we will set a time to see you. A notice will be posted on the door of this room on the days that we are here.

We hope to get to know you well enough in this last year of high school so that you will remember us when we write to you or come to see you during the five-year period after you leave high school. After you have been working in an occupation for five years we will want to know whether you think you made a good choice.

You may remember that this work with you is being done by Dr. J. W. M. *Rothney* and Mr. Paul *Danielson* of the University of Wisconsin, Department of Education.

On the reverse side the following mimeographed statement to parents appeared. The subjects were asked to read both of the statements at the beginning of the interview, to ask any questions they might have about the counseling, and to take the sheet home to their parents.

To Parents of Seniors

During this year your son or daughter, as a senior, must make one of his most important decisions—the choice of an occupation or a place for training beyond high school.

During the past two years we have talked with your son or daughter about his plans for the future. We have given tests to determine his proficiency in various fields and have prepared a cumulative record for each of the seniors. You might like to discuss the record of your son or daughter with the counselors. If you would like to do so please make an appointment by calling (a given telephone number) at the high school.

This counseling service is sponsored by the Department of Education of the University of Wisconsin. It is directed by Dr. J. W. M. *Rothney* and Mr. Paul *Danielson.* The high school is coöperating fully and all major decisions are considered by school officials and parents before any action is taken. *All* seniors have been interviewed and tested during the past two years and it is the intention of the counselors to keep in touch with these young people for the next five years in order to check on their progress.

We would like to have at least one conference with you this year about the plans for your son or daughter. Since the choices they make this year are of great importance to you and to them we would be very pleased to make an appointment to discuss them at your convenience.

It will be noted that in these statements, and in those presented previously, the subjects were reminded frequently of the names of the investigators, the university from which they came, and of the plan to follow their progress for at least five years after they left high school. These statements were used in the belief that follow-up procedures would bring better returns than are obtained when subjects are not well informed about the plan.

As in previous interviews, guide sheets were used and student responses to the questions were recorded on them. The guide sheet used for the first interview of the senior year is presented below. As in previous years *the guide sheet was discarded if the student preferred to talk about some other topic or wished to elaborate on any of the topics covered by the questions.* As might be expected the seniors were much concerned about their plans for work or training after graduation and much of the time was spent in discussion of them. Further comments about the interviewing methods have been made in the section of this chapter headed General Discussion of Procedures.

Are there any important changes in your family situation this year?

What occupation have you decided to enter? Do both your parents approve your plans? If not, what do they suggest?

What are your plans for training after you finish high school?

If you could drop one of your current subjects now, which would it be? Why?

Which of your current subjects would you like to spend all your time on? Why?

If you could make any changes in your present program what would they be? Why?

What school activities do you really spend much time on? How much time? Worth your time?

How do you spend your out-of-school time?

Jobs: Summer? What did you actually do?

Part-time now? Want to continue either after graduation? Why?

Is there anything about your health that keeps you from doing the things you want to do?

Who are some of your closest friends?

If asked, how would they describe you?

What are your strongest points?

What are your weaknesses?

Do you have any problems now on which you would like help? Any with which you think you will need help later on?

What problems do you have about your education now?

What kind of educational problems do you expect in the future?

What problems do you have about the choice of a vocation?

What problems do you have in getting along with anyone else?

If things worked out just as you wanted, what would you like to be doing five years after you leave high school?

SENIOR REPORTS

One month before graduation each student was asked to fill out a Senior Report, or questionnaire. The students, in groups of 35 to 40, were asked to indicate their postschool plans in terms of one of six categories: *Education, Employment, Armed forces, Working on parents' farm, Uncertain,* and, for girls only, *Married within one year.* Different forms of reports were then distributed to each student in terms of the choice he had indicated. Thus, if a student had said that he intended to obtain employment as soon as he had been graduated, he filled in a two-page report about his occupational plans. If he had decided that he would go on to post-high school training, he chose a report form containing questions about his educational plans. It was possible in this manner to ask more specific questions about plans than could be asked on a general questionnaire designed for use with all students.

The last three pages of each *Senior Report* were identical for all students regardless of the category in which their postschool plans fell. On these pages questions were asked about their long-term plans, their attitudes toward certain kinds of work or training, their feelings about school as they looked back on it, and their attitudes toward the future. They were also asked to estimate their standing on 12 items in comparison with other members of the senior classes. On the last page they were invited to make any comments about the past or future as they saw it. A sample copy of the complete *Education Report* (which was to be filled out only by those who planned to continue their education immediately after graduation) follows.

EDUCATION SENIOR REPORT Your Name____________
City ____________
Date____________

Give the name and address of someone who will always know where you will be so that they can send mail on to you.

NAME__________ADDRESS____________CITY ________

1. What is the name of your *first* choice of school or college or training institution?____________________
   Where is it located? ____________________
2. When did you decide on the place? Year_____Month______
3. Have you applied for admission?__________ Have you been admitted?__________
4. Have you applied for a scholarship? ______________
5. How long is the course you plan to take? ____________
6. How much do you think it will cost the first year? ________
7. What *percent* of the cost of your training do you expect to earn? ________How? ________________
8. Why did you select the school as your first choice? ________
   ____
   ____
   ____
9. If something keeps you from attending this place what are your second and third choices?
   Second choice__________________
   Third choice__________________
10. Who, if anyone, helped you in your choice of school?______
    ____
11. If more than one person helped you, who helped you most?
    ____

12. What is there about *you* that will make you successful in the training you have chosen? ______________________________

____

____

13. What is there about *you* that might keep you from being successful in your training? ______________________________

____

14. Name any friends of yours who are planning to go to the same place for their training. ______________________________

15. What arrangements have you made about a place to live? ______

____

16. Which of the activities that you carried on in high school are you planning to continue? ______________________________

____

17. What course do you plan to take? ______________________________

____

18. What, if anything, would change your mind about wanting to take the training you had planned for next year? ______________

____

____

____

(The following questions were answered by *all* students regardless of post-high school plans.)

1. Regardless of what you have said on the other pages, what would you like to be doing for a living:

Five years from now? ______________________________

____

Ten years from now? ______________________________

____

2. What training will be needed to get the job you listed on the first line on *this* page? ______________________________

____

____

3. Are there any kinds of *training* you would strongly object to taking? ____________________

____

4. Are there any kinds of *work* you would strongly object to doing? ____________________

____

5. Looking back at your last three years of senior high school do you think they were (put a check on the lines that tell how you feel).
   A. Generally pleasant? ________ or *un*pleasant? ________
   B. Generally worth while? ________ or *not* worth while? ________
   C. Generally useful? ________ or *not* useful? ________

6. Are there any subjects you took in high school which you wish you hadn't?
   Subject ________ Why? ________
   Subject ________ Why? ________
   Subject ________ Why? ________
   Subject ________ Why? ________

7. Are there any subjects you didn't take in high school which you wish you had?
   Subject ________ Why? ________
   Subject ________ Why? ________
   Subject ________ Why? ________

8. Are there any subjects you wanted to take that were not offered?
   Subject ________ Why take it? ________

   ____

   Subject ________ Why take it? ________

   ____

9. Are there any subjects on which you would like to have spent more time?
   Subject ________ Why didn't you spend more time on it?

   ____

   Subject ________ Why didn't you spend more time on it?

   ____

10. Looking toward the future do you think that things are going to work out well for you? ____________________

11. Why or why not? ____________________

____

12. How has the international situation (war) affected you?
13. How do you think it will affect you in the future? ______

______

______

14. Do you think there is as much chance for people to get ahead today as there was when your parents were the age that you are now? ______
15. Why? ______

______

16. What organizations or clubs would you want to belong to when you are working *or* a married member of the community? List in the order of your choice.

______

______

______

17. What *social problems* do *you* plan to do something about after you have finished high school?

______

______

18. How do *you* plan to work on them? ______

______

19. In each of the twelve headings below, show where you think you stand compared to other high school seniors by putting a check (√) mark in the column at the right.

   First Example: If you know that your scores on intelligence tests were above the 75th percentile, you would be in the upper quarter and you would put a check mark across from intelligence test scores and *under* Top Quarter.

   Second Example: If you have been a member of the first team in football you would be in the top quarter of your class in sports and you would mark it like the example below.

In the item given below I would be, compared to other high school seniors, in the	Top Quarter	Third Highest Quarter	Second Lowest Quarter	Lowest Quarter
Example: Skill in sports	√			

1. Achievement in my special field of interest (write it below)

---

2. Reading achievement

---

3. Intelligence test scores

---

4. Achievement in arithmetic and mathematics

---

5. Confidence that I will succeed in the work I have chosen to do

---

6. Getting along with people

---

7. Rank in *this* senior class

---

8. Confidence that I have chosen the right career

---

9. Knowing my own strengths

---

10. Knowing my own weaknesses

---

11. Readiness for life after high school

---

12. Getting along in new situations

---

20. Suppose you had a choice between (*A*) a safe steady job working for someone else with steady average pay for the job or, (*B*) running your own business with the chance of either going bankrupt or getting rich.
Would you choose *A* or *B*? __________ Why? __________

____

____

21. Do you believe that you will ever want counseling again?
____

22. If you do, where will you get it? ______________________
____

23. This last page is to be used to give more information on any of the questions asked on the other pages or to write anything you want to about school experiences or your plans for the future. You might want to comment about the counseling you have had, your preparation for the life that is ahead, the way in which schools could be improved, or any other matter that interests you. Write on the back of the page if you need more space.

The first sections of the Senior Reports for those who chose the forms for Employment, Armed forces, Working on parents' farm, Uncertain, and Married within one year are in Appendix III.

POPULATION LOSSES

At the time of graduation in June, 1951, the original population of 870 subjects had been reduced to 690. The reasons given for leaving and the numbers who gave them are presented in Table 17. Examination of the table reveals that approximately one-fifth of the initial population was lost during the three years of the study.

There could be no control by the schools or counselors over such factors as the moving of a family out of the city, serious health disorders, death of a student, or the marriage of a girl. The cases that fell in those categories will not be described as dropouts in the following discussion. One hundred and eight of the subjects (83, or 77 percent of them boys), including those who transferred to other schools, who enlisted, who were suspended, and who went to work will be considered as dropouts. They are the cases whom the school might presumably have kept in school if their needs had been met.

There is considerable evidence that those who left school to go to work or to enlist were doing so because of dissatisfaction with

TABLE 17. Losses from Original Population of the Study

Reason for Leaving School	Number Leaving from School *W*	School *X*	School *Y*	School *Z*	Total
Work	28	27	4	3	62
Family moved out of city	23	9	8	5	45
Transferred to other schools	11	16	1	–	28
Married	9	8	2	–	19
Enlisted	4	10	–	2	16
Reason unknown to school	2	–	–	1	3
Suspended	1	1	–	–	2
Ill health	1	1	–	–	2
Deceased	–	1	–	–	1
Accelerated graduate	–	1	–	1	2
Total	79	74	15	12	180
Original pop.	392	298	114	66	870
Percent of loss	20.2	24.8	13.1	18.2	20.7

school. Of the 16 boys who enlisted, 13 were failing in half or more of their courses in school and all were having trouble in adjustments. With rare exceptions those who left to work were having academic, disciplinary, or other difficulties, and some of the girls who dropped out of school to marry had expressed dissatisfaction with school. The transfers often went to parochial, private, or vocational schools because they or their families felt that their needs would be better met in the other institutions.

That school procedures had some effect on the drop-out rate is evidenced by the fact that one of the schools had a real drop-out (work, enlistment, transfer) rate of 4.4, one a rate of 7.6, another of 10.9, and the other a rate of 17.8 percent. The school with the drop-out rate of only 4.4 percent made a determined effort to adjust to individual differences by permitting the election of courses that seemed best for the child or by making adjustments when courses seemed unsuitable. Failing marks were very rarely given. In the school with the drop-out rate of 17.8 percent, election of courses was severely limited even though that fact was not indicated in printed statements, no student was permitted to change a course after he had attended it for a week, and the failure rate was high. It seems clear that the probability of students remaining to graduate was higher in some schools than in others and that the school practices and policies did influence the rate at which students left.

Of the 106 students who left school to work, to enlist, or to attend other schools, 50 were experimental subjects and 56 were controls. This difference can hardly be considered important in view of the number of factors involved, and cannot be considered as evidence for or against the premise that counseling affects drop-out rates. Some of the dropouts and transfers occurred before counseling could have influenced the students or their parents, even if it had been desirable to do so. Again the fact that the counselors were itinerant made it difficult to work with many potential dropouts at the time when working with them might have been most effective.

The loss of some 20 percent of the original population of the study was not unexpected in view of what was known about the mobility of the people in the communities, military draft and enlistment policies at the time, and the attitudes of some of the parents toward education.

At the time the plans for the study were formulated, a decision had to be made concerning what was to be done with those subjects who would leave before graduation. There seemed to be only two choices. The first would require the following up of dropouts and therefore reduction of the time that could be spent on those who remained. The second would be the "writing off" of a subject when he left school. It was decided that time and budget limitations would not permit the following up of those who left school and that they would be dropped from the current study as soon as they left. The decision was made with much regret, since the problem of school population losses is an important one that needs much investigation. When comment is made about the 100 percent returns in the follow-up studies, the 100 percent figure refers to the 685 cases who remained throughout the three years of senior high school and were still alive five years after graduation from high school.

THE BASIC DATA

At the end of the third year a cumulative record containing the kinds of information described in this chapter had been completed for each of the experimental subjects. The cumulative record for the control group students usually contained only a list of marks for grades nine through twelve, test scores, addresses, verified birth dates, behavior descriptions for some cases, senior reports, autobiographies or other personal documents, clippings from school or local newspapers, and short notes made after the introductory interview. It will be shown that some of these data were valuable in personalizing requests for follow-up data after the subjects had been graduated from high school.

The chief differences between the cumulative records of the experimental and control group subjects lay in the greater amounts of information of the kind noted above on the records of the experimental students. There was, of course, much detail in the interview reports and in interpretations of data contained in the records. Although many of the data had been tabulated and collated in the process of making minor investigations, the basic data for the study were to be found in the 685 cumulative records of the graduates. These records and the follow-up data described in the following chapter constituted the basic data of the study.

CLINICAL PREDICTION

Immediately after the experimental subjects of the study had begun their post-high school careers in 1951 an attempt was made to predict their success in the kinds of post-high school activity they had indicated they would undertake. The writer and a graduate student, who had not participated in the counseling but who had become familiar with the data, proceeded to make the predictions independently after they had worked through a small sample of the cases in order to get some uniformity in practice.

The first step in the prediction process required the setting up of categories of possible performances in each of five post-high school activities that the subjects had chosen. They are listed below.

Post-High School Training

He (she) will:

_______A. be eligible for *major* awards based upon scholastic performances.

_______B. be eligible for *minor* awards based upon scholastic performances.

_______C. complete training. Will not be eligible for awards nor on probation.

_______D. take longer than usual time to graduate though never on probation.

_______E. drop out of training for reasons other than scholastic difficulty.

_______F. be a marginal student. Will be on probation at some time.

_______G. be dropped because of low grades.

Employment

He (she) will:

_______A. be promoted in pay and responsibility faster than usual schedule.

_______B. be promoted in pay and responsibility on schedule.

_______C. remain at same job level at which he began.

_______D. be reduced in pay and responsibility.

_______E. be dismissed from a job.

_______F. change jobs. Changes will be to better positions.

_______G. drift voluntarily from job to job. Changes will *not* be to better positions.

_______H. leave job to get business of his own.

_______I. depend on family for support. Will not work.

_______J. drift as a vagrant. Will not work.

_______K. live by breaking the law.

Armed Forces

He (she) will:

_______A. be promoted faster than usual rate.

_______B. be promoted on schedule.

_______C. leave service at level comparable to entry rank.

_______D. be dishonorably discharged.

_______E. desert the service.

Work on Relative's Farm

He will:

______A. achieve recognition as superior farmer.
______B. get increased responsibility as reward for good work.
______C. be retained at initial entry status comparable to a hired hand.
______D. take over farm but will lose it by bad management.
______E. leave farm to enter *training*.
______F. leave farm to enter another *occupation* offering *better* opportunities.
______G. leave farm to enter another *occupation* offering *lesser* opportunities.
______H. leave farm at relative's suggestion that he enter other occupation.

Marriage (Girls Only)

She will:

______A. report that she is happily married.
______B. report dissatisfaction with marriage situation but will tolerate it so that marriage is not broken.
______C. end marriage by desertion, separation, or divorce.
______D. her husband will end marriage by desertion, separation, or divorce.

The categories listed above were drawn up on the basis of the writer's previous experience with youths' post-high school activities, the suggestions of persons who were familiar with practices in a particular field, and after discussion of possible categories with many persons who had shown interest in youth activities. Specialists in agriculture, who suggested the categories for the *work on parents' farm,* and members of the *armed forces* considered and approved the items that were to be used for those classifications. Graduate students in guidance, workers in industry, housewives, and many others assisted in the arranging of items in the other categories. The items, then, compose a concensus agreed upon after many suggestions, discussions, and compromises. In each division they generally represent a scale, but it is recognized that persons might disagree on the order of placement of the items. In the final selection, the investigators were less concerned with the scaling of items than with the setting up of categories descriptive of the kinds of activities in which the subjects might later be found. It was recognized that some of the subjects might change their activities during the five-year period after graduation from high school, but the predictions had to be based on the choices that were indicated at the time they were made.

After the categories had been drawn up the two predictors working examined the cumulative record of each case with respect to the following factors.

1. Academic performances in high school
2. Performances on tests taken in high school
3. Strength of drive to succeed
4. Realism in self-appraisal
5. Realism in appraisal of opportunities
6. Flexibility, modifiability, adjustability to new situations
7. Handicaps
8. Factors unique to this individual

Separate mimeographed sheets contained the items for the general classifications of employment, education, farming, marriage, and armed forces. At the bottom of each sheet the eight factors given above were listed with space to write between them and there was an added space for general comment.

After the cumulative record had been examined and notes recorded on the sheet, a prediction was made by checking the item which the predictor thought would best describe the level of activity of each youth five years after completing high school. (In the case of those entering post high school training and the armed forces, the prediction was to apply to the usual time required to complete the training or service.) A sample of a completed prediction sheet follows.

Sample of a Completed Prediction Sheet

He will:

______ be eligible for *major* awards based on scholastic performance.

__√__ be eligible for *minor* awards based on scholastic performance.

______complete training. Will not be eligible for awards nor on probation.
______take longer than the usual time to graduate though never on probation.
______drop out of training for reasons other than scholastic difficulty.
______be a marginal student. Will be on probation at some time.
______be dropped because of low grades.

1. Academic performance in high school
   (Not as high as anticipated. Too many outside activities.)
2. Performances on tests taken in high school
   (High enough for what he plans to do)
3. Strength of drive to succeed
   (Unusually high—extremely high)
4. Realism in self-appraisal
   (Tends to overestimate himself)
5. Realism in appraisal of opportunities
   (Extremely realistic about plans and family finances)
6. Flexibility, modifiability, adjustability to new situations
   (Can make adjustments readily)
7. Handicaps
   (Vision—wears contact lenses that provide some relief but cannot study for long periods)
8. Factors unique to this individual
   (A swimmer—record holder but swimming was done in hope that he would get a scholarship to further his education)

Comment

Motivation for chosen career is so high that it seems likely that he will compensate for visual difficulty.

In the prediction process the investigators tried to use what might be called clinical judgments of the relationships between the data about the student and the activity that he was about to undertake. For many of those who planned to enter unskilled labor, for example, their *academic performances* in high school were usually considered to be relatively unimportant and the data provided by *tests* requiring high verbal performances almost superfluous. The opposite situation usually applied for those who planned to go to college although the importance of those factors was considered in terms of what was known about the academic requirements of the particular college that the student planned to enter.

Strength of drive to succeed was estimated from the interview notes of the counselors, descriptions by teachers or parents, and the records of activity participation of the student. Particular attention was paid to written and oral reports by the student during interviews and in personal documents. Records of continuous striving to succeed in any assignments undertaken by the student and repeated statements about goals were heavily weighted in the prediction.

Realism in self-appraisal was judged from statements made in interviews, in personal documents (particularly the autobiography), in a self-appraisal scale of 12 items on the Senior Report, and in answers to questions designed to evoke pessimistic-optimistic attitudes. Students' reactions to interpretations of their test scores and records were also given much consideration in the judgment of realism in self-appraisal.

Realism in appraisal of opportunities required consideration of such factors as the amount of financial aid available for going to college or getting into a business. The size of a father's farm was an important factor for those youth who planned to work with their parents, since small farms were unlikely to support two male adults. Opportunities for advancement in some local occupational situations were appraised. The willingness of the student to weigh the advantages and disadvantages of foregoing high pay immediately to accept jobs where low beginning wages might lead, after on-the-job training, to high ultimate income was examined. Students' recognition of the extent to which their own particular handicaps and strengths might limit or enhance their opportunities was considered.

The two categories described above overlapped the one on flexibility, adjustability, or modifiability. Subjects who held rigidly to the choice of an occupation or place of post-high school training, despite much evidence that the choice seemed highly unrealistic in terms of previous performances and handicaps, were not predicted as likely to succeed. The student who insisted that she planned to go into nursing despite low scores on tests similar to those given for selection of students by schools of nursing and despite very low grades in science courses was not predicted to succeed in training for that occupation. Students who had achieved very low grades over the whole high school period but who insisted that they would turn over a new leaf and study diligently when they went on to college were not placed high in the flexibility category.

Particular problems of health or physique, limitations imposed by family circumstances, inadequate preparation in fundamentals such as reading, uncorrected speech deficiencies, and obvious personality difficulties were considered in the handicaps category. As in all the other groupings the attitudes of the subject toward his handicap as well as his actual condition was given much consideration. If the handicap was accepted with resignation and used as an alibi, it was considered differently from those cases where knowledge of the handicap had resulted in vigorous and effective attempts to compensate for it. If a subject persisted in the choice of an occupation or plan for training that seemed to be completely unrealistic, the handicap category became very important in the making of predictions. The investigators were not unaware, of course, of the fact that some individuals might succeed when all the evidence about their handicaps seemed to suggest that failure was inevitable.

The category of factors unique to the individual was added to allow for the fact that some characteristics or combinations of them suggested that the subject might succeed or fail in a particular choice despite the evidence offered in the other categories. Thus the girl who had violent temper tantrums at the beginning of each menstrual period seemed unlikely to succeed in the particular post-high school activity she had chosen. The boy who thought that "driving a shiny white milk truck was the best job a man could ever have" and who had already demonstrated that he could do it well seemed likely to succeed. And for the boy who had worked and planned to continue to work closely with his father in a custom butchering business, and who spent much time convincing the counselor that butchering was a clean and an important occupation, success seemed certain.

The section headed "comment" was frequently left blank. At times the predictors indicated the extent to which they felt safe in their estimates, commented on the difficulty of assessing the data on an individual, or elaborated on one of the other categories.

It will be observed that no attempt was made to attach numbers to any of the judgments in any of the categories. The weight given to any datum in the clinical predictions varied from case to case as the evidence seemed to justify it. Undoubtedly the predictors' judgments were influenced at times by previous experience with statistical predictions (such as the effectiveness of test scores and high school rank in forecasting academic success at the University of Wisconsin) but at other times they were not aware of any statistical data that could have been used either consciously or unconsciously in prediction. The forecasting of the performance of a girl who took an apprenticeship with a florist, for example, could not be based on any known data about the relationship between academic record test scores or personality characteristics to success as a florist's apprentice. In the particular nursery she had entered she was the first apprentice to be accepted.

It is important to note, too, that the kinds of data used in the prediction process were those that high school counselors are likely to have about their subjects if they maintain cumulative records of the information that they collect and record. The investigator's data did not differ greatly from those commonly obtained by counselors who collect information about pupils' personalities, abilities, and interests.

SOME PROBLEMS IN MAKING CLINICAL PREDICTIONS

The prediction of human behavior is at best a hazardous undertaking. When predictions are based, as in this study, on information gathered by counselors with the occasional aid of parents and teachers over a three-year period, and condensed for recording on a cumulative record card, it is a particularly difficult process.

The problems in this kind of clinical prediction can be classified into the several large categories noted below but they vary for particular pupils even within the classifications. Lack of information on some aspects of the behavior of some pupils, for example, was a basic problem. At times the counselors who knew some of the subjects very well failed to record every item of insight or information as fully as they did for some of the subjects about whom they knew less. What seemed particularly important in one case seemed less so in others so that there was some unevenness in data throughout the population. When, as in some cases, the counselors did not develop full rapport with a subject, the data on motivation or strength of drive seemed to be inadequate for forecasting purposes.

Some of the records appeared to indicate conflicting evidence about the behavior of the subjects. Some subjects had not achieved a high level of integration, and they changed their goals and motivation drastically as they increased in maturity. The predictor was required to give consideration to the end product achieved at the completion of high school and the development toward it. Should he give greater weight to the integration achieved at the end of the high school period than to the years in which there seemed to have been conflict? Would the end product be a stable one or was it just a nonconflict stage of a long series of alternating conflict and nonconflict experiences? These kinds of problems in the use of longitudinal data for prediction were noticed especially when subjects entered into fields of work or a training situation never considered with them by the counselors or mentioned at any time during the interviews. The boy who enrolled at a college despite the fact that he had never mentioned that plan, or the girl who suddenly dropped all previous plans when she entered a hasty marriage presented some challenges for the forecaster. And those subjects who did such things after a long period of protesting that they would never do so were particularly difficult to appraise.

Lack of information about opportunities for advancement in particular jobs probably limited the effectiveness of the predictions. Occasionally, despite high performance and drive, a worker may find himself in a blind alley job, and family circumstances may require him to stay there despite his desire to leave. Nepotism rather than performance may determine promotion in other situations, and current practices (the boom for employees and service men at the time of the Korean War in 1951, for example) might result in promotional opportunities that were difficult to anticipate.

The subjects for whom forecasting was very difficult were those at extremes of the high school academic ladder who intended to enter post-high school training. Perhaps this bright student who planned to enter a certain college would find the work less challenging and perhaps this poor student could stick through to graduation in a college with less demanding standards. Would the change from a small high school to a large college, or vice versa, be too difficult an adjustment for this student? Would the release from a protected and regimented home life to the relatively free situation of a university provide too many difficulties in adjustment? Would life in a city provide too many distracting influences to the boy from the small town? And were the performances that seemed high in a small high school remain high in the more selective student body of a college?

Prediction of adjustment in marriage is a particularly hazardous business when the future husband is not known to the predictor. In fact, it may seem foolhardy to attempt it under such circumstances. It did seem, however, that some of the girls had weighed the issues with care, had shown that they could make adjustments to occasional difficult situations, and were so determined to make a go of whatever things they undertook that they seemed likely to be successful.

The problems in making clinical predictions have been described above in some detail to show the factors that needed consideration. The list of problems presented below includes those given above and others which need not be described in detail here.

1. Inadequate data about characteristics of subjects.
2. Unevenness in adequacy of data about subjects.
3. Inadequate information about post-high school occupational and educational opportunities.

4. Fluctuations in post-high school employment and training opportunities.
5. Inadequate evidence about general relationships of characteristics of subjects and achievements beyond high school.
6. Fluctuations in motivation of subjects.
7. Changes in post-high school opportunities resulting from war and economic conditions.
8. Spontaneous changes in goals of the subjects.
9. Lack of information about specific influence of environmental changes upon behavior of youth.
10. Changes in regulations concerning required military service for youth.

Despite all these difficulties, it was decided that clinical predictions would be attempted using the categories described above. The extent of agreement between two independent predictors is described below.

AGREEMENT BETWEEN PREDICTORS

Clinical predictions for 333 of the 346 experimental subjects were made independently by each of two predictors. (The discrepancy of 13 from the grand total of 346 cases was the result, in part, of the fact that some of the cases had been done together while methods of prediction were being developed. In the others, different forms of prediction sheets had been used because of differences in the interpretation of the kind of work undertaken by the subject. In one case, for example, one of the predictors used the *work on relatives' farm* sheet while the other used the *employment* sheet, since the boy was actually a hired hand on a farm.) One hundred and seventy-six of the 333 cases had chosen employment, 106 planned to enter post-high school training, 19 were to work on a relative's farm, 16 joined the armed forces, and 16 girls married.

The extent of agreement of the predictors is shown in Table 18. It will be observed in the table that the percentages of agreement in descending order by areas are *marriage, education, work on relative's farm, armed forces,* and *employment* and that the

TABLE 18. Agreement of Two Predictors of the Post-High School Performances of Youth in the Areas Indicated

Area of Prediction	Number of Subjects for Whom Predictions Were Made	Number of Times Predictors Agreed on Category	Percentage of Agreement
Married (girls only)	16	13	81.2
Education	106	71	67.0
Work on relative's farm	19	12	63.2
Armed forces	16	10	62.5
Employment	176	94	53.3
Total	333	200	60.0

range is from 53.3 to 81.2 with the overall total at 60 percent of agreement. If a leeway of one category is used, the overall percentage of agreement rises to 80.5 percent but, as will be observed from the reading of the categories at the beginning of this section, a one-step variation might represent a very important difference. The lack of high agreement between the two predictors results in part from the fact that one of them had personal contact with the subjects while the other worked entirely from the cumulative records. It is also partly caused by the difficulties in prediction described in the previous section. In any case it is evident that two predictors generally differed in 2 out of 5 cases when perfect agreement of categories was demanded and in 1 out 5 when a one-step leeway was given.

The extent to which the various categories were used by the two investigators may be observed from the tabulation that follows. The *A* column presents the predictions of the principal investigator who had worked with the subjects and the *B* column contains those of a graduate student in guidance who worked only from the records. The number of categories in the five areas totaled 35 and only nine of them were not used. These nine tended to fall at the lower extremes. The investigators were aware that the probabilities of such extreme behavior were not high and they did not, therefore, predict that any of the cases would fall into the lower ends of the scale.

Category	Employ-ment		Education		Farming		Armed Forces		Marriage	
	A	*B*	*A*	*B*	*A*	*B*	*A*	*B*	*A*	*B*
A	12	1	6	2	2	0	4	0	13	14
B	58	51	18	25	11	11	8	9	1	2
C	0	0	3	2	0	0	0	0	0	0
D	55	87	51	58	3	3	4	7	2	0
E	1	1	17	7	2	3	0			
F	39	27	10	9	1	2				
G	9	8	1	3	0					
H	2	1			0					
I	0									
J	0									
K	0									
Total	176	176	106	106	19	19	16	16	16	16

The results of the study of clinical predictions and of a comparison between clinical and statistical predictions is reported in Chapter VII.

SUMMARY

In this chapter the methods of collecting data and of using them in counseling have been described. The basic concepts and criteria that governed the data-collecting and counseling processes have also been presented briefly. It has been noted that the procedures are the kind that may be employed by persons who have the training commonly expected of high school counselors and it has been shown that attempts were made to simulate conditions in which such counselors are commonly required to work. With this background in mind the reader may turn now to the description of the methods used in follow-up studies of the subjects three times after their graduation from high school.

CHAPTER IV

Follow-Up Procedures

In the previous chapters the setting of the study was given, the subjects were described, and the methods employed up to the time when the subjects completed high school were outlined. In this chapter the methods used in the follow-up of the subjects into their post-high school activities are presented. They are described in detail because the reader must consider them in the interpretation of results presented in later chapters, and because they illustrate some of the problems encountered in follow-up studies. Descriptions of the methods that were used successfully may encourage others to try this essential but difficult step in the guidance process.

THE FIRST FOLLOW-UP STUDY

The students were graduated in June, 1951. The first follow-up study began in October of that year and was completed by the end of January in 1952.[1] This first follow-up was designed to remind the subjects of the investigator's intent to keep in touch with them. It also attempted to get information about the extent to which they had carried out the plans made while they were in school, their degree of satisfaction with what they were doing, and their plans for the future. Since the first follow-up was done so soon after graduation, and since the purpose was only to get

[1] For a report of the procedures used, see J. W. M. Rothney and R. A. Mooren, "Sampling Problem in Follow-Up Research," *Occupations, 30*:573–579.

a quick survey of the factors mentioned above, it appeared that a postal card questionnaire would be adequate.

Double postal cards were mailed to all the subjects four months after they had been graduated from high school. One side of the card contained the following message.

We are still interested in you as we were when you were in high school. We want to know where everyone in your senior class is now and what he is doing. Will you let us know what *you* are doing by filling in the other part of this card, tearing it off, and dropping it in the mailbox?

If you have forgotten us look us up on page ——— of your senior yearbook.

Dr. Rothney
Mr. Danielson

On the other side of the card the following questions were asked.

What is your address? (street address and city)
Name?
Married girls give maiden name.____________________________
If you are not working full time, what are you doing?
If working, where do you work? (name of company)
What do you actually do on the job?
If working or not do you like what you are doing?
What would you like to be doing in your *second* year out of high school?

The mailing of this double card brought returns from only 56 percent of the cases. One month later a second double card, identical with the first, but with a coding added to identify it as from the second mailing, brought returns from 23 percent of the subjects. This brought the cumulative response to 79 percent.

For the third mailing one month later, a card, similar to the first but coded differently, was enclosed with the following form letter.

Dear______________

We have *not* heard from you on the cards like the one enclosed. We *have* heard from nearly everyone else.

1. *Maybe* you just lost the card. If you did, here is another.
2. *Maybe* we didn't have your right address. If so, this card can be used now.
3. *Maybe* you didn't think it was important to send it in. It really is very important if we are going to find ways to make school a better place. And we *do* need to hear from *every one* of you.
4. *Maybe* you don't want to tell us what you are doing. If that is so will you send in the card with your name and address on it and tell us that you don't want to fill it out? Then we can save time for both of us.

We do need cards from every one of the members of last year's senior classes.

Don't let *your* card be the only one that is missing. Send it in *today*.

Yours sincerely,
J. Rothney
P. Danielson

To *parents:*

If your son or daughter is in service we would appreciate it if you would put the address on the card and mail it in.

This letter, which provided socially acceptable excuses for failure to answer, brought responses from another 10 percent of the subjects and raised the cumulative percentage total to 89.

The remaining 11 percent of the subjects who had not responded to the three requests over the three-month period were sent a personal handwritten letter asking them to return their cards. Six percent responded and they brought the total to 95 percent.

Returns were obtained from the last 5 percent by visiting the subjects at their homes or places of employment.

Since most follow-up studies yield percentages of returns significantly less than 100 percent (usually about 60), the data were examined to determine what kinds of subjects responded in what order to requests for follow-up information. Analysis of the responses makes possible a better evaluation of the usual questionnaire studies in which less than 100 percent of the subjects respond, and points up the kinds of bias found in incomplete samples. In the analysis that follows, early and later responders have been classified in terms of: amount of counseling contacts while the subjects were in high school, sex, city or rural residence, rank in high school graduating class, intelligence test scores, kinds of postschool activity, satisfaction with that activity, and three other miscellaneous variables that seemed to influence the rate of returns. The findings with their implications are presented below.

It is interesting to note in Table 19 that the experimental subjects responded more quickly than the controls. The data suggests that, in general, those students who had been given individual attention were more likely to respond quickly to follow-up attempts than those who had not.[2] Elaboration of this finding was obtained when responders in the experimental group were classified in terms of the number of interviews they experienced when they were in high school. Those students who had been most interviewed and those who had requested further interviewing were usually among the earliest responders.

TABLE 19. Cumulative Percentages of Returns by Experimental and Control Groups

Group	Returns by Mailings				Letter
	1st	2d	3d	4th	and Visit
Experimental	62.1	82.7	90.2	96.0	100.0
Control	49.9	75.3	88.1	94.5	100.0
Difference	12.2	7.4	2.1	1.5	0

Males and females had been distributed almost evenly between experimental and control groups. Classifications of returns by sex of the responders showed that girls tended to respond more quickly than boys to the first two requests for information. As shown in Table 20, the percentage of responses by the boys went ahead at the third mailing and remained there. It seemed that it took the boys longer to get around to sending in their cards.

[2] Computation of significance of the differences shown in the tables in this section did not seem warranted in view of the nature of the data and the particular conditions existing at this time.

TABLE 20. Cumulative Percentages of Returns of Males and Females

Group	Returns by Mailings 1st	2d	3d	4th	Visits
Females	61.9	82.7	88.2	95.1	100.0
Males	49.4	74.7	90.1	95.4	100.0

From the condition of many of them, it appeared that they had been carried in pockets for some time before they were mailed.

Rank in high school class seemed to be related closely to immediacy of response. As shown in Table 21, 36 percent of all those who responded to the first mailing had been ranked in the highest fourth of their graduating class. Twenty-eight percent ranked in the second quarter, 20 percent in the third, and 16 percent in the fourth quarter. Thus, approximately 64 percent of the first responses were obtained from subjects who had achieved the

TABLE 21. Percentages of Returns by Rank in Class

Class Rank by Quarters	Returns by Mailings 1st	2d	3d	4th	Visits
First (highest)	36.0	18.8	10.8	7.5	3.3
Second	27.9	22.7	18.5	25.0	23.3
Third	20.0	33.8	24.6	40.0	33.4
Fourth (lowest)	16.1	24.7	46.1	27.5	40.0

upper *half* of their graduating class. The fact that highest-ranking individuals were less inclined to be tardy is shown by the proportions of high and low ranking students in the most difficult to get (visits) group. Of that group, approximately one-quarter were graduated with ranks above the average of their class. The ranks of almost three-fourths of the subjects in this group were below the class average. In general, then, early follow-up responses were obtained from students who had achieved better-than-average school standing.

The subjects were classified into quarters on the basis of an average of raw scores achieved on two administrations of the

Henmon-Nelson Tests of Mental Ability. Analysis of their speed of response as shown in Table 22 indicates that the highest scoring youths tended to respond earlier than those who scored low. The results suggest that, if a follow-up procedure is not continued

TABLE 22. Percentages of Returns of Subjects Classified by Scores on the Henmon-Nelson Test of Mental Ability

Quarterly Classification Based on Average of Two Raw Scores on Henmon-Nelson Tests	Returns by Mailings 1st	2d	3d	4th	Visits
0–24 (dullest)	50.0	25.0	0.0	0.0	25.0
25–49	40.7	26.7	17.2	9.1	6.3
50–74	62.1	21.3	7.2	4.9	4.5
75–100 (brightest)	94.1	5.9	0.0	0.0	0.0

until 100 percent of the subjects respond, the returns will not be representative in terms of the distribution of mental test scores obtaining in the original population.

Does one get a bias in questionnaire returns on the basis of the postschool training or occupational activities of the subjects? An answer is indicated in Table 23 in which the subjects have been grouped by their post-high school educational and occupational

TABLE 23. Percentages of Returns of Subjects Classified by Postschool Activities

Post-High School Activity	Returns by Mailings 1st	2d	3d	4th	Visits
Training (not college)	78.1	17.1	0.0	4.8	0.0
Higher Education	76.1	14.9	5.8	1.9	1.3
Service occupations	64.1	18.0	5.1	5.1	7.7
Clerical workers	62.5	20.8	6.9	6.3	3.5
Agriculture	51.2	23.2	16.3	7.0	2.3
Sales	38.7	35.5	6.4	9.7	9.7
Armed forces	37.9	24.3	16.2	10.8	10.8
Unskilled laborers	37.3	33.9	18.6	6.2	4.0
Unemployed	30.4	4.4	4.4	21.7	39.1

pursuits. The results suggest that one does get biased results. Those subjects who were continuing their education tended to respond much more quickly than any other group, while those employed in unskilled jobs, and the unemployed, were slow to respond. Until one gets 100 percent response, then, it seems that a bias may appear in the results.

It has been indicated that first responses to questions about employment and activities were usually made by those who were most satisfied with what they were doing.[3] In order to check on this matter the subjects were sorted by their degrees of satisfaction indicated in the answer to the question, "If working or not do you like what you are doing?" into the five categories used in Table 24. The data in that table indicate that those subjects who were most satisfied with their postschool activity tended to answer first, and that there was a general tendency for the subjects to withhold responses longer if they were less satisfied with their activities. The noticeable exceptions are the cases who were very dissatisfied with their activity. They returned their cards immediately but most of them also wrote letters asking about opportunities to improve their positions. These subjects responded quickly because they wanted help.

TABLE 24. Percentages of Returns by Degree of Satisfaction with Post-High School Activity

Degree of Satisfaction	Returns by Mailings 1st	2d	3d	4th	Visits
Very satisfied	72.3	15.2	2.7	7.1	2.7
Satisfied	55.8	24.1	12.4	4.2	3.5
Not so bad	48.4	30.6	12.9	6.5	1.6
Not satisfied	45.4	32.7	12.7	5.5	3.7
Definitely not satisfied	100.0	0.0	0.0	0.0	0.0
No comment	38.9	13.0	3.7	18.5	25.9

[3] Examination of the data showed that an overwhelmingly large number (80 percent) expressed themselves as *very satisfied* or *satisfied* with their postschool activity. Since other studies indicate that many people are dissatisfied with their jobs, much of the satisfaction may be considered as youthful exuberance about a first job.

Tabulations of returns by several miscellaneous variables that appeared to be influencing speed of response are shown in Table 25. The figures indicate a comparatively slow response from rural

TABLE 25. Percentages of Returns Distributed by Three Variables

Variable	Returns by Mailings 1st	2d	3d	4th	Visits
Rural	51.8	25.7	13.1	4.7	4.7
Broken home	43.0	26.6	15.2	7.6	7.6
Uncertain about choice of vocation while in high school	35.0	25.0	20.0	8.3	11.7

youth, subjects from broken homes, and those who had expressed themselves one month before graduation as uncertain about their post-high school plans.

Before summarizing the above data it may be well to point out some other factors that seemed to be operating to determine quantity and sequence of returns. The decision to use the double postal card was not a wise one. In many cases parents thought that they were advertisements and tossed them away before the subjects had seen them. The response to the letters and comments by the subjects indicated that many of them were being reached for the first time, although it was the third mailing. Students who had the same first name as their fathers also were not likely to get the cards unless the "Jr." was added very conspicuously to the address. Male students who had entered the armed forces were slow to respond because cards were not forwarded to them or, if forwarded, they were not received promptly. In general, those of the subjects who had moved out of the state did not respond to cards but did respond to letters.

Most of the subjects of this study were very well known to the author. He observed that many personal and family factors not revealed by the statistical data were operating to determine rate of response. There are hints that such factors, other than those indicated above, operated to determine the speed of responses to requests for information.

The following general conclusions can be drawn from the above data.

1. Graduates of high schools in industrial communities tended to respond faster to follow-up requests for information than graduates of schools located in agricultural areas.
2. Subjects who had received intensive individual attention responded faster than those who had not.
3. Subjects who had been interviewed frequently in a counseling program and those who had sought out further counseling responded more quickly than those who had not.
4. Girls responded faster than boys.
5. Subjects who ranked highest in their graduating classes tended to respond faster than the lower-ranking subjects.
6. Subjects who scored high on intelligence tests responded faster than the lower scoring students.
7. Those subjects who were continuing education beyond high school responded more quickly than those who had entered employment.
8. Of employed subjects, those who were in the higher-level jobs responded faster than subjects who were unemployed at unskilled jobs.
9. Those subjects who reported satisfaction with their post-school activity responded more quickly than those who were dissatisfied.
10. Youth who had been uncertain about their vocational choice during the last month of senior high school did not reply as quickly as those who had indicated definite plans for post-school activity.
11. Youths from broken homes tended to be slower in response than others.

The general conclusion from the analysis is that incomplete samples of populations in follow-up studies provide biased data. That bias may be pointed up by fabricating a composite person from the separate characteristics of early (and, in most studies, the only) responders. That hypothetical person would be a girl who lived in an unbroken home in the city, who had been intensively counseled, who had ranked above the average in her graduating class, and who scored above the average on intelligence tests. She would be either in post-high school training or on a white-collar job that she had wanted and would be satisfied with her post-high school training or employment.

The results suggest that a follow-up study is likely to yield responses that are biased on the favorable side if less than 100 percent of the subjects respond. In the two follow-up studies of these subjects described later in this volume the suggestion is fully corroborated.

Information obtained from the first follow-up study about the subjects' postschool activities and satisfactions is presented in detail in Chapter V. In that chapter relationships between the data obtained in the follow-up studies and information about the subjects secured previously and subsequently will be reported.

THE SECOND FOLLOW-UP STUDY

The second attempt to check on the progress of the subjects began in November, 1952, two and a half years after they had been graduated from high school. It was decided that a questionnaire would be used so that more extensive data than had been procured in the first follow-up study could be obtained. The questions this time were designed to secure information about the following items:

1. Post-high school vocational or training activities over the two-year period since the last report.
2. Reasons for entry into the activities.
3. Advancement in the activities.
4. Satisfaction with vocation, training, armed forces experiences, or marriage.
5. Future plans and outlook toward the future.
6. Recognition of personal strengths and weaknesses.
7. Participation in social-civic-recreational activities.
8. Names and addresses of former classmates. (This question had been designed to discover whether school friendships had been continued after high school. It served another purpose

very effectively when it provided addresses of some subjects who had been hard to locate.)

The results obtained from reluctant subjects by the use of personal handwritten letters in the first follow-up study suggested that personalized appeals might be more effective than the usual form letter in bringing responses. Accordingly the second follow-up study was so designed that a check could be made on this matter. The approach was to use a form letter and general questionnaire for half of the group and to employ handwritten letters and specific questionnaires for the other half.

Using the total alphabetical list of subjects (control and experimental subjects together) the 688 graduates of the four schools who were still alive were assigned alternately to a *general* or *personal* category. This categorization was made regardless of sex and previous experimental or control group classification. The numbers of subjects in each of the *personal* or *general* groups and their previous experimental or control group status are indicated in Table 26. The figures show that control and experi-

TABLE 26. Distribution of Original Control or Experimental Group Members into Personal and General Questionnaire Groups

Kind of Letter and Questionnaire Sent	Number of Subjects of Original Groups		
	Experimental	Control	Total
Personal	173	171	344
General	173	171	344
Total	346	342	688

mental subjects were almost evenly distributed throughout the new classification. A count of the number of males and females in each of the new classifications indicated that 166 males and 178 females had been placed in the *personal* group while 157 males and 187 females were in the *general* group.

Each of the subjects in the *general* category was sent the following *form* letter.

Dear ______________:

You will remember that while you were in high school we began a study of counseling that was supposed to help you in the choice of work or training after you left school. You will probably remember, too, that all of you agreed to answer our questions when we asked for information several years after graduation. *Every one* of the 1951 graduates answered our questions two years ago and we would like to hear from you again.

Enclosed you will find a short but very important list of questions. If we find out from your answers that we need better ways of preparing young people for what is ahead of them perhaps we can do something about it. Won't you please take ten minutes to answer the questions and return them to me right away in the self-addressed, stamped envelope?

Sincerely yours,
Dr. John W. M. Rothney

P.S. If you have forgotten me, look me up in your senior yearbook.

Along with the form letter the following general questionnaire was sent.

(Page 1)

Post-Graduate's Report

General

1. Name ______________________________
   Married girls please give maiden name. ______________
2. What is your present address? ______________________
   Street No. City State
3. Give an address where letters will usually reach you
   ____
   Street No. City State
4. Check the *one* item below that best describes your present status
   ______Full-time employment ________Student
   ______Farming ________(Girls only) Married
   ______In armed forces
5. Answer only *one* of these
   If you work full time what is your job? ______________
   What do you actually do on the job? ______________
   ____

Employer's name__________________Address__________
If you are farming is it a full-time job? Yes________No______
If you are in the armed forces what branch are you in?
______________What is your rank?____________________
If you are a student what course are you in?______________
____________Where?______________________________
If you are a married *woman* are you working outside of home?
Yes________No________Doing what?____________________

6. Regardless of what you are doing show how you like it by checking below
   ________I really like it.
   ________My likes just balance my dislikes.
   ________I don't like it but I will have to put up with it.
   ________I hate it. (If you marked this one will you tell us why?)
   ____
   ____

7. What would you like to be doing *5* years from now?__________
   ____
   10 years from now?______________________________
   ____

8. What is there about *you* that makes you *successful* in what you are doing?______________________________________
   ____
   ____

9. If you are married are you still living with your husband or wife?
   Yes________No________
   If not are you Separated________Divorced________Widowed________
   Separated for any other reason______________
   Why?______________________________
   ____

(Page 2)

A. What is there about *you* that *handicaps* you in what you are doing?______________________________________
   ____

B. Looking toward the future do you think that things are going to work out well for you?

C. Why?______________________________________
   ____

D. Why not? ____
____

E. Looking back at your high school training tell us
How it helped you most? ________________________________
____
____

F. How it failed to help you? ____________________________
____
____

G. Looking back at the counseling you had in high school tell us
How it helped you? ____________________________________
____
____

H. How it failed to help you? ____________________________
____
____

I. If you could live over again the last two years since you left high school would you do the same thing as you have done? Yes ______
No ______

J. If not what would you do? ____________________________
____
____

Show what you did each six months since you told us about what you were doing in the fall of 1951.

K. ____
January to June 1952

L. ____
June to December 1952

M. ____
January to June 1953

N. ____
June 1953 to the present

O. If you are married (both men and women) when were you married? ______________________ How many children? __________
Month Year

P. What clubs, political organizations, social and church groups do you belong to? ______________________________________
____

List the names and current address of the three of your high school classmates whom you know best.

Q. ______________________ ______________________
Name Address

R. ______________________ ______________________
Name Address

S. ______________________ ______________________
Name Address

T. Please use the back of this page to give more information on any of the questions asked above or to write anything you want about your school experiences, your present plans, or your plans for the future. You might want to comment on the counseling you had, your future plans, the ways in which schools can be improved, or any other matter that interests you.

Each of the subjects in the *personal* category received a hand-written letter. The contents generally expressed a personal interest in the subject. Highlights of school experiences such as dramatic and athletic performances or any other unusual or interesting activities and experiences of the subjects were recalled. In writing the letters, use was made of the materials obtained about the subjects while they were in high school and described in previous chapters. A sample personal letter follows.

Dear Jane,

We saw your wedding picture in the paper. Congratulations! We hope it will be a very happy marriage.

We are enclosing a questionnaire with this letter. Will you please take a few minutes to fill it in and mail it back *right away?* Two years ago we heard from all the 1951 graduates and we want to hear from *every one* of you again. *No one else will read your answers.*

A few of the married girls answered late last time. They seemed to think that we were not interested in them because they were not employed outside of their homes. This isn't the case. We are equally interested in *all* of the 1951 grads.

Good luck, Jane, let's hear from you real soon.

Sincerely,
Dr. Rothney

Along with the personal letter each subject received a questionnaire. The second page was exactly the same as the one that had been sent to the subjects in the *general* group. The first page differed, however, from that of the general questionnaire. The questions applied particularly to persons who were in either of the following post-high school activities: *employment, training, member of the armed forces, farming* or, for girls only, *married.* Samples of the first pages of the questionnaire for each of these groups are presented below.

Employment
Postgraduate's Report

1. Name ____________________
   Married girls please give maiden name ____________________
2. What is your present address? ____________________
   Street City State
3. Give an address where letters will usually reach you. ____________________
   ____
   Street No. City State
4. What is your job? ____________________
   What do you actually do on the job? ____________________
   ____
   Employer's name ____________________ Address ____________________
   When did you get the job? ____________________
   Month Year
5. Why did you choose this job? ____________________
   ____
6. Regardless of what you are doing show how you like it by checking below.
   ________ I really like it.
   ________ My likes just balance my dislikes.
   ________ I don't like it but I will have to put up with it.
   ________ I hate it. (If you marked this one will you tell us why?)
   ____
   ____
7. If you had to have special training to get this job where did you get it? ____________________
8. Who, if anyone, helped you to get this job? ____________________
9. What promotions or wage increases have you had since you started to work? ____________________

10. Do you belong to a labor union? Yes______ No______
    Which one? ____________
11. If you wish to mention your weekly wages please fill in below.
    $ (Weekly to start) ____________
    $ (Weekly now) ____________
12. Do you plan to keep this job? Yes______ No ______
    Any other comments about your job? ____________
13. What is the best job you can get with this employer? ____________
14. What would you like to be doing *5* years from now? ____________
    10 years from now? ____________
15. What is there about *you* that makes you *successful* in what you are doing? ____________

Training

Postgraduate's Report

1. Name ____________
   Married girls please give maiden name ____________
2. What is your present address? ____________
   Street No. City State
3. Give an address where letters will usually reach you ____________
   Street No.
   ____
   City State
4. Check only *one*.
   I am in training
   ______ In college Where? ______ What major? ______
   ______ In nursing Where? ______ Specialization? ______
   ______ Job apprentice Where? ______
   Apprentice for what? ____________
   ______ Others Where? ______ For what? ______
5. Regardless of the kind of training you are in show how you like it by checking below.

______ I really like it.
______ My likes just balance my dislikes.
______ I don't like it but I will have to put up with it.
______ I hate it. (If you marked this one will you tell us why?)

____

____

6. Who or what helped you to decide to enter this training? ______

____

7. Why did you chose the school you are now attending? ______

____

8. When did this training begin? ______________________
   Month   Year

9. List any outstanding awards received or offices held ______

____

10. Have you ever been on probation? Yes ______ No ______

11. Have you ever changed your course of study? Yes ___ No ______
    When? ______________________

____

12. Have you transferred from one place of training to another?
    Yes ______ No ______ If yes, when? ______
    From ______ To ______

13. Who is paying for your training? ______

14. What problems do you have in connection with your training?

____

____

15. What kind of grades do you usually receive? (Check one)
    Excellent (A) ____ Good (B) ____ Fair (C) ____ Poor (D) ____
    Below D ____

16. What would you like to be doing *5* years from now? ______

____

    10 years from now? ______

____

17. What is there about *you* that makes you *successful* in what you are doing? ______

____

Armed Forces

Postgraduate's Report

1. Name______________________________________
2. What is your present address? ___________________________

   Street No. City State

   ____
3. Give an address where letters will usually reach you

   Street No. City State
4. Check one. I am in the

   ______Army Where?_____________________________

   ______Air Force Where?_____________________________

   ______Marines Where?_____________________________

   ______Navy Where?_____________________________
5. Show how you like being in the service by checking below.

   ______I really like it.

   ______My likes just balance my dislikes.

   ______I don't like it but I will have to put up with it.

   ______I hate it. (If you marked this one will you tell us why?)

   ____

   ____
6. Check one. I was drafted______I volunteered______

   If you volunteered, who or what helped you decide to enter the armed forces?________________________________

   ____
7. When did your present service "hitch" begin? ___________

   When will it end?___________
8. Do you plan to sign for another "hitch"? Yes______No______
9. Name any Armed Forces schooling you have received.________

   ____
10. If you served overseas tell us where and when___________

    ____
11. Have you been in combat? Yes____No____How long? ______
12. Have you been wounded? Yes____No____How seriously?

    ____
13. Have you been a prisoner of war? Yes______No ______
14. List promotions in service

    Rank__________How long at that rank? ___________

    Rank__________How long at that rank? ___________

    Rank__________How long at that rank? ___________

15. List any medals, ribbons, or citations you have received in the service. ______

______

16. In what way has your service experience helped you? ______

______

17. In what way has it hurt you? ______

______

18. What would you like to be doing *5* years from now? ______

______

10 years from now? ______

19. What is there about *you* that makes you *successful* in what you are doing? ______

______

______

Married

Postgraduate's Report

1. Name ___Mrs. ______
   Maiden Name ______
2. What is your present address? ______
   Street No. City State
3. Give an address where letters will usually reach you
   ______
   Street No. City State
4. Show how you like married life by checking below
   ______I really like it.
   ______My likes just balance my dislikes.
   ______I don't like it but I will have to put up with it.
   ______I hate it. (If you marked this one will you tell us why?)
   ______
   ______
5. When were you married? ______
   Month Year
6. How many children have you? ______
7. If, in addition to home duties, you work for wages outside the home, what is your job? ______
   Full time______Part time______
   Where? ______
   Doing what? ______

8. Are you buying a home of your own? Yes______No______
9. Are you living with in-laws? Yes______No______
10. Are you still living with your husband? Yes______No______
    If not are you Separated______Divorced______
    Widowed______ Separated for any other reason______Why?______
11. What is your husband's job?______
12. What would you like to be doing *5* years from now?______
    10 years from now?______
13. What is there about *you* that makes you *successful* in what you are doing?______

Farming

Postgraduate's Report

1. Name______
2. What is your present address?______
   Route No. City State
3. Give an address where letters will usually reach you
   ______
   Route No. City State
4. Show how you like farming by checking below.
   ______I really like it.
   ______My likes just balance my dislikes.
   ______I don't like it but I will have to put up with it.
   ______I hate it. (If you mark this one will you tell us why?)
   ______
5. Check one.
   I am farming Full time______Part time______
6. If you have a part-time job what is it?______
   When do you work at it?______

7. Check one. I am
   ______Farming on my own.
   ______Farming on shares.
   ______Working on a farm for wages.
8. Are you working on the family farm? Yes______No______
9. If you are on the family farm what arrangements have you made for payment of your share? ______
   ______
10. Have you attended the university short course in agriculture? Yes______No______Do you plan to do it? ______
    When?______
11. Who or what helped you to decide to enter farming? ______
    ______
12. What bulletins or other materials on farming have you read within the past year?______
    ______
    ______
13. Do you have an agricultural deferment from the draft?______
    ______
14. What would you like to be doing *5* years from now? ______
    ______
    ______
    10 years from now?______
    ______
    ______
15. What is there about *you* that makes you *successful* in what you you are doing?______
    ______
    ______
    ______

The decision about which form of personalized questionnaire would be sent to each of the subjects in the *personal* group was made on the basis of the investigator's knowledge about their postschool activities obtained from many sources. Some were known to be in attendance at colleges or taking apprenticeships and they were sent the *training* form. Others had written informally to say that they were in the *armed forces* or *employed* and the proper form was dispatched. Reading of newspapers had revealed many announcements of weddings of girls and they were sent the *married* form. When there was uncertainty about a subject's status, two or even three of the questionnaire forms were mailed with directions to send in the one that was most suitable and discard the others. Eighteen subjects who were sent a form wrote to say that the one they received was not suitable and they answered the right one when it was mailed to them. If two forms seemed applicable, as in the case of girls who were married and employed, or married and in training, the *major* occupation (married, in such cases) was used in classification. If a subject was only temporarily in training as, for example, a boy who farmed during the year but took a month or two of short-course training in agriculture, he was classified as a farmer.

THE RETURNS

All the 688 letters, personal and general, were mailed at the same time on the same day in November, 1953. The *general* subjects who failed to respond within one month were sent another questionnaire with a form letter similar to the one on pages 145 and 146, which offered socially acceptable excuses for failure to respond. The *personal* subjects received the same letter but a note was handwritten at the bottom of the sheet. It contained, again, some reference to school or postschool activities and reminded them that the counselors remembered and were interested in them as individuals. All the second letters, general and personal, were mailed late in December to the subjects' home addresses in the belief that they might be on furlough from the armed forces, or home from employment and training activities for the Christmas vacation.

Those who had not responded to the second letter within a month received the third letter, with a small party pencil attached. It read as follows.

Remember! When you were in high school you promised to answer our questions after you graduated. Now, we really need your answer.

Here's a pencil, form, and stamped envelope. Won't you please pull up a chair and answer right away?

Yours for better opportunities for youth,
Dr. Rothney

P.S. No one else will read your answers.

The letters to the subjects in the *personal* group again contained a short handwritten note added to the form letter.

Subjects who did not respond to the third letter received, one month later, a fourth one somewhat sharper in tone. It suggested that they might omit items which they did not want to answer. The letter follows.

Dear ______________:

This is my fourth letter to you. I wonder if you have received all the others? If you have received them, and you are one of the few who haven't answered, it must be because you don't understand how important this work is and how necessary it is to hear from *every one* of you 1951 grads.

Maybe we can help you to understand by coming to talk to you at your home or where you work. If there are any who don't answer right away *this time* we will be able to explain the importance of it when we come to visit you. (Of course we won't be able to go overseas to see the fellows who are in the service but, because of their experience in the armed forces, I know that they are the kind who will appreciate this type of work.)

It will save you and me many hours of time if you will answer *right away*. No matter what you are doing, married, unemployed, working, studying, or in the armed forces *your* answers are extremely important.

It is especially important to hear from you if you think the school or counseling *didn't* do you any good!

If there is anything you object to answering please leave that one item blank.

DON'T FAIL! DO IT NOW!

Sincerely yours,
Dr. J. W. M. Rothney

Subjects in the *personal* group were again given particular attention by the addition of a handwritten note at the bottom of the letter.

Thirty-three of the 688 subjects did not reply to any of the four letters within the four-month period. At the end of that time differences in appeals to subjects in *general* and *personal* groups were discontinued. The answers to questionnaires by the last 33 subjects were obtained by use of registered letters with return receipts requested, by special appeals to parents to send on letters to their children and, in some cases, by visits to homes. At the end of five months *all* 688 subjects who were still alive had responded.

The differences in effectiveness of the use of the personal and general appeals may be observed by examination of Table 27. The figures, rounded off to one decimal place, indicate that the

TABLE 27. Cumulative Percentages of Responses by Personal and General Groups

Form of letter and Questionnaire	Returns by Mailings 1st	2d	3d	4th
Personal (N 344)	52.9	78.8	88.4	96.8
General (N 344)	48.8	76.2	86.9	93.6
Difference	4.1	2.6	1.5	3.2

personals answered slightly more promptly to the first mailing and maintained a slight lead throughout. The differences are very small and it appears that the greatly increased work of writing personal letters and constructing specialized questionnaires would not have been justified unless the investigators had been determined to get 100 percent returns. They were interested in the post-high school activities of every subject.

The completeness of response to items common to all the questionnaires was determined by a count of the items to which they had replied. No significant differences were found in the quantity of responses from subjects who received the personalized questionnaires and letters and those subjects who received only form letters and the regular questionnaires. In general more complete returns were received from girls than from boys, from the upper intelligence test score group, from the highest class rank group, and from those satisfied with their post-high school vocation or training. No significant differences between quantity of responses of original control and experimental subjects were found. Detailed tables of the distributions and significances of differences in speed of replying and quantity of responses are too lengthy to present here. They may be found in the complete report of a special study.[4]

It seemed possible that the slight differences in speed and quantity of response to the personalized and general appeals might have resulted from the influence of the subjects' experimental (counseled) or control (uncounseled) status in the original study. On the recommendation of Dr. Julian C. Stanley of the University of Wisconsin a triple chi-square was computed. The findings of 14.82 with 13 degrees of freedom provided insufficient evidence to reject the hypothesis that there were no important relationships between original control or experimental status and speed and quantity of response to general or personalized appeals.

Analysis of all the general and personal responses revealed that, although girls tended to answer about 10 percent faster than boys initially, the difference had disappeared by the fourth mailing. Rural subjects answered a little faster than those from the city but more rural subjects had failed to respond at the end of the fourth mailing. The difference in speed of returns from the subjects who had lived in the two larger industrial towns and two agricultural communities was insignificant. Grouping of the returns of the subjects in terms of current activities revealed that those who were in training replied much faster than those in the armed forces, farming, employment, or the girls who were married. The subjects who had achieved higher scores on the Henmon-Nelson Test of Mental Ability and higher class ranks at graduation tended to respond sooner than those who had lower scores and ranks. These findings generally corroborated the results obtained in the first follow-up study and the third one which was to follow two and a half years later.

[4] Robert L. Mooren, *A Differentiated Technique in Questionnaire Procedure,* unpublished Ph.D. thesis, University of Wisconsin, 1954.

Detailed analyses of the questionnaire responses of the subjects are presented in Chapter V.

RESPONSES TO PARTICULAR ITEMS

One difficulty with the questionnaire procedure is that subjects may choose to omit answers to particular items for any reason that they may think justified. In some cases the subjects simply stated that they did not want to answer questions for reasons which they gave. In other cases the item was left blank with no reason given and therefore no clue as to whether it was omitted by error, rejected for reasons that the subjects did not choose to state,

TABLE 28. Percentages of 685 Subjects Responding to Items on the Two and a Half Year Follow-Up Questionnaire

Item	Experimental Girls	Control Girls	Experimental Boys	Control Boys	Total Experimentals	Total Controls
Residence	100.0	100.0	100.0	100.0	100.0	100.0
1953 job or training status	100.0	100.0	100.0	100.0	100.0	100.0
Information about marriage	100.0	100.0	100.0	100.0	100.0	100.0
Live over last 2 years	98.9	97.3	95.7	98.7	97.4	98.0
Looking toward the future	96.1	92.9	90.7	94.5	93.0	93.3
Choice of activity 5 years later	96.7	93.4	81.5	89.4	89.5	91.2
Choice of activity 10 years later	96.1	93.4	75.3	83.2	86.3	88.6
What makes you successful?	90.0	84.6	79.7	87.5	85.2	86.0
How high school helped	85.1	83.5	81.5	83.8	83.4	83.6
Organizational memberships	85.1	75.3	74.8	73.2	80.2	74.6
What handicaps you?	70.7	71.4	72.8	79.4	71.7	75.1
How counseling helped	75.7	66.5	72.8	64.4	74.3	65.5
How high school failed	53.0	46.7	53.7	52.5	53.3	49.4
How counseling failed	37.6	34.6	38.3	35.0	37.9	34.8

or whether they had no feelings to express on the topic covered by the item.

It is apparent from Table 28 that the negative items were answered less frequently than the others and that the items on the last page were usually answered less frequently than those on the first two pages. Comparison of numbers of responses by control and experimental subjects indicates that there are not enough substantial differences to permit the making of comparisons between the groups.

THE THIRD FOLLOW-UP STUDY

CONSTRUCTION OF THE QUESTIONNAIRE

In the construction of the instruments for the previous follow-up studies the author had used his own judgment about the form and number of questions that would be asked. Before beginning the third follow-up conducted in the autumn of 1956, five years after the subjects had been graduated from high school, he decided to seek the judgments of a sample of the members of the American Personnel and Guidance Association concerning the kinds of items they would recommend for use in a follow-up questionnaire five years after high school.

Members of the Association may join one or more of five subgroups. The three subgroups from which it seemed best to draw the sample are described as follows in the 1954 Directory of the Association.

Division 2: National Association of Guidance Supervisors and Counselor Trainers.
NAGSCT's purpose is to further the development of guidance services in educational institutions. Those eligible to apply for membership are state and territorial supervisors and assistant supervisors of guidance services, administrative and supervisory personnel officially concerned with such services on the national and state level, and counselor trainers in colleges who prepare counselors for work in guidance services.

Division 3: National Vocational Guidance Association.

NVGA is an organization of persons in schools, colleges, government and private agencies, business, and industry, who do vocational and educational counseling and student personnel work. NVGA has no special requirements for general membership.

Division 5: American School Counselor Association

ASCA is an organization of counselors, teacher-counselors, directors and supervisors of guidance, and other school personnel below the college level, concerned with providing and improving guidance services for children, youths, and adults.

A sample from Divisions 3 and 5 was selected by taking the name of the first person on each page of the directory who had membership in both. The number was 84. The sample from Division 2 was selected by taking the name of the first person from the top of each even-numbered page. Forty-two names were obtained. Since the names in the directory are listed by states, the geographic variable seemed to be controlled. Each of the 126 persons selected received the following letter.

Dear ____________:

Would you give me a few minutes of your time to help in a project of much concern to me and perhaps of general interest to guidance workers?

As you may know, in 1948 I took the 900 sophomores in four Wisconsin high schools as subjects for study in counseling. Half of them were counseled as well as we knew how for the duration of their high school careers. The other half were given no counseling. Six months, and two and a half years after graduation we followed up all those who had been graduated. This fall, five years after graduation from high school, we plan to find out about their current status by questionnaires and by interviewing a sample of the subjects. The purpose of this follow-up is to see if there are any differences between the counseled and the uncounseled subjects. In other words, I am seeking to discover whether or not counseling has any provable effects upon the students who have received it.

I have, of course, my own ideas on what might be included in the follow-up study. To eliminate my own personal bias and to obtain a wide range of viewpoints, I am seeking the aid of several persons, such as yourself, who are interested in the guidance field.

In your opinion, what are the effects or what should be the effects of guidance I should look for in this follow-up study?

Your answer could be in very general form or in terms of specific questions that might be asked. The usual questions about jobs, health, marital status, and education after high school would be asked, but what else should be included? You could just put down some ideas on the back of this sheet or you could elaborate at length.

Naturally any follow-up study should be in terms of what was done in the counseling sessions. For the purpose of your comments here consider the type of counseling that is usually given, that is, the counseling that would need to be done for a large number of youth who are representative of what you will find in American high schools (excluding perhaps those in very large cities).

I hope this study can contribute to a better understanding of the guidance process among the workers in the field. Perhaps an even more important use for a study of this type is in showing the general public the effect guidance has on the school child. Anything you can do to assist me will be appreciated.

Sincerely,
John W. M. Rothney

Three weeks after the letters were mailed to each member of the sample and replies had been received from only 18 percent, a postal card reminder was sent. In the following 60 days an additional 20 percent of the sample replied. This return is about half of that which can normally be expected to a letter of this kind, and the reasons for the small number of responses are not clear. The small number of responses and their general quality suggested that guidance personnel have not given much thought to evaluation of guidance practices.

It is interesting to note that 55 percent of the *Division 2* sample replied, but that only 30 percent of the combined *Divisions 3* and *5* group responded. The difference may be a further indication of the lack of interest in evaluation among personnel on the "firing line." But mere figures do not measure the full difference between the two groups. With a few exceptions, the quality of the replies from the *Divisions 3* and *5* sample was decidedly lower.

Two samples of responses of members of the APGA from which the list on the following pages was drawn up are given below.

From a Guidance Director

1. Somehow you need to get at the job satisfaction angle—is he in a job consistent with his abilities, attitudes, and interests and which is both challenging and rewarding to him? If he had it to do over again up to this point, what if anything would he have done differently?
2. Is the job he is in of a type he planned to be in (if he had plans) when he left school? You will also determine, I assume, whether he had carefully-thought-out plans when he left school (whether or not he had had any counseling). Seems to me it is important (1) to know whether he had any plans and (2) if so, were they objectively arrived at and were they feasible ones?
3. What about the relationship between his potential job level and the type of work he is now doing?
4. Did he avail himself of a suitable level and amount of training (college or other education beyond high school) to qualify him adequately for a vocation suitable to his potentialities?
5. Job-preparation programs offered by his school and community will also be a factor (whether anything much beyond the typical college-prep program is offered in his high school). Some question as to whether or not he desired training of a type he was unable to get might be helpful.
6. Some questions regarding the specific needs for help which could be or could have been provided through counseling might also help.
7. I have the feeling that many students and graduates get or got help from their counselors and teachers that they are not fully or even remotely aware of—and that, therefore, the number indicating they had assistance and the extent of that assistance is apt to be somewhat misleading if taken at its face value. Is there some way this might be weighted in your analysis of outcomes?
8. Some significance might be attached, too, to the number and type of different jobs held by the individuals. It would seem that the "guided" probably would have had less job changes than the "unguided" and that jobs taken by the "guided" should have

been more consistently in line with vocational interests and capacities.

9. I don't know how you could get at it, but if there could be some means of evaluating which group is the better adjusted both socially and emotionally, there might be something of real significance here. I have the feeling, based on some thirty years in the business, that many of the good outcomes of counseling are never recognized because they helped substitute order and organization for their opposites. I guess we know, or at least feel this, but of course the problem is to prove it somehow—which of course is what you are after. I don't suppose it would be at all feasible to develop any type of instrument, or to administer one anyhow even if you had it, in order to get at this.

From a High School Dean of Girls

Of course, idealistically we look for many intangible benefits from counseling. I should hope to find fewer job "hoppers" among the counseled and those whose vocational goals have been more nearly realized.

The outcome of counseling, I hope, will not be entirely vocational. I should hope to find the person quite active in community affairs and enjoying a happy family life. Then, too, I should hope that he would have fewer law violations.

I realize that this is a very vague reply, and the results which I should hope to find would be extremely hard to measure. In short, I would hope to find the counseled subjects leading a fuller, happier life than the uncounseled.

I shall be very anxious to know what you do discover in your follow-up study.

The general lack of interest of professional personnel in a study concerned with the evaluation of the effects of counseling may be a serious handicap if guidance is to "come of age," since continuous development of evaluation techniques will depend upon the application of sound methods to all aspects of the problem.

Analysis of the responses to the letter produced the following list of items. They represent, according to the responses of the groups described above, the differences one would expect to find between counseled and noncounseled youth.

Has more close friends
Belongs to more fraternal organizations
Understands others better
Gets along better with fellow workers
Gets along better with boss
More maritally compatible
Appreciates family ties more
Is happier
Understands himself better
Feels more able to cope with present problems
Assumes more civic interests and duties
Participates more in activities beneficial to society
Is a more active church member
Has more hobbies
Possesses more credit cards
Has better plans for financial security (insurance, etc.)
Assumes more responsibility for his actions
Less likely to use alcohol to excess
Less likely to use drugs to excess
Less likely to have a police record
Less likely to have a record of traffic accidents
More satisfied with high school course selection
Fewer wish they had quit school earlier to work
More satisfied with level of education received
More likely to continue educational activities after starting career
Received more college scholarships
More likely to graduate from college
Less likely to change college curriculum
Less likely to change colleges
More likely to support use of public funds for guidance programs in school
Parents have more favorable attitude toward high school
Is more satisfied with present job
Changes occupations less frequently
More likely to have occupational level consistent with aptitude level
Makes more money
Less likely to have chosen present vocation primarily because of salary
More likely to have chosen present vocation rationally

More likely to have chosen present vocation because of opportunities for promotion
More likely to have chosen present vocation for the personal emotional satisfaction it provided
More likely to have chosen present vocation because of social status
Is more satisfied with present socioeconomic job standing
Has more confidence in soundness of personal decisions
Makes better plans for the future
More likely to seek and secure counseling after high school
More likely to seek counseling when in difficult situations
More likely to discuss frankly his own talents and limitations
More likely to recommend counseling to others

In order to get opinions of others about whether the items given by the members of the American Personnel and Guidance Association should be used in an evaluation of a counseling program, the items were drawn up into question form and submitted to four groups of graduate students. One group was composed of members of a beginning class in guidance, another of members of a class in the philosophy of education, the third was composed of advanced students in a guidance seminar, and the last consisted of members of an introductory class in guidance in which all members were experienced teachers. The questionnaire was given to students in their regular classes near the end of the semester.

The questions were set up so that the graduate student was required to indicate whether he thought that the item would best describe a counseled or uncounseled student or would be equally descriptive of either. Thus if the student thought that the item, "Has more close friends" was more descriptive of a *counseled* individual, he circled the *C* after the item. If he thought it more descriptive of a *noncounseled* youth, he circled the *N;* and if he thought that it would describe *both* counseled and noncounseled youth equally well, he circled the *B.* In answering, the students were asked to consider the kinds of counseling that is usually done for the youth one finds in American high schools.

In general the four groups tended to respond similarly regardless of the various discrimination indices that were applied. Chi-square computations indicated that the probability of reaching the obtained degree of agreement by chance was less than one in a hundred. The fact that the four diverse groups of students agreed on the items given immediately below suggested that there was rather general concurrence on the objectives of counseling.

The results from the *four* groups indicated that they thought the following items should be used in attempts to discriminate between counseled and noncounseled students five years after high school.

1. Understands himself
2. Understands others
3. Frankly discusses his own talents and limitations
4. Has confidence in soundness of his personal decisions
5. Seeks counseling when in difficult situations
6. Does outside study to improve his present job standing
7. Wishes he had quit school earlier to start working
8. Continues educational activities after starting career
9. Graduates from college
10. Graduates from professional school
11. Receives more college scholarships
12. Seeks and secures counseling after high school
13. Recommends counseling to others
14. Supports use of public funds for guidance programs in schools
15. Has plans for financial security

Three of the groups added the following items:

16. Feels able to cope with current problems
17. Makes plans for the future
18. Has occupational level consistent with aptitude level
19. Chose present vocation rationally
20. Chose present vocation primarily because of salary
21. Changes occupation
22. Assumes civic interests and duties
23. Has a police record

Only *two* of the groups felt that the following items would also discriminate between counseled and noncounseled youth five years after high school.

24. Has high quality of present activity

25. Is satisfied with high school course selection
26. Assumes responsibility for actions
27. Participates in activities beneficial to society
28. Changes jobs
29. Uses alcohol to excess
30. Uses drugs to excess

Only *one* of the groups added the following items:

31. Is satisfied with level of education received
32. Chose present occupation because of opportunities for promotion
33. Chose present vocation for the personal emotional satisfaction it provides
34. Chose present vocation because of opportunity for social services
35. Parents have favorable attitude toward high school

None of the groups suggested that the following items would discriminate between counseled and noncounseled students five years after high school.

36. Is happy
37. Is maritally compatible
38. Appreciates family ties
39. Has many close friends
40. Gets along with fellow workers
41. Gets along with the boss
42. Changes college curriculum
43. Changes colleges
44. Chose present vocation because of its social status
45. Has many hobbies
46. Has record of traffic accidents

It was noted at the beginning of this section that the procedure described above was designed to secure some judgments from a sampling of members of the American Personnel and Guidance Association and others interested in guidance about the kinds of behavior that would discriminate between noncounseled and counseled youth five years after graduation from high school. They were intended to supplement the judgment of the author in his decisions about the kinds of items that might be used in the questionnaires and interviews that were to be employed in the third follow-up.

The extent to which the judgments were used may be determined by examination of the questionnaire that appears on the following pages. Study of it reveals that the following items are covered:

A. Job, educational, or armed forces activity and marital status
(Questions 1, 8, 13, 18, 19)
B. Satisfaction with activities
(Questions 2, 3, 9, 11, 15, 16, 18c, 21, 31)
C. Changes in educational, vocational, marital, and armed forces activities
(Questions 8a, 8b, 8c, 10, 14a, 17, 26, 31)
D. Future plans
(Questions 6, 7, 12, 15, 16, 29, 31)
E. Understanding of own strengths and limitations
(Questions 4, 5, 22, 23, 27, 31)
F. Reasons for choosing occupation
(Questions 14, 20c, 31)
G. Attitudes toward education
(Questions 19, 22, 22a, 23, 23a, 26, 29, 31)
H. Attitudes toward counseling
(Questions 23, 23a, 28, 31)
I. Civic participation
(Questions 24, 24a, 25, 26, 31)

Wisconsin Counseling Study
THE UNIVERSITY OF WISCONSIN
Department of Education

FIVE YEARS AFTER HIGH SCHOOL

Name______________________________
Married girls give maiden name____________________
What is your present address?____________________
Street No. City State
Give an address where letters will usually reach you__________
Street No.
____
City State

1. Check the *one* item that best describes your present status.
   ______Married (women only) ______Student
   ______Full time employment ______In armed forces
   ______Farming ______Other (tell what)____
   ____

2. Regardless of what you are doing show how you like it by checking below
   ______I really like it.
   ______My likes just balance my dislikes.
   ______I don't like it but I will have to put up with it.
   ______I hate it.

3. Will you tell me why you checked the one you did? __________
   ____
   ____
   ____

4. What is there about *you* that makes you *successful* in what you are doing? ______________________________________
   ____
   ____
   ____
   ____

5. What is there about *you* that *handicaps* you in what you are doing? ______________________________________
   ____
   ____
   ____
   ____

6. What would you like to be doing *5* years from now? __________
   ____
   ____

7. *10* years from now? ______________________________
   ____
   ____

8. If you are married (both men and women), when were you married? ______________________________________
   Month Year
   (a) How many children? ______________
   (b) Are you still living with your husband or wife? Yes______
   No______

If not, are you separated?____Widow or widower?____
Divorced?________Divorced and remarried?________

(d) What is your husband's occupation?________________

(e) If you are a married woman, do you have a job outside the home?________________

If so, what do you actually do on the job?________

9. Judging from your own experience, what could schools do to prepare young people for marriage?________________

10. Show what you have been doing each six months since you last wrote in 1953.
    First half of 1954________________
    Second half of 1954________________
    First half of 1955________________
    Second half of 1955________________
    First half of 1956________________

11. If you could live over again the last 5 years since you left high school, would you do the same things as you have done?
    No________Yes________
    If *not,* what would you do differently?________________

    If *yes,* why?________________

12. Looking toward the future, do you think things are going to work out well for you?
    *If yes*________Why?________________

    If *no*________Why not?________________

13. If you are *EMPLOYED* full time NOW, what do you actually do on the job?________________

    What is name and address (include city) of your employer?
    ____

14. Why did you choose the job you now have? ____________________

____

____

If you wish to mention your wages, fill in below.
Weekly (when you began to work) $__________. Weekly now $__________

15. What (if anything) would make you change jobs? __________

____

____

16. Do you plan to change jobs? Yes______No______
If so, why?______________________________

____

17. If you have worked more than one year, what is the difference between the work you did when you started and the work you do now?______________________________

____

____

18. If you were ever (or are now) in the *ARMED FORCES,* what was your highest rank?______________________
(a) When did you serve?______________________
(b) How have you used any of your armed forces training since you left?______________________

____

(c) How do you feel about your armed forces experience?

____

____

____

19. If you had any *TRAINING* after high school (special school, apprenticeship, college, short course, or any other kind)
Where did you get your training?______________________
Place City

When?______________________

20. What degree or certificate did you get?______________________
When?______________________
(a) What was your major field of study?______________________
(b) For what were you prepared when you finished your training? ______________________

21. How do you feel now about your training experiences?

____

____

____

22. Looking back at your high school training, tell us how it helped you most.
____
____
____
____

How it failed to help you_______________
____
____
____

23. Looking back at the *counseling* you had in *high school* tell us
How it helped you_______________
____
____
____

How it failed to help you_______________
____
____
____
____

24. Give the names of any political organizations, clubs, social, recreational, or church groups which you have attended regularly during the last 3 years._______________
____

What offices have you held in any groups?
____
____

25. Have you voted in any political elections?_______________
Why or why not?_______________

26. What self-improvement activities such as courses, on-the-job training, reading, home study, etc., have you been doing?
____
____
____

27. Do you have confidence in the actions you take when you have to make choices?_______________
____
____

28. If you needed help in the last 5 years in making decisions, to whom did you go? ____________________

____

29. Any interesting plans for the future? ____________________

____

____

30. List the names and current addresses of the three of your high school classmates whom you know best. (Give maiden name of married women)

Name	Address	City
Name	Address	City
Name	Address	City

31. Please use the back of this page to give more information on any of the questions asked above or to write anything you want about your school experiences, your present plans, or your plans for the future. You might want to comment on the counseling you had, your future plans, the ways in which schools can be improved, or any other matter that interests you.

QUESTIONNAIRE RETURNS

The questionnaire was mailed to 685 [5] subjects in September, 1956, five years after they had been graduated from high school. The letter they received contained a stamped addressed return envelope, the printed questionnaire, and the following letter.

Five Years After High School

Dear ____________:

It seems like a long time since you told me when you were in high school that you would answer my questions five years after high school. The years have passed fast and now the time has come.

It is really important to do it. This will be the first time that *all* the people from four high schools (except those who have died) can

[5] Five subjects had died during the period 1951–1956. Two were killed in automobile accidents, two died as the result of polio, and one from a kidney infection.

tell about their activities after high school, and what they think schools have done and should do to help young people. It is only from *your* comments that we can tell what improvements should be made.

The questions have been set up so you can check most of them quickly. In some of the parts you will answer *only* the questions that apply to *you*. It should not take too long to fill it out and mail it in the enclosed self-addressed stamped envelope.

We heard from *all* of you before, so we are most optimistic about hearing from you again. If you do it now before you forget it will help a lot.

Best of luck,
John W. M. Rothney

P. S. If you have forgotten me look me up in your senior yearbook.

At the end of one month 47 percent of the subjects had responded. A second letter similar to the one on pages 145 and 146 brought the cumulative return to 72 percent by the end of the second month. A third letter similar to the one on page 167 produced a cumulative return of 86 percent. At this point several teachers in the communities began to make inquiries about the subjects and to encourage them by personal visits and telephone calls to send in their questionnaires. The investigators visited some of the subjects, sent postal cards or special delivery and registered letters to others, and enlisted the support of parents and interested persons in getting responses until *all* were reached.

The securing of such high percentages of returns to questionnaires as have been obtained in the three follow-up parts of this study is a formidable task. In addition to the general factors previously described in this volume there are innumerable personal conditions and situations that militate against the securing of prompt and complete returns. The following unedited quotations from some of the subjects illustrate how these operate.

Please forgive the delay on my part in regard to mailing this questionnaire. I'm still busy trying to organize as I've just had a third child. I've very sorry I caused any inconveniences of having to mail several letters.

I filled this out in a moving car on the way to see my wife and brand new baby. Excuse the sloppy penmanship and spelling.

For some reason or another you continue to contact me. However I was never interviewed or counseled by you or your associate whom I remember worked with you. I feel very much lacking to give you any helpful evaluation of you counseling research. (Control subject)

I had better apologize for being so tardy. I've actually considered these questions several times and each time I would come up with a different answer. I cannot really say that my true feelings are recorded for if I were to answer the same questions tomorrow or next week some answers might be different. Then maybe this is imagination but that can best be judged by comparing these answers with those previously submitted.

You will have to excuse my penmanship and sloppyness because I did in between corn loads at my brothers where we are picking corn.

Sorry I am so late getting this back to your. I started it one night just after I received it and didn't finish it. I put it up and forgot all about it until I got your card yesterday.

I am sorry I failed to send in the questionnaire sooner. No, I did not loose the first copy, but when I received it, I was in the process of making plans for my wedding, which was Oct. 6.

After that, there were many things to be done, and we were away on our honeymoon. Then there was moving, etc.

I did not forget you, and hope you will excuse the delay. Thank you.

I'm sorry for not filling out your questionnaire as yet. Actually I haven't had time yet. Also I'm afraid you'll steal my story and out do Steinbeck. I'll fill the blanks out soon and also add my observations. The situation is that—my wife had a nervous breakdown after the the birth of our son and things have been in a uproar for 15 months now. I have been faced with attempting to save my marriage or being a business success. So far moral feelings have demanded that I save the marriage. In the next few days I'll have to re-examine the question. As soon as I've made my move I'll bring you up to date.

Ever since school began in fall I have so busy and that is the reason for the delay in answering this and am sorry that you had to send another letter to me. Since there has been so much to do here I haven't had time to think about the things I had wanted to tell you. When I do I will write them to you and not wait to hear from you.

I received 3 of your counsilling forms. One was at a military base in California on or about the 28th of Oct. At that time we were being processed and getting ready to ship overseas. I did not fill out your form and it got misplaced. After I arrived overseas I received another about the 20th of Nov. I filled it out promptly and mailed it to you. It must have got lost in the XMAS mail as many things did. Due to a train wreck here. My mother mailed me this one Jan. 4th. I'm a little slow getting this one out also.

Please forgive the delay in answering this. As per usual I had slight trouble in analyzing my feelings about some of the answers to the questions.

Am sorry there was a delay in answering this. We have been out of town for a month and did not have our mail forwarded.

I was quite pleased to hear from you and more than willing to fill in the questionnaire.

I am sorry that I haven't answered your letters befor but as I told you befor I get riled about nothing some say it is wonderful but it makes you a little lazy I think I worry about nothing from day to day it just lasts for a few minutes when I do worry because if it is necessary I rectify it.

Thanks for your patience with me will try to do better next time.

Very sorry again that I had to be begged to answer this questionnaire. Hoping that this isn't the last one received and I have enjoyed taking part in this survey the last 5 years. I think its a very wonderful thing and it will prove helpful in education for the future.

In addition to the circumstances illustrated by the quotations given above there were many reasons for hesitancy to respond that were intimated in answers or inferred from circumstances. Among them were the following.

One subject had just been sentenced to a long jail term

Several were divorced and hesitated to report on or reveal their difficulties

One girl was attempting to hide so that she could not be served with legal papers

Several had been dropped from educational institutions and were antagonistic to all university personnel
Several, whose high school or university experiences had been unsatisfactory, were unwilling to coöperate with staff members from educational institutions
One boy had changed jobs so often that he thought the counselor would be disappointed in him if he reported those changes
One girl, who seemed to be partially employed at the most ancient but least honorable profession, would not answer mailed requests

RESPONSES TO PARTICULAR ITEMS

Although responses were obtained from all the subjects, each one did not answer every item. Residence, occupational or training levels, and marital status items were answered by all the subjects, but the percentages of response to other than these three seemed to depend on the kind of question asked.

It seems apparent from examination of the percentages of responses reported in Table 29 that the asking of questions on how counseling and high school had failed these subjects was not a fruitful enterprise. Approximately two-fifths and two-thirds of the experimentals and controls respectively did not answer these questions. As a result it is really not possible to determine whether

TABLE 29. Percentages of 685 Subjects Responding to Items on the Five-Year Follow-Up Questionnaire

Item	Experimental Women	Control Women	Experimental Men	Control Men	Total Experimentals	Total Controls
Residence	100.0	100.0	100.0	100.0	100.0	100.0
1956 job or training status	100.0	100.0	100.0	100.0	100.0	100.0
Information about marriage	100.0	100.0	100.0	100.0	100.0	100.0
Post-high school training [a]	99.4	99.5	100.0	97.5	99.7	98.5
Satisfaction with 1956 status	99.4	97.3	98.1	97.5	98.8	97.4
Live over again last 5 years	99.4	97.3	98.8	96.9	99.1	98.1
Satisfaction with						

TABLE 29 (*Continued*)

Item	Experimental Women	Control Women	Experimental Men	Control Men	Total Experimentals	Total Controls
armed forces experience [a]	—	—	93.3	92.3	—	—
Looking toward the future	97.2	95.6	90.7	94.4	94.2	95.0
Choice of activity five years later	97.2	96.2	90.1	87.5	93.9	92.1
Choice of activity ten years later	97.2	96.2	86.2	85.8	92.1	91.2
Voted in political elections	91.2	86.8	93.8	85.6	92.4	86.3
Confidence in making choices	88.4	84.1	94.4	85.6	91.3	84.8
What makes you successful?	84.6	81.9	85.8	89.4	84.1	84.4
How high school helped	82.3	76.4	82.8	76.3	82.5	76.7
Reason for choosing current job [a]	83.2	88.6	72.2	71.3	79.2	75.1
From whom advice sought	81.8	84.1	72.8	71.9	77.6	78.4
Satisfaction with training [a]	85.1	88.6	69.3	66.2	74.8	76.3
What handicaps you?	69.1	64.8	82.1	78.7	75.2	71.3
Weekly wages [a]	83.2	77.2	59.3	62.3	65.3	65.6
How counseling helped	70.2	64.3	75.3	65.6	72.6	64.9
Plans for the future	68.0	67.0	74.1	64.4	70.8	65.8
Number of self-improvement activities	69.6	62.1	73.5	63.1	71.4	62.6
Number of organizations	69.1	65.9	67.9	61.9	68.5	64.0
Number of offices held	65.7	61.5	65.4	59.4	65.6	60.5
How high school failed	55.9	52.8	61.7	55.0	58.0	55.8
How counseling failed	40.9	41.8	42.6	36.2	41.7	39.2

[a] The percentages for these items are based only on the number of cases to which the item applied. The weekly wage item, for example, applied only to those who were employed full time in 1956.

they hesitated to express complaints or had none. In view of the frankness of expression in response to many other questions, it seems likely that the latter explanation may hold, but one cannot be sure. The results do suggest that the use of such items does not now seem justified.

Differences between controls and experimentals in numbers of items to which responses were made may be observed in the table. None of them is big enough to suggest that the differences between the numbers of responses of the two groups has materially affected the interpretation of the results obtained from the questionnaire.

CONSISTENCY OF RESPONSE TO THE QUESTIONNAIRES

As the responses to all three follow-up attempts were received the dates of their receipts were stamped on each questionnaire. From these records it was possible to determine the consistency of response of each subject. A figure designating the consistency of each subject was obtained by subtracting his slowest response in weeks from his fastest response. Thus the three responses of the subjects listed in the first row of Table 30 were received within a two-week interval for each follow-up study. This does not mean that they always answered within two weeks after the first mailing. Thus a subject may have answered, say, in the fourth, fifth and sixth week after the first mailing on all three follow-up studies and still be in the top category. Responses of persons in the last row of Table 30 were at least 12 weeks apart on the three questionnaires.

Figures based on dates of reception of returns cannot be entirely accurate since time of reception and delivery was influenced by distance, and perhaps by the speed with which a letter was forwarded by relatives, but the figures in the table give a general idea of the consistency of the subjects in responding to the questionnaires. They indicate that prediction of time taken to respond to a second or third questionnaire based on speed of replying to the first questionnaires would not be highly accurate. Approximately one-quarter of the subjects were consistent if a one- to

TABLE 30. Consistency of Responses to Three Follow-Up Questionnaires

Intervals (Weeks)	Experimental Women	Control Women	Experimental Men	Control Men	Total Experimentals	Total Controls
1–2	32.0	27.5	18.5	18.8	25.6	23.4
3–4	23.8	19.2	32.1	20.6	27.7	19.9
5–6	16.0	18.7	15.4	20.6	15.7	19.6
7–8	12.2	13.2	16.7	20.6	14.3	16.7
9–10	7.2	9.3	9.3	5.0	8.2	7.3
11–13	8.8	12.1	8.0	14.4	8.5	13.1
Total	100.0	100.0	100.0	100.0	100.0	100.0

two-week interval was used and nearly one-half could be so classified if a three- to four-week interval was employed. There was a slight tendency for the women and the experimentals to be more consistent than the men and the controls, but no groups were highly so. The quotations presented in the section immediately above suggest that many factors were operating to produce the inconsistency in response indicated in Table 30.

REPORTS FROM EMPLOYERS ABOUT POST-HIGH SCHOOL EMPLOYMENT

Those subjects who had been employed were asked to indicate on the questionnaire the names and addresses of their employers, their weekly wages and, inferentially, the progress they had made on their jobs. To check on the validity of the responses of a sample of the subjects it was necessary to obtain a statement about their work experiences from their employers.

The names of 50 employed subjects were drawn randomly from the experimental group and the names and addresses of their employers listed. Each employer received the following letter.

Dear Sir:

In connection with research in vocational guidance sponsored by the University of Wisconsin we are studying the post-high school activities of a sample of youth from four Wisconsin cities. It is essential to obtain information about their employment status at certain times after they finished high school.

(Name of subject) __________ has indicated that he (she) was in your employ as a __________ in __________. He (she) has stated that the wages were approximately __________ per week.

A rating scale of the employee's performance is on the enclosed card. A number for the subject is used to preserve anonymity. We would appreciate it if you would put a check (√) on the rating that fits the person and mail it.

All information is, of course, completely confidential. No names or other identifying data are used in final reports.

Thank you for your coöperation in this matter.

Yours truly,
Dr. Rothney

Enclosed with the letter was a return postal card addressed to the investigator. It contained a number that identified the subject without revealing his name. The card also contained the following text.

No. __________ December, 1956

☐ (Check) The information given is substantially correct. If it is not correct indicate in what respects your records differ from what the worker reported. __________

____

Rating of Employee Performance (Check one)

☐ Promoted in pay and responsibility more rapidly than usual.
☐ Promoted in pay and responsibility at usual rate.
☐ Remained at same job level.
☐ Was dismissed from job.

__________ __________
Organization Company officer

Replies were received from 49 out of 50 employers and, since they confirmed what the subjects had said, it was concluded that the responses to the employment questions could be used for the purposes for which they are employed throughout this report.

RECORDS OF POST-HIGH SCHOOL EDUCATIONAL PERFORMANCES

Evidence about academic achievements of those subjects who went on to college or nursing schools was obtained. Through the assistance of Dr. Paul Trump, registrar of the University of Wisconsin, transcripts were obtained from the registrars of the institutions represented. Sixty-two out of 64 colleges and nursing schools reported.

The transcripts, in addition to providing complete lists of grades and credits achieved by the subjects, provided verification of periods of attendance, degrees awarded, honor or probationary status, rank in graduating class in some cases, and reasons for withdrawal or expulsion when a student left before graduation.

INFORMAL FOLLOW-UP PROCEDURES

The questionnaire returns, letters, and interviews were supplemented throughout the entire five-year period of the follow-up by informal methods. These have been described by Putman.[6] The following quotation from his report illustrates the techniques which he used in keeping informed about the subjects of this study who had attended the school in which he was a teacher.

> All of the information from personal sources was gained by chance meetings, either with the persons themselves or interested parties. Other sources included classmates, friends and relatives, spiritual advisers, employers, local or state newspapers, and college publications. Some information about graduates attending institutions of higher learning was gleaned from chance meetings with college instructors. By knowing something of close bonds of friendship among members of the studied class, the writer was able to gain information about not only the person talked to but also close friends as well.
>
> The information sought was similar to the information that is usually sought in a questionnaire study. Without stating items spe-

[6] John A. Putman, "Use of Community Resources in a Follow-up Study," *The Personnel and Guidance Journal,* March, 1954, 409–410.

cifically, the gist of the conversation with persons contacted was centered on the following items.

(1) What are you (or the graduate being discussed) doing now?
(2) How do you like what you are doing?
(3) Is that what you had planned to do when you graduated?
(4) If not, why the change?
(5) Are you glad (or sorry) to be out of school?
(6) What did you like about school?
(7) What did you dislike about school?
(8) What are your future plans?
(9) What and how is ________________ (a classmate) doing?

None of the persons from whom information was gathered was aware of the reason for conversation other than a mutual interest in the person or persons discussed. The writer did not seek out parents, friends, and employers. They were already acquainted with him so rapport had already been established. Contacts were made from the sidelines of a school dance to the local golf course; from chance meetings on the street to the steps of church after morning services; from across the table during a bridge game to across the table at the local soda fountain hangout.

In addition to the direct method of securing information by contact with individuals, publications provided valuable information. The local newspapers were the best sources. Clippings from school papers as well as out-of-town papers also proved fruitful sources of information about students who were attending schools or living out of the city.

A file was kept on each graduate. In that file a running account of the person was faithfully kept. Anything that person had said to the author about one of the graduates, anything he had heard from another person about the individual and the source was recorded. Newspaper clippings about the individual were kept in the file. The files of more than one-half of the subjects contained only one entry but many of the files contained numerous references.

The author used the techniques described during the period from September, 1952, to July, 1953. He found out valuable and usable information about the post-high school activities of 124 of the 158 graduates. Ninety-six of the 124 were "interviewed" in person. Thus, in the year following graduation, information was gathered for 79 percent of the graduates and 61 percent of them were seen personally.

The percentages seem gratifying when one considers that no complex planning was required and no funds were expended. It is also gratifying to reach such numbers since many of the graduates were unable to be contacted in person because of military service.

INTERVIEWS

Up to the time of the five-years-after-high school study the only elaboration of questionnaire responses obtained was in occasional letters and informal interviews when some of the subjects dropped in to see the investigator. The interviews seemed to yield so much more information than the questionnaire that it seemed desirable to add them as follow-up techniques.

It was impossible to interview all the subjects, but it seemed that a carefully chosen sample might serve the purpose. Every seventh subject on alphabetical rosters of the experimental and control subjects was chosen to provide a sample representative of the population and small enough so that the cost of interviewing them was within the budget. When the sampling method produced the name of a subject who was overseas or at a point in this country where the expense of reaching him did not seem justified, the next name on the list was substituted. Contingencies of time and convenience finally reduced the numbers who were interviewed to 25 control and 25 experimental subjects.

Forty-six interviews were conducted in the homes of the subjects and four were held at the University of Wisconsin at times convenient to the subjects. Each one had been informed by letter that the interviews were to be recorded, why each had been chosen, and why the interviews were being conducted. All letters were of the same form except for the second paragraph. That one referred to personal matters as in the sample below.

Dear____________:

Five years after high school did roll by in a hurry, didn't they? Thanks for completing the questionnaire. You have helped us to get replies from everyone, which is so necessary. Keeping in touch with 700 graduates has been a fascinating job as you can well imagine. Even more important, it will give your high school and others real help in making high schools better.

It sounds as though you have quite a family, Mary. I'll bet those three children keep you pretty busy. You were a fine student in high school, and I would expect you to be an excellent mother. You mention wanting to sing in a church choir. Have you had a chance to do anything with your musical training?

In this study we have one other project with which you could help. We expect to visit about fifty of you personally and talk with you in more detail about what you are doing. You might wonder why you have been chosen. We listed all the names of the graduates alphabetically and took every seventh name. Yours happened to come up. My assistant would visit you at *your* convenience and tape record an interview with you about your ideas of high school and any other experiences you might want to talk about. (It will take less than an hour of your time.) That will give me a first-hand report even though I can't be there myself.

Would you check on the enclosed card which date and hour would be most convenient for you? If there are none on the card please suggest one that is. An afternoon or morning hour would permit us to spend our evenings with those who work outside the home during the day. Thanks a lot for your help.

Sincerely,
Dr. Rothney

After preliminary remarks the tape recorder was set up and the interviewer asked the questions which had appeared on the questionnaire that the subject had filled out several months earlier. The interviewer had memorized the questions. He was not familiar with the subject's questionnaire responses and it was assumed that there had been a sufficient interval so that the subject might not have remembered all his answers to the items.

The subject was permitted to elaborate on his responses as fully as he wished, and questioning by the interviewer encouraged him to respond at much greater length than the questionnaire permitted. No time limit was placed on the sessions and they ranged in length from 30 minutes to an hour in length.

A SAMPLE FOLLOW-UP INTERVIEW

The following interview with one of the experimental subjects was taken directly from the tape. It has been edited only to prevent identification. The *I* indicates the interviewer who was a counselor-in-training and the *S* is the subject.

I—This is Bob Jackson interviewing on March 5, 1957. And your name is?

S—Jane Doe.

I—Um-hmm, and your maiden name?

S—Jane Rowe.

I—You didn't change the sound too much.

S—No, the spelling quite a lot.

I—Yes, quite a lot . . . and your address?

S—2056 Jones Avenue, Jonesville.

I—And if we wanted to reach you in a few years, at what address will mail usually reach you?

S—I think I could always get it from my parents at 109 Smith Street.

I—That's in your former home town?

S—Yes.

I—And you're married?

S—Yes.

I—Could you . . . (subject laughs) . . . Could you show how you like it by selecting one of these four categories: I really like it; my likes just balance my dislikes; I don't like it but I'll have to put up with it; and I hate it?

S—Well, I would take the first one. I really like it.

I—Uh-huh, and could you tell me why you named the one you did?

S—Well, I've always liked kids. (*)[7] And I've got a very nice husband, (*) and I think that's the only two things I could say.

I—Uh-humm. What is there about you that makes you successful in what you are doing?

S—Well, I don't know how successful I am (both laugh). I like housework.

I—You do, hmm?

S—I don't care for cooking too much, but I'm learning. (*) And I like to bake. (*) Otherwise I don't know if I am successful.

I—Uh-hmm. And what is there about you that handicaps you in what you are doing?

S—Well, I was used to having all my own money. And now it is

[7] An asterisk indicates uh-hmm or some other indication of verbal acceptance or agreement by the listener.

kind of hard to fall back on just one income. (*) But we're getting over that too (subject laughs). We've got that licked pretty much.

I—Uh-hmm. It's an interesting comment, and it hasn't come up before. I would think it would be a problem in almost any couple where the wife has been working. . . . Used to an independent . . . (cut off).

S—Yes, I was always used to when I wanted anything, you know, just going down and getting it, (*) and now we have to think about it a little more. (*) I think that's our biggest problem.

I—Uh-hmm. You mentioned that you like kids. Have you had a lot of experience with younger people?

S—Just with neighbors and I have a lot of little cousins. (*) And we've always been rather close on my mother's side of the family, so I mean that's the only experience I've had, so. . . .

I—Uh-hmm, what would you like to be doing five years from now?

S—Oh, possibly the same thing I am doing now . . . being a mother.

I—Uh-hmm, and ten years from now?

S—Maybe ten years from now I could be working. (*) By that time the children would probably be going to school and I could . . . ah . . . (unintelligible words) I could just work.

I—Uh-hmm. What was the last type of work that you did before you . . . (cut off).

S—Office work, typing and stenography.

I—Uh-hmm. Now you worked for a shopping news here in town, didn't you?

S—Oh, that was in my home town. I worked there, ah, during school (*) and then for about six months, I think, after I graduated.

I—Uh-hmm, and then you went from there to where?

S—To a fountain pen manufacturing company.

I—And is that where you worked up until (*) the end?

S—Yes (laugh), until the end (laugh).

I—(Laugh) . . . until the end . . . kind of dramatic . . .(laugh What kind of organization is that?

S—Well, it's really very nice as far as I'm concerned and I work with younger people and older people. (*) And with men and women . . . I mean I've got a . . . (unintelligible) you might say. (*) Everybody's really nice. You have to work but you have a lot of fun too (*) I liked it real much.

I—You mentioned going back to work. Would you like to go back to office work, or. . . .

S—Well, I've always sort of had it in the back of my mind that I'd like factory work. I don't know (*) and I'd maybe like to take up a chance at that . . . I don't know.

I—Is there better pay in that or would you get about the same?

S—I really don't know.

I—Just the kind of work that you'd like to try?

S—Yeah, I'd like to just try it.

I—Sure . . . what was the date of your marriage?

S—May 25, 1956.

I—Uh-hmm, and if we asked the number of children, you could almost say one then.

S—Yes (laughs).

I—And you're living with your husband. What's his occupation?

S—Well, right now he's an attendant at an institution. (*) But, ah, we think he's going to change and be a . . . a route salesman for a milk company. Hmmm, As it is now his hours are so long he . . . like this morning he left about ten minutes to six and he won't get home until about twenty after six so we don't see too much of each other . . . and a . . . a he works six days a week. . . . So that's kind of nasty.

I—That is a lot of hours.

S—Yes, it is. So we hope he is going to do something different. (*)

I—The route sales would be in this city area then too?

S—Yes, uh-huh. (*)

I—And you do not have a job outside the home at present?

S—No.

I—How long ago did you leave your job at the pen company?

S—Let's see, I left at Christmas time.

I—At Christmas time.

S—Yes. (*)

I—Judging by your own experience, what could high schools do to prepare young people for marriage?

S—Well, I really couldn't answer that too good. I think, ah, girls should take more of an interest in their home economics courses. I didn't and I'm suffering from it, right now. And ah, otherwise I really don't know. I think the problems come up and they're always different. (*) You just have to work them out. (*)

I—It isn't the kind of thing that could be taught in the high school for instance?

S—I really don't see how it could be. (*) I suppose you could talk to people about getting along with somebody, but until it really happens to you, . . . I know I often said that if that were my husband . . . this was before I was married. (*) (laughs) . . . I'd do different, and I'm finding out that I'm not doing any different. (*)

I—I see a fish over there on top of the television set, is your husband a fisherman too?

S—No, his father had those made. Where he worked some fellow made them so he brought them home (*) and we just have them sitting on there.

I—They are very good replicas . . . just like fish. (*) We'd like to keep track of your status over the last two and a half years. Beginning in January of 1954 . . . at that time you were working?

S—Yes.

I—At the pen company?

S—Uh-hmm.

I—And you continued to work there, as you mentioned, up until this last Christmas?

S—Yes.

I—Now you've been staying home. (*) Anything else happen over that period that was outstanding or real important or significant?

S—Oh, I think the only thing I did, I think it was during that time, I took a trip to Florida one summer. (*) Otherwise I don't think I did anything.

I—What did you think of Florida?

S—Oh, I liked it real well.

I—Would you like to live there?

S—No, I don't think I'd like to live there. It was fun to go and come home.

I—Why? (Asked after "like to live there" above.)

S—Oh, I don't know if it was just that my family was all back here or what. (*) Maybe that had something to do with it. (*) It was nice though.

I—Was your husband from this area too?

S—Well, we went to school together, and ah, then his father died and he, ah, moved to Illinois . . . a little town in the northern part of the state. (*) And he joined the army and, and then after he got out of the army he worked in Milwaukee . . . and then he started to come down and see me (laughs), and so (laughs).

I—Does he ever have the yen to go back to Illinois?

S—Oh, I don't think he particularly cares to go back, but he's forever bringing up the wonderful football team they have (laughs).

I—Well, they do have some pretty good teams over there. If you could live over again the last five years since you left high school, would you do the same things as you have done?

S—No, I think I recognize that question. (*) I would have liked . . . now that I think about it I think it would have been nice to have gone to school for a couple of years. (*)

I—What kind of school?

S—Oh, I always thought I'd like to be a teacher and so I would probably have picked something like a state college near my home.

I—Why do you say specifically teaching?

S—Oh, at one time I had, I think Dr. Rothney sort of talked to me about it . . . about being an elementary teacher. (*) But that all fell through. (*)

I—Does your interest in that reflect back on the fact that you said you liked children? . . .

S—Oh, I think that might be, yeah. . . .

I—Any other reasons that you? . . .

S—Well, I don't know, maybe the three months' vacation you get. . . . (*)

I—Looking toward the future, do you think things are going to work out well for you?

S—All I can say is that I hope that they do.

I—Why do you say that?

S—Oh, I don't think anyone really knows, and . . . I know it would be kind of too bad if you had the kids and they didn't.

I—Talking about this job again, you mentioned that you were doing office work. What did you actually do on the job?

S—Well, I worked in the trade department. (*) And ah, it was my job to type up all these corrections that would come in for different countries . . . like their importation duties and things like that. (*) And then the girls all followed country sheets, they called them, and we had to find out, oh, their currency for all the different countries and then I typed those up for them (*) and filed and did things like that. (*)

I—Why did you choose the job?

S—I didn't really choose it (laughs).

I—How do you mean?

S—Well, I was just, ah, picked (*) and then I could have changed if I didn't like it, you know. (*) But I mean we didn't have a list and we could choose export or domestic. We just got picked and that was it.

I—I see. If you wish to mention the wages you received, and you may not want to, this is one of the questions that you may not want to answer, what were they when you left work?

S—I don't mind saying. I was getting a hundred and five dollars clear every two weeks. (*) and I wasn't one of the highest paid girls by far. (*) I consider that quite good for a . . . a woman.

I—Yeah, and how did that compare with when you began working?

S—Well, let's see. My friend just started now and I believe she is making $70 every two weeks. (*) And she just began a few months ago.

I—Uh-hmm, and that was about what you were making at that time?

S—Well, I believe it must have been; I really can't remember. (*) But I think that they must start everybody out at about the same rate. (*)

I—Was there any difference between the work you did when you started and the work you did when you left?

S—Oh, yes, uh-huh, when I first started I was in the domestic department and I was doing odds and ends, rush jobs you know, (*) that they would bring in and it was terribly nerve-racking, and ah, then I got moved to export where you had your own job (*) no odds and ends you know. (*) It's much nicer. (*)

I—A lot of pressure on the other job, then?

S—Oh, terrific, it was awful.

I—Gosh . . . and you weren't in the armed forces?

S—No.

I—Uh-hmm. Did you receive any sort of training after you left high school . . . like college or? . . .

S—No, I didn't.

I—Okay, looking back at your high school training, could you tell us how it helped you most?

S—Well, you know, a friend and I were talking about that the other day (*) and the school has a commercial department, I think, that's just wonderful (*) and as far as I was concerned, we had, ah, one hour a day for shorthand *and* typing in our junior year and then the senior year the same . . . and as far as I know every girl from our town who has gone down to the pen factory is equal to the girls down there who had an hour of shorthand and an hour of typing (*) and I can't see where the girls from a neighboring city are doing any better job (*), not just comparing them to me but I know a lot of girls down there from my home town and I think the commercial teacher was just wonderful.

I—A very fine teacher then.

S—Yes, I do. (*) Otherwise I suppose, oh, your English would enter in quite a bit. (*) If I remember correctly we had good English teachers. (*) Otherwise . . . what was the question again? . . . I was rattling on and on. . . .

I—How high school helped you most.

S—Oh, I would say my commercial and English helped me the most. (*)

I—Had you made up your mind to get into commercial early in your high school career or at what time did you decide that you were going to? . . .

S—Well, I think I took typing in my sophomore year just because everybody said, "Be sure and take typing; you can always fall back on it." (*) And I liked it a lot and I liked the commercial teacher (*) and I think I just went on from there; I don't think I had too many ideas *what* I wanted to do. (*)

I—Could you tell us how high school failed to help you?

S—Well, I don't think the high school failed, (*) at least I know that it would have to have been me. (*) Offhand I can't . . . I don't know of anything. (*)

I—Looking back at the counseling you had in high school could you tell us how it helped you?

S—Do you mean from Dr. Rothney or from any teacher?

I—Well, both.

S—Well, like I did say, Dr. Rothney had talked to me about being an elementary teacher. (*) And I wish now I had done it. (*) But as it was I got earning my own money (*) and that's always bad (laughs) saying I'll go to school after I've worked so and so. You usually don't end up doing it. (*) So, ah, I don't think *that* counseling failed in that respect. It was just me. (*) No, I don't think the counseling failed.

I—Could you tell us how it helped you?

S—Well, as I look back at it, it was kind of fun getting out of class (both laugh). It was nice talking to him too. (*) And then I think we took quite a few of those tests, intelligence tests, and, ah, aptitude tests, I think they were. That was kind of fun, ah, knowing what you were really fitted to be. You know sometimes you think I can do this, and actually you're not cut out for it at all. (*) It was fun taking those tests. (*)

I—Were you able to put them to any specific use? I mean did they help you particularly, do you think?

S—No, I don't think so, in my own case, that they did help. (*)

Both talk

I—Go ahead.

S—I was just going to say I think one of the girls in our graduating class followed through that . . . she's a girl friend of mine, graduated from the U. (*) And I think it must have helped her (*) because she worked her way through (*) . . . helped out a lot by herself. (*) So in that case I think it helped a lot. (*)

I—You mentioned the fact that you had been working probably kept you from going on to school. Do you mean the part-time work before you finished school?

S—No. That didn't enter in . . . it was after I, ah, finished school (*) and then I was going to work and save my money (*) and as it was I started to buy a car and then I (laughs) just didn't get to school. (*)

I—Could you give the names of any political organizations, clubs, social activities, church, or any kind of group or activity which you have attended regularly during the last three years?

S—Well, I don't belong to any clubs. I don't belong to anything. (laughs) . . . nothing.

I—Have you voted in any political elections?

S—No, much as I hate to admit it, I didn't vote in this last election, (*) and it was just because I had forgotten to register, but I have voted.

I—You have voted.

S—Yes (laughs) and my brother will never let me forget it because I'm a staunch Republican and then I didn't vote. So now he . . . (both laugh).

I—Referring back to the fact that you have voted, may I ask why?

S—Why did I vote? (*) I think it was a little election at my home town at the time I was living there, I think it was a city election, (*) and my folks were voting so I just went along. (*) I didn't really have any good reason. (*)

I—You didn't have a registering problem?

S—No, ah, not down there. My husband registered and voted though. I can say that and give him that much credit. (*)

I—What self-improvement activities such as courses, on the job training, reading, home study, have you been doing?

S—You'll have to look right down there on that little stand. I have been reading my baby book. And ah, let's see, I read my cookbook a lot. (*) Otherwise I haven't been doing too much. (*)

I—Do you have confidence in the actions you take when you have to make choices?

S—Ordinarily, I do. (*)

I—And if you needed help in the last five years in making decisions to whom did you go?

S—Well, I usually just made up my own mind, and I never, ah, after I made up my mind I might have talked it over. I usually talked it over with my mother. I don't believe I ever talked anything over with my dad. But otherwise I usually just made up my own mind and then did it. (*)

I—Would you characterize yourself as kind of an independent person then?

S—Maybe I'm a little too independent (both laugh). Oh, I wouldn't say exactly independent, but, ah, I don't know what other word to use. I fall back on my husband quite a lot now. It's pretty much half and half with us. We discuss everything; even if we are going to buy a mop (laughs) . . . now we discuss it. (*)

I—Any interesting plans for the future?

S—About the only plans we really have right now is getting a down payment for our own home. (*) Then after we get that we'll just have to go on from there.

I—What kind of home do you have in mind?

S—Well, I've always liked an older home. Preferably brick; that's what I've always had my heart set on. But I usually set my heart on something and then get something altogether different (laughs). It'll probably be a ranch or something. I've always liked an older home though. We'll just have to wait and see.

I—Could you list the names and approximate addresses of the three of your high school classmates whom you know the best?

S—Let's see, um, Mary Smith is one and she recently got married and they're living in this city now. I don't know their address. I think it's on Ferry Street. And Jane Jones. She's living here. Those are the two and then I suppose I could say Doris Williams. She's in her home town. She lives on Main Street. I don't know what her address would be. Those would probably be the three most . . . (*)

I—What factors do you think have made certain of your classmates remain closer than others? Is there anything? . . .

S—Oh, I think, ah, if they went to college together I think they sort of stayed together. (*) As it was, ah, as I say I didn't go to college and I started being friends with all those kids at work and I never saw the girls who I had gone to school with. (*) And I think if they go to school together or even if they go to another college but they get together during their vacations, I think that keeps them together a lot. (*) And I think boys are more inclined to stay together than girls. (*)

I—For what reasons?

S—I don't know. I always thought boys were, ah, how should I say it, easier to get along with. (*) And they kind of overlook each others faults more than girls did. Girls are terribly picky (laughs). And I don't think boys are generally. (*)

I—If you were to give one bit of advice on the basis of your experiences to a high school student, what would it be?

S—I'd say study.

I—Anything in particular or just work hard?

S—Just study. Absorb everything you can and just plant it away because you can always dig it out and sometimes if you, ah, sometimes you get your facts all mixed up if you didn't exactly pay attention (*) but I think if you study and do the best you can that's the best (*) the best thing to do.

I—This last question is kind of a philosophical one. What things in life give you the greatest satisfaction and happiness?

S—What things in life give me? . . . I think this baby is going to give us an awful lot of satisfaction (*) I think that's the biggest thing right now. (*) When my husband and I go out and have a real nice time . . . without spending much money, that's always nice. I think the most important is the baby. (*)

I—Funny how they can be so important even before they are born (she laughs). Your whole life seems to center around them, doesn't it?

S—Yes.

I—Are there any other comments you would like to make about high school, counseling, or any experiences you have had?

S—No, I really can't say that I have any. (*)

I—How do you feel about high school?

S—At the time it was just something I went to. I could hardly wait to get out of it. (*) And everybody said it was the best years of your life. Maybe they were too. They are to me, now that I look back and think of all the fun I had and the kids I saw and now I don't see them. (*) So I think high school is wonderful.

I—Were you ever tempted to drop out?

S—No.

I—Do you want your own children to finish?

S—Oh, yes. I'd want them to go on to school. (*) No, I would be very, very heartbroken if my kids dropped out of high school.

I—Fine.

SUMMARY OF THE DATA OVER THE EIGHT YEARS OF THE STUDY

In order to show the various kinds of data collected on each subject from the time he was a sophomore in high school till he was interviewed five years after high school, the following report on *Will* has been prepared. It has been edited only enough to prevent identification. Will's own construction and spelling have been retained in his written responses.

THE CASE OF WILL

Birth date: October 25, 1932   Age at entering high school: 15–10

Academic Record [a] (Semester Grades)

	Grade 10		Grade 11		Grade 12		
English	C^2	C^1	B^2	B^2	C	D	(Ninth grade
Speech					D	C	marks were
Spanish			D^2	D^2			3 C's and 1
Algebra	D^2	D^2					D)

	Grade 10	Grade 11	Grade 12	
Geometry		D^2 F		
Biology	C^2 B^2			
World history	B^1 B^2			(Rank in
U.S. history		C^1 D^2		graduating
Geography			C C	class of
American problems			D C	353 students
Choir	Credit			was 242)
Typewriting			No credit	
Physical education	Credit	Credit	Credit	

[a] Letters attached to marks in grades 10 and 11 are teachers reports on effort graded on a scale of 1 for excellent, 2 for good and 3 for poor.

COMMENTS BY WILL ON HIS ACADEMIC EXPERIENCES

Grade 10. Likes history best and algebra least. He said that he just "loved" the ancient part of world history but that he just couldn't do mathematics and wanted to avoid it in the future.

Grade 11. Will said he liked history best but couldn't learn geometry. "I learn too slow." He wished that he had considered what counselor had said about election of geometry rather than followed the advice of a class advisor who was a mathematics teacher. He found Spanish difficult and felt quite sure that he would not elect it again.

Grade 12. He enjoyed his speech class most this year. He found it difficult to do his homework in his other classes. He said that he felt that college work would be difficult but that his parents wanted him to try it.

When Will was in the ninth grade his IQ score on the Otis Self-Administering test was 99. His score on an algebra aptitude test was at the 30th percentile.

COMMENTS ON TESTS

When his ninth grade test scores were interpreted to Will he seemed disappointed. He said he might have done better if he had the glasses he now has at the time he took the tests. When he saw his eleventh grade test scores he was again very much disappointed. He said that he did not expect to accomplish much in school. He was told

TEST RECORD

	Grade 10 Percentile	Grade 11 Percentile	Grade 12 Grade Placement
Henmon-Nelson Test of Mental Ability	31	31	
Primary Mental Abilities			
Verbal	17		
Space	24		
Reasoning	32		
Number	15		
Word Fluency	47		
Differential Aptitude Tests			
Verbal reasoning		15	
Number		25	
Spelling		15	
Sentences		30	
Progressive Reading			
Vocabulary			12.7
Comprehension			10.6
Total			11.9

that low scores on the tests did not completely preclude accomplishment of some of the things he wanted to do.

INTERESTS AND EXPERIENCES REPORTED

Grade 10. Read anything he could find about the Romans and ancient times. Enjoyed many sports, particularly skiing. Liked choir and listening to music.

Grade 11. Liked to read fiction. One teacher reported that he showed a keen appreciation of literature. Still a sports enthusiast and particular interest this year was in shooting with a bow and arrow. Still liked to listen to music. Liked cars but did not tinker with mechanical parts. Did not participate in school activities because he said he did not have time.

Grade 12. Still read fiction and was enthusiastic about watching sports teams. Lost interest in hunting. Bought a 1937 coupe. Played a minor role in a school dramatic production. Joined a naval reserve unit in a neighboring city.

WORK EXPERIENCE

Grade 10. Helped in a meat market and was glad to have the job as a source of income. Worked on a truck farm during two summer vacations. Did not like farming.
Grade 11. Got a job as doorman at a movie theater three evenings and one afternoon each week. Liked it well enough to continue.
Grade 12. Dropped work at the theater at parents' insistence to get time to do his homework, but really wanted to keep it so that he could earn enough money to operate his car. During the summer between the eleventh and twelfth grades he worked in a farm machinery plant where he earned 71 cents per hour for doing such jobs as painting and labeling machine parts.

EDUCATIONAL AND VOCATIONAL CHOICES

Grade 10. Some outdoor work such as conservationist or archeologist. His parents encouraged him to go on to college but left the choice of vocation to him.
Grade 11. Traveling salesman, with policeman or other outdoor work as second and third choices. Still interested in attending college. Said he planned to attend the extension center of the state university nearest his home. Parents approved. He said that if things worked out well for him in five years he would be a salesman or policeman.
Grade 12. Sales work of some kind after attending the extension center. Parents approved of his plans.

HEALTH AND PHYSICAL CHARACTERISTICS

Several teachers and counselors described Will as a handsome well-groomed boy. He was tall and slender. His clothes were well-pressed, his hair always neatly combed and his shoes shined. Such words as "immaculate" and "well-groomed" appeared frequently in the record. He had a very slight lisp and he needed glasses for reading and study. In response to all questions about his health he indicated that it was OK. He walked in a slow sedate manner.

Usual Behavior

The school which Will attended did not keep records of personal development. One teacher who did report on him while he was in the eleventh grade said that he was conscientious, that he habitually influenced the activities of his associates, that he seemed secure in his social relationships, and that he was concerned about the welfare of others. Another said that he was a little mischievous but very nice. She said that he tried to do the right thing.

Various observers of Will said that he seemed mature, poised, serious, and dignified. He talked freely during interviews, asked many questions, and said that he wanted to talk over his plans with somebody. Observers suggested that he seemed to feel insecure or uncertain and disturbed, particularly about his level of academic performance. He seemed determined to try and was dissatisfied with the results. Generally he was described as a, "nice guy even if he is not a good student." He had many friends who, he said, would describe him as OK or average.

The autobiography that Will wrote when he was in the eleventh grade follows. It has been edited only enough to prevent identification. His original errors in spelling and construction have been retained.

My Autobiography
(October 7, 1949)

In the state of New York in the year 1932 Oct. 25, I was born. My father came to this country from a country in Europe and my mother from another one. I am one of four other children so I do not consider myself a spoiled child. I have a brother and two sisters and I am the second oldest of the four.

My mother and father met each other in this country and were married. My oldest sister was born, and the family lived in another state for two years before moving to Wisconsin. The reason for moving was the transfare of my Dads job.

On the whole I have lived a very normal unexciting life. Except for a few accidents I can't remember anything else tradgic or exciting.

In the pocess of education I have gone to two grade schools, Junior High and now high school. One grade school I went to in another city, and the other in this county when we moved out there in 1941.

When I was thriteen I started making my first real money working for a truck farm bunching radish. There I worked for three summers, the third summer I worked in the washhouse packing. The winter of 1948 I worked for a butcher shop. I now work for a theater.

My favorite sports are skiing, swimming, and hunting. That is about all I have of importance to write.

HOME SITUATION

Will's father, who had received the minimum education in the country from which he came, worked as a maintenance man in a foundry. His mother had completed only an elementary school education. She was not employed outside the home. The family bought a new house in 1949 and they were very proud of it.

In conference with a counselor the parents expressed great interest in Will's progress and were insistent that he go on to college. They seemed to know their son's strengths and weaknesses and, although they had some doubts about the possibility of his success in college, they were willing to risk the expenditure necessary. Will had indicated that he wanted to earn part of his own expenses.

COUNSELING

During interviews with the counselor the following activities were carried out.

1. Will was encouraged to talk about his problems and plans.
2. Some of his questions were answered and he was directed to sources for the answers to others.
3. His choices of electives were discussed.
4. Test scores were interpreted.
5. College entrance requirements were discussed.
6. Requirements of the particular university extension center he had chosen to enter were considered.
7. A two-year certificate course in business offered by the university was examined with Will.
8. Time for consideration of occupations that he had chosen and others was provided. The pros and cons of each were discussed.
9. Arrangements were made for Will's visit to the university extension center with a friend during a spring vacation period.
10. Information about the navy classification system and ways of advancing was given at the time he was going to join the Naval Reserve Unit.
11. Some assistance in study habits and scheduling of time was provided.

12. He was given the chance to satisfy his desire "to talk over my plans with somebody."
13. He was complimented on his appearance and given encouragement when he most seemed to need it.

SENIOR REPORT

One month before graduation from high school Will completed the Education form of the Senior Report. His answers in their original form, with only enough editing to prevent identification, are given below.

1. What is the name of your *first* choice of school or college or training institution? University Extention
   Where is it located? Milwaukee Wisconsin
2. When did you decide on the place? Year 1951 Month ______
3. Have you applied for admission? No Have you been admitted? No
4. Have you applied for a scholarship? No.
5. How long is the course you plan to take? Two years
6. How much do you think it will cost you the first year? not more than $500
7. What *per cent* of the cost of your training do you expect to earn? Percent 50% How? Work during summer
8. Why did you select the school as your first choice? It offers the subject I wish to practice, and it is the closest school.
9. If something keeps you from attending this place what are your second and third choices? Second Choice radio or television work
   Third Choice active duty in the Navy
10. Who, if anyone, helped you in your choice of school? Dr. Rothney suggested the same school I had in mind.
11. If more than one person helped you, who helped you most? Dr. Rothney
12. What is there about *you* that will make you successful in the training you have chosen? determination
13. What is there about *you* that might keep you from being successful in your training? I am one of the stupid people in existence

14. Name any friends of yours who are planning to go to the same place for their training. Tom________.
15. What arrangements have you made about a place to live? I shall live with my parents at home.
16. Which of the activities that you carried on in high school are you planning to continue? English and Speech, only this time I am going to get my money's worth.
17. What course do you plan to take? Marketing and Advertising. Salesmanship.
18. What, if anything, would change your mind about wanting to take the training you had planned for next year?
If I had a chance to make good money by signing a radio or television contract, I would forget about selling.

1. Regardless of what you have said on the other pages, what would you like to be doing for a living:
Five years from now? Hollywood actor
Ten years from now? I don't know
2. What training will be needed to get the job you listed on the first line on *this* page? Theatrical Training
3. Are there any kinds of training you would strongly object to taking? Preparation for active duty in enemy waters.
4. Are there any kinds of *work* you would strongly object to doing? Work in dusty areas
5. Looking back at your last three years of senior high school do you think they were? (Put a check on the line that tells how you feel.)
   A. Generally pleasant? 12th *OR un*pleasant? Junior
   B. Generally worth while? 10th *OR not* worth while? 11th
   C. Generally useful? 10th *OR not* useful? 12th
6. Are there any subjects you took in high school which you wish you hadn't? Subject Geometry Why? Waste of time for me
7. Are there any subjects you didn't take in high school which you wish you had? Subject Business Law Why? (No answer)
8. Are there any subjects you wanted to take that were not offered? (No answer)

9. Are there any subjects on which you would have liked to have spent more time? Yes
   Subject Spanish Why didn't you spend more time on it?
   I was working after school and didn't have time.
10. Looking toward the future do you think that things are going to work out well for you? I haven't the slightest idea.
11. Why or why not? (No answer)
12. How has the international situation (war) affected you?
    It puts me in a hazardous position
13. How do you think it will affect you in the future? I may not live to tell, I may come back half a man, and I know it won't do me any good.
14. Do you think there is as much chance for people to get ahead today as there was when your parents were the age that you are now? More
15. Why? There is a wider field of jobs and positions
16. What organizations or clubs would you want to belong to when you are working or a married member of the community? List in the order of your choice. This is one of the few things that concerns me.
17. What *social problems* do *you* plan to do something about after you have finished high school? I haven't thought about it
18. How do *you* plan to work on them? (No answer)
19. In each of the twelve headings below, show where you think you stand compared to other high school seniors by putting a check mark in the column at the right.

In the item given below I would be, compared to other high school seniors, in the	Top Quarter	Third Highest Quarter	Second Lowest Quarter	Lowest Quarter
1. Achievement in my special field of interest (write it below) (No answer)				
2. Reading Achievement		X		
3. Intelligence Test scores			X	

4. Achievement in arithmetic and mathematics				X
5. Confidence that I will succeed in the work I have chosen to do		X		
6. Getting along with people		X		
7. Rank in this senior class			X	
8. Confidence that I have chosen the right career				
9. Knowing my own strengths		X		
10. Knowing my own weaknesses				
11. Readiness for life after high school		X		
12. Getting along in new situations	?			

---

20. Suppose you had a choice between (A) a safe steady job working for someone else with steady average pay for the job, or (B) running your own business with the chance of either going bankrupt or getting rich. Would you choose A or B? B Why? I would take a crack at the jackpot, providing I was still single.
21. Do you believe that you will ever want counseling again? Yes
22. If you do where will you get it? That's a good question because it depends upon where I am at the time.
23. This last page is to be used to give more information on any of the questions asked on the other pages or to write anything you want to about school experiences or your plans for the future. You might want to comment about the counseling you have had, your preparation for the life that is ahead, the way in which school could be improved or any other matter that interests you. Write on the back of the page if you need more space.

    This student counseling is one of the better things the school has to offer. It should be continued in the future, for it is a great help throughout high school.

(Special)

The *attendance office* should be cleaned out and replaced with people who know that every person who walks in there is not a lier.

Prediction of Post-High School Performance

Soon after Will had been graduated from high school the counselor and a counselor-in-training made the following predictions of his post-high school performance and wrote the following comments.

COUNSELOR-IN-TRAINING'S PREDICTION AND COMMENTS

He will:

_____A. be eligible for *major* awards based upon scholastic performances.

_____B. be eligible for *minor* awards based upon scholastic performances.

__X__C. complete training. Will not be eligible for awards or on probation.

_____D. take longer than usual time to graduate though never on probation.

_____E. drop out of training for reasons other than scholastic difficulty.

_____F. be a marginal student. Will be on probation at some time.

_____G. drop because of low grades.

Academic performances—Less than adequate for course
Test performances—Less than adequate for course
Strength of drive—Drive is so high it may compensate for above limitation
Realism in self-appraisal—Highly realistic
Realism in appraisal of opportunities—Same
Flexibility, adjustability, modifiability—Can make adjustments
Politically wise
Handicaps—Slight lisp
Unique Factors—Serious fellow
Comment—None

COUNSELOR'S PREDICTION AND COMMENTS

He will:

______A. be eligible for *major* awards based upon scholastic performances.

______B. be eligible for *minor* awards based upon scholastic performances.

__X__C. complete training. Will not be eligible for awards or on probation.

______D. take longer than usual time to graduate though never on probation.

______E. drop out of training for reasons other than scholastic difficulty.

______F. be a marginal student. Will be on probation at some time.

______G. drop because of low grades.

Academic permormances—Not quite adequate
Test performances—Not quite adequate
Strength of drive—Very good
Realism in self-appraisal—Realistic
Realism in appraisal of opportunities—Perhaps aiming a little high
Flexibility, adjustability, modifiability—Excellent
Handicaps—None
Unique factors—Dignified manner, excellent grooming
Comment—Will have more difficult time than most and may run into impossible scholastic problems—however, drive and determination will carry him through any situation.

FIVE MONTHS AFTER HIGH SCHOOL GRADUATION

Although Will had been invited to respond only to the items on the postal card questionnaire he chose to write the following letter. Original spellings and constructions have been retained.

Home address
November 7, 1951

Dear Dr. Rothney,

I was very glad to receive your little questionnaire and was not surprised when it arrived. I expected to hear from you sooner or later. It so happens that I did register at the University Extention, and enrolled in the Marketing and Advertising course.

So far all the courses are agreeable except the one requiring accounting. I can't say its difficulty caught me completely unawares, because I expected it to be more of a hinderance than an aid. A majority of my classmates have had bookkeeping and this is to their advantage. My instructor is an easy going understandable fellow; but he still has to cover a required amount of chapters in as specified time. Just as I am begining to understand one chapter we proceed to another. I must admit the fourth week I sought escape and asked the advisor if there was any way I could possibly get the certificate without taking accounting. He said he knew of no substitute for the course. Naturally he advised me to study harder; but this is easier said than done. If you know of any way I could drop the course I would appreciate your advice. I know it isn't solving the problem by trying to avoid it but thats how it is. The other subjects seem quite interesting, and I have had no trouble with them. I thank you very much for your concern, and hope to hear from you soon.

Sincerely yours,
Will

UNIVERSITY RECORD IN CERTIFICATE COURSE IN BUSINESS

The record which Will made at the extension center of the state university in the two-year certificate course in business was obtained from official records. It appears below.

First Semester 1951–1952		*Second Semester 1951–1952*	
Business economics	C	Statistics	F
Business English	C	Marketing practice	C
Business law	C	Business law	D
Business management	C	Business correspondence	C
		Economic geography	D

Note entered on record in June, 1952—May continue on final probation. Must earn grade points equal to credits in each semester henceforth or withdraw.

First Semester 1952–1953

Advertising	C	Public speaking	C
Salesmanship	B	Sales writing	B
Report writing	B		

Second Semester 1952–1953

Sales management	B	Sales promotion	B
Market research	C	Personnel management	C
Personal adjustment to business	B	American government and politics	F

TWO AND ONE-HALF YEARS AFTER HIGH SCHOOL GRADUATION

In January, 1954, Will answered the second follow-up questionnaire as follows:

Jan. 25, 1954

POSTGRADUATE'S REPORT

GENERAL

1. Name Will
2. What is your present address? (Home address)
3. Give an address where letter will usually reach you (Home address)
4. Check the *one* item below that best describes your present status
   - ____ Full-time employment
   - ____ Farming
   - X In armed forces
   - ____ Student
   - ____ (Girls only) Married
5. Answer only *one* of these
   If you are in the armed forces, what branch are you in? Army
   What is your rank? (No answer)
6. Regardless of what you are doing show how you like it by checking below
   - ____ I really like it.
   - X My likes just balance my dislikes.
   - ____ I don't like it but I will have to put up with it.
   - ____ I hate it. (If you marked this one will you tell us why?)
7. What would you like to be doing *5* years from now? Selling for a wholesale concern
   10 years from now? Selling for a wholesale concern
8. What is there about *you* that makes you *successful* in what you are doing? (No answer)

A. What is there about *you* that *handicaps* you in what you are doing? lack of self-confidence

B. Looking toward the future, do you think that things are going to work out well for you?

C. Why? To some extent, yes

D. Why not?

Looking back at your high school training tell us

E. How it helped you most? I can't think of any way

F. How it failed to help you? I can't say it failed me either. It was all up to me.

Looking back at the counseling you had in high school tell us

G. How it helped you? It helped me to decide to go on to school. It also showed me what profession suited me best.

H. How it failed to help you? (No answer)

If you could live over again the last two years since you left high school would you do the same thing as you have done?

I. Yes X No

J. If not what would you do? (No answer)

Show what you did each six months since you told us about what you were doing in the fall of 1951.

K. Went to Extension

January to June, 1952

L. Went to Extension and Worked

June to December, 1952

M. Went to Extension and worked

January to June, 1953

N. Am working part time waiting for draft

June 1953 to present

O. If you are married (both men and women) when were you married? (No answer)

P. What clubs, political organizations, social and church groups do you belong to? None yet

List the names and current addresses of the three of your high school clasmates whom you know the best.

Q. (Listed the names of three boys—one of whom was the Tom mentioned in the senior report.)

T. Please use the back of this page to give more information on any

of the questions asked above or to write anything you want about your school experiences, your present plans, or your plans for the future. You might want to comment on the counseling you had, your future plans, the ways in which schools can be improved, or any other matter that interests you.
(No answer)

Five Years After High School Graduation

In October, 1956, Will answered the follow-up questionnaire in the following manner.

Oct. 18, 1956

Name Will
What is your present address? (Home address)
Give an address where letters will usually reach you. (Same as above)
Check the *one* item that best describes your present status.

___	Married	___	Student
X	Full-time employment	___	In armed forces
___	Farming	___	Other (Tell what)

Regardless of what you are doing show how you like it by checking below

___ I really like it.
X My likes just balance my dislikes.
___ I don't like it but I will have to put up with it.
___ I hate it.

Will you tell me why you checked the one you did? I am not settled yet
What is there about *you* that makes you *successful* in what you are doing? (No answer)
What is there about *you* that *handicaps* you in what you are doing? I lack the power of concentration on my day to day work.
What would you like to be doing *5* years from now? Undecided
10 years from now? (Not answered)
If you are married (both men and women) when were you married? (No answer)
Judging from your own experience, what could schools do to prepare

young people for marriage? stress fun and entertainment less and serious thinking more.

Show what you have been doing each six months since you last wrote in 1953.

First half of 1954 army

Second half of 1954 army

First half of 1955 army

Second half of 1955 army

First half of 1956 army and civilian life

If you could live over again the last five years since you left high school, would you do the same things as you have done? No ____ Yes X

If *yes,* why? I have had no serious difficulties

Looking toward the future, do you think things are going to work out well for you? Yes

If yes ____ Why? I never make predictions about the future in regard to myself.

If you are *employed* full time *now* what do you actually do on the job? Write export orders.

What is name and address (include city) of your employer? Gave name of a tractor export firm.

Why did you choose the job you now have? convience

If you wish to mention your wages, fill in below.

Weekly (when you began to work) $74.00 Weekly now $77.00

What (if anything) would make you change jobs? Boredom and sitting in one spot day after day.

Do you plan to change jobs? Yes X No ____

If so, why? I want a job where I can move about.

If you have worked more than one year, what is the difference between the work you did when you started and the work you do now? (No answer)

If you were ever (or are now) in the *armed forces,* what was your highest rank? corporal

When did you serve? 1954–1956

How have you used any of your armed forces training since you left?
no

How do you feel about your armed forces experience? very worth while

If you had any TRAINING after high school (special school, apprenticeship, college, short course, or any other kind) Where did you get your training? Extension (University) Milwaukee
Place City

When? 1952–1953

What degree or certificate did you get? none

What was your major field of study? Marketing and advertising

For what were you prepared when you finished your training?
Selling

How do you feel now about your training experiences? It's too bad I wasn't intelligent enough to be able to learn more in a higher college.

Looking back at your high school training, tell us how it helped you most. I can't think of any way it did.
How it failed to help you (No answer)

Looking back at the counseling you had in *high school* tell us how it helped you. To make up my mind about going to extension. It showed me that truth about myself, that I was not as smart as I thought I was.
How it failed to help you (no answer)

Give the names of any political organizations, clubs, social, recreational, or church groups which you have attended regularly during the last 3 years. (No answer)

Have you voted in any political elections? no
Why or why not? army

What self-improvement activities such as courses, on-the-job training, reading, home study, etc., have you been doing? none

Do you have confidence in the actions you take when you have to make choices? Yes

If you needed help in the last five years in making decisions, to whom did you go? (No answer)

Any interesting plans for the future? Marriage

List the names and current addresses of the three of your high school classmates whom you know the best. (Three names of boys were listed.)

Interview Five Years After Graduating from High School

On February 28, 1957, four months after he had completed the questionnaire responses described immediately above, the following interview conducted by a counselor-in-training was tape recorded at Will's home.

Interview with Will in March, 1957, Five and a Half Years After High School Graduation

Preliminary comments:

Will lived with his parents in a comfortable middle-class home tastefully decorated in early American style. Will (according to the interviewer who had not seen him before) was a smooth, good-looking fellow who made an excellent impression. His voice, with its excellent quality and pitch, made the interviewer comment about the possibility of its use in radio. He wore glasses, talked freely and confidently, and the jerkiness that may be observed in the following record was *not* noted at the time of the interview. He was relaxed and seemed to enjoy the session. He seemed to be positive about his relationship with the counselor, who had worked with him when he was in high school, and he commented favorably on the interviews the counselor had held with his parents. The interview is edited only enough to prevent identification.

The interview:

I—This is Bob Jackson, interviewing on February 28, 1957, and your name is?

S—Will.

I—And your address?

S—Route 7, Box 115, Wellsville.

I—Do you mind if I call you Will?

S—No, sir.

I—And I'm Bob.

S—Bob, O.K.

I—If we wanted to reach you in a couple years, Will, at what address will mail usually reach you?

S—Well, I can say that it will be the state of Wisconsin, either in Milwaukee County or Wellsville. (*) . . . Within a year's time. . . . (*)

I—What address will we put on the . . .

S—Well, the address I wouldn't know because I intend to get married this fall and naturally I'll be living someplace else rather than here.

I—If we forward it to your folks will they pass it on?

S—Yes, they will.

I—Married in the fall?

S—Uh-huh, September 14.

I—September 14, boy (laughs), and you're employed now?

S—Yes.

I—What do you actually do on the job?

S—Well, I'm in the export department for a machine manufacturing company and actually I'm an export order clerk. I write up orders for these export companies that send in orders to the company.

I—By export does that mean out of the country?

S—Out of the country, yes. The company has dealerships all over the world, and these dealers send in orders from their customers . . . for repair parts and ah, diesel tractors mainly, and ah, all kinds of road machinery, and ah, just about anything the company does (*) in the tractor line.

I—In the tractor line. (*) And then your employer is the company that is near Wellsville?

S—Right.

I—I worked there three summers so I know the place (*) . . . tractor shop and turbine. Could you show how you like what you are doing by selecting one of these four categories: I really like it; my likes just balance my dislikes; I don't like it but I'll have to put up with it; and I hate it.

S—Well, my likes just balance, I mean my likes balance my dislikes. I can say that. (*)

I—Why did you name the one that you did?

S—Well, ah, it's a good outfit to work for, I ah, as far as benefits are

[8] The asterisks refer to some sort of verbal assent such as an uh-huh by the listener in each case.

concerned, and ah, working conditions, but ah, the department I happen to be in, which is the repair department, there doesn't seem to be much of any spot for advancement (*) from ah, I can tell that by ah, just by ah, surmising things myself and by looking at things myself and by, ah, what other people in the department have said . . . of course gossip, there's a lot of that . . . (*) . . . like in any office, (*) and from what people have said in other departments on the same floor. (*) It's boring work actually; you're doing the same thing every day . . . (*) . . with slight variations, but you're doing the same thing every day. (*) And I like a job, I think I want a job where I can move around . . . all day long. So that's why I'm definitely interested in selling, (*) and traveling, traveling and selling. (*)

I—What is there about you that makes you successful in what you are doing?

S—(laughs) Well, that, ah, that is a little hard to answer. Actually, I, ah, I can't say I'm successful, I'm just, ah, because I don't, ah, I don't particularly like it, so ah, I don't consider myself being successful at it. Being successful to me, ah, is doing something you like and doing it well. And I can't say I do it particularly well because my mind is on other things most of the time. It's a kind of thing you can do, ah, fairly well and have your mind some-place else.

I—What is there about you that handicaps you in what you are doing?

S—Well, ah, I suppose I get bored too easy. Maybe not too easy, but I get bored (laughs), and ah, I don't like the idea of sitting in one spot. (*)

I—What would you like to be doing five years from now?

S—Well (laughs to himself), that's . . . actually nothing in particular, just that, ah, I'd like to be doing something that I like, (*) and doing something that I'm going to make enough money on to satisfy myself. It probably would be selling. I don't know. Unless I, ah, . . . somebody comes up with something else or I find something else, or somebody offers me something that I have never even thought about . . . and all of a sudden I might decide that that's it. (*)

I—You've had this interest in selling for quite a while, haven't you?

S—Yes, that, ah, . . . that interests me . . . quite a bit, although, ah, I sold shoes part time while I was going to the University

Extension,[9] and ah, I've sold them part time, ah, since I've been home from the army. Within the last year I've sold them for four months . . . (*) . . . from the end of August till the end of December (*) to pick up, ah, some extra money.

I—For whom did you sell?

S—A large retail store in Milwaukee, (*) and I made, ah, fairly good money. I did all right there. Of course that type of selling is . . . that's retail selling . . . to the . . . direct to the customer, and ah, you don't go out and get them of course. They come in to you and there's the difference. There's an awful lot of difference because you don't do any canvassing. They're there for shoes and you show them what you have and that's it.

I—You think you would be interested in the canvassing type?

S—Well, I'm going to try it to find out whether I am or not. I intend to try it.

I—As one fellow I've talked to said, creative sales . . . creating a market.

S—Yeah, well, ah, I was, I'm interested in life insurance right now, (*) and ah, I hear there is, there is a market for life insurance. You just have to make the people realize they need insurance but ah, you have to realize, I mean make them realize that they can afford it and, ah, need as much as they should have. (*)

I—Within the matter of five minutes since I met you, my first reaction is very favorable. You would be the kind of person that if you came into my home, I would be inclined to listen to you . . . that first reaction, which would be awfully essential, I would say, to a fellow selling insurance. (*) How about ten years from now, anything. . . .

S—(laughs) Now that, ah . . . Then I would like to be firmly, fairly well settled in something. I mean, I figure by that time I, if I'm not then I'm, I've been lost. (*) I think I should be firmly settled in something ten years from now. (*) Like I said before, I, I can't say just what but . . . but two years in the army did put me behind. There's no doubt about that, because I was contemplating that before I graduated from high school because Korea had broken out, ah, while I was in high school; nobody knew how long it was going to last then, and then the draft was

[9] Extension, as it is used here and throughout the interview, refers to that branch of the University of Wisconsin that was formerly operated by the University Extension Division.

in effect then anyhow, so I knew I was going to have to go. (*) So, but, ah, I went to the University Extension anyhow because that was a, that was a two-year course. It kept me out of the army for a year anyhow, I think, from what I can see. I mean it delayed it a year.

I—Judging from your own experience, what could schools do to prepare young people for marriage?

S—Well, I don't think it would hurt at all to have a, an extracurricular or if not, ah, ah, what's the word for it . . . they should . . . I'm trying to think of the word . . . not extra, extracurricular, and ah, maybe even, maybe have it even in the schedule . . . (*) . . . as a, as a required course. That's what I was trying to get . . . and have it as a required course. Just have a mixed class and, ah, just ah, discuss, ah, marriage and how to prepare for it and what to expect, and ah . . . the facts of life I think are important (*) naturally. I don't think that would hurt at all. Because I'm, I know there's an awful lot of young people that don't get the, the education, and the training, and the facts at home that they should have because of parents being embarrassed or, ah, they don't have the time. And there are an awful lot of people who get married thinking they're in love and aren't. I think it would help a lot.

I—We'd like to keep track of your status over the last two and a half years, so beginning with January of 1954 what, and where were you doing it, and then we'll trace it up to the present.

S—Well, in January of 1954 I was working part time. I had just gotten out of, ah, University Extension in the summer, June, and I was working part time in Milwaukee . . . selling shoes, (*) and, ah, in March, March 8, 1954, I was drafted in the army, (*) and ah, I just, I got out of the army February 23, 1956. (*)

I—And then you began with . . .

S—The machine manufacturing company.

I—The machine manufacturing company.

S—Three weeks later I started.

I—If you could live over again the last five years since you left high school, would you do the same things as you have done?

S—Well, relatively speaking, I can say that I probably would. Two years I would have nothing to do with anyhow . . . (*) . . . being I was drafted. I had nothing to say about that.

I—Why? I mean, why would you do these same things?

S—And ah, the two years at University Extension Center: I wasn't sorry for that. Although I wish I had been a little more qualified to have taken a four-year course. I would have done that instead if I had felt that I was intelligent enough to, ah, take a four-year course without, ah, working, I mean, ah, studying continually. I, ah, the way it was I had to, ah, pay my own tuition, and ah, if I had gone for the four years I would have had to have done the same thing, and ah, I don't think I could have had enough time to study it as much as I would have had to. If my parents had been able to afford the four years, why I'm pretty sure I could have gotten in a four-year course, but it would have taken a lot of work. I know that, (*) and that would have been the only way I could have done it probably.

I—Well, those first two years have a reputation of being the toughest. If you get through those why . . .

S—Yeah, that's what I understand.

I—Looking toward the future, do you think things are going to work out well for you?

S—Well, I'm a, I'm a natural born skeptic or whatever you want to say so I don't, I don't count my chickens before they hatch. I just plan ahead as much as possible and think about the future a lot but I don't come to any conclusions about something like that. I don't want to be sorry later for shooting off my big mouth about what I'm going to do and (laughs) . . . and what I think I'm going to do. I just say what I'm planning on doing.

I—Why did you choose the job you now have?

S—Well, ah, after I got out of the army, of course, you feel a little lost for two or three weeks because you're . . . things have naturally changed. I wasn't home . . . I was home once while I was in the army . . . on leave, so I hadn't been home in a, about twenty to twenty-one months, and ah, I thought I could stay home maybe, well, maybe a month and then look for something, but I, I realized that after the second week I was getting pretty restless and I just wanted to get back into the swing of things . . . as soon as possible. So, my father worked at a machine company, and my sister worked there at the time, and I had worked there one summer when I was in high school. (*) So, ah, that was the second place I looked for a job. I went down to the Electric Company in Milwaukee and, ah, just to see what they had to offer, and they weren't hiring anybody so I went to the machine manufacturing company two days later. They offered me this so I took it. I figured, well, I'll take this and I can always look around for something else (*) while I'm doing it, but I wanted to make some money because, ah, I was pretty broke, naturally, and ah, it's one thing you have to have.

I—Was it anything like you had in mind when you took your training? Was it the thing you thought you were working for at the time?

S—Well, ah, I thought that at this machine manufacturing company, and I even mentioned when they hired me, that, ah, I had heard about the tractor sales department, of course, and I told the fellow that interviewed me that that was what I would like to get into in the future . . . (*) . . . tractor sales . . . but he didn't encourage me any at all in, ah, during the interview, and I thought there was something funny about that. He didn't encourage me so, I figured, well, I'll see what happens anyhow, (*) and then now I realize, and I realized later it's virtually impossible to get a transfer out of that department. (*) No matter, the better you are, it seems, the less chance you have of getting out. And it seems like the ones, the undesirables, are the ones that get transferred. And I, that's what I've heard. Since I've been there nobody has been transferred at all, and it's, ah, it's, ah, export repairs and there's the correspondence, export sales correspondence, export pricing, and ah, export credit (*) on that floor, which actually makes up . . . all the other floors are actually connected with it. The export sales manager is on the sixth about . . . well, it's just the next desk away from me in his office. I can see him at his desk. (*) Well, I haven't tried to get a transfer yet and ah, I ah, think I probably will try to get one, but first I'm going to have something else lined up, in case my trying to get a transfer is going to cause some, cause, ah, some trouble, dissension or whatever you want to call it. (*) Because this fellow I work for, he seems to have the idea that, ah, if he transfers anybody out of his department, and I guess that can be a logical way of thinking about it, it's a detriment to him or it's a bad reflection on him because a lot of people do quit because they get tired of doing what they do actually. I know that's the reason, and ah, I've heard a couple of them who have tried to get a transfer, one fellow who had been there for awhile, he'd been there for about sixteen or seventeen years and he jumped the chain of command, that is he didn't go to his immediate boss first, he went higher up first to get a transfer. The word is now that he has had it as far as our company is concerned. They'll keep him on, sure, but he just made a bad move there. (*) So he's a . . .

I—A lot of politics then?

S—Yes, it's, it's a, it seems to be that, ah, in order to get a transfer you have to be assured of a job someplace else in the company. That is, you have to be desired and wanted before you apply for a transfer. Otherwise you're wasting your time (both talk). Pardon me, . . . in this particular department, I'm not saying that all our company is like that, but, ah, where I am, and ah, it's across the street from the main plant.

I—If you wish to mention your wages, what are they weekly now?

S—Well, I, ah, make about $80 a week now.

I—And when you began to work?

S—It was about $75.

I—What if anything would make you change jobs?

S—Well, if somebody offered me a job selling life insurance, I would take it.

I—Do you plan to change jobs?

S—Yes.

I—Why?

S—Well, for all of the reasons I mentioned before, and ah, I want to take a crack at selling, to determine if that's for me, and I figure I'm not going to find out if I don't try it, so . . . I'm going to try it.

I—It may seem ridiculous to ask something that you have already answered but it has to be done that way. Is there any difference in the work you did when you started and the work you do now?

S—No, there's no . . . no, wait a minute, there is a . . . in the beginning I checked and priced the orders that came in for repair parts and now I do less of that and more writing the orders, (*) and a lot of them have to be duplicated.

I—And you were in the army?

S—Right.

I—What was your highest rank?

S—Well, corporal, or when I left it was specialist three; they've changed it, but actually it's the same thing.

I—And could you repeat the dates that you served?

S—From, ah, March 8, 1954, to February 23, 1956.

I—How have you used any of your armed forces training since you left?

S—Well, I haven't used any of it because I was an International Morse Code radio operator (*) and, ah, I haven't used that at all.

I—Did they send you to school for that?

S—Yes, I was in Florida for six months at the Southeastern Signal School they have down there.

I—What kind of work would that be?

S—Well, that's radio communication and with International Morse Code, (*) and I used that . . . of course. I was a radio operator and they sent me to Germany, the second armored division; I was a radio operator.

I—On a company level?

S—No, it was at battalion level.

I—Battalion. You were in Germany; how long were you there?

S—Fourteen months.

I—What are your reactions to Germany?

S—I like it. If you're in the army and you can go to Europe you've got it made. (*) It's good. You travel a lot, see a lot, and the duty is exceptionally better than you would have in the states. (*) I still wouldn't recommend anybody join the army and to enlist for three years. I wanted to go to Europe and I was lucky. I got sent.

I—How do you find the people accept the Americans?

S—Well, they take them more or less as a necessary evil. I guess you would say that. The women, of course, they get along with you (laughs) better than the older people. I'm quite sure they realize that we are more of a benefit to them than a hindrance. I think the majority of people think that way. Of course, there are a lot of them that don't. They ah, they'd like to see us go, of course, any country would, because we're foreigners, and them being a proud people anyhow they . . . but ah . . . they'll miss us when we leave, I'm quite sure of that. (*)

I—How do you feel about your armed forces experience?

S—Well, I'm not sorry I spent two years in it, I mean, if I could have gotten out of it I undoubtedly would, but ah, I can't say I'm sorry I . . . traveled around quite a bit . . . saw a lot of things and learned quite a few things and . . . I met, met an awful lot of people, types of people that I never would have met in civilian life because you just don't come across that variation in civilian life like you do in the army. (*)

I—And you had college training after high school. You had your training where?

S—University Extension in Milwaukee.

I—And what were the dates of that again?

S—Let's see . . . I graduated in 1951 . . . well, the fall of '51 I started . . . until ah, well, it would be June of '53. (*)

I—And what degree or certificate did you receive?

S—Well, I didn't receive any degree or certificate, because I didn't take a few of the courses that were necessary . . . for a certificate.

I—And your major field of study was what?

S—Well, it was in marketing and advertising.

I—And for what were you prepared when you finished your training?

S—More or less as a salesman. (*)

I—What type of courses did you take, Will?

S—Well, I took economics; I took business English; I took, ah, personnel management; I took advertising, and ah, I had some accounting, statistics, and ah, business law, which was interesting. If I had studied more I'd have gotten a lot more out of it.

I—Not an easy course by any means, then, was it?

S—Well, ah, it wasn't a hard course, except that the only thing that was hard for me was accounting, (*) accounting and statistics, but I'm miserable at math anyhow so, ah, anybody who was, anybody who was a little better than average at math shouldn't have too much trouble with accounting if they, if they study. It takes a lot of studying, accounting, a lot of work.

I—How do you feel about your training experiences?

S—Well, ah, some of the teachers weren't exactly what I would have liked to have. They were a little too easy on us. But, ah, college is, ah, college is up to the individual. They don't force you to study because you're there because you want to be and if you don't want to learn that's up to you. So I can't blame any of them if I didn't learn anything, but some of them didn't seem to be as sharp as I was expecting, (*) and if I would have . . . I didn't study as hard as I should have . . . I got fairly good grades but if I had studied . . . maybe if I had studied accounting harder and statistics, maybe I could have gotten that. (*) But, ah, it didn't interest me, and that's one of my faults. If things don't interest me then I, I don't work at them hard.

I—Looking back at your high school training could you tell us how it helped you most?

S—Well, ah, actually I can't recall anything about it that helped me most. There wasn't anything in particular that helped me most. (*) It was a high school course. The only fellow that really did me any good was Dr. Rothney. He, he interviewed me and he told me what he thought I was . . . had the aptitudes in after taking . . . of course we took a lot of examinations and . . . he, ah, told me what he thought I would be good in and what I could do, and ah, he was actually the, the fellow that did me the most good in high school. (*)

I—How accurate was he, or how well do you think he diagnosed you?

S—He diagnosed me pretty well.

I—Can you tell us how high school failed to help you?

S—Well, I don't think, I don't think I can blame anything on high school either. (*) It didn't do anything detrimental to me.

I—This next question is repetitive, but maybe you would like to add something to it. Looking back at the counseling you had in high school could you tell us how it helped you most?

S—Well, like I said, it helped me, period. That's all there's to it, because it made me think a lot about my future and, ah, it gave me an idea of what my aptitudes were, (*) and ah, it just helped.

I—Could you tell us how it failed to help you?

S—Well, I can't say it failed to help at all. It may . . . one thing it did make me realize was that I wasn't as . . . I wasn't as, ah, intelligent as I thought I was. Because I was disappointed when I took the exams. I, ah, was disappointed in the grades I got. It made me realize I wasn't as well educated as I thought I was.

I—Well, now, exams aren't always right. They can be way off the mark.

S—Well, that might of, that might of hurt me . . . those exams might have hurt me more than they helped me because it, ah, it slowed me down quite a bit, you know. I (*) . . . and then of course when I went to the University Extension I had to take some examinations there too. I was disappointed in the results of those. More I should say; I think I can say more, because I . . . of all the college preparatory students that took the exam I fell in the lower third. They had it divided into three thirds and I fell in the lower third, and I expected to be in the middle. (*) And that's when they told me that, ah, they didn't, they discouraged me more than anything from taking a four-year course, because they said that I'd have to work awful hard and chances were that I wouldn't make it. (*)

I—Do you agree with the diagnosis, or prognosis, or prediction?

S—Yes, I think so. (*) Maybe if they hadn't told me that I would have gone in and maybe I would have made it and maybe I wouldn't have. Maybe I'd have been hurt later on that someone didn't tell me. Then again maybe I would have . . . maybe being dumb to that would have helped me . . . maybe I would have. . . .

I—You raise an awfully important question.

S—Because it killed, it killed . . . it killed a little ambition actually.

I—Yes.

S—That's what it did.

I—I'm not supposed to do much talking here, but I wonder if we have the right to do that to anybody, because our tests aren't perfectly accurate. Is it worth taking that chance with people?

S—I don't remember what type of test I took in high school, but I, I do remember the one we took, I mean I took, at the University Extension: (*) The College Preparatory Exam (*) that they give to everybody before they sign them up as a student. (*) Maybe I just happened to hit a morning when the interviewer was in a bad mood, because I remember that too, that he wasn't, he wasn't very friendly.

I—He wasn't. . . .

S—He wasn't discourteous but he wasn't friendly. You know he didn't make me feel like I should have been there at all (laughs).

I—That's right.

S—But, ah, before I, before I saw him I had my mind made up on the two-year course anyhow, and I told him that after he gave me (*) his ideas . . . on what I was capable of (*) but even I was enlightened quite a bit. (*)

I—Could you give the names of any political organizations, clubs, social, recreational, or church groups which you have attended regularly during the last three years?

S—Well, I, . . . the last three years, no, I can't. When I was in the army I didn't belong to any club because I . . . whenever I had a leave or anything I traveled . . . I saved my money so I could travel. That's what I wanted to do.

I—And before or after the army?

S—And after the army, well, during this year I've been . . . it's been a pretty busy year (*) and I haven't, I haven't belonged to any club.

I—Any activities?

S—Well, ah, the only activity I have is my fiancée (both laugh).

I—That's a good one.

S—Yeah, I think so.

I—Have you voted in any political elections?

S—Yes, this last one. I voted.

I—Why?

S—Why? (*)

I—Not particularly the last election, but why have you voted?

S—Well, I wanted to see the man that got in get in, (*) and ah, voting is a privilege and I figure as an American it's my duty (*) to vote.

I—Did your army experience strengthen that in any way or was that pretty well resolved in your mind before it?

S—It was resolved in my mind before.

I—What self-improvement activities such as courses, home study, on-the-job training, reading, have you been doing?

S—Well, I do some reading, but that's, that's about it. (*)

I—Any particular area or type of reading?

S—Well, I like *Time* magazine. I read that whenever I get a chance because there are always quite a few interesting things on international events which I like to read about. (*) And *Holiday* magazine is one of my favorites because, ah, it deals with traveling and Europe and a lot of those places I've been and I like to read about them and places that I haven't been. (*) Then, of course, *Life* magazine. (*) Those three. *Newsweek* also. *Time* and *Newsweek* are practically the same magazine anyhow.

I—Do you have confidence in the actions you take when you have to make choices?

S—Yes, I think . . . I think I do.

I—If you needed help in the last five years in making decisions, to whom did you go?

S—Well, ah, I didn't ask anybody for any help. I just made them myself, because nobody at home ever forced me to do anything I really didn't want to, like going to school or, or anything like that. They left it up to me.

I—Then you've been pretty independent?

S—Yes, independent thinking anyhow. (*)

I—How do you evaluate that, now that you . . .

S—Well, sometimes I wish I hadn't been so independent. My father gives me all sorts of advice and what I could do, (*) but, ah, he, I don't seem to derive any confidence out of it. He means well, you know, he . . . and then, ah, if I do something usually he's got something critical to say about it, so, ah, actually . . . it doesn't help too much.

I—How would you . . .

S—He could of . . . I just feel as though, ah, he could, ah, he should know me better or could know me better than . . . and know . . . know more like a lot of fathers know just what their sons are cut out for, and they can guide them into it, you know. (*) In fact, a lot of fathers even tell their sons what they should do, you know, or almost make them do it. I know a couple of my friends whose fathers just make sure they are going to do that thing if nothing else and then after that they can do what they want but they're going to do this (*) or learn this or take that trade. And maybe, maybe that's a good thing, but still a little more push like that probably would have helped me.

I—Is that how you would structure, looking ahead to your own family, is that . . .

S—Yes, I think I'll be able, my father maybe couldn't recognize it in me but I think I'll be able to . . . in my children I'll be able to, ah, detect natural abilities and, ah, natural interests, and I'm going to encourage them in what they are able to comprehend or that which interests them more than anything else, I'll try to cultivate them in that direction and, ah, (*) maybe that'll help them. (*)

I—Any interesting plans for the future? You mentioned your marriage as one.

S—Yes, and ah, a change of jobs in the future. (*) I think if I decide to undertake life insurance, of course, I have to have a license. I probably will go back to the University Extension and take a life insurance selling course. I know they have that. It'd probably be at night. (*) While I'm still working at my present job I'll take that (*) . . . take the exam and then, ah, undertake it. I have a couple of . . . I have one lead anyhow that . . . in fact a fellow offered to get me started in it so. (*)

I—Do you have to be pretty careful in selecting a company in life insurance or isn't that a factor?

S—I imagine it is. I don't know an awful lot about it. But I imagine it is. This fellow that I'm . . . that offered to get me into it, he has an agency of his own. (*) So he sells for seven or eight companies: life insurance, automobile insurance, everything. And he's been selling it for the past eight years part time, and he's been doing quite well, and he's not the type of fellow that is a, is a braggart. I can see by his home and the way he talks that he's an honest fellow. He's not giving me any, any big line, and he intends to go into it full time because of his health. He's not able to work at his regular job. So the way . . . he's been doing awfully good part time so I imagine he'll do really good full time, and ah, he's said he's thinking about. . . . I told him that if he ever, ah, decided to hire any salesmen that he could call me and I'd come over and talk to him. (*)

I—Could you list the names of the three of your high school classmates whom you know the best.

S—Well, there's ah, Jim, who lives in a small town near here. He's the one I've had the most contact with since I've been out of the army. Actually, ah, the first year after I got out of high school . . . the first year at University Extension . . . I chummed around with fellows I had gone to school with and, but after that I, I more or less stopped that and spent my free time in Milwaukee with fellows I met at Extension and I hadn't had anything to do with anybody in Wellsville until after I got out of the army . . . and then I met . . . I, of course, looked up those fellows I had known during high school and that year immediately after high school, (*) and Eddie is one of them. I, ah, chummed around with him after I got out of high school. (*) He got married in April and I went to his wedding, and ah, . . . the other one is . . . that I looked up is Bill.

I—If you were to give one bit of advice on the basis of your high school experiences, what would it be?

S—Well, if the high school student is interested in going to college and definitely has a mind to go on to college, he by all means should go, (*) because today . . . in this . . . in the world today and in the future . . . ah, college is the thing. You just aren't going to get anywhere without a college education. If you want to get someplace, you have to have it. It's becoming more and more important every year, because more and more people are going, and therefore companies . . . and there is such a demand for college educated people . . . and if, ah, there are more of them then naturally the companies are going to prefer those people, and those who haven't gone or can't go are just going to have to be content with the mediocre. (*)

I—One more formal question here, a sort of philosophical question: what things in life give you the greatest satisfactions or happiness?

S—Actually I can truthfully say I've never given that too much thought. I probably will now that somebody asked me, (*) but, ah, self sat[isfaction] . . . well, I could say . . . an untroubled mind are the things that make me the most happy. (*) Free of worry . . . that makes me the happiest, but ah, if, ah, . . . I'm becoming more and more aware of the freedom we have in this country, (*) and the importance of it, and, ah, the importance to keep it. Even though I haven't known anything else I can still look over the fence that so many people don't have it (*) . . . so many things that we take for granted that other people don't have. Now you talk to a lot of people, a lot of these foreigners, D.P.'s, or other than D.P.'s, that have come over to this country; you talk to them and you see in their face and in their talk how much they appreciate the little things we take for granted. It makes you feel good that they're . . . that they appreciate those and it makes you realize that there are . . . it makes you realize what you have.

I—Any other comments that you'd like to make, Will, about high school, counseling, or any of your experiences?

S—Well, . . . no, that's about it; I can't think of anything else.

I—How do you feel about high school, looking back on it?

S—Well, I, ah, I was more intent on education the first two years, ninth and tenth grade, than I was in my junior and senior years because, ah, I started to open up more and I was working part time in high school then because I had a car, of course. . . . I had to work part time to keep it running, (*) but I can say that my last year in high school was my best, because up until that time I was too self-conscious (*) and after that . . . I mean my last year . . . and after that, that's when I started to open up and enjoy myself more.

SUMMARY

Since follow-up is perhaps the most neglected part of guidance work, it seemed desirable to report the procedures used in this study in detail. The methods used in getting post-high school information about the status and progress of all the subjects have been described completely enough so that others who plan follow-up studies may see what is involved. Construction of questionnaires and techniques for getting 100 percent of the subjects have been outlined. Methods for checking questionnaire returns against employer reports and official records of subjects in post-high school training have been described. The use of the follow-up interview as a supplement to the questionnaire method has been illustrated with complete recorded interviews. A summary of all the data collected upon each individual during the whole eight-year period of the study can be observed by reading the case of Will, which appears immediately above.

Upon completion of this chapter the reader will have become familiar with the subjects, their setting, their problems, and the methods that were used in putting the information obtained about them to use in counseling. The results will be presented in the following chapters.

CHAPTER V

Interim Evaluations

The title of this chapter contains the word "interim" to indicate that it will be concerned with evaluations made before the completion of the study. The "final" evaluation of the experiment conducted five years after the subjects had been graduated from high school will be presented in Chapter VI.

The interim evaluations are reported in four sections. The *first* and *second* are composed of evaluations of high school academic achievements and responses to a Senior Report which were made at the close of the students' high school careers. The *second* contains brief reports of a six-months-after-high-school postal-card survey of the subjects' job or training activities and their satisfaction with them. The *third* is a report of a questionnaire survey of their occupational or training experiences and their social adjustments two and a half years after the subjects had been graduated from high school. A final report on the five-year-after-high-school study, in which data on all the topics noted above were obtained, is reserved for Chapter VI. In each of the interim evaluations 100 percent of the subjects (excluding five who had died) constitutes the population.

METHODS OF REPORTING RESULTS

In reporting analyses of data obtained by the techniques described in previous chapters, an attempt has been made to present them so that readers at various levels of statistical sophistication may get the message they tell.

Most of the follow-up results in the second half of this chapter and throughout Chapter VI are presented by percentage of the number of subjects who responded to the items on the questionnaires. The decision to use percentages (rounded off to one decimal place to save space) was based on the belief that most of the readers would be teachers, counselors, principals, parents, and others who are concerned about youth but who cannot be expected to keep up with the many new developments in statistical method. It seemed desirable to compute the percentages on the basis of the numbers who actually responded to the items because it was not possible in all cases to determine the reasons for failure to respond. The inclusion of frequencies in addition to percentages for the usual six groups (experimental women, men, and total experimentals and control women, men, and total controls) in all the categories would have produced unwieldy tables, so they have been omitted. Those who wish to obtain the frequencies for each group and category may do so by computing them from the percentages given across from each classification and under each heading in the tables.

In order to get significance of differences, the chi-square test was used when it was appropriate.[1] In general the procedure was to set up fourfold tables in which the *numbers* of responses in each group and category were compared with numbers of responses made by the subjects in all other groups and categories in the table. The procedure is illustrated in the following sample.

In the 1956 follow-up study all 685 subjects were asked to respond to the following item, *Looking back at the counseling you had in high school, tell how it helped.* Usable responses were obtained from 68.7 percent or 471 subjects. Of these, 249 were experimentals and 222 were controls. Twenty-four and nine-tenths percent, or 62 experimental subjects, said that counseling had helped them in their personal development, while only 13.1 percent or 29 control subjects answered in the same way. Thus

[1] See Quinn McNemar, *Psychological Statistics,* 2d ed., New York, John Wiley & Sons, Inc., 1955, pp. 212–240.

187 experimentals and 193 controls did not indicate that counseling had helped in their personal development. From these *numbers* (not percentages) the following fourfold table was set up.

	Counseling Helped in Personal Development	All Other Responses to Question on How Counseling Had Helped	Total
Experimentals	62	187	249
Controls	29	193	222
Total	91	380	471

The chi-square computed from the table was 10.549. Since it must be 10.827 to be significant at the .001 level and since the 10.549 comes very close to that figure, the difference is reported as significant at the 1 percent level. The conclusion drawn from the result was that the difference was statistically significant. There was, therefore, enough evidence to permit the rejection of the hypothesis that there was no difference between the experimentals and controls in reporting that counseling had helped in their personal development.

In some cases it was impossible to indicate whether differences were statistically significant by the chi-square test even though huge differences appeared. Thus in answer to one item only 1 percent of 300, or three experimental subjects who answered the item, fell in one category while 27 percent of approximately the same number of controls fell in that category. The chi-square test should not be employed when the number of cases is as small as three in any group. It could not be employed in this situation to determine the significance of the difference obtained although a matter of 26 percent disparity when such large populations had been studied certainly seemed to be important.

Occasionally the chi-square test was used in 2 by 5 tables. This was the regular contingency rather than the goodness-of-fit test. If the latter test had been used, many more significant differences between the counseled and uncounseled subjects could have been reported. Had it been possible, for example, to use the responses of the control group members as theoretical distributions, the use of the goodness-of-fit test would have been justified. The first person to do a study such as the one reported in this volume cannot consider his obtained control group distributions as theoretical arrays [2] because he cannot estimate his sampling error. In order to obtain enough distributions to get reasonable estimates of the errors, longitudinal studies such as the one described here would have to be repeated many times. And as time went on, changes in such factors as economic conditions, military requirements, marriage customs, training requirements, and others might prevent the securing of *meaningful* estimates of sampling errors of the activities of youth and young adults even if they were statistically adequate. Thus, as in many cases, the common statistical procedures that are suitable for quick studies of fruit-fly genetics, manurial treatments of soils, and the drawing of markers from jars are not adequate in original longitudinal studies of the development of human beings. Those who wish to assume that the activities or responses of the members of the control group do constitute an adequate theoretical distribution against which the responses of the experimentals could be arrayed can find considerable justification in the stand they take. They can, from the data presented in the tables, work out goodness-of-fit chi-squares which will produce more significant differences than are reported in the following pages. The results that are presented here may be considered as minimum.

Occasionally it has been necessary to report results in other than percentages and to employ significance tests other than the chi-square. The analysis of variance procedure was required, for example, in the study of responses to the Senior Report. Those who do not understand that procedure will just have to accept the statement that it is widely accepted as statistically respectable. In the particular case in which it was used here the work was done under the supervision of Professor C. W. Harris of the University of Wisconsin, who is recognized as an authority in this field.

At times correlation methods were utilized when there seemed to be no simpler way of indicating the extent of certain relation-

[2] This is done very frequently, however, in educational research.

ships. Means, critical ratios, and, occasionally, more technical procedures were required in the analysis of data. When they are employed attempts are made to provide verbal interpretation that the lay reader may grasp without getting involved in the intricacies of the methods.

The reader should note that when rigorous standards for significance of differences between groups are applied, many of them must be separately rejected as insignificant. When, however, a vast majority of computed differences that are separately insignificant point consistently enough in one direction to indicate definite trends, they cannot collectively be rejected. As the reader goes through the following pages on evaluation, he will observe such a strong trend for the counseled subjects to respond differently from the controls in the direction hypothesized by guidance people generally (and by the sample of them used in setting up the criteria for this study) that it cannot be rejected.

Finally it has not been possible to do all the longitudinal studies that the data might have permitted. At this time new methods for treatment of longitudinal data are being developed and it is anticipated that they will be used in further analyses of the materials collected over the eight-year period of this study.

EVALUATION AT THE TIME OF COMPLETION OF HIGH SCHOOL

At the time of graduation from high school two sources of data for comparisons between control and experimental subjects were available. The first was the academic record of each subject, which contained rank in class, number of failures, and achievement in courses. The second source of data was the students' Senior Reports described in Chapter II. The reader may recall that these reports were obtained approximately one month before graduation and that they provided data on the students' plans, their knowledge about opportunities in areas in which they had chosen to work or train, and their attitudes toward school and the future. In the following sections results obtained from examination of academic records and Senior Reports are reported.

ACADEMIC ACHIEVEMENT

Since achievement in school is a matter of concern to most students and their parents it must become a matter of conern to counselors. The chief symbols of achievement in the American high school are the marks a student has obtained. They may or may not be reliable and valid. They may indicate real achievement or they may reflect compliant behavior, but regardless of their validity, they are the coin of the school realm—the publicly-accepted evidence of achievement or lack of it. They open and close doors of educational institutions, determine eligibility for scholarships, and delimit vocational opportunities, since high school graduation is frequently required as a condition for employment or post-high school training. Since the American public seems to be generally agreed that high marks are better than low marks, it is often indicated that they can be used as criteria of the effectiveness of counseling. It is debatable whether *all* well-guided students should make better grades than those who are unguided, since high marks may be obtained at too great a sacrifice of other valuable experiences. Counselors cannot, however, ignore the fact that they must work with many members of school faculties who do consider marks as evidence of good adjustment and high achievement. It seems, then, that part of the evaluation of their efforts should be in terms of the coin of the realm in which they work. The following description of the difference between the academic achievements of the control and experimental subjects of this investigation is presented for that reason.

It was the practice, in the four schools from which our subjects were drawn, to compute a rank in class for each student near the time of graduation. In general, the procedure was one of counting the numbers of letter grades made on the courses taken during grades nine to twelve inclusive, and ranking each student in terms of the number of grade points he had obtained. Fowler [3] has pointed out the limitations of the rank in class figure as a measure

[3] B. H. Fowler, "Are We in Need of a New Plan for Evaluating Student Qualifications for College Entrance?" *Bulletin of the National Association of Secondary School Principals,* 35:92–98.

of anything significant and the writer is fully aware of the validity of his argument. Despite its limitations, rank in class is still used widely, and it is particularly important when such matters as college entrance are considered.[4] It seemed desirable, therefore, to compare the ranks in class achieved by the control and experimental students.

Since our subjects attended schools of different sizes, it was not possible to make direct comparisons of ranks for the total group. In order to make the comparisons, each rank was converted so that every subject was given a rank of 1 to 100 regardless of the actual size of his graduating class.

Ranks in class of the experimental and control groups are presented in Table 31. Examination of it reveals very similar distri-

TABLE 31. Ranks in Graduating Class of Experimental and Control Subjects

Rank	Experimentals		Controls	
	Number [a]	Percent	Number [a]	Percent
1–10	41	11.8	29	8.5
11–20	31	8.9	41	12.0
21–30	36	10.4	28	8.2
31–40	39	11.2	36	10.5
41–50	27	7.8	42	12.2
51–60	35	10.1	29	8.5
61–70	42	12.1	30	8.7
71–80	34	9.8	34	9.9
81–90	35	10.1	34	9.9
91–100	27	7.8	40	11.6
Total	347	100.0	343	100.0

[a] The graduating classes in all the schools contained students who entered the schools during their *junior* and *senior* years but who were not subjects of this study. Ranks in class were computed in the schools on the basis of the whole graduating class. In the above table of ranks only the subjects of this study are listed.

butions, and there is no marked tendency for the experimental group to achieve higher ranks than the control group subjects. The difference of 3.8 percent between the percentages in the lowest category suggests that counseled students were slightly

[4] A. E. Traxler and A. Townsend, *Improving Transition from School to College,* New York, Harper & Brothers, 1953.

less likely to fail or come close to failures in courses. The greater percentage of experimentals over controls (3.3) in the top category may indicate that some experimental subjects were encouraged to work just a little harder. There is, however, no clear-cut and important difference except in the extreme categories of final rank in class.

This finding does not indicate that counseling did not influence school performance, since the rank in class was computed on the basis of four years of grades while intensive counseling was done only during the last two years.

Tabulation of the number of failing marks revealed that 77 had been given to the 347 subjects of the experimental group while 102 had been given to the 343 members of the control group while they were in the eleventh and twelfth grades. Considering that each subject usually took four basic subjects per year, the failing marks obtained by the control groups were greater by approximately 1 percent. This difference is probably insignificant except to the additional students who received the failing grades.

As another check on the differences between the academic performances of the control and experimental subjects, their grade point averages achieved during the eleventh and twelfth grades were computed. The grade-point system is widely used in schools and colleges despite its many limitations and it was used here simply because it is so commonly accepted.

Values of 5 for A, 4 for B, 3 for C, 2 for D, and 1 for grades lower than D were allotted to all marks except those for physical education, earned each half year while the subjects were in their last two years of high school. The last two years of high school were used because it was during that period that the most intensive counseling was done with the experimental subjects. The procedure of assigning the numbers arbitrarily is a rough technique that does not permit (as the T-score procedure used later in this section does) consideration of differences in grading practices among schools and within subject areas in the same schools. In addition to such limitations, two additional factors reduced the dependability of the technique. One of the large schools, although it gave full credit toward graduation for music courses, entered only credit or failure on the students' records rather than letter grades. One of the small schools did not use grades of failure regardless of what the student did in any course in which he was enrolled.

Regulations concerning the number of courses that a student could elect varied from school to school and, regardless of regulations, exceptions were occasionally made for some students in three of the four schools. In general the subjects had enrolled in four courses each semester. Thus, during the two last years of high school, a student with grades of C in all courses would earn 48 grade points. Study of Table 32 indicates that the average differed by several points from that theoretical average, because some students who had fallen behind in the first two years of high school attempted to make up their deficiencies by carrying extra credits. Others increased their loads for such reasons as the desire to win scholarships or development of interest in subject areas that led them to study beyond the requirements of the school. Certain students chose to carry less credit than the usual junior or senior carried because they had built up surpluses and were now interested in jobs or school activities that did not carry credit, and a few students chose to carry the minimum course load all the way through their high school careers. Some students failed to earn credit in courses they elected, and others were encouraged or discouraged by school personnel, parents, and others to add to, or subtract from, their course loads.

Distributions, means, sigmas, and differences between earned grade points of the control and experimental subjects are presented in Table 32. It will be observed that for cities *W*, *X*, and *Y*, and for the total group, the average grade-point scores for the experimentals were slightly higher than for the control groups. In city *Z* (with the smallest population), the reverse of the common trend was found. The differences between the means are not large enough to permit rejection with a high degree of confidence of the hypothesis that there are no differences between the groups.

Study of gains or losses in grade point averages of the subjects grouped by city, sex, and experimental or control group status

TABLE 32. Differences in Means of Combined Eleventh and Twelfth Grade Point Averages of Subjects of the Control and Experimental Groups

Groups	N	Mean	S.D.	*t*	Approximate Level of Significance
City *W* Controls	148	48.95	12.34	.327	.37
City *W* Experimentals	163	49.37	10.24		
City *X* Controls	118	51.10	11.40	.890	.17
City *X* Experimentals	108	52.57	13.30		
City *Y* Controls	51	64.07	16.64	.535	.30
City *Y* Experimentals	48	66.77	17.44		
City *Z* Controls	26	60.38	14.59	.342	.37
City *Z* Experimentals	28	58.93	15.92		
Total Controls	343	52.98	14.13	.349	.35
Total Experimentals	347	54.17	14.14		

indicated that there was no important tendency for the experimental subjects to make consistently higher gains than the controls. The figures presented in Table 33 were obtained by computing the grade point average for each student for the tenth grade and then for the eleventh and twelfth grades combined. Since the most intensive counseling of the experimental subjects occurred in those last two years, it would seem likely that, if the counseling had influenced their academic performances, it would be revealed in greater gains during the last two years of high school. The figures in the table indicate that there is no clear-cut superiority of the counseled subjects in every case. The differences are small but in most of them the experimental subjects show the greater gains.

T-SCORE PROCEDURES

Differences in marking procedures in the four schools and inequalities in distribution of marks within subject areas make any direct comparisons of students grades of doubtful value. In order to determine the extent of differences, distributions of grades by subject areas in each school and in all four schools

TABLE 33. Average Gains or Losses in Grade-Point Averages from the Tenth Grade to Eleventh and Twelfth Grades

Subjects	City	N	Average Gain or Loss in Grade-Point Average
Experimental girls	*W*	93	.03
Control girls	*W*	87	–.13
Experimental boys	*W*	70	–.12
Control boys	*W*	61	–.10
Experimental girls	*X*	63	.21
Control girls	*X*	60	–.07
Experimental boys	*X*	45	.10
Control boys	*X*	58	.05
Experimental girls	*Y*	18	.04
Control girls	*Y*	25	.18
Experimental boys	*Y*	30	.10
Control boys	*Y*	26	.21
Experimental girls	*Z*	9	.13
Control girls	*Z*	11	.18
Experimental boys	*Z*	19	.05
Control boys	*Z*	15	.04

taken together were made. It was found that, while the distributions of grades by subjects for *all* schools were symmetrical and normal, the subject area distributions of marks in *separate* schools were not always normal.

Chi-square tests of goodness-of-fit of distributions of marks in English and commercial subjects in all four schools for seven semesters were made.[5] Using the theoretical percentage mark distribution of 4–24–44–24–4 as the criterion, the following x^2 values were obtained. From this evidence it appeared that differ-

Subject	x^2	Degrees of Freedom	Level of Significance
English	1.112	2	50%
Commercial	3.781	2	20%

[5] Details of the procedures used in this section are given by Robert A. Heimann in his unpublished Ph.D. thesis entitled *Intra-Individual Consistency of Performance in Relation to the Counseling Process,* 1952. It is on file at the University of Wisconsin.

ences in the compared distributions were not significant. The marks tended to follow a normal distribution.

To determine whether marking distributions differed *in school years* the English marks in the tenth grade, where the subject was required, were compared with those of the twelfth grade, where it was an elective. Using the tenth grade marks as the criterion, distribution the x^2 of 2.190 indicated that there was insufficient evidence to conclude that the distributions differed significantly.

Since the two procedures produced the results indicated above, it seemed that the most meaningful method of utilizing the marks for the comparisons of control and experimental groups would be that of using distributions of marks by school subjects and by separate schools but without differentiation between semesters or years.

In order to use the marks separately by subject and school, it was decided to "normalize" each of the distributions of marks for each of the separate schools. The T-score, or normalized score technique, was used for this purpose. The value of the mean for the T-score distribution was 50 and the standard deviation was set at 10. From Table 34 it will be seen that, since it is relatively

TABLE 34. Selected Examples of T-Score for Marks in Four Schools

Subject	Marks	School *W*	School *X*	School *Y*	School *Z*
	A	70	66	67	67
	B	60	56	58	60
English	C	49	50	48	52
	D	38	41	39	42
	F	27	31	—	27
	A	71	67	64	67
	B	59	59	57	59
Commercial	C	49	49	48	51
	D	39	39	37	41
	F	25	27	—	—

easier to get an A in English at school *X* than at school *W*, the weighted T-score for that subject in school *X* is lower than in school *W*. It will also be noted that marks of D are given with greater frequency in English in school X than at school W with resulting difference in each of the T-scores for this mark. By assigning to each individual the weighted T-score, so determined for the particular subject taken and for the school he attended, fairly equivalent scores for academic performances were obtained.

To reduce the labor involved in assigning T-scores to all the 690 subjects, a sampling procedure was used. Every seventh control and experimental case was taken from the files to produce 50 cases for each group. The ranges of average T-scores assigned to the cases, their means, standard deviations, and the significance of the differences between the means are presented in Table 35.

TABLE 35. Means, Ranges, Standard Deviations, and Difference of Means of Average T-Score on Academic Performances of Control and Experimental Subjects

Group	N	M	Range	S.D.	*t*	Level of Significance
Control	50	50.42	40–64	5.71	.501	not significant
Experimental	50	50.98	39–60	5.34		

The figures reveal marked similarity in the average T-scores achieved. The *t* of .501 is near the 30 percent level, which is not high enough to permit rejection of the hypothesis that there are no significant differences between the groups. The slight differences in extremes of range similar to those found in the rank-in-class computations reported earlier appear again in the ranges and standard deviations. In view of the finding from the computations with 100 randomly obtained cases, it seemed that the time required to compute T-scores for the total population would not be justified.

SUMMARY ON ACADEMIC ACHIEVEMENT

It appears that the differences between the academic achievements of the control and experimental subjects are so small that they cannot be considered significant. All the computations, however, point to slightly higher achievements of the counseled subjects, and the regularity of this occurrence suggests that there may be a slight relationship between academic performance and membership in the control or experimental group.

The writer has shown previously that intensive counseling specifically designed to improve academic achievement can accomplish that purpose.[6] The counselors in the study reported in this volume did not set the raising of marks as a goal for every experimental subject but, as indicated above, they were aware that high marks are considered by many persons in and out of schools as evidence that a student has achieved one of the goals that is set up *for* him. There is some suggestion in the consistency of the findings given above that counseling has played a small part in the achievement of that objective.

ANALYSIS OF SENIOR REPORTS

CHOICE OF POST-HIGH SCHOOL ACTIVITIES ONE MONTH BEFORE GRADUATION

The reader will recall that a questionnaire described in Chapter III and hereafter referred to as a "Senior Report" was filled out by each of the subjects one month before graduation. It was administered by the writer and his assistants to groups of approximately thirty-five students. To get uniformity in its administration the following directions were read to the students.

The Senior Reports which I will give you in a moment will be filled out by every senior in the high school. They will help in planning future school programs and they will aid us to keep in touch with you after you leave high school.

Six kinds of reports are listed on the blackboard, but you will fill out *only the one* that suits you. Listen carefully while I tell you about them and then decide which one you should choose.

1. *Employment*—This report will be filled out only by those who plan to go to work as soon as they graduate.
2. *Education*—Only those who plan to continue their education beyond high school will fill out this one. Those who plan to go to

[6] John W. M. Rothney and B. A. Roens, *Guidance of American Youth*, Cambridge, Harvard University Press, 1950, Chap. 4.

college, nurse's training, vocational school, business colleges, or any other place of training will choose this report.

3. *Work on Parents' Farm*—This will be filled out only by those students who plan to work full time on their parents' farm. (You will choose this one even if you expect to work there only until you enter the armed forces.)
4. *Armed Forces*—If you expect to enter the army, navy, air corps, or marines (including WAC and WAF) *within the next six months,* you will fill out the armed forces report.
5. *Married Within One Year*—(girls only)—This report will be chosen only by girls who have definite plans to marry within the coming year.
6. *Uncertain*—Students who are not sure about what they want to do after they finish high school will fill out this report. It will be chosen only by those who have no idea of what they want to do during the next year.

After you have chosen the report that best fits your plans, I will give each of you a report form. On the last page there is room to write any comments you wish to make. Take as much time as you need.

Please check to see if you have left out any items. If you have nothing to say about the item put a line in to show that you have read it.

Exceptionally good rapport had been achieved with the subjects at this time and they worked diligently at the reports. (At this point the reader should examine the items in the Reports presented on pages 123–128 in Chapter III.)

The numbers of subjects who selected each of the six kinds of Senior Reports are presented in Table 36. It will be seen by examination of the table that the selection of reports in order of frequency was employment, education, uncertain, work on farm, armed forces, and married within one year. The percentages of subjects choosing them in descending order ranges from 43.7 to 4.0. The differences between the two groups are not significant and it would be difficult to establish the fact that the small differences obtained were due to counseling.

That education was the chief distinguishing area of choice between experimental and control subjects is indicated by the fact that 15 more experimentals than controls planned to go on for further training. (As will be seen later, a much greater proportion

TABLE 36. Numbers and Percentages of Subjects Who Indicated Their Choice of Post-High School Activity by Selection of the Senior Reports Indicated

Kind of Report	Number Experimental	Number Control	Percent Experimental	Percent Control	Total	Percent of Total
Employment	150	149	43.6	44.0	299	43.7
Education	118	103	34.3	30.1	221	32.3
Uncertain	27	33	7.9	9.7	60	8.8
Farming	19	23	5.5	6.8	42	6.1
Armed Forces	13	22	3.8	6.5	35	5.1
Married (Girls Only)	17	10	4.9	2.9	27	4.0
Total	344	340	100.0	100.0	684 [a]	100.0

[a] Six subjects of the 690 were either ill at the time the Senior Reports were done or had been graduated at mid-year.

of experimentals than controls actually did go on.) The difference in the numbers who planned to go into the armed forces may represent in part the counselors' discussions with students about the various methods of entry into military service. It would be questionable to assume that the differences in numbers of control and experimental subjects who planned to be married or to work on their parents' farms were determined by counseling although, in particular cases, the discussions with the counselors about such choices may have had some influence.

Interpretation of the figures in Table 36 is difficult. It requires the examination of the circumstances of each case before the differences can be attributed to the work done by the counselors and, further, it must wait for the determination of whether the individuals carried through with the plans they had made. At this point it was possible to indicate that there seemed to be only minor differences between the choices of control and experimental subjects, which may have been due to chance. The reader may appraise the consistency and appropriateness of the choices by study of the follow-up data which appear later in this volume.

The following sections deal with analysis of the differences between responses of the control and experimental subjects to selected items in the Senior Reports. The response to some of the items in the first pages were made by small groups of subjects (such as the 27 girls who intended to marry within a year) and they did not warrant extensive statistical analysis. Several items were employed only to facilitate follow-up procedures and were not constructed to permit the making of comparisons between control and experimental groups. Still others (such as those which asked specific questions about the particular occupations chosen or training opportunities selected) were designed to make the subjects think further about their plans and, since they applied to so many specific work or training opportunities, it was impossible to check the accuracy of the answers. Finally, as will be shown in the following two sections of this chapter, a careful and thorough statistical analysis of certain kinds of questionnaire responses indicated that their worth in evaluating the effectiveness of counseling was seriously limited. In view of such limitations, analysis of the responses to the Senior Reports were limited to those described in the following pages.

A METHOD FOR TREATING RESPONSES ON THE SENIOR REPORTS

One of the assumptions of this study was that the influence of counseling at the end of the high school period would be partially reflected in the outlook of the persons who had been counseled. Effective counseling, it was assumed, would be reflected in the individual's understanding of his strengths and handicaps, information about the occupation for which he felt that he would be most suited, knowledge of the training that was required for the work he planned to do, and his attitude toward the future. A sound outlook, therefore, would be based upon realistic self-concepts, suitable choices of occupation, knowledge about the selected occupations, and a realistic awareness of opportunities for post-high school training.

In order to set up criteria for evaluating the students' responses to the whole Senior Report, ten persons were asked to coöperate by acting as judges.[7] They were in the process of their work for a

[7] Most of the materials in this section are taken from an unpublished Ph.D. thesis at the University of Wisconsin by Carol Carlson now of the University of California Counseling Center.

Ph.D. in guidance or had recently completed their degrees. They had obtained similar training or experience in the field of guidance and it was felt that their rating of responses could be treated similarly in setting up the criteria.

Five hundred and thirteen usable Senior Reports of subjects who said that they planned to seek *employment* or enter *training* were used in the process of obtaining criteria for evaluating the responses. The first step was to pull 50 of the Reports at random from the total of 513. Responses to 25 questions from each of the 50 Reports were recorded on separate cards and these 25 sets of cards (50 in each set) were given to each judge at the rate of two or three sets each day for ten days. The judges rated each response on a four-point scale, denoting whether they thought it was indicative of "very good," "good," "poor," or "very poor" counseling. The arithmetic averages of the ratings of the ten judges on each of the responses were then to be used to establish criteria for rating the responses on the total 513 Reports.

Before the ratings could be used, however, it was necessary to make a check on the internal consistency of the judges to determine the extent to which each of them would repeat his ratings when given the same responses a second time. One month after the completion of the first ratings for the total set of responses each judge rated three sets of responses named as factual, rational (denoting a reason), or attitudinal. The question, "What kinds of jobs do beginners get in the kind of work you plan to do?" for example, was considered to be a *factual* item. "Why did you choose this work?" is a sample of a *rational* question, and "Do you think that there is as much chance to get ahead today as there was when your parents were the age that you are now?" is a sample of an *attitudinal* item in the following analysis.

The correlation coefficients between first and second ratings determined by Pearson product-moment correlation coefficients are reported in Table 37. Examination of the table indicates that the reliability for factual items was generally high with the average at .90. The averages of the coefficients for rational and attitudinal items, .66 and .67, were so low that their usefulness in

TABLE 37. Reliability Coefficients (Test-Retest Coefficients) of Each Judge for Three Types of Questions on the Senior Reports

Judge	Reliability Coefficients for kinds of items indicated Factual	Rational	Attitudinal
1	.88	.59	.68
2	.93	.84	.59
3	.93	.85	.63
4	.60	.65	.79
5	.98	.67	.55
6	.92	.62	.71
7	.75	.59	.59
8	.89	.40	.68
9	.88	.62	.68
10	.95	.52	.75
Average [a]	.90	.66	.67

[a] The averages were computed through the use of Z-score transformations of the correlation coefficients.

the evaluation of counseling by rating of senior report questionnaires was seriously questioned.

To measure the extent to which the judges agreed with one another, a series of intercorrelations among the judges' ratings were computed. The data for the first set of intercorrelations in Table 38 were taken from the total responses. Separate intercorre-

TABLE 38. Coefficients of Correlation Between the Ratings of Total Responses to Senior Report Questions by Ten Judges

Judges	1	2	3	4	Judges 5	6	7	8	9	10
1										
2	.74									
3	.72	.82								
4	.54	.54	.53							
5	.67	.78	.79	.51						
6	.68	.70	.74	.44	.68					
7	.60	.65	.67	.43	.60	.70				
8	.65	.72	.72	.52	.68	.60	.56			
9	.21	.61	.57	.52	.55	.54	.44	.54		
10	.63	.71	.67	.44	.69	.57	.56	.58	.51	

lations reported in Tables 39, 40, and 41 were then computed for each of the three (factual, rational, and attitudinal) types of questions described above.

Examination of Table 38 indicates that external consistency was not high for the *total* responses. The coefficients ranged from .21 to .82 with the median at .60. Such coefficients indicate that even persons with similar backgrounds do not agree closely with one another on their total ratings of questionnaire responses. This finding should be a matter of some concern to those who use questionnaires in the usual manner.

When the coefficients of correlation in Table 39 between the judges' ratings of *factual* responses are examined, it can be seen

TABLE 39. Coefficients of Correlation Between the Ratings of *Factual* Responses to Senior Report Questions by Ten Judges

	Judges									
Judges	1	2	3	4	5	6	7	8	9	10
1										
2	.83									
3	.83	.93								
4	.83	.87	.93							
5	.75	.89	.94	.90						
6	.83	.88	.93	.92	.88					
7	.87	.86	.88	.89	.85	.88				
8	.85	.86	.90	.87	.89	.85	.83			
9	.76	.88	.85	.87	.86	.87	.88	.82		
10	.72	.85	.88	.90	.92	.87	.81	.81	.83	

that the ratings are very similar for the ten judges. The coefficients vary from .72 to .94 with the median at .87. Only 3 of the 45 are below .80, and 8 of the 45 are above .90.

The greater variability and generally smaller size of the coefficients of correlation between the ratings of *rational* and *attitudinal* items may be observed in Tables 40 and 41. The range of coefficients for the rational items is from .11 to .81 with the median at .47. Only 8 of the 45 are above .60 and 14 are below .40.

The coefficients of correlation between ratings of *attitudinal* responses approach in size those described immediately above.

TABLE 40. Coefficients of Correlation Between the Ratings by Ten Judges of Responses Giving a *Reason* in the Senior Report

Judges	Judges 1	2	3	4	5	6	7	8	9	10
1										
2	.40									
3	.34	.68								
4	.59	.63	.55							
5	.30	.59	.61	.52						
6	.40	.66	.64	.58	.62					
7	.30	.45	.72	.38	.50	.45				
8	.49	.51	.30	.46	.23	.43	.11			
9	.58	.49	.34	.40	.14	.47	.24	.21		
10	.33	.81	.59	.58	.71	.58	.44	.37	.28	

They ranged from .24 to .83 with the median at .56. Only 9 of 45 are above .60 and 11 are below .40.

It appeared, then, that the ratings of the *factual* responses were the only ones of all those in the Senior Reports consistent enough to justify their use in this attempt to evaluate counseling by questionnaires at the time the subjects were graduated. The reasons for the failure to get consistent ratings of the *rational* (giving a reason) and the *attitudinal* items appeared to result from the fact that similar verbal responses on the Senior Reports may have

TABLE 41. Coefficients of Correlation Between the Ratings of *Attitudinal* Responses to Questions on the Senior Report by Ten Judges

Judges	Judges 1	2	3	4	5	6	7	8	9	10
1										
2	.42									
3	.56	.41								
4	.72	.60	.47							
5	.24	.35	.57	.22						
6	.83	.55	.51	.81	.31					
7	.60	.28	.50	.57	.32	.57				
8	.70	.39	.56	.61	.33	.68	.58			
9	.58	.23	.53	.58	.32	.59	.58	.56		
10	.79	.53	.52	.81	.28	.79	.49	.62	.58	

meant different things to the subjects themselves and to the raters. Read and rated by the judges in isolation and without knowledge of the subjects' background, they may have reflected quite different rates of progress of individuals.

APPLICATION OF THE SCORING METHOD TO THE EMPLOYMENT SENIOR REPORTS

The procedures used to set up the criteria for judging responses and the techniques for using them in the total evaluation have been described above. The subjects were the 144 experimental and 146 control group students who responded fully to the *employment* form of the questionnaire, and the 119 experimentals and 104 controls who answered the *education* form in detail.

Analyses of the data in the Senior Reports were made in two parts: (1) an analysis of variance of the response ratings for the experimental and control groups who chose the *employment* forms; (2) an analysis of variance of the response ratings for members of the experimental and control groups who responded to the *education* report.

As explained in the section above, the judges were first given 25 sets of cards with 50 responses in each set. They rated the responses on a four-point scale, and the average rating for each response was used to establish the criteria. These criteria were then used as a basis for scoring the responses for the total of 513 subjects.

Inspection of the raw score data showed variation in the response ratings among the total group of subjects. The problem, therefore, was to account for this variation. It might have been caused by random inconsistencies of the individual subject, by differences between the experimental and control groups evoked by counseling, or by the different types of questions for which the responses were made. In order to test the significance of these variations and to determine the interaction among them, an analysis of variance was completed.

In this study there was independence between the experimental and control groups, but not among the ratings for the various questions within each group. Therefore, an analysis of variance model, described by Edwards,[8] that would allow for repeated measurements of the same individuals within groups was required. Another factor that had to be taken into consideration was that the number of subjects in the experimental group (144) differed from the number of subjects in the control group (146). To take care of this difference, the computational formulas given by McNemar [9] were used to compute the sums of squares.

In this comparison of the experimental and control subjects it would be expected that the individuals within each group would differ somewhat from one another in the realism of their responses. The question then became whether the differences in responses between the two groups was significantly greater than the differences among individuals within the same group. In addition it was found that each individual had ratings for the 28 [10] items that differed according to different questions. A tally of the 290 subjects who used the employment form of the questionnaire showed that 255 of the 290, or 88 percent, had ratings that ranged from 1 to 4. Thirty-one subjects (11 percent) had ratings ranging from 1 to 3. Four subjects (1 percent) had ratings from 2 to 4, and none had ratings that covered less than three of the four points on the scale for the 28 questions. The question then became whether the variation of ratings for each individual was a random or chance variation, or whether there was some pattern for the various ratings that was similar for all individuals. The analysis of variance technique attempts to answer these questions.

The F score of the mean square of between groups divided by the mean square of between subjects within the same group equalled .406. The F was insignificant. This finding means that the difference between ratings in the experimental and control

[8] Edwards, Allen L., *Experimental Design in Psychological Research,* New York, Rinehart & Company, Inc., 1950.

[9] McNemar, Quinn, *Psychological Statistics,* New York, John Wiley & Sons, Inc., 1949.

[10] Question 9a was omitted from this analysis because it was dependent upon a previous question and could not be answered by all subjects. It states: "If you do not have a job promised, name some places where they hire people to do the work you want."

groups had less variation than the ratings of subjects within the same group.

In the next part of the analysis the variation between questions was compared to the interaction, or error term, of the pooled subjects and questions. In this case F equaled 72.057, which is significant at the .001 level. The interaction of questions and groups as compared to the interaction of pooled subjects and questions (F 1.011) showed no significant difference.

In view of this analysis, therefore, it appeared that there was no difference in the variation of response ratings between the two groups as compared to the variation of ratings within each group. The factor that made the difference in the variation of ratings appeared to be the difference in questions asked in the questionnaire. In other words, the variation of individual ratings was not haphazard, but followed a pattern according to the question.

An examination of individual questions revealed that the majority of responses to a particular question tended to be limited to one or two categories. The responses to some questions, for instance, would all be given ratings of "3" and "4," while to others the majority would be "1" and "2," or "2" and "3." These ratings were directly dependent upon the original ratings of the ten judges, which had been used to set up the evaluation criteria. For questions where the judges' ratings were skewed one way or the other, the ratings of responses for the total group reflected the original distribution.

Another important consideration is the fact that ten of the 28 questions used in this analysis of variance were factual questions rated arbitrarily on a two-point scale, "1" or "2," to indicate whether the subject knew or didn't know the required information. These ten questions were not given to the judges to rate because it was felt that there was no justification in setting up criteria for these on a four-point scale. Only a two-point scale could be used to indicate knowing or not knowing the information. The factual questions given to the judges were rated in a similar way, so that the ratings were high or low indicating a specific response or a negative response, as "no response" or "don't know." The large number of "no response" and "don't know" items that appeared in response to factual questions along with specific information tended to increase the variance of the ratings for these questions.

The ratings for questions that required expressions of reasons and attitudes were more evenly distributed and had smaller variances among subjects. The majority of ratings fell in the "3" and "4" categories, depending upon whether the responses were general or more specific. In some cases, however, the "2" and "3" categories were used to differentiate the general and specific responses, and a rating of "4" was seldom used.

An analysis of variance using selected experimental subjects who had received the most counseling and who, in the judgment of the counselors, had benefited most from counseling, was made. Since some of the subjects in the experimental group had come for only the minimum number of interviews, it was felt that perhaps the control and experimental groups were not distinct enough to show differences in the responses of the two groups. By comparing the responses of the control group with those of a selected group of 48 subjects who were thought to have been helped by counseling, significant differences between the groups might be found.

The analysis of variance indicated, however, that the results were very similar to those obtained from the analysis when the total experimental group was used. The F test of 1.218 showed that there were no significant differences between the two groups as compared to the variance within the same group. The ratio of the interaction of the questions and groups to the interaction of the pooled subjects and questions was likewise insignificant. On the other hand, as was found when the entire experimental group was used, the *between* questions were the only items that made a significant difference. To make this analysis, 48 subjects from the control group were selected by random procedures so that the size of the two groups would be equal since, when the size of the two groups differ greatly, the F test is weakened. An additional analysis comparing the total control group with the selected experimental group was made as a check, and the results were very similar. It appeared that if differences resulting from counseling did exist between the experimental and control groups, these differences were not revealed by responses to the senior reports.

APPLICATION OF THE SCORING METHOD TO THE EDUCATION SENIOR REPORTS

The analysis of responses to the *education* form of the Senior Reports followed the same statistical design that was used for the analysis of the *employment* form. The results were similar. The ratio of the mean squares of the *between* groups divided by the mean squares of the subjects *within* the same group have an F equal to 1.046, which is not significant. The ratio of between questions to the error term, the interaction of pooled subjects and questions, resulted in an F equal to 56.751, which was significant at the .001 level. The F ratio of the intersection of questions and groups divided by the interaction of the pooled subjects and questions (1.513) was not significant. A tally of the range of individual ratings showed that 213 of the 223 subjects (95.5 percent) ranged from 1–4, 9 (4 percent) from 2–4, and 1 (0.5 percent) from 1–3. This tally revealed that the ratings of individuals within the same group varied and that there was great variation within the same individual.

These results might be expected to resemble those obtained from analysis of the *employment* form of the questionnaire in view of the fact that the second halves of the two forms were identical. The first parts of the two forms were alike in content, but different to the extent that one had to be applied to future employment and the other to such post-high school education as colleges, schools of nursing, business colleges, and vocational schools.

The questions on the *education* Senior Report required facts, reasons, and attitudes. The distribution of the ratings of responses were very much the same as those of the employment form. The factual questions not rated by the judges were on a two-point scale of "1" and "3." The questions asking for reasons and expressions of attitudes were more evenly distributed than the factual questions, and the majority of the responses fell in category "3." The differences in the criteria for rating the different types of questions accounted in part for the significant variability between questions.

Again following the plan used in the analysis of the *employment* groups, a selected number of experimental subjects were used to compare with the control group. The selected subjects were those who had received a great deal of counseling and the counselors believed they had benefited most from it. Forty subjects, approximately one-third of the 119 in the experimental group, were compared to 40 control subjects chosen at random from the 104 in the entire control group. In this analysis the F ratio of the *between* groups compared to the subjects *within* the same group was 1.189. It was not significant. The F value for the *between* questions was 24.267, significant at the .001 level, and the interaction of questions and groups (1.291) was not significant. An analysis of variance using the 40 experimental subjects and the total control group produced similar results. They are not presented here because of large differences in the size of the two groups.

These analyses of the responses to the *education* form of the Senior Reports, as with the *employment* form, indicated that if there were differences in the responses of the subjects in the two groups resulting from the counseling given to the experimental group, this difference was not manifested in the responses to the Senior Reports.

SATISFACTION WITH HIGH SCHOOL COURSES

Studies of the Senior Reports described on the previous pages suggested that further work with an overall score derived from it would not be productive. The combining of scores from factual, rational, and attitudinal items did not produce scores that differentiated between control and experimental subjects. There remained, however, the possibility that separate items of the Senior Reports might indicate whether differences existed.

Frequently in studies of evaluation of guidance or other educational procedures, students are asked to report their feelings toward courses they have taken at various times in their careers.

This practice is always questionable since subjects do not have much choice after requirements have been met (see pages 45 and 46) and have little opportunity to change courses after the school year is well under way. In addition there are always the limitations caused by faulty memory, rationalization, and deliberate misrepresentation. At best the technique can produce only questionable results.

Despite the limitations indicated above, it seemed desirable to get information about the subjects' attitudes toward their high school programs as revealed in questions 6, 7, and 8 of the first common page of the Senior Reports. The first of these asked, "Are there any subjects you took in high school that you wish you hadn't?" The second asked, "Are there any subjects you didn't take in high school that you wish you had?" The third asked, "Are there any subjects you wanted to take that were not offered?"

The numbers and percentages of control and experimental subjects who named courses in answer to the three questions are indicated in Table 42. It will be seen that the differences between the groups were small. Only 162 of the 344 experimentals and

TABLE 42. Numbers and Percentages of Subjects Who Named Courses in Answer to Questions 6, 7, and 8 of the Senior Reports [a]

Responses	Experimentals N	Experimentals %	Controls N	Controls %
Named courses that they wished they had not taken in high school	162	47.1	161	47.4
Named courses that they wished they had taken in high school	215	62.5	223	65.6
Named courses that they wanted but which were not offered by high school	84	24.4	62	18.2

[a] It should be noted that the students had already chosen their programs for the sophomore year before the counseling study began.

161 of the 340 subjects who filled out the Senior Reports responded to the first question. It is not known whether the approximately 53 percent of the total group who did not reply were completely satisfied with their high school programs or were

indicating only indifference, submission to school procedures, or lack of thought about the matter. The answers to the second question suggest that a slightly larger number of experimental subjects wished that they had taken courses that they did not take. This could mean that they were dissatisfied with the choices they had made *or* it could mean simply that they wished that they could have had more freedom of choice. Less than a quarter of the total group named courses that they had wanted to take but which were not offered by the school and approximately 6 percent more experimentals than controls named such courses. This difference might suggest that they felt that their needs had not been met. Courses most frequently mentioned in the answers to the third question were agriculture for girls, anatomy, astronomy, business law, child care, conservation, farm machinery, first aid, Italian, Norwegian, penmanship, photography, and salesmanship.

There is a very slight indication that the experimental subjects may have been more satisfied with the programs they had experienced, since they named fewer courses that they wished they had not taken. There is some evidence also that they had thought more about what courses they had needed but could not get. The significance of these findings must not be overestimated by the reader, because many factors influence the answers to such questions. To a large percentage of these students, the high school courses they were required to take, and the few electives they were permitted, seemed to be matters of little concern. They attended high school, they said, to get a diploma and were not vocal (especially near the time of graduation) about what they had accepted in order to achieve that end. One of the subjects put it well when he was asked how high school had aided him. It had, he said, "Helped to pass the time while I was growing up."

Some of the students were concerned about their high school programs and particularly their electives, and these are the subjects whose responses provided the data in the table. They were more likely to have well-formulated plans (such as college attendance) and they believed that specific programs of study were required. This awareness of requirements was not simply a function of counseling but of well-publicized statements of teachers, principals, parents, and others. Important differences between counseled and uncounseled students with respect to such matters were not likely, therefore, to be apparent in their answers to the questions under consideration.

Finally, in addition to all the difficulties mentioned above, there is a real problem about the value of stated client satisfaction as a measure of difference among groups of high school students. There is ample evidence all about us that persons can become satisfied with, and even enthusiastic about, circumstances or procedures that do not seem to merit such expressions of appreciation. Attempts to appraise the value of educational procedures by polling of subjects' opinions *after* they have been experienced are fraught with so many difficulties that results must always be questioned.

SELF-APPRAISAL AT TIME OF HIGH SCHOOL GRADUATION

It has been indicated previously in this volume that all the information which had been obtained about the experimental subjects was shared with them. Basic to this sharing procedure was the belief that one important function of high school counseling is the development of more valid self-concepts by the counselee. Evidence about the accomplishment of that objective from several sources will be presented in the results of follow-up studies in later chapters, but the first evidence is contained in question 19 of the Senior Reports.

Question 19 was stated as follows.

In each of the twelve headings below, show where you think you stand compared to other high school seniors by putting a check (√) mark in the column at the right.

First Example: If you know that your scores on intelligence tests were above the 75th percentile, you would be in the upper quarter and you would put a check mark *across from* intelligence test scores and *under* Top Quarter.

Second Example: If you have been a member of the first team in football you would be in the top quarter of your class in sports and you would mark it like the sample below.

In the item given below I would be, compared to other high school seniors in the	Top Quarter	Third Highest Quarter	Second Highest Quarter	Lowest Quarter
Example: Skill in sports	√			
1. Achievement in my special field of interest. (Write it below)				
2. Reading achievement				
3. Intelligence test scores				
4. Achievement in arithmetic and mathematics				
5. Confidence that I will succeed in the work I have chosen to do				
6. Getting along with people				
7. Rank in *this* senior class				
8. Confidence that I have chosen the right career				
9. Knowing my own strengths				
10. Knowing my own weaknesses				
11. Readiness for life after high school				
12. Getting along in new situations				

Since numerical scores were available for items 2, 3, 4, and 7, definite comparisons between the students' ratings of themselves and their actual standing could be made.

During the counseling of the experimental subjects their test scores had been interpreted to them in terms of percentiles. In the two smaller schools no satisfactory reading test scores were available, but in the other schools reading, mathematics, and mental ability test scores had been interpreted for the experimental subjects at least twice. Differences in scores achieved on tests with similar labels often made the interpretations difficult.

And the fact that the correlation between test scores in mathematics and marks in that field were low further complicated the interpretation process. Despite such difficulties, it appeared to the counselors that the experimental subjects might know their approximate standing on test scores better than the controls.

Policies about informing students of their rank in class differed in each of the schools. In the largest school students were encouraged by the administration to go to the office during the last month of their senior year and obtain a figure designating their approximate rank in class. In the two smaller schools, students were not urged to seek their rank but they could obtain the information if they persisted. In the second largest school the students were not informed about their ranks under any circumstances. Student estimates were based, therefore, on what they remembered about their marks. Such variations in practices made comparisons in the rank-in-class category very difficult, but the conditions were comparable for controls and experimentals within each school.

Three groups were used for comparison purposes. The original experimental and control groups were supplemented by a third group composed of the 116 experimental subjects who had more than the average number of contacts with the counselors. Although these additional contacts had not always been concerned with interpretation of tests, they had dealt with the concerns of the counselees and some self-appraisal had usually been involved in the process.

The comparisons that follow are in terms of the extent to which the subjects estimated, overestimated or underestimated their actual standing in quarters of their classes when they placed themselves in any one of the quarters. Thus, a student who placed himself in the top quarter of his class of 300 students and whose official rank was less than 75 had, for these purposes, estimated his position correctly. One who scored twice near the 60th percentile on the Henmon-Nelson Test of Mental Ability but who had ranked himself in the first quarter of his class was listed as an overestimator. If he had listed himself in the lower quarter he had underestimated.

A summary of the number of cases that fell into the various categories is available in Table 43. Examination of the figures contained in it suggests that there are important differences in the

TABLE 43. Accuracy of Estimates of Their Standing in Reading, Mathematics, Intelligence Test Score, and Rank in Class of Three Groups of Senior High School Students

Accuracy of Estimates	Controls N	Controls %	Experimentals N	Experimentals %	Most-Counseled Experimentals N	Most-Counseled Experimentals %
Correct estimate of standing	130	37.9	151	43.3	51	44.2
Overestimate of standing	116	33.9	103	29.8	33	28.0
Underestimate of standing	59	17.3	68	19.7	26	22.7
No estimates available	38	10.9	25	7.1	6	5.1
Total	343	100.0	347	100.0	116	100.0

accuracy of self-estimates of the control and experimental subjects. The contingency chi-square [11] of 5.64 with three degrees of freedom for the total groups indicates that the hypothesis that there is no difference between the self-estimates of the experimental and control group subjects may not be rejected with a relatively high degree of confidence. The difference in size of populations in the control and *special* experimental groups does not permit similar methods of comparison, but the difference in percentages suggests that the differences might be greater. The percentage in favor of the experimental group is apparent in the distributions.

The percentages of subjects whose estimates fell into the various categories have been presented together in Table 44. They have been rounded off to whole numbers to save space. Study of the figures presented suggested that there might be important

[11] Some goodness-of-fit chi-square tests have been used later in this section. It is the only time they are used throughout, but they seemed suitable here. See the discussion of the chi-square method on pages 245 and 246.

TABLE 44. Percentages of Estimates of Control, Experimental, and Most Counseled Experimentals in the Four Areas Indicated

Accuracy of Estimate	I.Q. Test Score Percent Con.	Exp. 1	Exp. 2[a]	Reading Percent Con.	Exp. 1	Exp. 2	Mathematics Percent Con.	Exp. 1	Exp. 2	Rank in Class Percent Con.	Exp. 1	Exp. 2
Correct estimates	30	45	48	38	36	37	38	44	40	46	46	52
Over-estimates	36	32	32	41	39	33	30	21	17	30	30	29
Under-estimates	19	14	16	13	19	25	23	30	37	14	16	13
Refused to estimate	15	9	4	8	6	5	9	5	6	10	8	6

[a] Experimentals in second columns are in regular experimental group. Those in third columns of each section are most counseled experimentals.

differences in the accuracy of the estimates of control and experimental subjects with respect to the first three categories.

Chi-square from the actual figures[12] of the distribution in the intelligence test score category for the total experimental groups was 18.12. It is significant at the .001 level. The hypothesis that there is no difference between the experimental and control groups can be rejected with a high degree of confidence. Procedures for interpreting intelligence test scores to students, described on pages 83 and 84, appear to have produced significantly greater realism in self-appraisal of performances on such tests. Whether or not such realism is of importance to the individual is not, of course, answered by these findings.

The chi-squares computed from the distributions of estimates for the large total control and experimental groups show no significant differences for reading, mathematics, and rank in class. This finding is of interest because relationships between test scores and achievement, as measured by teachers' marks, are not high and the correlation between tests bearing similar labels is

[12] Although percentages are frequently used in the tables throughout this volume for the benefit of those who are not familiar with other statistical procedures, actual computations were done with numbers rather than percentages.

low (see Table 13). Students who achieved low marks in mathematics, for example, could make high scores on the number section of the Primary Mental Abilities test because it deals only with simple addition, and students who scored high on the numerical ability section of the Differential Aptitude Test might have low marks in a course on mathematics where the subject matter was not adequately sampled by that test. Similar factors may also have been operating to determine students' estimates of their proficiency in reading.

As indicated above, information about a student's rank in class was available to him in most cases simply by asking about his status or by making deductions from knowledge of his marks. Students, either experimental or control, who had achieved high marks as shown by their standing on published honor rolls and those who had been consistently at the bottom of their classes made the deductions readily. The very small differences in percentages of experimental subjects who estimated their rank in class accurately may result from the fact that the counselors suggested to experimentals who were going on to training that they seek out their rank in class as further information for use in self-appraisal.

It appears from the above data that the experimental students were significantly more realistic about themselves than the controls in only one of the four factors (mental ability scores) for which numerical ratings were available. There is just a hint that interpretation of scores on mathematics and reading tests to high school students during counseling, and suggestions that they seek out more information about themselves produce more realistic self-appraisals. The differences between the control and experimental subjects in these areas do not, however, reach significant levels.

For the remaining eight items of question 19, no figures that would permit comparisons of the subjects' ratings with their status were available. It was possible, however, to compare the numbers of controls and experimentals who had placed themselves in each of the quarters for each item. Chi-square tests of the significance of the differences for each of the items are presented below.

For items 1, 5, 6, 10, and 11 the computations reveal significant differences. Examination of the distributions indicated that the

No.	Item	Chi-Square	Approximate Level of Significance
1	Achievement in my special field of interest	10.84	$< .02$
5	Confidence that I will succeed in the work I have chosen to do	22.34	$< .001$
6	Getting along with people	13.20	$< .01$
8	Confidence that I have chosen the right career	1.79	$= .75$
9	Knowing my own strengths	3.88	$= .50$
10	Knowing my own weaknesses	13.95	$< .01$
11	Readiness for life after high school	14.47	$< .01$
12	Getting along in new situations	6.70	$= .20$

experimentals tended to rate themselves nearer the top. The results on item 8 may indicate that the consideration given to career choice during counseling had resulted in uncertainty about the word "right," which appeared in the question and produced almost as much doubt as when no counseling is given. No ready explanation can be given for the response to item 9, since considerable time had been given during the counseling to consideration of the strengths of the experimentals. It seems to have been forgotten, rejected, or consciously minimized.

In general, the answers to the question on the senior report designed to get a measure of self-appraisal one month before high school graduation revealed that the experimental subjects were significantly more realistic in only one of the four areas in which numerical checks could be made. In the eight areas in which no such checks were possible there were significant differences in five of the eight areas. Each of these five differences were in the direction that might be expected if counseling had been effective.

In his study of this section the reader is cautioned against too wide generalization from the figures presented. An effort has been made to describe the subjects, the question from which the results were obtained, the methods used, and the circumstances under which the data were secured. All these must be considered and their limitations recognized in the interpretation of the results.

INTEREST IN JOB SECURITY

Question 20 of the senior report was designed in part to determine whether differences existed between responses of the experimental and control subjects to a question about their interest in job security. It was asked at this time partly because a great many statements in current periodicals and newspapers had suggested that youth were primarily concerned about security and not interested in taking chances in the future. The question asked: "Suppose you had a choice between (A) a safe steady job working for someone else with steady average pay for the job or, (B) running your own business with the chance of either going bankrupt or getting rich. Would you choose A or B? Why?"

The distribution of responses of the 333 experimentals and 327 controls indicates that no important differences between the two groups were obtained.

	Experimentals	Controls	Total
Percent choosing A (security)	43.5	43.7	43.6
Percent choosing B (risk)	56.5	56.3	56.4

It is also evident that there is a tendency for this whole group of high school seniors to prefer risk to security when thinking about future employment.

Only a small sample of the subjects responded to the question about why they answered the way they did, and it was not possible to classify the responses meaningfully enough to warrant detailed analysis of the data.

The answers to question 20 should not be taken as conclusive evidence that youth prefer risks to job security. Many factors such as the form of the question, its place at the end of the Senior Report, the fact that many of the girls planned to marry so soon that they did not feel that the implied choice was of concern to them, and many other attitudinal or situational factors may have influenced the answers. The responses indicate only that, under the circumstances in which they were obtained, counseling had not influenced their answers to this question and that there is a slight preference for risk over job security. Certainly the results do not suggest that most youth have become so concerned with security that they are not willing to take risks.

SUMMARY ON SENIOR REPORTS

It appears in retrospect that the Senior Reports did not produce as valuable data as had been anticipated. At the time they were administered it seemed that they might serve the following purposes:

1. Give the counselors a last chance to meet the members of the experimental and control groups and to remind them about the follow-up studies that were to follow.
2. Get a final written statement of the subjects' plans for the immediate future and written statements about their attitudes just before they left school.
3. Stimulate the students to think over once more their plans for postschool activities.
4. Provide data to permit comparison of the choices and attitudes of control and experimental subjects.

The reports did serve the first purpose effectively as evidenced by the percentage of response on the follow-up studies. The second purpose was achieved only if one is reminded that the words "final" (for the school situation) and "written" are used. It had seemed previously that statements in interviews had produced better data (because the statements could be checked by further questioning), but it was impossible to interview all the subjects within a month before graduation. It is not known whether the third purpose was achieved except in the few cases where subjects sought interviews after administration of the senior reports.

That the fourth purpose could not be achieved became apparent only when the methods of analysis of the Senior Reports described above were attempted. It appeared that there was little agreement among students of guidance on the rating of those items in the reports that had to do with the giving of reasons for choices and those that required expression of attitudes. In a sense the finding does contribute much because it warns those who interpret questionnaire data alone that they may make serious errors. As a result of this finding, the author made several changes in his plans for the analysis of the follow-up questionnaire data that were obtained later. Finally, they did indicate some important differences between control and experimental subjects in choice of post-high school activity and in self-appraisal just before high school graduation. And although all the data did not permit elaborate statistical analyses they did offer a valuable link in the chain of data about these individuals that was to cover an eight-year period.

FOLLOW-UP SIX MONTHS AFTER HIGH SCHOOL GRADUATION

The first check on the post-high school activities of the subjects was begun during the autumn of the year after graduation from high school. The postal-card survey described in Chapter IV was designed to remind the subjects of the counselors' interest in them and to prepare them for later follow-up studies. It also provided data on their work or training activities, a measure of their satisfaction with what they had chosen to do, and an indication of their plans for the coming year. The subjects were asked what they were doing, specific details about what their jobs entailed (if they were employed), their feelings about their occupations or training situations, and their plans for the coming year. Responses from 100 percent of the subjects obtained by the methods described in Chapter IV permitted the analyses that appear in the following sections of this chapter.

In Table 45, which follows, the reader will find a summary

TABLE 45. Percentages of 685 Control and Experimental Subjects in Training and Occupations Six Months After High School [a]

Status	Experimental Girls N–181	Control Girls N–182	Experimental Boys N–162	Control Boys N–160	Total Experimentals N–343	Total Controls N–342
Attending college	22.1	19.2	30.1	18.1	25.8	18.7
Semiprofessional training	8.3	7.7	1.9	1.9	5.4	5.0
Clerical training	0.5	3.3	0.0	0.6	0.3	2.0
Skilled trade training	0.0	0.0	3.1	7.5	1.5	3.5
Clerical occupations	43.7	43.9	1.9	5.6	23.9	26.0
Sales occupations	5.5	3.3	1.9	3.8	3.8	3.5
Service occupations	4.5	3.8	1.2	0.6	2.9	2.4
Agricultural occupations	0.5	0.0	13.0	13.8	6.4	6.4
Semiskilled occupations	0.5	0.6	18.5	16.3	9.0	7.3
Unskilled occupations	3.9	5.5	17.9	19.4	10.4	12.6
Armed forces	0.5	0.0	9.9	11.2	5.0	5.3
Unemployed	1.7	2.8	0.6	1.2	1.2	2.0
Married (girls only)	8.3	9.9	0.0	0.0	4.4	5.3
Total	100.0	100.0	100.0	100.0	100.0	100.0

[a] Although responses were received from all 690 subjects, only the 685 who were still alive five years after the study was completed are used in this table. The use of the 685 figure will permit comparisons with tables obtained from the later follow-up studies.

picture of the employment or training status of the subjects distributed by experimental or control group status and sex.[13]

Examination of the table reveals that the chief difference between the experimental and control groups as a whole is in the

[13] See the report by Remstad in Chapter VII on the difficulties met in classifying the occupations which the subjects entered.

greater (7.1) percent of the experimentals who went on to college. The chi-square for the total group computed from the actual frequencies just borders the 5 percent level of significance. The difference for the girls of 2.9 percent is insignificant, but that for the boys of 12.0 percent approaches significance at the 5 percent level. In terms of actual cases, 89 out of the 153 who went to college at this time were experimentals. Of the total of 78 boys who went on, 49 came from the experimental group. Forty of the 75 girls who went to college were members of the experimental group.

Two hundred and thirteen of the 685 subjects went on to one of four kinds of post-high school training in colleges, schools for nurses, apprenticeships, or in clerical fields. Of these 213 cases, 113 were experimental and 100 controls. The differences between the groups are not significant for the total group nor for the numbers of boys and girls within the totals. The gain of the experimentals in college attendance is balanced by the numbers of controls who went into training below the college level.

The greater percentage of boys entering skilled training, usually in the form of apprenticeships, illustrated an interesting result of how counseling seems to have influenced vocational choices in a way that was not intended. At the time that these students were graduated there was a great demand for unskilled workers (since many laborers were in the armed forces) and wages were high. The experimental subjects who were informed by the counselors about the relatively low beginning wages for apprentices tended to reject the delayed value of apprenticeship so that they might take advantage of the current high wages for unskilled workers. Control subjects who had not considered all the pros and cons of apprenticeships were more likely to accept them. As will be shown later, the differences between the groups had decreased by the time the five-year-after-high school study was made and more normal differentials between wages for skilled and unskilled workers existed.

In the area of marriage, counseling of girls seems to have had no effect on the time at which it occurred. Nor does there seem to be any appreciable difference in the time of entry into the armed forces. It is possible, however, that although the numbers are similar, the reasons for the choice may have been different as the result of discussions with counselors about plans for marriage and entry into the armed forces. The differences in the numbers of girls who entered clerical work are not important. A girl who commits herself to the commercial course in high school, and thus takes the specialized work over the last two years, usually finds that she can make the most of her training by accepting clerical work.

SATISFACTION WITH ACTIVITIES SIX MONTHS AFTER HIGH SCHOOL GRADUATION

An attempt to assess the satisfaction of the subjects with their immediate postschool activities consisted of assigning numbers to responses to the item, "Regardless of what you are doing, tell how you like it," on a four-point scale. A very enthusiastic response such as "I love it" or "I really like it" was rated 4, a simple one indicated by an "It's O.K." was rated as 3, a negative response of a mild nature such as "It will be O.K. till I get something I like more" was numbered as 2. The 1 rating was reserved for subjects who might indicate extreme dislike of an activity, but no such expression of distaste appeared.

The extent to which the subjects as a whole liked their choices is indicated by the following tabulation.

Category	Percent Boys N-324	Percent Girls N-366
4 (Enthusiastic)	7.7	26.2
3 (Satisfied)	72.9	57.6
2 (Temporarily O.K.)	10.5	9.6
1 (Extreme dislike)	0.0	0.0
No answer given	8.9	6.6

The differences between girls and boys is apparent and the chi-squares at less than the 1 percent level indicate that the differences are highly significant. The finding that more than 80 percent of the subjects in both groups liked their first postschool activities is probably a result of the satisfaction derived from first pay checks and feelings that they were "on their own." Figures reported in Chapter V for the later follow-up studies show considerable decreases in satisfaction. The fact that more of the girls were in the very enthusiastic category may merely reflect the use of more expressive language. Approximately 10 percent of both boys and girls expressed distaste for their activities, but none displayed extreme displeasure, although there may have been some who felt it. They may have been represented in the 8.9 percent of the boys and the 6.6 percent of the girls who refused to answer. It was not possible at this stage, however, to determine the reasons why the persons in this category had not responded except in the few cases where subjects wrote supplementary letters.

Despite the limitations of data obtained from such instruments as a postal-card survey an attempt was made to determine whether there were any important differences between control and experimental subjects in satisfaction with their job or training activities. The following distribution of ratings reveals that small differences existed, but that they were not large enough to suggest that differences between counseled and uncounseled youth in satisfaction with their job or training activities six months after high school will generally be revealed.

Since it had been noted that the girls and experimentals had

Category	Percent Experimentals	Percent Controls	Differences
4 (Enthusiastic)	20.7	14.2	6.5
3 (Satisfied)	63.7	66.2	2.5
2 (Temporarily O.K.)	8.4	11.4	3.0
1 (Extreme dislike)	0.0	0.0	0.0
No answer	7.2	8.2	1.0
	100.0	100.0	

responded differently from the boys and controls a further breakdown by all four categories seemed necessary. The distribution presented below with the nonresponders eliminated again shows greater percentages in the top categories for the experimentals and particularly for the experimental girls but the chi-squares are not large enough to justify rejection of the hypothesis that there are no significant differences between the experimental and control groups.

Rating	Percent Experimental Girls	Percent Control Girls	Percent Experimental Boys	Percent Control Boys	Total Experimentals	Total Controls
4 Enthusiastic	33.1	23.0	10.1	6.9	22.3	15.6
3 Satisfied	59.8	64.1	78.5	81.3	68.6	72.0
2 Temporarily O.K.	7.1	12.9	11.4	11.8	9.1	12.4
1 Extreme dislike	0.0	0.0	0.0	0.0	0.0	0.0

It appears that there are no important differences between the total group of control and experimental subjects in satisfaction with their occupational or training activities six months after they had completed high school. The slightly greater satisfaction found for the experimental group does not permit generalization to the effect that they will appear in other situations. Perhaps there are no important differences simply because the novelty of post-high school activities, the opportunity to be "on my own," and the earning of wages developed uncritical attitudes toward nearly all the kinds of training opportunities and jobs that they had entered. In later sections of this and following chapters the satisfactions of the same subjects with their activities two and four and one-half years later will be reported.

THE SECOND FOLLOW-UP STUDY

In late autumn of 1953 when the subjects had been out of

school for approximately two and a half years, the second follow-up study, which employed the instrument and procedures described on pages 153 to 171, was begun. This was to be an interim appraisal of status between the more important six-month and five-year-after-high-school studies of the subjects. Its main purposes included a tryout of a questionnaire method and an attempt to keep in touch with the subjects in order to facilitate the main follow-up study that was to be done in 1956. The actual findings of the second study about the subjects' activities and attitudes are not as important as the tryout of the method and the maintenance of rapport, but they are reported in this section to maintain the continuity. Combinations and comparisons of findings from the first and following studies are presented in later chapters.

STATUS TWO AND A HALF YEARS AFTER HIGH SCHOOL GRADUATION

The reader has seen the distribution of the training and educational activities of the subjects six months after high school graduation in a previous section of this chapter. In Table 46 he will observe the training and occupational status of the same subjects two years later when they had been out of high school for two and a half years. Although the greater numbers of experimentals than controls in college appear as they did two years previously, and the difference in numbers of control and experimental group subjects in training remains substantial, the other differences between the groups are insignificant.[14]

The distributions reveal the influence of current social circumstances. In 1951 only 10.5 percent of the boys were in the armed forces and 18.7 percent were in unskilled occupations. In 1953 approximately 47.8 percent were in the services and some 6½ percent were in unskilled labor. It is apparent that the military draft drew heavily from this occupational level.

[14] Two subjects had died during the two-year period. Actually only 685 cases are in the table. The three subjects who died before the third follow-up study are omitted so that the same number of subjects appear in all three tables of occupational and training status in the three follow-up studies.

TABLE 46. Percentages [a] of 685 Control and Experimental Subjects in Training and Occupations Two and One-Half Years After High School Graduation

Status	Experimental Girls N-181	Control Girls N-182	Experimental Boys N-162	Control Boys N-160	Total Experimentals N-343	Total Controls N-342
Attending college	18.8	12.1	21.6	13.1	20.1	12.6
Semiprofessional training	7.2	5.5	0.6	3.8	4.1	4.7
Skilled training	0.6	0.0	3.2	4.4	1.7	2.0
Managerial positions	0.0	0.6	1.2	0.0	0.6	0.3
Clerical occupations	21.5	28.6	1.2	2.5	12.0	16.4
Sales occupations	2.2	1.1	1.2	0.6	1.7	0.9
Service occupations	2.8	1.1	0.0	1.2	1.5	1.2
Agriculture	0.0	0.0	8.0	11.9	3.8	5.5
Skilled occupations	1.1	2.2	1.9	1.2	1.5	1.8
Semiskilled occupations	0.0	0.0	5.6	5.0	2.6	2.3
Unskilled occupations	1.6	2.7	6.2	6.9	3.8	4.7
Armed forces	0.0	0.6	48.1	47.5	22.7	22.5
Married (girls only)	43.6	43.9	0.0	0.0	23.0	23.4
Unemployed	0.6	1.6	1.2	1.9	0.9	1.7
Total	100.0	100.0	100.0	100.0	100.0	100.0

[a] Rounded off to one decimal place.

Another significant change appeared in the number of girls who left clerical and other occupations to marry. In 1951 some two-thirds of the girls were employed and only 9.1 percent were married. In 1953 approximately 44 percent of the girls had become wives and the percentage of employed girls dropped to nearly 30 percent.

Study of the figures may stimulate some thought about high school programs for youth. Should college entrance requirements determine so much of what is done in secondary schools? Have teachers really considered the amount and kind of work in their fields that large percentages of graduates will need in their post-school activities? Are the usual career days in which opportunities in the professions are stressed realistic in their emphasis? Are counselors realistic in their vocational guidance? These questions and many others must come to those who scrutinize such follow-up results as those presented above.

SATISFACTION WITH OCCUPATIONAL OR TRAINING STATUS

The subjects indicated their satisfaction with employment or training status by responding to the following item on the questionnaire.

Regardless of what you are doing show how you like it by checking below.

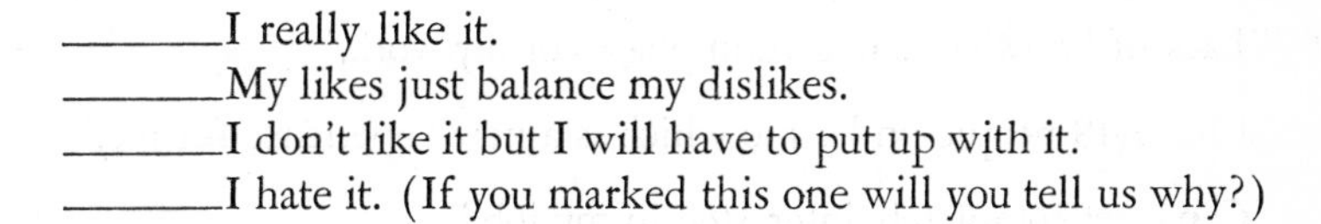
________I really like it.
________My likes just balance my dislikes.
________I don't like it but I will have to put up with it.
________I hate it. (If you marked this one will you tell us why?)

Percentages of the more than 97 percent of the subjects who responded to the item appear in Table 47. It appears that some of the satisfaction with employment and training opportunities

TABLE 47. Satisfaction with Occupational and Training Status Two and a Half Years After High School Graduation

Response	Experimental Girls	Control Girls	Experimental Boys	Control Boys	Total Experimentals	Total Controls
I really like it	83.7	84.6	41.6	43.2	63.7	65.3
Likes balance dislikes	15.2	12.5	26.1	28.1	20.3	19.8
I will have to put up with it	1.1	2.3	27.3	24.8	13.6	12.8
I hate it	0.0	0.6	5.0	3.9	2.4	2.1

revealed in the 1951 study had been reduced in the two-year interval. Although most of the girls really liked what they were doing, the boys had lost much of their enthusiasm. Perhaps the differences are caused in part by the fact that nearly half of the girls had been married in the two-year interim (and not to these boys since only ten subjects had married classmates), while almost half of the males were in the armed forces. Perhaps these factors had already begun to obscure any influence of counseling received during their high school careers.

Those who indicated that they were dissatisfied with their activities gave such reasons as the following for their responses.

"Some of the routine checks and jobs present no challenge to me, therefore I find them boring and have to drive myself to do them."

"The universal lack of knowledge of all things."

"My writing ability is not too good."

"Lack of knowledge in certain phases of my work."

"I have 48 people under me which is a new experience for me."

"Can't get completely interested in my job."

"I don't care for the so-called office manager and she knows it."

"Lack of time and money."

"My dislike of routine household chores."

"Sometimes the children make me very nervous."

"An inability to budget time and to procrastinate."

"Perhaps my greatest handicap is that some people say I take my work too seriously."

"I am quite reserved and find it difficult to be a good conversationalist to the public."

"Sometimes I'm too soft-hearted."

"It is rather hard for me to take criticism."

"I worry a little too much about getting my work out—but it seems that everyone has ulcers these days—so I don't think I'm doing too badly."

"Sometimes I wish I had more patience."

"I dislike the service!"

SATISFACTION IN RETROSPECT

Only 16 subjects of the total of 685 failed to respond to the item on the 1953 questionnaire that was designed to get information about satisfaction with their experiences in the two and a half years since they had completed high school. The figures in Table 48 reveal no important differences between the two total groups but the slight tendency for the experimentals to

TABLE 48. Percentages of Responses Two and a Half Years After High School to the Question, "If you could live over again the last two years since you left high school, would you do the same things as you have done?"

Response	Experimental Girls	Control Girls	Experimental Boys	Control Boys	Total Experimentals	Total Controls
Yes	79.3	77.4	55.5	51.2	68.3	65.1
No	19.0	20.9	42.6	46.2	29.9	32.8
Undecided	1.1	1.1	1.9	1.3	1.5	1.2
Yes and no	0.6	0.6	0.0	1.3	0.3	0.9

respond more favorably is again apparent. The difference between boys and girls is highly significant, but it appears again to be caused by the marital and martial situations which almost half of the subjects had experienced rather than their experimental or control group membership while they were in high school.

OPTIMISM—PESSIMISM

It is sometimes suggested that individuals who have made satisfying adjustments will look favorably toward the future. Since it is often stated that well-counseled subjects will have made better adjustments, it is inferred that they will be more optimistic than those who have not been counseled. The figures in Table 49 indicate that there are no important differences between the approximately 93 percent of the experimental and control subjects who answered this question in their attitudes toward the future.

TABLE 49. Percentages of Responses Two and a Half Years After High School to the Question, "Looking toward the future, do you think things are going to work out well for you?"

Response	Experimental Girls	Control Girls	Experimental Boys	Control Boys	Total Experimentals	Total Controls
Enthusiastic yes	33.9	34.3	20.0	19.3	27.6	27.3
Yes	56.3	57.4	53.1	64.7	54.9	60.8
Not clearly yes or no	8.0	7.1	22.1	15.3	14.4	11.0
No	0.6	0.6	4.8	0.7	2.5	0.6
Emphatically no	1.2	0.6	0.0	0.0	0.6	0.3
Total	100.0	100.0	100.0	100.0	100.0	100.0

It is interesting, however, to note that a marked and statistically significant difference beyond the 1 percent level ($X^2 = 16.64$) was found to exist between the enthusiasm expressed by boys and girls in the total group. It appears from the data that the girls were considerably more optimistic in their outlook toward the future two and one-half years out of high school than were the boys. This might be caused by the fact that the girls tended to marry and settle down earlier than the boys. The girls' enthusiastic response to this question may reflect a general satisfaction with married life in its earlier stages (for some, even the "honeymoon" stage) and a hope and expectancy that it would continue.

Samples of the reasons given for pessimistic and optimistic outlooks indicate some determiners of responses to this question.

"I am very happily married and my work has very favorable opportunities for advancement in my field. I believe I have the ability to succeed."

"Because I am ambitious and my husband and I have learned to discuss everything we do before doing it and agree to what we both feel is best."

"We (my husband and I) both want the same things. I believe I have a good start, I have a fairly good job and I'm willing to work for what I want."

"In my depressed moments I feel that things can't keep on working out as perfectly forever."

"Automation and decrease in farm machinery sales make the future look not so good."

One subject who thought things would not work out well for her said, "I have no interest in life."

MOBILITY TWO AND ONE-HALF YEARS AFTER HIGH SCHOOL GRADUATION

The extent to which subjects change their status during the first two and a half years after high school graduation may be observed in Table 50. It is apparent that, except in the case of the experimental boys, the most common pattern is to change

TABLE 50. Percentages of Subjects Who Made the Number of Changes Indicated in Vocational, Educational, Armed Forces, and Marital Status in the Two and One-Half Years Following High School Graduation

Number of Changes	Experimental Girls	Control Girls	Experimental Boys	Control Boys	Total Experimentals	Total Controls
No change	38.7	33.0	37.7	38.1	38.2	35.4
One	47.0	44.0	35.2	39.4	41.4	41.8
Two	10.5	18.1	16.6	11.9	13.4	15.2
Three	2.7	1.6	5.6	3.1	4.1	2.3
Four	0.0	0.0	1.8	1.3	0.9	0.6
Incomplete data	1.1	3.3	3.1	6.2	2.0	4.7
Total	100.0	100.0	100.0	100.0	100.0	100.0

only once during the period covered. The usual change was from job or training into the armed forces for men and from job or training to marriage for the girls. The slight difference in stability between experimental and control groups by sex and by total is caused by the greater numbers of experimentals in training.

A study of the mobility of these subjects by Schreiber[15] is too

[15] David E. Schreiber, *Some Problems in the Effective Utilization of the Threshold Worker,* unpublished Ph.D. thesis, University of Wisconsin, 1956.

detailed to present here. Those readers who are particularly interested in the *employer, exit, occupational, industrial, entrance,* and *geographic* mobility of young workers will find some interesting conclusions and implications in his report.

SELF-APPRAISAL (HANDICAPS)

Recognition of personal strengths and weaknesses is often said to be a desirable outcome of the counseling process. The well-counseled individual, it is claimed, will have greater awareness than the noncounseled person of his own strengths and limitations. There was some indication as reported on page 278 that the experimental subjects were more realistic in self-appraisal than the controls one month before graduation from high school. Two items on the second follow-up questionnaire were designed to determine whether this had been continued two and one-half years later. In order to avoid too direct questioning, the items were phrased as they appear in the headings for Tables 51 and 52. The open end question answered by 72 percent of the experimentals and 75 percent of the controls required classification of the responses by the investigators. Results of attempts to do so by teams of the research staff are indicated by the entries that appear in the first column of the two tables which follow.

Study of Table 51 indicates that there is little difference between the total responses of the groups. More control than experimental boys (7.6 percent) reported that nothing handicapped them, but this difference was insignificant. On the item concerning lack of skill, however, the difference was significant beyond the 5 percent level ($X^2 = 4.05$). Chi-square for the item about inadequacy of high school preparation could not be computed because of insufficient numbers in the categories.

The answers of the control and experimental subjects to this item on the questionnaire have not revealed any important differences between the groups in terms of self-appraisal. It should be noted that the responses to the item do not indicate whether or not the person *was* handicapped by any of the factors mentioned. They indicate only what the subjects said had handicapped them at the time they answered the question. And they might

TABLE 51. Percentages of Responses Two and One-Half Years After High School to the Question, "What is there about *you* that *handicaps* you in what you are doing?"

Category	Experimental Girls	Control Girls	Experimental Boys	Control Boys	Total Experimentals	Total Controls
"Nothing handicaps me."	34.4	33.1	36.5	44.1	35.4	38.5
"I don't know."	2.3	2.3	4.2	0.0	3.3	1.2
"My lack of skill." (Physical handicaps, can't follow directions, can't understand it.)	16.4	13.8	20.4	11.0	18.3	12.4
"My personal qualities." (Lack of self-confidence, bad temper, nervousness, procrastination, too easy-going, etc.)	26.6	33.1	14.4	15.0	20.7	24.1
"Inadequate high school preparation." (Did not take the right courses, enough courses, etc.)	0.8	3.1	1.7	6.3	1.2	4.7
"Inadequate preparation outside of high school."	1.6	0.0	3.4	2.4	2.4	1.2
"My failure to adapt to the job." (Lack of interest, dislike job, working conditions, etc.)	4.7	5.4	7.6	6.3	6.1	5.9
"Job is unsuitable." (Working conditions are not suitable, job is not interesting, challenging, etc.)	2.3	0.8	4.2	4.7	3.3	2.7
Irrelevant and unclassifiable responses	10.9	8.4	7.6	10.2	9.3	9.3
Total	100.0	100.0	100.0	100.0	100.0	100.0

be mistaken for any of many reasons. Since these subjects were in such a wide variety of occupational, educational, personal, and social situations, it was not possible to determine whether the subjects were realistic in their self-appraisal. Even if such information had been available, it would not have been possible to generalize about realism in self-appraisal since what might be a strength in one situation might be a limitation in another. It does seem clear, however, that the responses for the total groups of experimental and control subjects are not large enough to reject the hypothesis that there is no difference in the kinds of statements they make when they are asked to indicate what it is about them that handicaps them in what they are doing.

SELF-APPRAISAL (STRENGTHS)

Responses to the question about the qualities that made them successful in what they were doing were classified as far as possible with the same headings as those used in the handicaps table presented above. The question was answered most by the experimental girls (90.9 percent) and least frequently (79.6 percent) by the experimental boys. Only 15.4 percent of the control girls and 12.4 percent of the control boys rejected the question. One can only conjecture as to the reason for rejection of the question by such large numbers of experimental boys. It may have been modesty, failure to make self-appraisals, even unwillingness to express their feelings if they felt unsuccessful.

The three categories into which most of the responses fell were those concerned with skills, personal qualities, and adaptability to the demands of the job. In the first two of these the differences between the groups are not statistically significant. In the third, however, there are significant differences between the experimental and control girls but not between the two groups of boys. There are no significant differences in responses of the total control and experimental groups.

In general the answers to this question have produced inconclusive results. The differences in self-appraisal that appeared at the time of graduation from high school have been reduced in two and one-half years to the point where, with one small exception, they are insignificant. It is not known whether this finding results from real changes within the individuals or merely

TABLE 52. Percentages of Responses Two and a Half Years After High School to the Question, "What is there about *you* that makes you *successful* in what you are doing?"

Category	Experimental Girls	Control Girls	Experimental Boys	Control Boys	Total Experimentals	Total Controls
"Nothing" or *"I am not successful."*	4.3	3.2	10.8	7.1	7.2	5.1
"I don't know."	3.1	3.2	7.0	5.0	4.8	4.1
"The skills I possess." (Intelligence, manual dexterity, fast learner, etc.)	5.5	7.8	9.3	10.7	7.2	9.2
"My personal qualities." (Patience, perseverance, getting along with others, conscientiousness, etc.)	26.4	32.5	34.1	30.0	29.8	31.3
"My high school preparation."	1.2	3.2	0.8	1.4	1.0	2.4
"My preparation outside of or beyond high school."	0.6	0.0	0.0	2.2	0.4	1.0
"My adaptability to the demands of the job." (Like the working conditions, like the kind of work, like to learn new parts of the job, etc.)	53.4	42.9	26.4	33.6	41.4	38.4
"I find the job suitable." (Job is challenging, stimulating, etc.)	3.1	1.3	2.3	4.3	2.7	2.7
Irrelevant and unclassifiable responses	2.4	5.9	9.3	5.7	5.5	5.8
Total	100.0	100.0	100.0	100.0	100.0	100.0

changes in expressing themselves on such matters in reply to a questionnaire item.

Samples of the statements of the subjects in responding to the item are given below. They give some indication of the variety of reasons why the subjects answered as they did.

"I get along well with people and I am willing to accept responsibility."

"I think that the thing that makes me most successful in what I am doing is that I enjoy what I am doing and I am doing what I was trained to do."

"I try to make my job as pleasant as possible and coöperate with the people around me."

"I have set my goals in life, and I intend to accomplish said goals. Along with this I have a wife and two children to provide for—needless to say, my time is all but totally consumed with this!"

"It's determination to do what I have always wanted to do and that's to work with horses."

"I do the job that is laid out to me to the best I am able."

"I like to know what there is to do, to set up a proposed schedule for the job to be done, and follow it through to the finish."

"I like giving of myself."

"I get along with people I work with and I mind my own business."

"I know how to budget time for study and other interests."

"I like to cook, take care of children, play bridge, and work part time."

"I am willing to try and don't get discouraged easily."

"I don't believe I am far enough along in the course I am pursuing to say that I am succesful. If I am it will probably be due to the fact that I have been able to discipline myself to study."

"I think mechanical aptitude helps most."

"I can't really say I am successful but my experience before going to college helped a lot."

SATISFACTION WITH HIGH SCHOOL TRAINING

Presumably persons who had been well counseled in school should look back at their school experiences with more favor than those who had not. It was to test this presumption that the subjects were asked to respond to the question that appears in the heading of Table 53. Approximately 16 percent of the sub-

TABLE 53. Percentages of Responses Two and a Half Years After High School to the Item, "Looking back at your high school training, tell how it helped you most."

Responses	Experimental Girls	Control Girls	Experimental Boys	Control Boys	Total Experimentals	Total Controls
"*It did not help.*"	2.6	0.0	3.8	9.0	3.2	4.2
"*Helped in personal development.*" (Developed interests, ambitions, self-confidence, application, sense of duty, etc.)	7.8	12.5	11.4	14.9	9.4	13.6
"*Prepared adequately for vocation.*"	34.4	40.1	31.8	26.1	33.2	33.6
"*Prepared adequately for marriage and homemaking.*"	8.4	5.9	0.0	0.0	4.5	3.2
"*Prepared adequately for post- high school training.*"	19.5	11.2	12.1	11.9	16.1	11.5
"*Prepared adequately in social development.*" (Learned to get along with others, made friends, prepared for citizenship, etc.)	20.8	20.4	15.2	19.4	18.2	19.9
"*Developed values.*" (Learned value of an education, stimulated further study, stimulated planning for the future, learned how to think, broader outlook, etc.)	3.9	1.3	8.3	6.0	5.9	3.5
"*Don't know.*"	0.0	1.3	3.0	1.5	1.4	1.4
Irrelevant and unclassifiable responses	2.6	7.3	14.4	11.2	8.1	9.1
Total	100.0	100.0	100.0	100.0	100.0	100.0

jects almost equally distributed in the control and experimental groups did not respond to the question for reasons which are not known and the entries in the table are based on percentages of those who did reply. Since the item was of the open-end type, the investigators were required to assign the written answers into the categories given in the table. They were set up after a sample of the responses had been read and classified coöperatively by the writer and three graduate students in guidance. They were on a second page of the questionnaire and the readers did not know whether they were reading the answers of a control or experimental group subject.

The figures in the table reveal no startling differences between total control and experimental subjects, but they are generally in the direction to be expected if the basic presumption was correct. Some of the differences suggest that the control boys were less satisfied than the experimental boys with their preparation for a vocation but more pleased with their training in social and personal development. Control girls were slightly more satisfied than the experimentals with their preparation for a vocation and the assistance they received in personal development, while the experimental girls showed greater satisfaction with their preparation for post-high school training and marriage.

Samples of their unedited statements are given below.

"In a nutshell, I think the mere accumulation of a thorough educational and social 'backbone' while in high school has helped me most effectively in my work in college and the army, and has been most important in my pleasant relationships with so many interesting people and close friends. I feel that no phase of high school training has been misused or has remained undeveloped."

"Encouraged an interest in the field in which it now seems I will be happy to spend my life. I can't think of any particular trouble in which the high school, given our social and intellectual climate, could possibly have helped more. I think that on the level of teaching quality I was extremely lucky to go to ______________ H.S. I feel that the standards there were far above average."

"I had an excellent preparation for college and an excellent opportunity to develop any leadership ability I had. Also it seems that my understanding and tolerance of people increased."

"As far as academics go in high school, mathematics helped me the most in my present occupation but more than that, high school seemed to help my adjustment to life more than anything else."

"Besides the basic knowledge it gave me I consider it a stepping-stone without which I could have advanced no further in life. I don't think it failed me any place."

"It helped us by showing what we were best suited for even if some of our plans didn't turn like they did when we were in high school. I truthfully don't think it failed."

"Taught me to get along with and understand people. Taught me to do my job well. It did not fail me in any way."

"Comparing other college students I feel I had a very good background for college training. It took a while to adjust, but it wasn't as difficult for me as it was for other students."

"I can't give any reasons but I feel that I have gained much from my school training."

"I took the business course. Everything taught was used in everyday business. That's about all I can say."

"I feel the training I had helped me succeed on the job."

"It was good preparation for any college work—gave me a good foundation. It was weak in math causing me to have trouble in some advanced courses in college."

"It prepared me for the jobs that I have had since then. Also taught me how to get along with people and to do a job well. Didn't give me enough practical background for later life."

"My training for office work was supporting me and a very good work, I think too. Wish I would have had shorthand in school. Never really use it at work but could have had it."

"Well, I think it helped me understand better government and develop my study habits."

"I think the general education it gave me is invaluable."

DISSATISFACTION WITH HIGH SCHOOL TRAINING

The second half of the question, which attempted to elicit information about dissatisfaction with high school training, contained the item that appears in the heading of Table 54. It is not known why this question received the second lowest percentage of responses of all the items on the questionnaire. It was not answered by 46.7 and 50.6 percent of the members of the experimental and control groups respectively. It may be that these persons did not think that high school failed them but one would wonder why they did not write that it had not failed them as 25.1 percent of the experimentals and 16 percent of the controls did. It appears that direct questions about the lack of value of counseling and high school training do not elicit adequate numbers of responses.

The difference between the numbers of experimental and control boys who indicated that high school did not fail to help them is the only highly significant difference in the table. The other differences are not large enough to justify any generalization about the differences in groups with respect to the value of their high school training. In several areas the experimentals seem to be slightly more critical, but this may result from the fact that they felt that they knew the investigator well enough to feel safe in making their criticisms.

Samples of the responses to the question on how high school failed to help the subjects are given below.

"High school failed in teaching the importance of accepting and meeting responsibilities."

"I don't believe high school is too good. It doesn't prepare the student enough for college."

"I think they don't have enough on getting along with people. The training should be made true to life."

"I didn't study the way I should have and now I am sorry for it."

"It didn't help much because the training I took had nothing to do with the kind of work I wanted to do. I think it should have made

TABLE 54. Percentages of Responses Two and a Half Years After High School to the Item, "Looking back at your high school training, tell how it failed to help you."

Responses	Experimental Girls	Control Girls	Experimental Boys	Control Boys	Total Experimentals	Total Controls
"It did not fail."	19.8	17.7	31.0	14.3	25.1	16.0
"Failed in personal development." (See items in Table 53 above.)	5.2	4.7	5.8	7.1	5.5	5.9
"Failed to prepare adequately for a vocation." (Inadequate academic or vocational preparation for job, failed to show application of facts to jobs, etc.)	21.9	21.2	16.1	17.9	19.1	19.5
"Failed to prepare adequately for marriage and homemaking."	8.3	4.7	1.2	0.0	4.9	2.4
"Failed to prepare adequately for post-high school education." (Did not learn to study, did not learn essentials, inadequate prerequisites, inadequate curriculum, etc.)	21.9	17.6	21.8	15.5	21.9	16.6
"Failed in social development." (See items in Table 53 above.)	5.2	8.2	2.3	4.8	3.8	6.5
"Failed to develop values." (School was not inspiring, challenging, did not teach responsibilities, etc.)	7.3	14.1	5.8	19.0	6.6	16.5
"Don't know."	1.0	2.4	4.5	2.4	2.7	2.4
Irrelevant and unclassifiable responses	9.4	9.4	11.5	19.0	10.4	14.2
Total	100.0	100.0	100.0	100.0	100.0	100.0

more subjects mandatory. Subjects should be what you can do best not what you just like."

"It would have helped me if I had applied myself, but at the time my thoughts were of a different world. I took the wrong classes; had I taken the right ones I would have definitely gone on to school."

"Didn't do much to help me. Math was not required and the school was not strict enough. It was too easy."

"It failed to teach me things a person needs to know for advancement in later life. It is my belief that our schools should make mandatory such courses as math, trig, English, History, etc. Throughout the high school years as most young people don't know what they want to do when they leave school and I'm sure courses like these would be very helpful in later life."

"Ours was a poor school system. The teachers were incompetent. I can't spell or write."

"H.S. helped me none whatsoever. I took the college prep—when I discovered I couldn't continue my schooling I had a difficult time working in an office when I had no office training.

REACTIONS TO COUNSELING (HOW COUNSELING HELPED)

Statements of client satisfaction, which are often used in evaluation studies, have always provided questionable evidence. Such things as faulty memory, deliberate deception, unwillingness to admit dissatisfaction so that the investigator's feelings will not be hurt, failure to admit dissatisfaction since it may reflect on the responders, unwillingness to admit that a subject had really needed assistance at an earlier period, misinterpretation of the question, and many other factors may distort the data. This writer, although thoroughly skeptical of all evaluation studies that use client satisfactions as criteria, was interested in getting the reactions of the subjects even though it was known that such factors as those mentioned above might be operating to reduce their validity.

Unwillingness of many clients to indicate satisfaction with any procedure unless they are coerced or coaxed by comments or anticipated rewards to do so is reflected in the large percentage of subjects who did not answer this question. Approximately one-quarter (25.7 percent) and 34.5 percent of the controls and experimentals respectively made no response to the question. It is possible that the form of the item may have reduced the number of replies. A check list of possible responses might have

TABLE 55. Percentages of Responses Two and One-Half Years After High School to the Item, "Looking back at the *counseling* you had in high school, tell how it *helped* you."

Responses	Experimental Girls	Control Girls	Experimental Boys	Control Boys	Total Experimentals	Total Controls
"It did not help."	6.6	12.4	9.3	26.2	7.8	18.7
"It helped vocationally." (Helped to choose the right vocation, channeled thinking on vocation, established vocational goals, etc.)	21.9	16.5	14.4	9.7	18.4	13.4
"It helped educationally." (Helped to choose right courses, get better grades, stimulated educational planning beyond high school, etc.)	14.6	14.9	10.2	6.8	12.5	11.2
"It helped in planning for the future." (Made me aware of opportunities, made me think of the future, etc.)	17.5	9.1	23.7	22.3	20.4	15.2
"It helped my personal development." (Provided help in self-analysis, built self-confidence, helped with adjustment problems, made aware of assets and limitations.)	24.8	18.2	18.6	13.6	22.0	16.1

TABLE 55 (*Continued*)

Responses	Experimental Girls	Control Girls	Experimental Boys	Control Boys	Total Experimentals	Total Controls
"It gave me a chance to talk things over." (Provided someone to talk to, someone interested in me, someone who cared about me, etc.)	8.0	5.8	5.1	3.9	6.7	4.9
"I received no counseling."	0.0	13.2	0.0	3.9	0.0	8.9
"It helped me in school." (It kept me in school when I was going to leave.)	0.7	0.0	4.3	1.0	2.4	0.4
Irrelevant and unclassifiable answers	5.9	9.9	14.4	12.6	9.8	11.2
Total	100.0	100.0	100.0	100.0	100.0	100.0

brought more replies, but it would also have suggested responses which the subjects may not have thought about and have produced only rapid superficial answers. Those who took the trouble to answer probably did so because they had given consideration to the item and felt strongly enough about it to write out an answer.

Since 65.5 percent of the control subjects answered the question it appears that there was some difficulty in the interpretation of the word "counseling." The investigator might have avoided this difficulty by wording the items to define counseling as that activity carried on only by the investigators, but he chose not to do so since he wanted to see how many of the control subjects thought that they had obtained counseling from any source.

Only 8.9 percent of the controls who answered this question replied that they had received no counseling and 11.2 percent gave irrelevant and unclassifiable answers. The approximately 80 percent of the control group responders must have thought that the term counseling was descriptive of the advice given by class advisers, parents, teachers, religious advisers, and others. Some of the controls may also have considered as counseling the interviews with the counselor that were designed only to develop rapport for follow-up purposes.

In general the answers to this question may indicate the differences between subjects who have received what has been interpreted as counseling in an organized program and those who may have obtained what they considered to be counseling wherever they could find it. In every total category the percentages indicate that more experimental than control subjects thought that counseling had helped them but the chi-squares computed from the actual frequencies reached the 1 percent level for only the first item. Some of the comments that appeared on the questionnaires follow.

"I think it gave us broader views on what we would like to be, but yet we couldn't have."

"I believe it helped me to stop and think about things. Before deciding not to go to college I had thoroughly thought it over."

"Truthfully it only encouraged me to continue with my music, which my family couldn't afford."

"Sort of can't remember it, but it must have been very good."

"I was told frankly according to test results of my abilities and what I might expect in the future; it is then up to the individual as to what he does with this knowledge."

"It helped prove to myself I wasn't cut out to be a farmer although I wouldn't admit to anyone at the time."

"I never worked to the extent of my capiabilities in school. I say this because I never really worked at all. This may perhaps be due to my own personality lack; however, I never had a teacher (or counselor)—except when I asked for it and I never asked for it—who really instilled any desire to work in me. I feel that such inspiration (?) is a very necessary part of education especially on the secondary level. I honestly feel that the ability to work to the extent of one's ability is a more important asset (if a choice must be made) than further education.

"Most certainly your private and thoughtful counseling has been a rewarding realization in my years following high school. Though suggestions as to schools, interests, etc. were made you definitely did reserve the important decisions for the individual himself to make.

"Though I have answered the questions with some degree of completeness, I do desire to simply tell you again just how profitable and beneficial your counseling program was to me following high school graduation. Such an attraction to and belief in a program of consultation stems from the many ways I successfully applied the knowledge I learned from such advice and council. In addition, during the course of a four year college education, I did become a part and a working member of many school organizations and I do think that as a result of the deep-rooted counseling I received in high school, these responsibilities were more successfully met. And further, it is this same 'backbone' of confidence, developed through strong and specialized training, that I know will produce much personal success and happiness in the years of my future. I'm overly appreciative, Dr. Rothney, of the fine, devoted effort and concern you gave to my series of questions and problems while completing my high school education and preparing for college. I only hope that your type of program can expand further and that the personal concern of such individuals as you in the educational department of *many* schools can continue in an even greater circle and sphere of influence.

"If convenient, I do hope to find a timely opportunity to visit you shortly at your university office.

Sincerely,______________"

"I can't recall that I ever had any actual counseling from a high school instructor. Perhaps you could have helped me more if I had had the courage to open my mouth. However, my visits with you did help me to the extent that at least I knew that someone at high school was concerned about me as an individual."

"It helped in a lots of ways but the most important way was that it gave me there wisdom which took years for them to require. I sure have applied alots of that wisdom in only five years."

"In closing I want you to know you have my wish that your work is progressing smoothly there at the University and that you continuing to put as much spark and ambition for a well planned future into todays school children as you did for me and my classmates in 1951."

"It taught me the importance of looking ahead to plan a future. It gave me ambition and now I realize life is more interesting if you continue to reach for a higher goal."

"I really don't see very many of the people that I graduated with. It seems like after graduation you become friendly with the people you work with and then when you get married you again become acquainted with other married couples perhaps even friends of your husband or wife. I think you lose contact with school friends quickly.

"I was glad to have had the opportunity for all the worthwhile guidance that was given to me during high school. I sincerely think that my life was better planned because of it.

"Thank you again."

"My counseling would have helped me if I would have had enough sense to follow through with my plans—the counseling didn't fail—my own know-it-all did it."

"About the only counceling I can remember having in H.S. is that that you gave me and then several talks with the dean of girls. As I said, I don't think I ever had any serious problems. If I did, I discussed them with my parents. I don't know if I would have wanted counseling if it would have been available."

"About all I ever got was when you told me I wouldn't like factory work. Well, I tried it—and I never was so unhappy—you were so right!!"

"I help all of us to solve problems of all kinds while in school. I only wish there was someone to help us young married people that need counseling."

"I wouldn't say it has failed. It would have been interesting to talk over the fact that we might not succeed in the career chosen and then what means of livelihood would be undertaken."

"It helped me to the extent that I realized someone was interested in my future and willing to counsel me. If it wasn't for the counseling, I don't believe I would have finished college—in spite of my high school scholastic achievement."

"Had it not been for Dr. Rothney I probably would not have taken Medical Technology at Madison and I know of no other course that I could have liked so much or would have been so good for me."

"Counseling in high school is of great advantage since, it is a rare family who can offer objective help to a child in chosing a suitable vocation or profession. Therefore, where else can a teen ager receive this much needed aid, but from an adequately prepared counselor? If more intense and personal help were available, the wary and defensive teenage person might develop more faith in the counselor thereby becoming more receptive to the information and help offered."

"I recall a time when in High School I wanted to quit and get married but was 'talked into' finishing at least my high school education. Which now I'm glad I did. When your in school you only plan a few weeks a head; but later you plan for years a head; which without an education you would probably still keep thinking in terms of days instead of a future."

"I feel that your counseling was very helpful. We have love in my family (mama, Papa, Brother) and are interested in helping each other to do the right things by using experiences we have gained, when a person is sincere in trying to help in choosing another person occupation and this person is also outside the family. One is able to discuss the problems involving that occupation by looking at both sides."

"I believe that if I had more counseling before I came to high school and then a great deal more while I was in high school it would have helped me a great deal more than what it did."

"The counseling that I did receive started me thinking. Before I met you I had no thoughts for future employment, my only thought was that I was going to be drafted and that was it. But after I met you and was asked varies questions on what I would like to do and the many advantages I had with a good education I began to think."

"In the service I could and did start plans for the future. I knew I liked construction work the best, so I got into a branch of the service where I learned how to read a slide rule, did a little surveying, and even took a correspondence course in Algebra from the University of Wisconsin, before I left service.

"All the counseling I received did me more good than I can tell you. I think it should be continued and it should be begun in the earlier grades.

"Thank you for your deep concern in mine and every students future success."

REACTIONS TO COUNSELING (HOW COUNSELING FAILED TO HELP)

Fewer subjects responded to this question than to any other in all the follow-up attempts. Approximately 62 and 65 percent of the experimentals and controls respectively rejected this item. Perhaps they could think of no reason why it failed them because they were not clear about what it might have done. Others may have intended to indicate, by refusing to answer, that counseling had not failed them and the factors mentioned in the section above may also have influenced this client evaluation item.

In Table 56 it will be seen that 43.1 percent of the experimentals and 19.3 percent of the controls said that counseling did not fail. This is a highly significant difference on a very important item. Whether or not they were actually helped, the feeling that it did not fail them is an important statement. Since it has been quite obvious from data in the previous tables that the subjects did not hesitate to express dissatisfaction when they felt it, we may conclude that the obtained difference indicates that the counseled subjects more than the controls had not felt let down in their counseling.

It is interesting to note that 12.3 and 9.3 percent of the responses of the experimentals and controls respectively thought that counseling had failed them because it did not establish a *definite* goal. These subjects seemed to reflect a point of view about counseling that is rather commonly expressed among laymen and one that was not changed for 12.3 percent of the experimental subjects in their interviews with the counselor.

Some of the differences in the table are very large but their significance could not be computed because of the small numbers. The category, "received no counseling," shows differences of

TABLE 56. Percentages of Responses Two and a Half Years After High School to the Item, "Looking back at the *counseling* you had in high school, tell how it *failed* to help you."

Response	Experimental Girls	Control Girls	Experimental Boys	Control Boys	Total Experimentals	Total Controls
"It did not fail."	44.1	17.5	41.9	21.5	43.1	19.3
"It failed to establish a *definite* educational or vocational goal."	13.2	11.1	11.3	7.1	12.3	9.3
"It directed me toward the wrong educational or vocational goal."	7.4	4.7	8.1	10.7	7.7	7.6
"It failed to stimulate planning for the future."	7.4	11.1	1.6	12.5	4.6	11.8
"It failed to help in the solution of personal problems."	1.5	1.6	1.6	0.0	1.5	0.8
"Counselors didn't provide enough chance to talk things over sympathetically."	1.5	0.0	1.6	0.0	1.5	0.0
"Received no counseling."	1.5	20.6	0.0	7.1	0.8	14.3
"Did not get enough counseling."	13.2	15.9	11.3	14.3	12.3	15.1
Irrelevant and unclassifiable responses	10.2	17.5	22.6	26.8	16.2	21.8
Total	100.0	100.0	100.0	100.0	100.0	100.0

19.1, 7.1, and 13.5 percent respectively for experimental and control girls, boys, and totals, but the small numbers of experimental subjects in each group precluded the use of the chi-square test.

In general the figures in the table suggest that the experimental more than the control subjects felt that counseling had not failed them. Some of the unedited comments from experimental and control subjects presented below indicate their reactions to the process.

"I don't think I helped me because I didn't let it help me. I was as a lot of guys were my age, I thought I knew it all. Now I know differently."

"At a high school age you try to get away from counciling."

"I think I was too immature at that time to be able to use the counselling to think for myself. I just blindly accepted it."

"The only comment I have is that I wish there were some way you could have made me study more than what I did. Looking back now I can see my mistakes and they sure seem foolish."

"This isn't very flattering but I was so wrapped up worrying about whether or not I was going to be a invalid that I'm afraid I only listened half heartedly and consequently have had to rely on my own feeble powers of reasoning which as hinted above are not always the wisest."

"I feel the time to counsel and try to inspire teens is not when they are juniors or seniors but as they enter high school. Too many girls I know feel as I do that the professions might have been more satisfying surely than office work but no one (teacher, counselor, what have you) ever told them that there are satisfactions in life other than merely drawing a good wage. In my opinion there would be no teacher shortage if the teachers there are now would only attempt to present thier lot as a rewarding career instead of uninteresting drudgery."

"I can only say I do not believe I took advantage or interest in it when it was available. I was suspiscious of *your* interest and questions."

"I never had an interview with any of the salaried counselors who supposedly help youngsters plan their future."

"Due to the lack of time available, I don't think the students made the most of the counseling program."

"At the time I thought it was a good place to go as a change from study hall. I couldn't imagine myself being very interesting, like the big wheels, so I never really told anyone all my troubles, which seemed so big at the time."

"I think counseling gives each child the urge to do what they want to do most. Sometimes it doesn't work as sometimes the individual doesn't have the knowledge or money to go ahead. Perhaps if I had had the money I would have done what I wanted to do. My greatest wish was to be a doctor but after knowing I could never afford the expenses I gave up."

"*All* girls should be briefed in marriage and be given the thought that it will probably end up as first or second choice of careers. Undoubtedly it is in the back of every girls mind, tho, not given a chance to express it."

"I thought the interviews were very pleasant and I can still see my counselor's smiling face. It made me think of the future but I was already planning marriage."

"I think I shall always regret that I didn't continue my education after high school—If there would have been someone there to push me into college—or to explain how one could work their way through —I would have gone on. As it was there wasn't anyone who really cared if I finished high school, But I am now giving my husband all the encouragement one needs to get through—And will definitely do the same with our children when the time comes."

"It told of only what I could not do—not what I might be able to do."

"I feel it could have helped me more in the choice of schools—the few who advised me did a good job but more information could have been had."

"I am sorry to say, but I must repeat from your first questionnaire, I did not feel that you encouraged me to pursue the course that I did decide upon. I realize that I have not started my own practice and many things can happen but I do feel confident that I will complete the course and be able to establish a practice. I remember your discouraging my desires and suggesting teaching of some kind. I will agree that teaching is the only other vocational interest I would have."

"One incident of counceling stands out VERY CLEARLY in my mind. One of my teachers advised me not to try to go to college because I could never make the grade. I happened to be poor in that particular subject but if I had taken that teachers advice I would be very sorry today. I will never forgive that teacher and I often wonder how many other peopels confidence she deystroyed or if anyone took that kind of advice from her and was sorry later."

"I can't say it did. I think you should give tests every year to see what a person is suited for, then show it to them in *black* and *white,* then do the counseling. You seem so afraid to show results of tests you take. I can see where in some cases showing I.Q. tests, no well balanced person would get a complex from that."

"I did not take enough science courses. I wish we would have had a counselor to help us decide on our courses. I feel that there were some courses—Business Practice and Geography which were slide courses which I shouldn't have taken.

"I didn't take all the courses I wish I had. As far as I can remember I never had any counseling other than about going to college."

"At the time I was in high school, I think the counseling failed me most in not guiding me socially as well as educationally. As far as I'm concerned, almost all emphasis was put on educational guidance while little thought or time was given to social guidance. And to me these two factors are almost equally important in our world of today. Perhaps the opportunities for social development were evident and abundant, but the question was how to pick and choose wisely and correctly."

SUMMARY

In this chapter some interim appraisals of counseling obtained by comparing performances and attitudes of the control and experimental subjects at the time of graduation, six months later, and two and one-half years after completing high school have been reported. Since the findings have been given at the end of each section it is not necessary to repeat them here. In general it has been shown that few statistically significant differences between the counseled and uncounseled subjects appeared. Most of the smaller differences, however, tended to be in the direction hypothesized by guidance workers and their frequency suggests that they cannot be attributed to chance alone. The reader may now turn to the following chapter in which the final evaluations of the counseling program are reported.

CHAPTER VI

Five Years After Graduation from High School

In the initial planning of the study reported in this volume the decision was made to follow up the subjects until they had been out of high school for five years. This period was chosen because it seemed to cover a span of years long enough to permit the subjects to get well started in their careers. The work has proved so fascinating that the writer will continue to keep in touch with the subjects for many more years, but the preparation of this report marks the official end of the study as it was planned. Further treatment of the complete cumulative and follow-up records of the subjects will be conducted with new techniques for analyses of longitudinal data that are now in the process of development.

In this chapter an attempt is made to present descriptions of the activities, attitudes, and adjustments of the large representative group of high school graduates five years after they had left school. Differences and similarities between those subjects who had been counseled in the manner described in previous chapters and those who were not given such special counseling are presented in detail.

The chief source of the statistics used in this chapter was the questionnaire response received from 100 percent of the 685 subjects who were still alive in 1956. The data from the questionnaires were supplemented by intensive interviews of a sampling of 50 of the subjects, reports of employers of a sample of those subjects who were at work, and the official transcripts of all those subjects who went on to training in institutions of higher education. The wealth of information made possible many more analyses than those reported here, but an attempt has been made to cover as many of the most important findings as time and space have permitted.

MARRIAGE AND FAMILY

Five years after high school graduation 78.5 percent of the women and 45.7 percent of the men were married. Times of marriage in terms of yearly intervals after high school graduation are listed in Table 57. Only ten of the 685 subjects had married

TABLE 57. Percentages of Men and Women Subjects Married During Yearly Intervals After Graduation from High School

Married within	Women	Cumulative Total	Men	Cumulative Total	Total Group	Cumulative Total
1 year	14.9	14.9	1.6	1.6	8.6	8.6
2 years	17.3	32.2	5.3	6.9	11.7	20.3
3 years	16.8	49.0	8.7	15.6	13.0	33.3
4 years	11.8	60.8	9.3	24.9	10.7	44.0
5 years	13.8	74.6	12.7	37.6	13.3	57.3
6 years	5.0	79.6	8.1	45.7	6.4	63.7
Not married [a]	20.4		54.3		36.3	
Total	100.0		100.0			

[a] This includes four subjects who are now divorced.

classmates who were subjects of the study. Three of the 321 male subjects and nine of the 324 women had obtained divorces or were separated from their husbands or wives. Four of the divorced women had remarried but none of the men had done so. Ninety-three or 33.5 percent of the 278 women who were living with their husbands had full-time jobs outside of the home.

Two hundred and sixty-one children had been born to the married couples. One hundred and forty-five persons indicated that they had one child, 89 reported that they had 2, 26 said they had 3, and one woman reported that she had 4 children. Of the 685 subjects, 61.9 percent said that they had no children, but their written comments suggested that many were expecting to have some in the near future.

The extent to which the girls had married men whose vocations was similar to their fathers' occupations may be observed in Table 58. The 259 cases used in the table are all the married girls except those who reported that their husbands were in the armed forces and who did not designate their regular occupations. Considerable mobility is indicated since only 48, or 18.5 percent, of the 259 cases are found in the diagonals. It seems likely that

TABLE 58. Number of Women Who Married Men Employed in Same and Different Occupational Areas as Their Fathers

Fathers' Occupational Area	Number of Husbands in Areas Indicated [a]										
	Prof.	Semi-prof.	Man.	Cler.	Sales	Serv.	Ag.	Sk.	Semi-sk.	Unsk.	Total
Professional	*4*	–	1	–	1	–	2		2	–	10
Semiprof.	1	*1*	–	–		–			–	2	4
Managerial	15	1	*2*	–	3	1		5	2	3	32
Clerical		–	–	–	1	2	1	5	1	2	12
Sales	2	–	1	1	*2*	–	2	4	–	–	12
Service	4	–	–	1	2	*3*	1	5	3	3	22
Agriculture	5	–	1	2	1	1	*9*	8	3	5	35
Skilled	9	4	4	5	3	7	6	*18*	18	12	86
Semiskilled	3	–	1	1	1	2	2	6	*6*	1	23
Unskilled	6	–	–	1		2	4	5	2	3	23
Total	49	6	10	11	14	18	27	56	37	31	259

[a] Husbands were either employed in, or in training for, occupational areas indicated.

there will be changes as time passes resulting from such factors as the movement of husbands from other classes to the managerial level and from the unskilled or semiskilled to the skilled level. Currently a general trend may be observed for these high school graduates to marry men in what are commonly described as upper occupational levels although an exception to the trend may be noted in the last category. The general tendency may be noted in the following summary abstracted from the figures in Table 58.

The fathers of four of the 49 girls who married professional workers were professionals.

The father of one of the six girls who married semiprofessional workers was semiprofessional.

The fathers of two of the ten girls who married managers were managers.

The fathers of none of the 11 girls who married clerical workers were clerical workers.

The fathers of two of the 14 girls who married salesmen were salesmen.

The fathers of three of the 18 girls who married service workers were service workers.

The fathers of nine of the 27 girls who married farmers were farmers.

The fathers of 18 of the 56 girls who married skilled workers were skilled workers.

The fathers of six of the 37 girls who married semiskilled workers were semiskilled workers.

The fathers of three of the 31 girls who married unskilled workers were unskilled workers.

Girls who came from farm homes and those whose fathers were skilled workers tended to marry men employed in those areas more than girls from the other groups.

It appears that the girls who graduated from high school tended to marry men in occupational categories different from those of their fathers. The changes are probably the result of both economic and educational developments that have occurred over the period of one generation.

Three hundred and eighty-four of the 685 subjects responded to the question, "Judging from your own experience, what could schools do to prepare young people for marriage?" Of these, 99 favored a course in marriage as a school subject, 96 said more attention should be paid to the problem of getting along with others, 69 suggested that more home economics training with emphasis on child care should be required, 64 indicated need for more training in such matters as insurance, budgeting, home finances, and loans, and 41 said that specific sex education was needed. Only 15 responders said that they thought the school was doing an adequate job of marriage preparation.

GEOGRAPHIC MOBILITY

Five years after high school graduation, 87 percent of the subjects were living in their home state and almost three-fifths of them were living in the town in which they had attended high school.[1] The figures in Table 59 show that those who left Wisconsin tended to remain in the midwestern states. The slight

TABLE 59. Percentages of Subjects Residing in Geographic Areas Five Years After High School Graduation

Residence	Experimental Women	Control Women	Experimental Men	Control Men	Total Group
Home town	45.3	52.2	64.8	68.7	57.2
State of Wisconsin	38.7	30.8	22.9	25.6	29.8
Midwest	6.1	8.3	6.8	1.9	5.8
Southwest	5.0	5.5	1.9	0.6	3.4
Southeast	3.3	1.1	1.2	0.6	1.6
Northeast	1.6	1.1	0.6	1.3	1.2
Northwest	0.0	0.5	1.2	0.0	0.4
Foreign	0.0	0.5	0.6	1.3	0.6
Total	100.0	100.0	100.0	100.0	100.0

tendency to go west is seen in the 3.4 percent who had moved to the southwestern states, particularly California. Less than 1 percent had taken up residence outside the country. There is a greater tendency for girls to leave their home town and state but this difference is attributable to the number of married women who go with their husbands.

Only two differences between the control and experimental

[1] In the cases of those who were temporarily away from home in the military service or college but who gave a home address to which they intended to return, the permanent place of residence was used.

groups approached significance. More control than experimental girls remained in their home towns and slightly more of the counseled girls were living in their home state but not in their home towns.

OCCUPATIONAL AND TRAINING STATUS FIVE YEARS AFTER HIGH SCHOOL GRADUATION

Six hundred and eighty-five of the 690 graduates were still alive five years after they had completed high school. The percentages of the 685 who were in various occupational and training activities are presented in Table 60. It should be noted that the last two columns refer to sex rather than experimental or control group status. The decision to use this form was made because married women were placed in the married category re-

TABLE 60. Percentages of Subjects in Post-High School Training and Occupations Five Years After Graduation from High School

Status	Experimental Women (N-181)	Control Women (N-182)	Experimental Men (N-162)	Control Men (N-160)	Total Women (N-363)	Total Men (N-322)
Attending college	1.1	2.2	19.8	11.1	1.6	15.4
Semiprofessional training	0.0	0.6	1.2	2.5	0.3	1.9
Skilled training	0.0	0.0	2.5	4.4	0.0	3.1
Professional positions	8.8	4.9	4.3	2.5	6.9	3.4
Semiprofessional positions	0.6	1.6	1.2	5.0	1.1	3.1
Managerial positions	0.0	0.6	4.3	4.4	0.3	4.3
Clerical occupations	6.6	9.8	3.1	5.7	8.3	4.7
Sales occupations	0.6	0.0	0.6	3.1	0.3	1.9
Service occupations	0.6	1.1	1.9	1.9	0.8	1.9
Agriculture	0.0	0.0	4.9	7.5	0.0	6.2
Skilled occupations	0.0	0.0	11.1	10.0	0.0	10.6
Semiskilled occupations	0.0	0.0	13.0	15.0	0.0	14.0
Unskilled occupations	2.2	0.6	14.2	10.6	1.4	12.4
Armed forces	0.0	0.0	14.2	13.8	0.0	14.0
Unemployed	0.6	0.6	3.7	2.5	0.5	3.1
Married (girls only)	78.9	78.0	0.0	0.0	78.5	0.0
Total	100.0	100.0	100.0	100.0	100.0	100.0

gardless of whether they were working outside their homes. The large percentage of married women distorts any distribution of percentages in the various categories when men and women are combined in total experimental and control groups.

The differences between control and experimental groups of women were very small. Since more than 78 percent were married, only some 22 percent were distributed over the other categories. The small numbers left do not permit any important generalizations about such differences as appear in the professional positions category where 3.9 percent more experimentals than controls may be found, and the clerical classification in which there are 3.2 percent more controls than experimentals. It appears that, for those women who had not married, the original choice of going on to training was the determining factor in the activity carried on five years after graduation. The fact that approximately four out of five girls were married within five years (newspaper reports and other sources indicate that at least another 5 percent have been married since these data were collected) and that only a third of them were temporarily employed outside their homes suggests that the education of girls in high school must still be considered primarily as preparation for careers as homemakers.

The differences between the post-high school activities of men and women is made very clear by comparison of the last two columns of Table 60. By the end of the fifth year after high school graduation the percentages of women exceed those of men in only the marriage, clerical, and professional positions categories. In the others the percentages of men exceed those of women by significantly large amounts. The task of vocational counseling for male high school graduates would seem to differ materially from that for women.

The one important difference between the control and experimental boys appeared in the "attending college" category. In all the other classifications there are no other differences that can even be considered as indicative of a trend for one group to exceed the other. It was apparent in the questionnaire responses that many of the men were still in transition stages resulting in large part from the interruption caused by military service requirements. For that reason the occupations and training activities of a large group of the men five years after high school cannot be considered as final placements. Perhaps by the time another follow-up study is conducted five years hence it will be possible to determine whether or not there are really significant differences in the post-high school activities of counseled and uncounseled men.

PROGRESS FIVE YEARS AFTER HIGH SCHOOL

In order to set up criteria for the prediction studies described in Chapter VII the transcripts for all the subjects who attended colleges were obtained. From the transcripts it was possible to set up the six categories listed at the left of Table 61, and to

TABLE 61. Percentages of 201 Subjects Who Entered College and Performed at the Levels Indicated Within Five Years After High School Graduation

College Performances	Experimental Girls (N-52)	Control Girls (N-52)	Experimental Boys (N-56)	Control Boys (N-41)	Total Experimentals (N-108)	Total Controls (N-93)
Won honors	21.2	9.6	7.1	2.4	13.9	6.5
Made usual progress	48.1	46.2	37.5	34.1	42.6	40.7
Put on probation or took longer than usual to graduate	9.6	15.4	25.0	17.1	17.6	16.1
Dropped for low grades	3.8	5.8	12.5	17.1	8.3	10.8
Left for reasons other than low grades	15.4	19.2	10.7	9.8	13.0	15.1
Still in college as undergraduates in 1956 [a]	1.9	3.8	7.2	19.5	4.6	10.8
Total	100.0	100.0	100.0	100.0	100.0	100.0

[a] These were not probation or failing students. Most of them started college later than the others or had returned to college after absences for marriage, work, or military service.

classify each of the subjects accordingly. The honors and probation categories included any student where those circumstances were clearly indicated on the transcript. If the subject took an extra semester or summer session to complete work for his degree and the delay was caused by his low academic performance, he was placed in the third classification. When a subject was clearly dropped for low grades he fell in the fourth group but if he left for illness, marriage, work, or military service while he was in good academic standing he was placed in the fifth group.

The figures in the table show the kinds of differences between the experimental and control groups that have appeared throughout this study. There is a trend toward superiority by the experimentals but the differences do not meet the test of significance in any of the subgroups or when the two upper groups (which might be described as successful) and the third, fourth, and fifth categories (those who had difficulty) are used for comparative purposes. Although more than twice as many experimentals won honors, fewer were dropped for low grades, more graduated in the usual time, and fewer experimental women were put on probation or had their graduation delayed, the differences do not reach the statistically significant levels that have been utilized.

The differences in progress of groups of subjects who entered employment may be observed in Table 62. Their progress was determined from their own reports and checked by reports of a sample of employers five years after high school. The methods

TABLE 62. Percentages of 392 Subjects Who Were Employed and Who Performed at the Levels Indicated Within Five Years After High School Graduation

Employment Performances	Experimental Girls (N-106)	Control Girls (N-98)	Experimental Boys (N-93)	Control Boys (N-95)	Total Experimentals (N-199)	Total Controls (N-193)
Owns business, better jobs, faster than usual promotions	19.8	15.3	33.3	20.0	26.1	17.6
Promoted on schedule	15.1	13.3	12.9	13.7	14.1	13.5
Remained at same job level	59.4	66.3	43.0	49.5	51.8	58.0
Reduced in level or dismissed from job	5.7	5.1	10.8	16.8	8.0	10.9
Total	100.0	100.0	100.0	100.0	100.0	100.0

of classifying subjects by progress in employment is described in the section on prediction studies in Chapter VII. It will be seen that the differences are of much greater magnitude than those previously reported for those subjects who entered college. The largest one between counseled and uncounseled boys is 13.3 percent, which is significant at the 4 percent level. When boys and girls are grouped for a comparison of totals in the top category the test of significance again meets the 5 percent level employed. It will be noted that in all the comparisons the differences are in the direction hypothesized by guidance workers. There seems to be ample reason to reject the hypothesis that there is no difference between the experimental and control subjects in the progress they made in employment in the five-year period after they received their diplomas.

The persistency with which a few significant differences and many small significant differences in the direction hypothesized appears throughout the five-year-after-high school data suggests that the differences cannot be attributable to chance alone. The differences noted in this section were drawn from comparisons of the experimentals and controls in areas on which the counselors had spent much of their time. It appears that their efforts are reflected in the differences observed.

REASONS FOR CHOOSING JOBS

Those subjects who were employed full time at the period of the 1956 follow-up were asked to answer the question, "Why did you choose the job you now have?" In tabulating the responses to the question all married women, full-time students, and members of the armed forces were omitted. Seventy-nine and two-tenths and 75.1 percent respectively of the experimentals and controls who were currently employed, and who did not fall into the three categories listed above, answered the question in a manner that permitted unequivocal interpretation when their replies were read by three staff members of the study.

In Table 63 the percentages of subjects who gave the responses that could be classified into the seven categories are presented and

TABLE 63. Percentages in Rank Order of Responses Five Years After High School to the Question, "Why did you choose the job you now have?"

Experimental Women	%	Control Women	%
Satisfactions with work conditions	43.3	Satisfactions with work conditions	41.9
Best obtainable	13.4	Advancement	19.4
Geographic location	13.4	Geographic location	9.7
Chance for advancement	10.0	Best obtainable	9.7
Salary	10.0	Salary	9.7
Preparation [a]	6.6	Preparation	6.4
Opportunity for social service	3.3	Social service	3.2

Experimental Men	%	Control Men	%
Satisfactions with work conditions	27.4	Satisfactions with work conditions	33.3
Advancement	26.2	Salary	20.7
Best obtainable	19.0	Advancement	17.2
Preparation	16.7	Best obtainable	16.1
Salary	8.3	Preparation	10.4
Geographic location	1.2	Geographic location	2.3
Social service	1.2	Social service	0.0

[a] Usual answer here was that the subject felt prepared by experience or training for the job.

arranged in rank order by groups. The satisfactions with work conditions category contained answers which suggested that the responder obtained much pleasure from his work. This was reflected in such statements as, "I enjoy my work," or "This is just what I wanted." The best obtainable category contained responses such as, "This isn't what I wanted but jobs are scarce," or, "I wasn't prepared for anything better." In the geographic location group there were references to climate or other features of a particular part of the country. In the fourth category the subjects indicated that the job was a promotion or that opportunity for promotion was available. In the category of salary, references to such fringe benefits as insurance and retirement as well as actual pay checks were made. In the last category of the first column references to helping unfortunates, young persons, and others who needed assistance appeared. Some element of self-sacrifice for social welfare was usually implied in the last category for all groups.

The items in the table make it very clear that working conditions were the most commonly given reason for choosing a job and that social service was definitely in last place. Salary ranked fifth for three of the groups but second for the control men. Geographic location seemed rather important for the women but was a matter of slight consequence to the men.

Using the categories for the experimental and control men which contained enough cases to justify the use of the chi-square procedure, the differences just verge on the 5 percent level of significance. There is, then, some reason to reject the hypothesis that there is no difference between these groups of counseled and uncounseled men in the reasons they give for choosing their current jobs. Whether or not one believes that the differences are in a desirable direction will depend on one's philosophy. The differences between the experimental and control women were insignificant.

WAGES

All the subjects who were in *full-time* employment were invited to report on their earnings by responding to the item, "If you wish to mention your wages, fill in below your weekly wages." Only 65.3 and 65.6 percent of the total controls and experimentals responded to the invitation, but those figures were derived from responses that were given from 15 to 23 percent more frequently by women. Only 59.3 of the employed experimental men replied to the item.

The mean weekly wages for 30 experimental women, 27 control women, 64 experimental men, and 76 control men were $70.50, $69.70, $87.47 and $89.76 respectively. None of the critical ratios of the differences between the experimental and control groups reached significance, so there is no reason not to reject the hypothesis that there were no differences between the weekly earnings of these groups five years after they had completed high school.

The distributions of wages reported by the subjects appear in Table 64. To save space in the table (but not in the computations), the 17 experimental and 18 control men who were earning more than $100 a week were grouped in the top category. The highest wage reported was $250 per week. A check on the

TABLE 64. Percentages of Subjects Five Years After High School Reporting the Following Weekly Wages

Weekly Wages $	Experimental Women	Control Women	Experimental Men	Control Men	Total Experimentals	Total Controls
100 or more	0.0	3.7	26.6	23.7	18.1	18.4
90–99	3.3	3.7	6.2	15.8	5.3	12.6
80–89	20.0	11.1	18.7	26.3	19.1	22.3
70–79	40.0	37.1	23.4	21.0	28.7	25.3
60–69	16.7	22.2	14.1	5.3	14.9	9.7
50–59	10.0	11.1	9.4	5.3	9.6	6.8
49 or less	10.0	11.1	1.6	2.6	4.3	4.9
Total	100.0	100.0	100.0	100.0	100.0	100.0

earnings reported in the questionnaire was obtained by asking a random sample of 50 employers to report on the subjects' earnings. It revealed that the subjects had reported correctly in every case.

SATISFACTION WITH STATUS

The same form of the question that was used in the 1953 follow-up study appeared in the 1956 questionnaire. Following the question concerning their status the subjects were asked to show how they liked what they were doing by checking one of the items that appear on the left side of Table 65. Clearly interpretable responses were obtained from 98.8 and 97.4 percent of the experimentals and controls respectively.

Analyses of the data in the table indicated that more women than men *really* liked their current status. Approximately 20 percent more women than men chose the top category and about 10 percent more women's responses were in the upper two groups. Only 2.3 of the women indicated dissatisfaction while 12.7 of the men used the dissatisfaction categories.

TABLE 65. Percentages of Subjects Expressing Indicated Degrees of Satisfaction with their Status Five Years After High School

Response	Experimental Women	Control Women	Experimental Men	Control Men	Total Experimentals	Total Controls
I really like it.	88.9	83.0	67.3	57.1	78.8	70.9
My likes just balance my dislikes.	10.5	15.3	20.1	30.1	15.0	22.2
I don't like it but I will have to put up with it.	0.6	1.7	12.0	12.2	5.9	6.6
I hate it.	0.0	0.0	0.6	0.6	0.3	0.3

The differences between the experimentals and controls were in the direction expected if it were assumed that counseled subjects would express greater satisfaction with their current status. The numbers in the bottom row for all groups and in the second lowest category for the women are too small to permit use of chi-square methods so the computations were made with the figures in the top two classifications for women. The figures in the top three groupings were used for the men and for the totals. The differences between the control and experimental men and women separately were not significant, but the chi-square for the totals was beyond the 5 percent level. The finding suggests that there is ample reason to reject the hypothesis that there is no difference between the stated job and training satisfaction of counseled and uncounseled subjects five years after the counseling was completed.

Some of the factors that were operating to influence statements of satisfaction and dissatisfaction may be observed in the quotations below. They were given in response to the request to tell why they had indicated the degree of satisfaction that they did. They indicate that satisfaction is a composite of many factors.

"I am very happily married and have a swell husband and a wonderful little boy. We have a good life together."

"The rewards of a wife and mother are small materially but spiritually they are the greatest."

"I have a wonderful boy baby and a very nice house but my husband is very unreasonable 95 percent of the time."

"I have been forced by marital trouble to prostitute my abilities."

"Married life is OK and I love my two children but I hate life on a farm and my husband loves it so I gave in."

"My husband and I have very little common interests except our children."

"I enjoy my work. We have good working conditions and the time goes quite fast."

"I guess I like my work because it gives me a chance to think for myself. It's interesting, consuming and creative work."

"I enjoy working with young. As a kindergarten teacher I have an opportunity to work with the age groups I enjoy."

"I enjoy the feeling of being able to work for myself (be my own boss) and make a sizeable income. It also offers self-improvement and builds confidence."

"I guess there are parts of any job people dislike."

"The more time I spend on the drawing board the more I dislike it. When I get more of a variety of work I like it."

"It's piece-work. Some jobs are good and some are bad."

"I was always interested in farm life and having a wonderful offer by my daddy I have an ideal set-up."

"It isn't the type of work I like but the money is good."

"I am interested in the work and I can be sure of a secure future."

(From a barber) "I like to be with the public and talk with them."

"It's a well paying job. There's room for advancement. Because I feel I have the ability and interest in this field that out-weights any other, also it is a medium where one can express himself. It's interesting, expressive and it is less uninhibiting."

"The job isn't just what I want but an opportunity to go to foreman's school has kept me at it."

"I like it because I am making enough money to support my mother."

"I'm a little upset because of my present status—having to support my children by myself."

"My boss has a chip on his shoulder."

"I don't enjoy the process of getting an education but I realize that it will give me a better status for the future."

"I am still young enough to learn so it will help me face the problems of tomorrow. I think the more education a person can get, the better off he will be."

"Before I entered service I never realized how much an education meant. Now I think I do, and I really want one."

"I was drafted into the army so I have to serve the 2 years whether I like it or not."

"It's been a wonderful experience for me (army) but now I want to get out and go to school."

"The army to me is an easy life for a person who has no ambitions in life. I get no satisfaction what so ever in my job."

SATISFACTION IN RETROSPECT

It might be assumed that subjects who had received special counseling in high school would be more satisfied with their activities during their early post-high school years than those who had not been counseled. The figures in Table 66 indicate that there is a slight but not statistically significant difference between the total

TABLE 66. Percentages of Responses Five Years After High School Graduation to the Question, "If you could live over again the last five years since you left high school, would you do the same things as you have done?"

Responses [a]	Experimental Women	Control Women	Experimental Men	Control Men	Total Experimentals	Total Controls
Yes	79.3	77.4	55.5	51.2	68.3	65.1
No	19.0	20.9	42.6	46.2	29.9	32.8
Undecided	1.7	1.7	1.9	2.6	1.8	2.1
Total	100.0	100.0	100.0	100.0	100.0	100.0

[a] Only 20 controls and six experimentals did not answer this question.

groups. More of the experimentals reported that they would do the same things that they had done for the past five years if they could live the years over again. The breakdown by sex groups indicates that there is more than twice as much difference between the experimental and control men as between experimental and control women. The differences, while in the general direction that has been found in previous analyses, are not large enough to permit rejection of the hypothesis that there is no difference in retrospective satisfaction between the counseled and noncounseled subjects.

Some of the comments that followed their answers to the question are given below.

"I would have saved my money, stayed home a lot more, and would have picked my friends a little more carefully, because for a while we sure did have a wild time. Of course your first real paycheck and a little bit of freedom did seem like the thing for a teenager."

"It's been a muddling process, but I have learned much from my mistakes, and I think I'm a better person for it."

"I wouldn't have had a child so soon after we were married. I would have waited until we had a house and I didn't have to work."

"I wouldn't marry so soon. I know now it was a big mistake marrying so soon."

"I probably would enter the service right after graduation."

"I would do construction work in different parts of the country instead of in one place."

"Work in town where I could work my way up."

"Try a job other than farming."

"Although I've five years wiser, having a college education would have helped me quite a few times."

"While a B.A. in international relations, 3 semesters of law school and flying in the Air Force appear quite disjointed, a broad background arises which I consider invaluable."

"We did not have it easy these past 5 years financially, but I would do it over again because we have gained so much from some of the hardships we have had."

"I'm proud to have served my country in time of war."

CUMULATIVE RECORD OF POST-HIGH SCHOOL OCCUPATIONAL AND TRAINING ACTIVITIES

The three follow-up studies have provided data for the cumulative record of vocations and training experiences that appears in Table 67. It is a composite table and the same persons are not necessarily in the same categories at each period. The data from which it was compiled are presented in Appendix II. Study of the material reported there will make it possible for the reader to observe the variations of choices of each individual over the eight-year period of the study. The following discussion refers to the composite picture obtained by counting the numbers and computing the percentages of the subjects in each category at the time the follow-up results were obtained. Thus the data in Table 67 are used in a cross-sectional manner even though the same individuals were used. Those in Appendix II are longitudinal.

The differences in the activities of males and females, regardless of their control or experimental group classification discussed in previous sections, become more striking the longer the subjects are studied. Marital and martial factors produce the largest percentages for the women and men in the whole table. The marital

TABLE 67. Percentages of Experimental and Control Subjects in Occupation and Training Six Months, Two and a Half, and Five Years After High School Graduation

Status	Experimental Girls (N-181)			Control Girls (N-182)			Experimental Boys (N-162)		
	1951	1953	1956	1951	1953	1956	1951	1953	195
Attending college	22.1	18.8	1.1	19.2	12.1	2.2	30.1	21.6	19.
Semi-professional training	8.3	7.2	0.0	7.7	5.5	0.6	1.9	0.6	1.
Skilled training	0.5	0.6	0.0	3.3	0.0	0.0	3.1	3.2	2.
Professional positions	0.0	0.0	8.8	0.0	0.0	4.9	0.0	0.0	4.
Semi-professional positions	0.0	0.0	0.6	0.0	0.0	1.6	0.0	0.0	1.
Managerial positions	0.0	0.0	0.0	0.0	0.6	0.6	0.0	1.2	4.
Clerical occupations	43.7	21.5	6.6	43.9	28.6	9.8	1.9	1.2	3.
Sales occupations	5.5	2.2	0.6	3.3	1.1	0.0	1.9	1.2	0.
Service occupations	4.5	2.8	0.6	3.8	1.1	1.1	1.2	0.0	1.
Agriculture	0.5	0.0	0.0	0.0	0.0	0.0	13.0	8.0	4.
Skilled occupations	0.0	1.1	0.0	0.0	2.2	0.0	0.0	1.9	11.
Semiskilled occupations	0.5	0.0	0.0	0.6	0.0	0.0	18.5	5.6	13.
Unskilled occupations	3.9	1.6	2.2	5.5	2.7	0.6	17.9	6.2	14.
Armed forces	0.5	0.0	0.0	0.0	0.6	0.0	9.9	48.1	14.
Married (girls only)	8.3	43.6	78.9	9.9	43.9	78.0	0.0	0.0	0.
Unemployed	1.7	0.6	0.6	2.8	1.6	0.6	0.6	1.2	3.
Total	100.0	100.0	100.0	100.0	100.0	100.0	100.0	100.0	100.

Status	Control Boys (N-160)			Total Girls (N-363)			Total Boys (N-322)		
	1951	1953	1956	1951	1953	1956	1951	1953	195
Attending college	18.1	13.1	11.1	20.7	15.4	1.6	24.2	17.4	15.
Semi-professional training	1.9	3.8	2.5	8.0	6.3	0.3	1.9	2.2	1.

ABLE 67 (*Continued*)

Status	Control Boys (N-160)			Total Girls (N-363)			Total Boys (N-322)		
	1951	1953	1956	1951	1953	1956	1951	1953	1956
killed training	8.1	4.4	4.4	1.9	0.3	0.0	5.6	3.7	3.1
rofessional positions	0.0	0.0	2.5	0.0	0.0	6.9	0.0	0.0	3.4
emi-professional positions	0.0	0.0	5.0	0.0	0.0	1.1	0.0	0.0	3.1
Ianagerial positions	0.0	0.0	4.4	0.0	0.3	0.3	0.0	0.6	4.3
lerical occupations	5.6	2.5	5.7	43.8	25.0	8.3	3.7	1.9	4.7
ales occupations	3.8	0.6	3.1	4.4	1.7	0.3	2.8	0.9	1.9
ervice occupations	0.6	1.2	1.9	4.1	1.9	0.8	0.9	0.6	1.9
griculture	13.8	11.9	7.5	0.3	0.0	0.0	13.4	9.9	6.2
killed occupations	0.0	1.2	10.0	0.0	1.7	0.0	0.0	1.6	10.6
emiskilled occupations	16.3	5.0	15.0	0.5	0.0	0.0	17.4	5.3	14.0
nskilled occupations	19.4	6.9	10.6	4.7	2.2	1.4	18.6	6.5	12.4
rmed forces	11.2	47.5	13.8	0.3	0.3	0.0	10.6	47.8	14.0
Iarried (girls only)	0.0	0.0	0.0	9.1	43.8	78.5	0.0	0.0	0.0
nemployed	1.2	1.9	2.5	2.2	1.1	0.5	0.9	1.6	3.1
Total	100.0	100.0	100.0	100.0	100.0	100.0	100.0	100.0	100.0

percentage was highest at the five-year follow-up and the martial reached its peak at the two and a half year after high school period. The rapid decline in the numbers of women in the clerical occupations is particularly noticeable. The steady decrease in percentages of the women in training is attributable in part to drop-outs and completion of courses. There are higher percentages of men in training at the end of the five-year period because their education was interrupted by military training, and because many did not have enough financial resources to begin training immediately after high school graduation or to continue it without interruption. The post-high school pattern for four out of five girls is to go into commercial work or enter post-high school training and to marry within five years. The pattern for boys in general is not as simple since the only large concentration is in the armed forces category two and a half years after completing high school.

The reader who is interested in sex differences will note the following, and other, comparisons.

1. At the end of five years 15.4 percent of the men and only 1.6 percent of the girls were still in colleges or universities.
2. Twice as many girls as boys were in professional positions (mostly in teaching) at the end of the five-year period.
3. Armed forces experiences had been obtained by two women and 194 men.
4. Of the girls, 43.8 percent started careers in clerical work but only 8.3 percent remained after five years. Only 3.7 percent of the boys started in clerical work, but 4.7 percent were in that occupation five years later.
5. No girls were working in a skilled occupation in 1956 but 10.6 percent of the boys were employed at that level. The semiskilled category contained no girls five years after high school but 14 percent of the boys were in that group. In the unskilled group the boys outnumbered the girls by percentages of 12.4 to 1.4.
6. Only one girl became a farmer and she left within two years, but 6.2 percent of the boys were employed on farms.

Comparisons between control and experimental subjects did not produce as clear differences as those obtained when sex groupings alone were used. The chief difference between experimental and control girls was in the numbers who went to college, remained to graduate, and entered professional work. The other differences were small and they tended to remain so throughout the whole period as the marriage factor became more important.

The chief difference between counseled and uncounseled men lay in the numbers who went to college and persisted in their training. Small differences appeared in the greater number of controls who took skilled training or remained on the farm, and even lesser differentials appeared in the other occupational areas.

OCCUPATIONAL MOBILITY AFTER HIGH SCHOOL GRADUATION

The figures in Table 67 give the overall picture of occupational and training mobility for the group as a whole. The data obtained from the three follow-up studies made it possible, however, to determine the number of changes each of the individuals had made from the time he received his high school diploma to a period five years later. In compiling the data which appear in Table 68 it was considered a change if the subject moved from one job to another but not if it was simply a promotion on the same job. Movement of a girl from employed worker to housewife or from marriage to working divorcee was reported as one change. A boy who worked before he was drafted and then returned to the same job after military service was credited with two changes, and if he took a quite different job later three changes were recorded. Entry into training and leaving it was recorded as two changes. The percentages of subjects who made the number of changes indicated appear in Table 68.

The data were complete enough to permit valid statements about the mobility of 96.8 percent of the experimentals and 92.1 percent of the controls, but complete verifiable records over the five-year period were not available for 9.6 percent of the control men. The range of changes was from zero to nine. Reading of

TABLE 68. Percentages of Subjects Making Number of Changes Indicated in Occupational, Training, Marital, and Martial Status Within Five Years After High School Graduation

Number of Changes	Experimental Women	Control Women	Experimental Men	Control Men	Total Experimentals	Total Controls
More than 4	1.1	1.8	6.5	2.1	3.6	1.9
4	1.1	1.8	10.4	8.9	5.4	5.0
3	8.4	12.8	22.7	29.4	15.1	20.5
2	32.6	33.9	26.0	25.3	29.5	30.0
1	48.4	39.2	27.3	23.3	38.6	31.9
0	8.4	10.5	7.1	11.0	7.8	10.7
Mean	1.49	1.62	2.23	2.10	1.83	1.84

the data in the table reveals that these individuals were not highly mobile. The most common pattern for women was to make only one change (usually from a job to marriage) and for experimental and control men the mean number of changes were 2.23 and 2.10. The distributions for the men are markedly different from those for the women. Nine and a half percent of the women and 9.1 percent of the men entered into an occupation, marriage, or training experience and remained there during the whole five-year period.

The critical ratios of the differences between the means of the experimentals and controls when grouped by sex are insignificant and, since the means of the totaled groups are identical to the first decimal place, it is apparent that there is no statistically significant difference between them. There is, therefore, no reason not to reject the assumption that there is no difference in the amount of occupational and training mobility of counseled and uncounseled subjects in the five-year period following high school graduation. Factors other than experimental or control group membership in this study have influenced the mobility of these 685 subjects. Marriage, military service, financial conditions, and economic circumstances of the period under consideration may have been much more potent factors than the efforts of their high school counselors.

CONSISTENCY IN VOCATIONAL CHOICE (SPECIFIC OCCUPATIONS)

The data obtained from each subject over the eight-year period made it possible to determine the extent to which expressed choices of vocations and training for them were realized at later times.[2] Choices were obtained for the experimentals during interviews held during the tenth, eleventh, and twelfth grade years of high school. The final choice of each year expressed in the last interview was used in the computations of percentages given below. Since no interviews were held with the controls in the eleventh and twelfth grades, the choices for those years are given for the experimentals only. One month before high school gradu-

[2] See the details for each subject in Appendix II.

ation all subjects expressed their choices on the Senior Report. Data about actual occupational experiences and training were obtained on the six-month, two and one half-year and five-year post-high school follow-up studies. Finally the subjects from both control and experimental groups indicated choices for periods ahead by answering the question, "What would you like to be doing five years from now?" on the Senior Report and on the follow-up questionnaires two and one half and five years after high school graduation.[3]

In reading the figures in Table 69 it must be noted that the same persons are used throughout but the percentages apply only to the two periods indicated. Thus from the first percentage given in the fifth row of the table one learns that six months after high school graduation, 59.1 percent of the experimental girls were employed in (or were in training for) the occupation they had expressed as a choice on the Senior Report.

To ensure that all computations were done in the same manner it was necessary to set down certain guides for interpretation of choices. Thus a man who had chosen an occupation other than the armed forces, who was drafted and returned to the occupation was classified as consistent even if he was in the armed forces at the time he answered the questionnaire. Students who were in specific training for an occupation for which they had expressed a choice but who had not yet entered the occupation were considered to be consistent. Girls who said that they planned to be married at the time indicated in the first entry of each pair and who were married at the time of the second part of the entry were also classified as consistent but they were not so classified unless choice of marriage had been clearly expressed. Office workers such as file clerks, office machine operators, typists, stenographers, and those who held positions in small offices where they were required to carry on several of such activities were put in the consistent group if they had named one of the jobs as a choice and were employed in another of the same group. Occasionally it took

[3] They answered this question for ten years also on the two-and-one-half-and five-year after high school questionnaires. Their responses are indicated in another section of this chapter.

TABLE 69. Percentages of Subjects Who Were in Occupations or Training for Occupations at Certain Periods After Occupational Choices Were Given

Period covered: From	To	Experimental Girls (N-181)	Control Girls (N-182)	Total Girls (N-363)	Experimental Boys (N-162)	Control Boys (N-160)	Total Boys (N-322)
10th grade interview [a]	11th grade interview	54.3	–	–	54.7	–	–
11th grade interview	12th grade interview	50.6	–	–	50.8	–	–
12th grade interview	1 month before graduation	43.2	–	–	56.4	–	–
10th grade interview	1 month before graduation	19.9	32.7	26.3	23.1	18.8	21.0
1 month before graduation	6 months after graduation	59.1	57.4	58.3	46.7	36.3	41.5
6 months after graduation	2½ years after graduation	49.2	46.9	48.1	37.9	38.8	38.4
10th grade interview	5 years after high school	7.7	5.6	6.7	15.9	12.5	14.2
11th grade interview	5 years after high school	6.1	–	–	14.2	–	–
12th grade interview	5 years after high school	11.0	–	–	18.1	–	–
1 month before graduation	5 years after high school	17.7	13.6	15.7	23.1	16.3	19.7
6 months after graduation	5 years after high school	12.2	19.1	15.7	21.4	19.4	20.4
2½ years after high school	5 years after high school	48.6	59.9	54.3	25.8	18.1	22.0
5-year future choice given 1 month before graduation	5 years after high school	47.0	45.1	46.1	15.9	15.6	15.8
5-year future choice given 2½ years after high school	5 years after high school	74.6	77.8	76.2	23.6	26.3	25.0
5-year future choice given 5 years after high school	5 years after high school	77.9	79.1	78.5	30.2	34.4	32.3

[a] No interviews with controls in the eleventh and twelfth grades.

considerable effort to determine consistency, but the answers to the question on the follow-up questionnaire about what employed subjects actually did on the job, and the transcripts of those who went on to training, made it possible to classify all subjects adequately.

The figures in Table 69 show that variability rather than consistency is the rule in vocational choices. Perhaps the women could generally be described as consistent if one assumes that most of them had only the major goal of marriage throughout and that their expressed vocational preferences were not choices in the same sense as those made by men. It seems likely that the assumption is a safe one, but if it is, the variability in temporary choices is still high. Without introducing the difference between controls and experimentals at this time, it will be seen from Table 69 that only about three-fifths of the girls were doing six months after graduation what they had indicated they planned to do one month before commencement; that approximately half were still carrying on the same activities two years later, and that about half were doing the same thing five years after high school that they had been doing two and a half years previously. The other figures show such great changes that good prediction of activities from stated choices would not be possible. Yet it is interesting that almost half of the girls were doing, five years after high school, what they said they planned to do five years in the future when they filled out their Senior Reports one month before graduation. It seems clear, however, that marriage makes the problem of vocational choices much less significant for men than for women. Variability rather than consistency is the rule for men as well as for women during the eight years covered in this study. The percentages in the table indicate that only one in seven men was doing, five years after high school, what he had chosen to do while he was in the tenth grade and only one in five made, a month before graduation, the same choice that he named in an interview while he was in the tenth grade.[4] These figures sub-

[4] It should be noted that tenth grade interview choices were recorded only after discussion with the subjects about the occupations they had named. The choices are

stantiate over a longer period of time the findings of Schmidt and Rothney [5] and they suggest that complete planning of high school programs of study based on stated vocational preferences of tenth graders can hardly be justified.

Only 41.5 percent of the boys were doing in the autumn of the year in which they graduated what they planned to do one month before they received their diplomas. Less than one in five (19.7 percent) of the boys followed through the one-month-before-graduation choices to five years after graduation. The post-high school occupations of the boys are not stable since only 38.4 percent of the boys followed through in the same kind of work from the six-month to two-and-one-half-year after graduation periods, and only one in five (20.4 percent) had carried through to the five-year follow-up study. Even after the subjects had been out of school for some time they had not settled down since only 22 percent were in the same occupational area two and one-half and five years after graduation. The fact that they still did not consider their choices final is indicated by the fact that three-quarters of them, when asked in the second follow-up questionnaire what they would like to be doing five years hence, indicated an occupation other than the one they were in at that time.

There is no strong trend for greater consistency among the controls than among the experimentals. Study of the figures in the table reveals small differences except in five categories. The differences between experimental and control boys in consistency of choices one month before graduation and work entered six months later approach significance at the 5 percent level, which would seem to indicate that the experimental boys were more likely to go into the post-high school choices that they had made on their Senior Reports. This might suggest that they had more certain choices for the first post-high school step. The significant differences do not hold, however, for the senior report and five-year-

---

not of the snap judgment type that are often obtained when the subject is asked to fill in a blank in a questionnaire.

[5] John F. Schmidt and John W. M. Rothney, "Variability of Vocational Choices of High School Students," *Personnel and Guidance Journal,* Vol. XLVII, No. 4, 297–300, 1953.

after-high school consistency nor for the two-and-one-half- to five-year choices even though the percentage differences were substantial.

The control girls were significantly more consistent in reporting the same choices from the tenth grade to the senior report. This difference may reflect the efforts of the counselor to have the experimentals consider more occupational and training opportunities. The control girls were also significantly more consistent in their two-and-one-half- to five-year-after-high school activities, which may mean that they saw fewer opportunities for change.

In general the evidence seems to show some difference between counseled and uncounseled subjects in consistency of the choices named and implemented. It should be noted that consistency as used here does not necessarily imply something commendable. One may consider inconsistency as desirable exploration for those young people who were not yet encumbered by family responsibilities. On the other hand, some persons might suggest that the sooner a young man or woman chooses an occupation and settles down to it the better it will be for him. The latter point of view was expressed by one of the experimental boys who had tried several activities. He said (perhaps reflecting parental pressures) that he thought we would be very disappointed in him because he had changed plans so frequently.

While admitting that the generalization might be modified for certain individuals under varying circumstances, the writer tends to favor the longer exploratory period. This may have been reflected in his counseling and sensed by some of the experimental subjects, but the pressure of parents and school personnel to "make up your mind" was certainly operating. The variability noted throughout this whole section may reflect general effects of the parental, economic, marital, martial, and other pressures which these people met in the process of coming of age. The influence of counseling is seen only in exceptional cases.

Seventy-five of the 685, or 11 percent of the subjects, remained completely consistent in their five choices and activities recorded in the tenth grade interview, on the Senior Report obtained one month before graduation, and on the three follow-up studies. Of these 75, 23 were farmers, 18 were teachers, and 13 were clerical workers. Physicians, machinists, and draftsmen each had two consistent choosers and several other occupations had one each.

The figure of 11 percent consistency was obtained from the data for girls and boys combined and is reduced by the fact that so many of the girls had married. Forty-five of 322, or approximately 14 percent of the boys, remained consistent throughout. The 23 who chose farming constitute almost half of the 45 boys who were consistent.

CONSISTENCY IN VOCATIONAL CHOICE (OCCUPATIONAL AREAS)

The discussion in the preceding section has centered around the choosing of, training for, or actual employment in specific occupations. It may be said that these are too specific and that counselors should be concerned with areas or levels of choices, so the data presented below pertain to levels or areas. It should be noted, however, that the time must come for all youth to choose a specific job and go to work at it or to choose a particular course of study to pursue. A youth cannot continue to choose or work in a general area. He must choose specifically within one.

In order to determine the extent of consistency of the subjects by occupational areas, all their choices for, and actual employment in them were classified in the areas used previously in this report. They are professional, semiprofessional, managerial, clerical, sales, service, agriculture, skilled, semiskilled, and (for girls only) married. The consistency of choices and activities in the occupational areas and over the periods indicated in Table 70 were then computed.

When the broader occupational categories are used the subjects appeared to be more consistent than when specific occupations had been named. Comparison of the percentages for the comparable periods listed in Tables 69 and 70 shows that some of them are doubled. It is apparent that the important differences in consistency between the control and experimental subjects disappear, but slightly greater consistency of the counseled group may be noted in all except two of the comparisons.

TABLE 70. Percentages of Subjects Who Were in Occupational Areas or in Training for Them at Certain Periods After Occupational Level Choices Were Given

Period Covered: From	Period Covered: To	Experimental Girls	Control Girls	Experimental Boys	Control Boys	Total Experimentals	Total Controls
Tenth grade interview	Choice one month before graduation	45.9	48.4	39.5	35.0	42.9	42.0
Tenth grade interview	Five years after high school	12.7	9.9	29.0	25.0	20.4	17.0
Choice one month before graduation	Activity six months after graduation	68.5	68.1	58.6	47.5	63.8	58.5
Choice one month before graduation	Activity five years after graduation	22.1	17.6	30.9	24.4	26.2	20.8
Choice for five years after high school given one month before graduation	Activity five years after graduation	45.9	41.8	22.2	22.5	34.7	32.7

In general it appears that the consistency of the subjects (regardless of whether they were in the experimental or control group) in choosing and entering occupational *areas* can be expressed as follows:

Approximately two out of five	made the same area choice in 10th and 12th grades.
Approximately one out of five	was, five years after high school, in the occupational area chosen in the 10th grade.
Approximately three out of five	entered immediately into the occupational area (or training for it) chosen one month before graduation from high school.
Approximately one out of five	was in the occupation area that he chose one month before graduation five years after he was graduated.
Approximately one out of three	who said, one month before graduation, that he wanted to be in a certain occupational area five years after graduation, was actually employed in or in training for employment at that level five years after completing high school.

It appears from comparison of consistency of specific vocational choices and choices of occupational areas that these youth were less variable in the latter than in the former. It appears also that such variability is little influenced by counseling. Whether or not the finding of small differences between counseled and uncounseled subjects are considered important will depend, as indicated in the previous section, upon the point of view of the reader. But whether or not he prefers consistency to variability, expressed choices in terms of specific occupations or general occupational areas, and whether he counsels or does not do so, it appears that he will find that it is difficult to forecast a young adult's occupational activity from his earlier choices.

VOCATIONAL ASPIRATIONS

In the 1953 follow-up study and again in 1956 the subjects responded each time to the two questions, "What would you like to be doing five years from now?" and, "What would you like to be doing ten years from now?" In 1953 and 1956 the total percentages of responders were 90 and 92.5. Distributions of the vocational aspirations presented in Table 71 reveal some interesting developments.

It will be observed that the vast majority of the women of both experimental and control groups aspired to be married or to remain married. These choices seem realistic in view of the fact that almost 80 percent were married, that many were engaged, and that the divorce rate was very low. The second most common choice in 1953 for the women was professional work or training for it, but by 1956 that choice had dropped almost to the vanishing point along with all the others. Differences between control and experimental women are obviously insignificant.

There is no such all-inclusive category for men as marriage is for the women. The choices of the *men* are listed in rank order in Table 72, and study of the percentages (rounded off to the nearest whole number) reveals that the greatest concentration of choices lies in the field of professional work, but the range for the groups at the various times extends from 35 to 18 percent. The armed forces, unskilled labor, and clerical areas were not selected by more than 3 percent at any one time. What may seem to be a heavy concentration of choices at the upper end of the occupational scale does not suggest as much lack of realism as some previous researchers have suggested when it is considered that these men were high school graduates, that approximately 60 percent of them had gone on to post-high school training or were planning to begin or continue further training when their military obligations were completed. The managerial group contains large numbers. However, from the progress that these men had already made, it seems probable that many of them may reach their goals. There is always the possibility that some of them made their choices with tongue in cheek and that a few were doing a bit of wishful thinking.

Generally it appears that the experimental men tended to choose the professional and skilled areas more frequently than the controls while the latter tended to choose agriculture more often and to show greater signs of indecision. In the other areas the numbers of counseled and uncounseled men are either very similar or so small that dependable comparisons cannot be made.

TABLE 71. Percentages of Subjects Who Chose Occupations Indicated Two and One-Half and Five Years After High School Graduation in Response to the Question, "What would you like to be doing five years from now?" and, "What would you like to be doing ten years from now?"

Occupations Chosen	Choices Made 2½ Years After High School: Experimental Women 5 Yrs.	Experimental Women 10 Yrs.	Control Women 5 Yrs.	Control Women 10 Yrs.	Experimental Men 5 Yrs.	Experimental Men 10 Yrs.	Control Men 5 Yrs.	Control Men 10 Yrs.
Professional work or training for it	9.7	4.6	7.0	2.9	34.8	23.0	20.3	13.5
Semiprofessional work	0.0	0.0	0.6	0.0	5.3	7.4	8.4	9.0
Managerial positions	0.0	0.0	1.2	0.0	9.8	15.6	11.2	19.5
Clerical occupations	1.7	1.1	0.6	0.0	1.5	0.8	2.8	1.5
Sales occupations	0.0	0.0	0.0	0.0	2.3	1.6	4.2	3.8
Service occupations	1.1	0.0	1.2	0.6	3.8	4.1	1.4	0.8
Agriculture	0.6	0.0	0.0	0.0	9.1	9.8	15.4	15.0
Skilled work	0.0	0.0	0.0	0.0	18.9	20.5	11.2	12.8
Semiskilled work	0.0	0.0	0.0	0.0	0.8	0.8	4.9	3.8
Unskilled work	0.0	0.0	1.2	0.6	0.8	0.0	1.4	0.8
Armed forces	0.0	0.0	0.0	0.0	1.5	0.0	0.7	0.0
Married (girls only)	83.4	91.4	84.1	94.7	0.0	0.0	0.0	0.0
Undecided	3.4	2.9	4.1	1.2	11.4	16.4	18.1	19.5
Total	100.0	100.0	100.0	100.0	100.0	100.0	100.0	100.0

TABLE 71 (*Continued*)

Occupations Chosen	Choices Made 5 Years After High School: Experimental Women 5 Yrs.	Experimental Women 10 Yrs.	Control Women 5 Yrs.	Control Women 10 Yrs.	Experimental Men 5 Yrs.	Experimental Men 10 Yrs.	Control Men 5 Yrs.	Control Men 10 Yrs.
Professional work or training for it	1.7	1.1	1.7	2.3	28.8	23.6	18.6	17.5
Semiprofessional work	0.0	0.0	0.6	0.6	7.5	5.7	10.7	5.8
Managerial positions	0.6	0.0	1.7	0.6	11.0	17.2	12.2	18.3
Clerical occupations	0.0	0.0	2.6	0.0	1.4	0.7	1.4	1.5
Sales occupations	0.0	0.0	0.0	0.0	3.4	2.8	2.1	2.2
Service occupations	0.0	0.0	0.6	0.0	2.1	1.4	5.0	5.1
Agriculture	0.0	0.0	0.0	0.0	7.5	7.9	12.1	12.4
Skilled work	0.0	0.0	0.0	0.0	16.4	17.9	17.2	13.1
Semiskilled work	0.0	0.0	0.0	0.0	4.8	3.6	5.8	5.1
Unskilled work	0.0	0.0	0.0	0.0	2.7	2.8	1.4	1.5
Armed forces	0.0	0.0	0.0	0.0	5.5	5.0	2.8	2.2
Married (girls only)	96.0	97.2	94.2	94.8	0.0	0.0	0.0	0.0
Undecided	1.7	1.7	0.6	1.7	8.9	11.4	10.7	15.3
Total	100.0	100.0	100.0	100.0	100.0	100.0	100.0	100.0

PLANS FOR THE FUTURE

It was known from informal contacts with some of the subjects after they had left school that they had many different kinds of plans for the future. In view of their wide variety it was impossible to provide a check list of plans on the questionnaire, but it seemed desirable to get evidence about their plans by inviting them to respond freely to the question, "Any interesting plans for the future?" This was the last of the regular items in the ques-

TABLE 72. Vocational Aspirations of Men Subjects Five and Ten Years Later

Percentages of Choices of Experimental Men							
Choices Made in 1953 for the Years				Choices Made in 1956 for the Years			
1958		1963		1961		1966	
Professional	35	Professional	23	Professional	29	Professional	24
Skilled	19	Skilled	20	Skilled	16	Skilled	18
Undecided	11	Undecided	16	Managerial	11	Managerial	17
Managerial	10	Managerial	16	Undecided	9	Undecided	11
Agriculture	9	Agriculture	10	Agriculture	8	Agriculture	8
Semiprofessional	5	Semiprofessional	7	Semiprofessional	8	Semiprofessional	6
Service [a]	4	Service	4	Unskilled	6	Unskilled	5
Sales	2	Sales	2	Semiskilled	5	Semiskilled	4
Clerical	2	Clerical	1	Sales	3	Sales	3
Armed forces	2	Unskilled	1	Armed forces	3	Armed forces	2
Semiskilled	1	Semiskilled	1	Service	2	Service	1
Unskilled	1	Armed forces	0	Clerical	1	Clerical	1

[a] Service refers to service occupations, *not* to armed forces.

Percentages of Choices of Control Men							
Choices Made in 1953 for the Years				Choices Made in 1956 for the Years			
1958		1963		1961		1966	
Professional	20	Undecided	20	Professional	19	Professional	18
Undecided	18	Managerial	20	Skilled	17	Managerial	18
Agriculture	15	Agriculture	15	Managerial	12	Undecided	15
Managerial	11	Professional	14	Agriculture	12	Skilled	13
Skilled	11	Skilled	13	Undecided	11	Agriculture	12
Semiprofessional	8	Semiprofessional	9	Semiprofessional	11	Semiprofessional	6
Semiskilled	5	Semiskilled	4	Semiskilled	6	Service	5
Sales	4	Sales	4	Service	5	Semiskilled	5
Clerical	3	Clerical	2	Unskilled	3	Sales	2
Service	1	Service	1	Sales	2	Unskilled	2
Unskilled	1	Unskilled	1	Clerical	1	Clerical	2
Armed forces	1	Armed forces	0	Armed forces	1	Armed forces	2

tionnaire and only 70.8 percent of the counseled and 65.8 percent of the controls responded to it.

Answers to the question were classified coöperatively by three investigators into the categories reported in Table 73. It will be seen that 25.9 and 30.2 percent of the experimentals and controls respectively said that they had no interesting plans for the future.

TABLE 73. Percentages of Response to the Question, "Any interesting plans for the future?"

Response	Experimental Women	Control Women	Experimental Men	Control Men	Total Experimentals	Total Controls
Plans for marriage, family, or improvement of home situation.	58.5	52.5	22.5	29.1	40.7	41.8
Plans to begin or continue full-time education.	8.1	3.3	17.5	11.7	12.8	7.1
Plans for improvement on current job or change to new one.	4.1	6.6	23.4	21.4	13.6	13.3
All other plans (travel, self-improvement, community service, etc.)	7.3	9.0	6.6	5.8	7.0	7.6
No interesting plans	22.0	28.6	30.0	32.0	25.9	30.2
Total	100.0	100.0	100.0	100.0	100.0	100.0

These subjects actually wrote that they had no specific plans and they should not be confused with those who did not answer the question. Of those who had plans, the most common for each group except the experimental men had to do with marriage, home, and family. More than half of the women and approximately a quarter of the men referred to these areas. The men, much more than the women, indicated plans for occupational changes and the continuation or beginning of training.

Differences between the total experimental and control subjects and between women and men of the two groups are indicated by chi-squares of 4.609, 4.962, and 2.467 respectively. With four degrees of freedom none of these reaches the 5 percent level of significance. These figures indicate, despite the interesting percentage differences apparent in the table, that there is no reason to reject the hypothesis that there is no difference between the stated plans of counseled and uncounseled subjects five years after completion of the counseling. The significant differences that did exist one month before high school graduation had disappeared within the five-year period.

Samples of the responses to the questionnaire item are given below.

"I want a business of my own someday. I have the spot picked out if I can get my hands on it."

"Yes, I want to become a head football coach in a big high school around the Milwaukee area."

"More children—company I work for is growing and I feel I will better myself with it."

"As I said before I getting married in November."

"Never ask a planner if he has plans. My work as a professional will keep me very happy and occupied. Enjoy travel very much, hope to do a lot. Eventually marriage, of course."

"Our house will be our biggest plan for awhile."

"I am buying 10 or 15 head of beef feeders which will be my first real investment on the farm."

OPTIMISM—PESSIMISM

The question that appears in the title of Table 74 was designed to determine whether the counseled were more optimistic about their futures than the uncounseled subjects. Behind the question was the assumption that if the counseled subjects were more satisfied with their current status and the progress they had made during the past five years, they would look forward to continuing satisfaction. The question was answered by 94.2 percent of the experimentals and 95.0 percent of the controls.

TABLE 74. Percentages of Subjects Responding to the Question, "Looking toward the future, do you think things are going to work out well for you?"

Response	Experimental Women	Control Women	Experimental Men	Control Men	Total Experimentals	Total Controls
Enthusiastic yes	46.6	43.1	34.0	33.8	40.9	38.8
Yes	49.4	52.3	56.5	59.6	52.6	55.7
Yes and no	2.8	2.8	7.5	6.6	5.0	4.6
No	0.6	1.2	2.0	0.0	1.2	0.6
Emphatically no	0.6	0.6	0.0	0.0	0.3	0.3
Total	100.0	100.0	100.0	100.0	100.0	100.0

It is apparent from the figures given in the table that there are no marked differences between the counseled and uncounseled subjects, and computations indicate that the small differences are statistically insignificant.[6] The differences are smaller than those usually found in previous comparisons but even they are in the general direction that was hypothesized. The women were slightly more optimistic than the men, but more than 90 percent of the responses for all groups fall into either the optimistic or highly optimistic groups. Regardless of satisfaction with their current status, these young men and women felt that things were going to work out well for them in the future. Such feelings were not related to their experimental or control status during the period of this study. Perhaps their optimism was related to the interesting plans for the future that were reported in the previous section of this chapter.

CONSISTENCY IN OPTIMISM—PESSIMISM

At three times during a five-year period all the subjects were asked to respond to the question, "Looking toward the future, do you think things are going to work out well for you?" Responses to the question were obtained on the Senior Report one month before high school graduation and on questionnaires two and one-

[6] See also the report on this subject in the section by Peter Merenda in Chapter VII.

half years and five years after the subjects had been graduated. The replies tabulated in Table 75 indicate the extent to which the subjects were consistently optimistic over the five-year period. Responses to the item on at least two occasions were obtained from 99.4 percent of the subjects.

It is interesting to note that only 3.9 percent of the total experimental and control groups were *highly* optimistic all three times, but a general air of optimism is apparent if the first three sets of

TABLE 75. Consistency in Expression of Optimism One Month Before High School Graduation and Two and a Half and Five Years Later

Responses	Experimental Women	Control Women	Experimental Men	Control Men	Total Experimentals	Total Controls
Highly optimistic three times	6.7	6.2	0.6	1.3	3.9	3.9
One highly optimistic and two optimistic responses	47.2	43.2	27.1	40.4	37.9	41.9
All three responses optimistic but none highly so	16.7	18.8	20.0	16.0	18.2	17.5
Not consistently optimistic or pessimistic	28.9	31.8	48.4	40.4	37.9	35.8
Responses not clearly classifiable	0.5	0.0	3.9	1.9	2.1	0.9
Total	100.0	100.0	100.0	100.0	100.0	100.0

figures in each column are added. It should be noted that not a single subject was completely pessimistic over the five years, although 37.9 and 35.8 percent of the experimentals and controls respectively swung from pessimism to optimism over the span of years covered.

There are no consistent significant differences between the counseled and uncounseled subjects. If there are differences in the outlook toward the future they have not been discovered by the procedure that has been used in this study. The general optimism of youth is something that is, perhaps fortunately, not readily influenced by persons or circumstances. The fact that not one of these young persons was consistently pessimistic over the five-year period when they were beginning their careers and during the period that many had met serious setbacks suggests that faith in themselves and in society has not been lost.

POST-HIGH SCHOOL TRAINING

By the time the subjects had been out of high school for five years 36.7 percent of the experimental women and 50.6 percent of the experimental men had entered post-high school training of some kind other than in the armed forces. Only 33.2 percent of the control women and 46.2 percent of the control men had received such training. The figures in Table 76 also show that approximately one-third of the total group of women and almost half of all the men went on to some kind of instruction after they left high school.

TABLE 76. Percentages of Subjects Five Years After High School Who Completed or Were Enrolled in Post-High School Training

	Experimental Women	Control Women	Experimental Men	Control Men	Total Experimentals	Total Controls
Hold bachelor's degree	17.7	10.0	8.6	9.0	13.4	9.5
College undergraduate	0.6	2.8	14.2	9.0	7.0	5.6
Postgraduate study	0.6	0.5	6.2	2.6	3.2	1.5
Graduate nurses	5.0	5.0	0.0	0.0	2.6	2.7
Completed apprenticeship	0.0	0.0	3.1	5.7	1.5	2.7
Apprenticeship in progress	0.0	0.0	2.5	3.8	1.2	1.8
Obtained certificate [a]	5.6	5.5	3.7	4.5	4.7	5.0
In certificate training	0.0	0.0	0.6	2.6	0.3	1.2
Began training but did not complete it	7.2	9.4	11.7	9.0	9.4	9.2
Total	36.7	33.2	50.6	46.2	43.3	39.2

[a] Includes beautician, practical nursing, normal school teacher training, technical and commercial school graduates.

In order to determine the significance of the differences between the control and experimental women in post-high school training a 3 by 2 table was set up for chi-square computation. This was done by combining the numbers in the first three (college attendance) categories in the table, by grouping those who completed nursing and certificate training, and by using the last category. The chi-square indicated that the difference between the experimental and control groups was not quite significant at the 5 percent level. A similar comparison for the men, in which the numbers in the first three (college) groups, in the fourth, fifth, sixth, and seventh categories, and the last classification were used, was just at the verge of significance at the 5 percent level.

Although the differences do not quite meet the rather rigorous level of significance that has been set, there are some very interesting differences between the groups. It can be observed from the table that 17.7 percent of the experimental women held the bachelor's degree while only 10 percent of the uncounseled women had reached that level. Nine percent of the control men had been graduated from colleges or universities while only 8.6 of the experimentals had done so, but the percentages of experimental men who were still attending college as undergraduate or graduate students far exceeded the percentage of controls who were doing so. Other differences are so small that generalizations from them are not possible.

It will be another five years before the data on post-high school training can be really evaluated. Plans to continue training were commonly expressed in answers to the question about the plans for the future. Seventeen and five-tenths percent of the experimental and 11.7 percent of the control men said that they planned to go on for further training (Table 71). Eight and one-tenth percent of the experimental women and 3.3 percent of the control women also planned to go on. If these plans are carried through, it seems likely that the differences revealed in this five-years-after-high school study will probably approach highly significant levels within the next five years.

SATISFACTION WITH POST-HIGH SCHOOL TRAINING

Those subjects who indicated that they had entered post-high school training were asked to express their satisfaction by answering the question, "How do you feel about your training experiences?" The answers were classified coöperatively by three investigators into the categories that are used in Table 77.

TABLE 77. Percentages of Responses Five Years After High School to the Question, "How do you feel about your training experiences?"

Category	Experimental Women	Control Women	Experimental Men	Control Men	Total Experimentals	Total Controls
Highly enthusiastic	55.4	39.2	45.1	45.4	50.5	42.1
Satisfied but not enthusiastic	21.4	35.3	43.1	34.1	31.8	34.7
Showed both satisfaction and dissatisfaction	17.8	9.8	5.9	9.1	12.1	9.5
Dissatisfied	5.4	13.7	3.9	11.4	4.7	12.6
Extremely dissatisfied	0.0	2.0	2.0	0.0	0.9	1.1
Total	100.0	100.0	100.0	100.0	100.0	100.0

The numbers in the last category were too small to permit use in chi-square computations, but when the numbers in the first four classifications were used, the chi-square verged on significance at the 5 percent level for the women. For the men and the totals the chi-squares are also close to that level. There is some reason to believe that rejection of the hypothesis that there are no differences between counseled and uncounseled subjects is possible.

The differences between counseled and uncounseled subjects are particularly noticeable in the categories of high enthusiasm for and dissatisfaction with the post-high school training that these subjects had undertaken. These are particularly noticeable in the case of the women. The experimental men tended to report satisfaction but not enthusiasm. There seems to be reason to believe, from the figures given in the table in this section and the one in the previous section, that the time spent with the experimental subjects in discussing opportunities for post-high school training was time well spent in terms of the numbers who went on to it and in their satisfaction with decisions to do so.

The following quotations drawn at random from the questionnaires give some of the reasons for satisfaction or dissatisfaction with post-high school training.

"Did not enjoy my practice teaching—undecided as to whether I will ever teach."

"Should have taken typing and shorthand. Commerce School would have been more practical for me, but I don't think I would have enjoyed it."

"Not concrete. Didn't really prepare me for a specific job."

"Invaluable—I intend to finish my education when I receive my separation from active service in January, 1959."

"I enjoyed every minute of college."

"Beyond literal evaluation."

"It has aided me quite definitely in my work with personnel and their problems in the Army. I hope to enlarge on my ability to supervise personnel and direct their efforts in business upon discharge from the service."

"I could have used more 'practice teaching' than 'book learning' education courses."

"The experiences of my training have helped me in everyday living."

"I think they made me appreciate things more and expanded my viewpoint."

"I am glad that I went to the University that one year. I had thought about going there all through H.S. and would have felt I had missed something had I not gone."

"Inadequate. I learned more in an art studio. I worked part time in, the last year in art school."

"I wish I had taken those things in high school. However, I do think it was a good experience for me to get away from home."

"Far too specialized."

SATISFACTION WITH ARMED FORCES EXPERIENCES

At the time of the five-year follow-up, 194 subjects reported that they had served or were now serving in the armed forces. They indicated their reaction to their tour of duty by answering the question, "How do you feel about your armed forces experience?" Their responses were classified into the groups listed in Table 78. Interpretation of the written responses was done cooperatively by three investigators and a fourth one was asked to make an interpretation when there was disagreement about the placement of a response. The interpretations were usually unequivocable.

TABLE 78. Numbers of Responses of Control and Experimental Subjects to the Question, "How do you feel about your armed forces experiences?"

Responses	Experimental Men	Control Men	Total Men
Enthusiastic about armed forces experience	44	37	81
Expressed satisfaction but not enthusiastic	36	38	74
Stated satisfaction and dissatisfaction	10	9	19
Expressed only dissatisfaction	4	10	14
Expressed extreme dissatisfaction	4	2	6
Totals	98	96	194

It will be observed from study of the table that there are no significant differences between control and experimental subjects in their reactions to armed forces experiences. It will also be observed that 155 out of 194 men looked back favorably and only 20 of the total responded unfavorably to their tours of duty. Nineteen or approximately 10 percent of the group expressed both satisfaction and dissatisfaction in such equal amounts that it was not possible to classify them as clearly satisfied or dissatisfied.

This high expression of satisfaction in retrospect is interesting when it is compared with the high expression of dissatisfaction made by the men who were actually in the armed forces two and a half years previously. At that time 142 who were then in the armed forces had indicated their satisfaction with the experience. Only 15 percent said that they really liked it, 31 percent said their likes just balanced their dislikes, 45 percent said they didn't like it but would just have to put up with it, and 8 percent said they hated it. It seems apparent that these men followed the rather common pattern of persons who often claim dissatisfaction while they are in an enforced experience but express satisfaction with it after it is completed.

The following comments were taken directly from the questionnaires. They give a good sampling of the statements made.

"I gained a lot of knowledge plus a lot of experience, plus a lot of travel. It really wasn't so tough now that I look back at it."

"Rough at times, but pleasant to look back on now that its done. I would not consider returning to a peace time Navy."

"It was a Experience."

"I glad to have it."

"It was largely a waste of time, but I feel the leadership experience was valuable."

"Beneficial, as is most any experience one might conjure up."

"Makes a man out of a boy."

"I hated it."

"It's good for a guy, but do believe they should go in very soon after you get out of high school."

SELF-APPRAISAL (STRENGTHS)

It is frequently suggested that counseling should help a subject to recognize his own limitations and strengths. It has been shown in a previous section that it did seem to do that at the time the counseling was completed. The item on the questionnaire that is repeated in the table below was used in an attempt to discover whether it had carried over to a period five years later.

Perhaps insufficient analysis of self, modesty, misinterpretation of the question, and other factors noted previously were operating in the cases of the 14.9 percent of the experimentals and 14.6 percent of the controls who did not answer the question. Since 85.1

ABLE 79. Percentages of Responses Five Years After High School Graduation to the Question, "What is there about *you* that makes you *successful* in what you are doing?"

Responses	Experimental Women	Control Women	Experimental Men	Control Men	Total Experimentals	Total Controls
nswered "Nothing," or "I am not successful."	2.6	3.4	5.8	4.9	4.1	4.1
don't know."	2.0	3.4	4.3	6.3	3.1	4.8
he skills I possess." (Intelligence, manual dexterity, fast learner, etc.)	8.5	7.4	14.4	16.1	11.3	11.6
ly personal qualities." (Patience, perseverance, getting along with others, conscientiousness, etc.)	37.9	36.2	37.4	32.2	37.7	34.2
ly high school preparation."	0.0	1.3	0.0	0.0	0.0	0.7
ly preparation outside of or beyond high school."	0.6	0.7	1.4	1.4	1.0	1.0
ly adaptability to the demands of the job." (Like the working conditions, like the kind of work, like to learn new parts of the job, etc.)	39.9	42.9	31.6	34.9	36.0	39.1
elevant and unclassifiable answers.	8.5	4.7	5.1	4.2	6.8	4.5
Total	100.0	100.0	100.0	100.0	100.0	100.0

and 85.4 percent of the subjects did answer the question, the numbers are sufficiently large to permit comparisons of the responses of the experimentals and controls, particularly in the three areas of skills, personal qualities, and adaptability to the demands of their jobs.

The placing of the responses in the categories was done by three counselors-in-training who worked coöperatively with the author.

It may seem strange to separate adaptability from personal qualities, but the use of the separate adaptability category seemed justified because some responses referred to specific jobs or training situations while others seemed to refer to general characteristics. If the responses in these two categories of personal qualities and adaptability to a job are combined they include 73.7 percent of the responding experimentals and 73.3 percent of the controls who answered the question. Apparently these subjects felt that such personal qualities as patience, perseverance, conscientiousness, and adaptability to working and training conditions were of much greater importance than their skills, their preparation for jobs, or for post-high school education.

None of the differences between the total, sex, or control and experimental groups is statistically significant. The insignificant differences that may be obtained by doing some subtractions with the percentages given in Table 79 reveal reversals of the trends that have usually been found throughout this study. More, but not significantly more, of the controls than experimentals mentioned their skills, and adaptability to the demands of their jobs.

The percentages in Table 79 and computations of difference from the raw data indicate that there is no reason to reject the hypothesis that there is no difference between counseled and uncounseled subjects in their judgments of what makes them successful five years after the counseling was completed. It appears that the analyses of personal strengths that the counseled subjects had carried on with the counselor when they were in high school had been forgotten. Perhaps these subjects now thought that former strengths were unimportant in their current situations as, in fact, they may have been. And perhaps they had not carried on the process of self-analysis that was begun during counseling. Their comments were similar to those given in answer to the same question on the 1953 follow-up study. Some samples are given below.

"I thoroughly enjoy my work! Also I can leave it behind me—when work permits—and come home without my school problems, ready to settle down for an evening with my husband."

"If I ever did anything right in my life I did it when I got married.

I don't know what makes me successful in my marriage—It's probably because I married the right person for me."

"If man knew of his intellect that which makes him successful or unsuccessful there would be little need of a counseling study or an educational field. 'I don't know.' "

"I don't know if I am successful. My husband and I were separated and although he did some pretty bad and unexplainable things, I felt maybe I could do something to change him, so I took him back."

SELF-APPRAISAL (HANDICAPS)

As indicated previously, the question in the table heading below was designed to get an indication of self-appraisal without asking it so directly that it might be rejected. Actually only 24.8 and 28.7 percent of the experimentals and controls respectively refused or neglected to answer the question. The control girls rejected it most (35.2 percent) and the experimental boys (82.1 percent) responded most frequently. The amount of response seems particularly good when one considers that this was an open-end question that required the individual to admit that he had a handicap and to name it.

It will be observed in Table 80, however, that of those who did respond almost one-third of the total controls and slightly more than one-third of the experimentals wrote in the statement that nothing handicapped them. Again the experimental men stood out from the other groups with 41.3 percent suggesting that they had no handicaps. The direction of the differences between the total groups is again similar to what has been found previously, but again the differences are not statistically significant.

Sufficient numbers were available in only two categories to justify acceptable computations of significance of differences. The most common response given by 30.6 percent of the experimentals and 34.4 percent of the controls was concerned with handicaps in such personal characteristics as lack of self-confidence, exhibiting temper, nervousness, procrastination, too easy-going and similar qualities. The women gave such responses twice as frequently as the men. This may indicate more self-analysis, more of the charac-

TABLE 80. Percentages of Responses Five Years After High School to t[illegible] Question, "What is there about *you* that *handicaps* you in what you are doing[illegible]

Responses	Experimental Women	Control Women	Experimental Men	Control Men	Total Experimentals	Total Contr[illegible]
"Nothing handicaps me."	28.0	26.3	41.3	36.5	34.9	31.[illegible]
"I don't know."	0.0	0.8	0.0	0.8	0.0	0.[illegible]
"My lack of skill." (Physical handicaps, can't follow directions, can't understand job, etc.)	10.4	11.9	17.3	20.6	14.0	16.[illegible]
"My personal qualities." (Lack of self-confidence, bad temper, nervous, procrastination, too easy-going, etc.)	42.4	45.8	19.5	23.8	30.6	34.[illegible]
"Inadequate high school preparation." (Did not take the right courses, enough courses, etc.)	0.8	0.0	2.3	1.6	1.6	0.[illegible]
"Inadequate preparation outside of high school."	0.0	2.6	3.7	0.8	1.9	1.[illegible]
"My failure to adapt to the job." (Lack interest, dislike job, working conditions, etc.)	1.6	0.8	2.3	3.2	1.9	2.[illegible]
"Job is unsuitable." (Working conditions not suitable, job is not interesting, challenging, etc.)	0.8	0.8	5.3	4.0	3.1	2.[illegible]
Irrelevant and unclassifiable responses	16.0	11.0	8.3	8.7	12.0	9.[illegible]
Total	100.0	100.0	100.0	100.0	100.0	100.[illegible]

teristics noted, or perhaps just more willingness to admit them. Fewer experimental than control responses, in total and by sex groups, fell in this personal qualities category, but the differences did not reach the size required to indicate statistical significance.

The second category in which sufficiently large numbers for analysis appeared was concerned with lack of self-satisfying performances resulting from stated physical or mental handicaps. The differences between the groups were again so small that it was not possible to permit any generalization about differences between the total or sex groups.

In general the answers to the question that was posed did not reveal any important differences between the counseled and uncounseled subjects. During the five years that the subjects had been out of high school many may have chosen to move out of training or occupational areas in which they felt handicapped, and it appears that the controls had succeeded in this almost as well as the experimentals. If there were significant differences between counseled and uncounseled subjects in reporting of their handicaps at any time, they had almost completely disappeared in the five-year period. The differences between young men and women, regardless of their control or experimental status in this study, were significant and merit further investigation.

SATISFACTION WITH HIGH SCHOOL EXPERIENCE

In this section we are concerned with what this good sample of high school graduates reported as the most helpful contribution of their high school experiences. Eighty two and one-half percent of the experimentals and 76.3 percent of the controls responded to the open-end question stated in the title of Table 81. Their answers indicated that they thought that the most valuable contributions of high school training were in preparation for a vocation and for post-high school training, in social adjustability, in personal development, in development of values, and in preparation for marriage, in that order. The order of the first two, and to some extent the last, may have been determined by the post-high school activities of the subjects. The others, since they are common to all subjects, may be considered as their choices regardless of their post-high school activities. They do seem to have reflected the relative emphases of the schools as they were revealed in curriculum practices and teachers' statements.

The subheadings in parentheses behind the main entries in the

TABLE 81. Percentages of Responses Five Years After High School to the Item, "Looking back at your high school training, tell how it helped you most."

Responses	Experimental Women	Control Women	Experimental Men	Control Men	Total Experimentals	Total Controls
"It did not help."	2.7	5.0	9.7	10.7	6.0	7.6
"Helped in personal development." (Developed interests, ambitions, self-confidence, application.)	6.1	6.5	7.5	9.8	6.7	8.0
"Prepared adequately for vocation."	34.2	33.1	26.9	31.1	30.7	32.2
"Prepared adequately for marriage and homemaking."	9.4	9.3	1.5	0.0	5.7	5.0
"Prepared adequately for post-high school training."	20.8	16.5	14.9	16.4	18.0	16.6
"Prepared adequately in social adjustability." (Learned to get along with others, made friends, prepared for citizenship obligations, etc.)	15.4	14.4	19.4	12.3	17.3	13.4
"Developed values." (Learned value of an education, stimulated further study, stimulated planning for the future, learned how to think, broader outlook, etc.)	6.1	6.5	8.2	8.2	7.1	7.3
"Don't know" and irrelevant or unclassifiable answers.	7.3	8.7	11.9	11.5	8.5	9.9
Total	100.0	100.0	100.0	100.0	100.0	100.0

table indicate the guides for placing the responses in the categories. The division into personal and social categories represented an attempt by four workers to separate the "getting along with others" type of responses from those concerned with personal characteristics that might be developed even if one did not learn to get along with others. If the reader prefers to put these categories together, the combined totals would still be less than the combination of preparation for vocation and post-high school training responses.

It is worth noting that more men than women said that high school did not help them at all. Although only 6 and 7.6 percent of the total groups of experimentals and controls respectively said that it had not helped them, it will be observed that only 2.7 percent of the experimental girls and 5 percent of the control girls made such statements. In some cases the subjects seemed to give grudging credit to the school.

The largest difference in the table is that between responses of experimental and control boys which fell in the social adjustment category. The difference of 7.1 percent does not quite reach the five percent level of significance. All the lesser differences are not statistically significant. In general the computations indicate that there is no reason to reject the hypothesis that there are no important differences in the reactions of these counseled and uncounseled five-year graduates to their high school experiences. If the addition of counseling to their regular program made differences in the way that they thought high school helped them most, those differences appear to have almost vanished by the time they had become citizens eligible to vote for school appropriations. Samples of the reasons they gave for responding to the question in the way they did are given below.

"Of course high school training helped me most in preparing me for my four years of college, inasmuch as I selected courses which would be of most value toward my college education. But I cannot neglect the fact that it was in high school that I developed a definite desire to advance socially as well as educationally."

"I believe that the high schools should provide more instruction in crafts for the boys and more general practical training for girls. From my own experience, I've seen many of the girls that I went to school with doing mediocre jobs and wishing that they had training in some line of work that would provide them with a living. The fellows are the same—taking factory jobs and the like—although they dislike the work—because they have to make a living. I would have liked to have gone on to college but found it impossible as I had too many financial responsibilities when I graduated from high school, so I'm glad that I took the one and only course provided by the school where I could go out and support myself."

"I think that in addition to the academic preparation, the extra-curricular activities helped me the most. I spent my first eight years of schooling in a parochial school, which was wonderful academically but not much else—it certainly didn't help much in development of the personality."

"How can high school training help anyone?"

"It seemed to make it easier in meeting people plus its made me a lot of lasting friendships which I cherish very much."

"Not too much as far as studies went, but very much as to meeting people and getting along with people."

"Practically everywhere that I have been I had to use my high school training one way or another and especially in the service."

"I feel my high school training helped me the most by serving as a place of maturing completely and learning to make decisions and becoming socially aware of life time obligations."

"I would say mostly by the broadness of choice in various fields."

"It taught me office training and therefore I never would have to be completely dependent on someone else for my livelihood."

"Agriculture helped me in my line of work in feeding, seeding and soil building. Woodworking helped me in building things around the farm."

"I was better prepared scholastically for college than most people I have checked with. The school also offered an extensive extra-curricular activity program which helped general development."

"My clerical training helped me get a very good job as a bookkeeper and filing clerk. Home Ec. helped me manage my home. Everything else has helped me to have a broader understanding of world problems, English to write better and appreciate reading."

"It built my self-confidence which can be more helpful than anything."

"It gave me a fairly good background in social sciences and literature. Some teachers I still feel close to and can talk things over with."

DISSATISFACTION WITH HIGH SCHOOL EXPERIENCE

All items in the questionnaire used in the 1953 and 1956 follow-up studies that were designed to get evidence of dissatisfaction were poorly answered. Whether the subjects were afraid to write them on a questionnaire which they had signed, did not feel any dissatisfaction, or were simply unwilling to express any that they had is not known. In any case 58 and 53.8 percent of the experimentals and controls chose not to write an answer to the open-end question which appears in the title of Table 82. The experimental men made the best record with a 61.7 percent response and the control women the poorest with only 52.8 percent. It appears that the negative type of item is not a good one in the follow-up questionnaire.

Of those who did respond, 26.1 percent of the counseled and 20.7 percent of the controls said that high school had not failed to help them. If we assume that a large proportion of those who did not respond did feel satisfied, add the proportion who said that it had not failed, and add a few from the I-don't-know category, it can be assumed that at least more than half of these graduates felt that their high school had not failed to help them.

Those subjects who did respond said that the school failed them with respect to the following factors in descending order: adequate preparation for post-high school training and development of values in approximately the same amounts, adequate preparation for a vocation, marriage and homemaking, personal growth, and social development. It should be noted that the question on how high school had failed to help these subjects followed im-

TABLE 82. Percentages of Responses Five Years After High School to the Item, "Looking back at your high school training, tell how it failed to help you."

Responses	Experimental Women	Control Women	Experimental Men	Control Men	Total Experimentals	Total Controls
"It did not fail."	21.2	25.0	31.0	15.9	26.1	20.7
"Failed in personal development." (See Items in Table 81 above.)	5.0	7.3	4.0	4.5	4.5	6.0
"Failed to prepare adequately for a vocation." (Inadequate academic or vocational preparation for job, failed to show application of facts to job, etc.)	16.2	10.4	12.0	20.5	14.1	15.2
"Failed to prepare adequately for marriage and homemaking."	9.1	14.6	4.0	0.0	6.5	7.6
"Failed to prepare adequately for post-high school education." (Did not learn to study, did not learn essentials, inadequate prerequisites, inadequate curriculum, etc.)	16.2	15.6	17.0	20.5	16.6	17.9
"Failed in social development." (See items in Table 81 above.)	5.0	4.2	0.0	1.1	2.5	2.7
"Failed to develop values." (School was not inspiring, challenging, did not teach responsibilities, etc.)	17.2	14.6	25.0	20.5	21.1	17.4
"Don't know" or unclassifiable answers.	10.1	8.3	7.0	17.0	8.6	12.5
Total	100.0	100.0	100.0	100.0	100.0	100.0

mediately after the question on how high school had helped them most. It seems likely that the response to the previous question may have influenced the answer that was given to the second one.

The most striking difference of responses in the table is that of 15.1 percent between experimental and control boys who answered that high school had not failed to help them. This difference is significant beyond the 5 percent level. Almost equally significant is the difference in responses of counseled and uncounseled men (8.5 percent) who indicated that the high school had failed to prepare them adequately for a vocation. These two differences are the only large ones in the table. The lesser differences are usually in the direction that might have been anticipated from the data of the previous follow-up study and other computations from the data of this five-year study, but they are not significant.

Many of the subjects who responded to this item wrote at great length and with much feeling. Some of their feelings are reflected in the unedited quotations that follow:

"I could say a lot about school improvement if I wished to (in reference to *public* schools), however, I think you will get the point when I tell you that my children will go to parochial schools. There is more difference here than merely the teaching of religion."

"We were not given enough work. You became lazy and then did a mediocre job. There wasn't enough work to hold our interest. The kids resent work at the time but *give it to them.*

"Kids should be given more work. Keep them on the go. Doing things. If you don't, you stagnate. There is too much mediocrity in this country now. Don't train them to be that way!

"Kids with any inclination toward further study should be required to take two or three years of Math, four years of English, one or two years of a foreign language, typing, chemistry, physics, speech, basic psych. and be given reading training. A course should be developed to teach kids how to study."

"I can't remember really wanting to learn my subjects in high school. I did the work and got good grades but don't remember any inner desire to learn a subject—the only class I remember more than vaguely now (subject treated and manner in which conducted) is my college prep. English class in my senior year—could the real enthusiasm of a child first learning be somehow capture and continued in his late elementary and secondary education—and on?"

"I only regret that I didn't 'apply' myself—It seems as though I wasted a great deal of time in school—I think now of what I could have done with some of those extra hours.

"Another thing, I never really learned to comprehend reading until after I was out of school—I read but didn't always know what I was reading. I learned fast after I was 'working for a living'—Ha! Ha!"

"Whether this is due to me or my education I don't know, but I think I'm just now learning the correct attitudes of study (that is intellectual curiosity, not being afraid to give the wrong answer). The lack of good attitudes like these have been my biggest drawback on a college level."

"The absence of comprehensive final exams prevented me from getting what I feel was necessary training in preparing for and taking this sort of test. The lack of this training proved almost overwhelming during my first year of college."

"I feel the greatest essential need in the high school program is the actual on the job experience of doing something instead of just reading and studying and hoping you can apply this study when you graduate."

"I feel that the courses in high school need to have more emphasis on actual experience in doing something instead of so much reading and trying to really understand just from books."

"Although this failure may revert back to my nature, I feel that my high school failed to stress the importance of the social opportunities available. I think I myself could have developed much more socially if I only had realized what could be gained by participating in many of the activities which I permitted to slip through my fingers."

"I only wish I could have the chance to have the school I had five years ago, I sure would make better use of it. I think I could have avoided the mistake of having one failure in marriage."

"I have one comment on the 'improvement of schools.' If the salary of teachers were to be raised, it might encourage more people to take up the profession, hereby eliminating the over-crowded class-room conditions now existing."

"You probably heard this before from other students. I wish I studied harder. Its the same with me. During that time, I didn't have my goal to make. So naturally, I didn't pick the right subjects. Guess I was one of the unusual ones who didn't know what he wanted to be."

"I have always and still think the ways most school subject are forced in a High School Student is unfair—to teachers—pupils—tax-payers alike. Several of us girls have talked of this many times. Of the time a person is in high School he usually has some idea of what he's interested. me—clerical or office work, Alright, I would have been much better to have spent 2 times as much study on that than on old world History for example I don't give a hoot whether Cleopatra was a little Sirem or a damsel in distress. Sure I remember it but have no need for it and never will as I'm not a teacher. I had it cramed down my throat in Grade School. Turned right around in High School and had it cramed down again. Not only old World Histry but Citizenship, History of the U.S., Science, English Literature. Could have used and benefited much more with that time spent in office training. My particular interest. I had to take 3 subjects not of my choosing and chose one that I wanted. Why not reverse that I'd be happier in School and a much better trained person out. I know life isn't always what one wants but doesn't a person get enough of that in normal life without it in School. You are a highly educated man and won't agree I know. I haven't met or heard of one that has. But I believe I'm average—not going on to school with an average job and life. I think most of us will agree. I sincerely believe that that system will be used but will be years yet. I hope my son has his choice."

"I wasn't an excellent student. Mostely, because I was too busy fooling around and having a good time. I've never regretted it."

"I believe I lost much in my high school education because of an inferior-complex acquired early in my freshman year do to the loss of several front teeth. This has not been confirmed by any medical society but I have studied sychoanalyst and believe I have reached an unprejudice answer. What I think I have lost, I tried to pick up on my own. As far as studies are concerned I believe I have done a fair job, but something I find hard to achieve is the social association I missed. I believe I still suffer from the complex in this respect, but believe in time it will remedy itself."

SATISFACTION WITH COUNSELING

The reader is referred back to the discussion of the limitations of reports of client satisfaction that appeared in the section with the same title as this one in Chapter V. Those limitations should be considered in the study of the figures in Table 83. It is apparent that the generally favorable reaction that appeared in the two and one-half year after high school follow-up has again been found. Only 27.4 and 35.1 percent of the experimentals and controls respectively failed to respond to the item and even some of those who did not answer this item made comments about the counseling or lack of it on the last page of the questionnaire. Such responses are not incorporated in the table in this section.

Of those experimentals who replied to the question, 1.2 percent said that they had received no counseling despite the fact that not one of them had had less than three interviews. Twelve percent of the comments in answer to the item, "Looking back at the counseling you had in high school, tell how it helped you," could not be interpreted meaningfully and they were put in the irrelevant or unclassifiable answers category in the table. The percentage of the responses of the experimental group, then, who answered the question and who agreed that they had received counseling and who gave relevant and classifiable responses was only 59.4.

The usable responses indicated that the experimental subjects felt that the counseling had helped them in personal development, in vocational choices, educational adjustment, future planning, and providing a chance to talk things over, in that order. The controls who had obtained their counsel from sources other than the investigators arranged their responses in the same order. The percentages were higher in all cases for the total group of experimentals and they were so much higher in the category of assistance in personal development that the difference was significant well beyond the 1 percent level. This significant difference was attributable in part to the fact that more than twice as many ex-

TABLE 83. Percentages of Responses Five Years After High School Graduation to the Item, "Looking back at the counseling you had in high school, tell how it helped you."

Responses	Experimental Women	Control Women	Experimental Men	Control Men	Total Experimentals	Total Controls
"It did not help."	12.6	15.4	21.3	21.9	16.9	18.5
"It helped vocationally." (Helped to choose the right vocation, channeled thinking on vocation, established vocational goals, etc.)	14.2	12.8	13.9	7.6	14.1	10.3
"It helped educationally." (Helped to choose right courses, get better grades, stimulated educational planning beyond high school, etc.)	15.7	9.4	10.7	14.3	13.3	11.7
"It helped in planning for the future." (Made me aware of opportunities, made me think of the future, etc.)	12.6	7.7	12.3	14.3	12.4	10.8
"It helped my personal development." (Provided help in self-analysis, built self-confidence, helped with adjustment problems, made me aware of assets and limitations.)	29.1	13.7	20.5	12.3	24.9	13.1
"It gave me a chance to talk things over." (Provided someone to talk to, someone interested in me, someone who cared about me, etc.)	7.1	1.7	3.3	1.0	5.2	1.3
"I received no counseling."	0.8	27.3	1.6	14.3	1.2	21.2
"It kept me in school." (It kept me in school when I was going to leave.)	0.0	0.9	0.0	1.0	0.0	0.9
Irrelevant and unclassifiable answers	7.9	11.1	16.4	13.3	12.0	12.2
Total	100.0	100.0	100.0	100.0	100.0	100.0

perimental as control girls felt that they had been helped in personal development. It should be noted also that twice as many experimental as control boys felt that they had received help in their vocational choices.

The responses of the control group indicate that they were not particularly pleased with what counseling they had received. Of the controls, 35.1 percent did not reply, and this may indicate that they did not feel that counseling had helped. Of those who did respond, 21.2 percent said they had received no counseling, and 12.0 percent made irrelevant or unclassifiable responses. Actually then, only 195 of 342, or 57 percent of the control subjects, expressed satisfaction with the counseling that they had obtained from sources other than those provided by the special counselors of this study. They were least satisfied with their chance to talk things over, vocational assistance, planning for the future, educational development, and personal development, in that order.

The responses to the direct question about how counseling had failed to help are presented in the next section. They indicated even more convincingly than the above figures that the control subjects who had no special counselors felt that the advisers they had chosen had failed them.

DISSATISFACTION WITH COUNSELING

As in the 1953 follow-up study, the question which asked the subjects to tell how counseling had failed to help them was the item most frequently omitted. Only 41.7 percent of the experimentals and 39.2 percent of the controls answered the question. It was not possible to determine the reason for this failure to respond. It may have been the fault of the form in which the item appeared, the subjects' feelings that they had no dissatisfaction to report, forgetting, inadequate comprehension of the term "counseling," or some other factor of which the investigators were completely unaware.

The responses of the subjects who did answer the question are reported in Table 84. Study of the figures in it suggests that there are some important differences between the experimental and

TABLE 84. Percentages of Responses Five Years After High School Graduation to the Item, "Looking back at the counseling you had in high school, tell how it failed to help you."

Response	Experimental Women	Control Women	Experimental Men	Control Men	Total Experimentals	Total Controls
"It did not fail."	44.6	22.4	47.8	29.3	46.1	25.4
"It failed to establish a *definite* educational or vocational goal."	8.1	7.9	8.7	1.7	8.4	5.2
"It directed me toward the wrong educational or vocational goal."	10.8	3.9	8.7	5.2	9.8	4.6
"It failed to stimulate planning for the future."	4.1	1.3	1.5	5.2	2.8	3.0
"It failed to help in the solution of personal problems."	2.7	3.9	4.3	0.0	3.5	2.2
"Received no counseling."	1.3	22.4	1.5	15.5	1.4	19.4
"Did not get enough counseling."	8.1	23.7	10.1	10.3	9.1	17.9
Irrelevant or unclassifiable responses	20.3	14.5	17.4	32.8	18.9	22.3
Total	100.0	100.0	100.0	100.0	100.0	100.0

control subjects. The difference between the total number of controls and experimentals who said that counseling had not failed them is significant well beyond the 1 percent level, the difference between girls near the 1 percent level and between the boys near the 5 percent level. There are many other large percentage differences in the table, but the small numbers in some of the response categories did not permit use of the chi-square test of significance of differences that has been used throughout. Thus in the case of the response, "I received no counseling," by the women there is a difference between experimentals and controls of 21.1 percent, but the small number represented by the 1.3 of the experimental women who gave that response prevented satisfactory calculation of the significance of the difference.

It is apparent that small groups of both experimental and control subjects alike thought that counseling should have helped them to establish *definite* educational or vocational goals. They also said that counselors had directed them toward wrong goals, failed to help them in the solution of personal problems, and in stimulation of planning for the future. The control men are exceptional in these categories. Large percentages (19.4 and 17.9 percent of the controls who responded) indicated that they had none or not enough counseling, while 1.4 and 19.4 percent of the responding experimentals said that they had no counseling or not enough.

The responses to this item were small in number and difficult to evaluate. The fact that significantly greater numbers of controls said that counseling did not fail to help may mean only that they had not learned what to expect of counseling and, not expecting much, they were less disappointed with what they got. The finding that larger percentages of experimentals said that it had failed in the second, third, fourth, and fifth entries in the table may have meant only that the experimentals felt that they knew the counselors well enough to criticize their work. There may also have been some projection of reasons for failure onto the counselors by those who felt that they had been unsuccessful in reaching their educational and vocational goals or in solution of personal problems. In any case it seems quite clear that the subjects who had received the special counseling and who chose to respond to the item were more critical of the counseling than those who had obtained their counseling from other sources. The findings suggest that counselors should indicate the limitations of what they can do so that too much is not expected of them, and that if they fail to do so, many of their counselees will not hesitate to tell them that they have failed. The reader is referred to the comments about counseling quoted in the counseling evaluation sections of the previous chapter.

SOURCES OF ADVICE AFTER HIGH SCHOOL GRADUATION

In asking the question, "If you needed help in the last five years in making decisions, to whom did you go?" the investigators were trying to discover whether the counseled subjects tended to go to different sources than the uncounseled subjects for counsel after they had finished school. The hypothesis was that the counseled subjects might have learned different sets of values to guide them when choices had to be made. Although the item was near the end of the questionaire, 77.6 and 78.4 of the experimentals and controls gave answers that could be classified into the categories given in Table 85. When two sources of advice were given the first one was recorded.

Study of the percentages in the table indicates that the subjects tended to go to their families or spouses for advice most frequently. The second frequency of response was "no one." After

TABLE 85. Percentages of Subjects Who Went to the Named Sources for Advice in Making Decisions

Source	Experimental Women	Control Women	Experimental Men	Control Men	Total Experimentals	Total Controls
Member of family other than husband or wife	30.4	34.0	38.1	47.8	33.8	39.9
Husband or wife	42.6	37.9	15.3	11.3	30.5	26.5
Religious adviser	4.0	7.8	4.3	3.5	4.1	6.0
Staff member of high school	0.7	0.0	0.8	1.7	0.8	0.8
Former counselors of this study	2.0	0.0	2.5	0.0	2.3	0.0
Staff members of school or college attended	4.0	2.0	1.7	2.6	3.0	2.2
Employers or fellow workers	0.7	3.9	8.5	3.5	4.1	3.7
Professional persons (lawyers, bankers, doctors)	1.4	3.9	0.8	0.9	1.1	2.6
"No one" and miscellaneous [a]	14.2	10.5	28.0	28.7	20.3	18.3
Total	100.0	100.0	100.0	100.0	100.0	100.0

[a] This category includes a few cases where the person named was unknown to the readers of the questionnaires.

these they turned to employers or fellow workers, staff members of a training institution attended, professional persons such as bankers, lawyers, or doctors, former counselors in this study, and staff members of their high schools, in the order given. The family and "no one" categories in the table contain almost 85 percent of the responses.

The differences between the various percentages in the table seem to be produced by factors other than membership in the experimental or control group while the subjects were in high school. Almost 10 percent more of the control than experimental men turned to members of their families, but the difference for women is less than 4 percent. More than twice as many women as men turned to their marriage partners for advice, and more than twice as many men than women indicated that they went to no one for advice. Five percent more experimental than control men sought advice from employees or fellow workers, but more control than experimental women went to such sources. More than 2 percent of the experimental subjects reported that they had gone to the counselors of this study and no controls indicated they had used this source. (These latter figures throw some doubt on the responses to the item, since considerable numbers of both groups had come to the counselor for counsel during the past five years.) It is significant that less than 1 percent of the subjects had sought advice from their former high school teachers.

CIVIC, RELIGIOUS, SOCIAL, AND RECREATIONAL ACTIVITIES

On one item of the questionnaire the subjects were asked to name any political organizations, clubs, social, recreational or church groups that they had attended regularly during the past three years. Space did not permit listing of the many possible activities in separate categories on the questionnaire and the responses of the subjects, therefore, were only in terms of those which the subjects remembered and which they thought important enough to report. Sixty-eight percent of the experimentals and 64 percent of the controls answered the question. It may be safe to assume that failure to answer meant that the subjects did not participate in activities.

The number of activities mentioned by any one subject ranged from 0 to 8. To save space in the table, those who engaged in more

TABLE 86. Numbers of Subjects Five Years After High School Who Said That They Attended Regular Meetings of Stated Numbers of Political, Religious, Recreational, and Social Groups

Number of Organizations Regularly Attended	Experimental Women	Control Women	Experimental Men	Control Men	Total Experimentals	Total Controls
More than three	16	4	8	3	24	7
Three	9	9	9	6	18	15
Two	24	19	14	12	38	31
One	37	54	39	33	76	87
None	39	34	40	45	79	79
Total	125	120	110	99	235	219
Mean	1.58	1.13	1.17	0.88	1.39	1.02

than three activities have been grouped in the top category. The range in means of the six groups is from the 1.58 of the experimental girls to the 0.88 of the control boys. The numbers of participators may be obtained by summing the top four figures in each column, and the process reveals that women report more participation than men. The difference in numbers of participators in the control and experimental groups is not important. The mean number of activities are higher for experimentals than for controls, but the usual tests for significance of the differences such as the critical ratio can hardly be applied meaningfully to these data. The reader must not put too much emphasis upon the mean differences. It will be enough to say that it appears as if the counseled subjects tended to participate in more organizations of the kind named than the uncounseled subjects. No necessary cause-and-effect relationship has been established.

A question about offices held in organizations listed in the item above was answered by 65.6 percent of the counseled and 60.5 percent of the noncounseled subjects. It is probably safe to assume that those who did not answer the question were not officeholders, but that assumption has not been used in the analysis of the data.

TABLE 87. Numbers of Subjects Five Years After High School Who Reported Holding Number of Organizational Offices Indicated

Number of Offices Reported	Experimental Women	Control Women	Experimental Men	Control Men	Total Experimentals	Total Controls
More than two	6	4	4	1	10	5
Two	12	6	8	4	20	10
One	29	28	18	19	47	47
None	72	74	76	71	148	145
Total	119	112	106	95	225	207
Mean	0.66	0.47	0.49	0.32	0.58	0.40

The number of offices held ranged from zero to seven. In order to save space in the presentation of the table, those who held more than two offices have been placed in the top category. By adding the numbers in the three top rows it will be seen that 77 and 62 of the total numbers of experimentals and controls respectively were officeholders. Nine more experimental than control women and six more experimental than control men held offices in one or more organizations. These small differences in numbers who held any offices suggest that the generally higher means of the experimentals cannot be considered important. Perhaps the small differences result from the fact that more of the experimentals had attended institutions for advanced training where there was more opportunity and encouragement to hold offices. In any case the reader is cautioned against concluding that counseled subjects were more likely to develop leadership qualities than those who were not given special counseling in high school.

VOTING RECORD

In order to get additional information about the subjects' civic awareness, they were asked if they had voted in any political elections and their reasons for doing or not doing so. Only 7.6 percent of the experimentals and 13.7 percent of the controls failed to answer the question.

It is apparent from the figures in Table 88 that there are no significant differences between the counseled and uncounseled

TABLE 88. Percentages of Subjects Voting in Political Elections

Voting Record	Experimental Women	Control Women	Experimental Men	Control Men	Total Experimentals	Total Controls
Voted	58.8	58.9	55.9	54.0	57.4	56.6
Had not voted	41.2	41.1	44.1	46.0	42.6	43.4

subjects. It appears that the women reported a slightly better voting record than the men, but the difference is so small that it is unimportant.

At the time the question was asked, the approximate average age of the subjects was 23 years and 8 months so that most of them had reached the voting age about two years previously. All were old enough to vote if they had chosen to do so in the presidential election of 1956. Despite their ages and opportunities, only slightly more than half had chosen to vote. This finding suggests that much needs to be done to get these young electors to the polls.

Some of the most common reasons for voting and for failure to do so are revealed by the following quotations taken at random from the files of questionnaire returns.

"This is the only way a sensible American can voice his mind."

"I'm very interested. Always looked forward to it. Seems the right thing to do."

"I think it is my duty and my privilege."

"My vote is just as important as anyone else's."

"I was interested in who the leaders of my country would be."

"Personally thought it was a young American voter's principal duty as a devoted citizen."

"In my opinion good government starts with the individual getting out and voting."

"To help keep our country strong."

"We live in a new city which makes voting especially important."

"City election. Husband works for city. Vitally interested in outcome."

"Justifies my griping about politics."

"I have gotten so far out of touch with politics that when I became 21, I just haven't had time to refresh my training what with getting married and having a baby."

"Didn't become registered. I haven't been in any place long enough to register."

"I have moved several times during the past few years."

"No, no excuse."

"I just came of age last year and there hasn't been elections that amount to anything yet."

"I was always away from home and never registered at home."

"Failed to register for absentee ballot." (Student)

"Not interested till recently."

"Didn't feel well enough informed."

"I just haven't got around to registering."

"I was never in the right town at the right time."

"There hasn't been much to vote for since I was 21."

"With my intelligence I cannot decide which party or group is the best to have governing our country."

SELF-IMPROVEMENT ACTIVITIES

The survey of opinions of members of the American Personnel and Guidance Association about the differences between counseled and uncounseled persons indicated that they thought that counseled subjects would be more likely to participate in activities that might be classified as self-improvement. In order to determine whether such differences existed, our subjects were asked to respond to the question, "What self-improvement activities such as courses, on-the-job training, reading, home study, etc., have you been doing?" Seventy and six-tenths percent of the experimentals and 62.6 percent of the controls responded to the item. The percentages of the groups of responders who were carrying on such activities are reported in Table 89.

It is evident from the figures in the table that most of the subjects were doing something about improving themselves. The range is from the 75.4 percent of experimental girls to 55.5 percent of the control boys who were carrying out any of the stated activities. Of the total groups only 29.4 and 37.4 percent of the experimentals and controls reported no activity. The most common practice in both groups was to indulge in only one activity and relatively few, 7.7 and 4.2 percent of the experimentals and controls respectively, participated in more than two.

TABLE 89. Numbers of Subjects Five Years After High School who were Engaged in the Stated Numbers of Self-Improvement Activities

Number of Activities	Experimental Women	Control Women	Experimental Men	Control Men	Total Experimentals	Total Controls
More than two	13	5	6	4	19	9
Two	27	26	20	8	47	34
One	55	47	52	44	107	91
None	31	35	41	45	72	80
Total	126	113	119	101	245	214
Mean	1.22	1.01	0.93	0.73	1.08	0.87

The mean number of activities for each of the groups presented in Table 89 indicate that the experimental men and women were more likely to report participation in self-improvement activities. It is difficult to evaluate the significance of the differences in means because the assumptions inherent in common statistical procedures cannot be met with these kinds of data obtained under such circumstances. The critical ratio for the total group is significant near the 5 percent level. It appears that the experimentals belonged to a greater number of organizations but it would be dangerous to assume that the differences were attributable to counseling even though the counselors encouraged participation by the experimentals in those cases in which it seemed desirable. The reader is cautioned against overgeneralization, especially if a direct cause-and-effect relationship is implied, because too many factors have been and are operating to influence the responses to the question that was asked.

SELF-CONFIDENCE

In order to determine whether there was any difference between the experimental and control subjects in self-confidence, they were asked the question, "Do you have confidence in the actions you take when you have to make choices?" Ninety-two percent of the experimentals and 85 percent of the controls responded to the item.

It is evident from the figures in Table 90 that a great majority of the subjects (89.4 percent of the experimentals and 85.5 percent of the controls) were either highly or usually self-confident when choices had to be made. The differences between the groups throughout the table, while in the direction that has been found in previous comparisons, were insignificant.

Regardless of the results of the comparisons between experimentals and controls, it is interesting to note that less than 5 percent of the subjects lacked confidence in making choices five years after high school, and that more than 85 percent felt confident or very confident when choices were to be made. The figures suggest that this good cross section of the nation's young men and women have not lost faith in themselves. Perhaps they reflect an outlook that characterizes a period of what has been described as prosperity, since they differ markedly from those obtained from youth during a period of economic depression.[7] Perhaps they show a common characteristic of early adulthood, that period of life

[7] Walter F. Dearborn and John W. M. Rothney, *Scholastic, Social, and Economic Backgrounds of Unemployed Youth,* Cambridge, Mass., Harvard University Press, 1938.

TABLE 90. Percentages of Subjects Five Years After High School Expressing Varying Degrees of Self-Confidence

Response	Experimental Women	Control Women	Experimental Men	Control Men	Total Experimentals	Total Controls
Highly confident	7.5	3.3	9.8	9.5	8.6	6.2
Usually confident	77.5	77.8	84.3	81.0	80.8	79.3
Uncertain	8.1	11.1	5.2	6.6	6.7	9.0
Not usually confident	5.6	7.2	0.7	2.2	3.2	4.8
Definitely not confident	1.3	0.6	0.0	0.7	0.7	0.7
Total	100.0	100.0	100.0	100.0	100.0	100.0

which is challenging to the individual and rewarding to society. It seems to be so common that it develops regardless of the amount and kind of counseling received in high school.

SUMMARY

This chapter has dealt with the results obtained in the follow-up study conducted five years after the subjects had completed high school. In some instances cumulative data concerning choices and attitudes covering the eight years of the study have been presented. Since the findings have been interpreted at the end of each section, there is no need to repeat them separately at this time. In general it will be seen that the differences between the control and experimental subjects are in the directions that are commonly hypothesized by guidance workers. With some exceptions, the differences are usually small and insignificant when considered separately. When, however, so many of them point so consistently in the same direction, they cannot be ignored. They do seem to suggest that membership in the experimental group might have made some difference in the post-high school performances and attitudes of these young men and women.

Before reading the final summary of the results of the study the reader is referred to the reports of several sub-studies which appear in the following chapter.

CHAPTER VII

Miscellaneous Studies

The materials collected during the eight years covered by this study have been used at various times in by-product studies by some 45 graduate students for special projects, seminar papers, and Ph.D. theses. Many of those done in the earlier years of the study could use only the incomplete data available at the time, and the findings were of less value than the training in research obtained by the students. The reproduction of all such studies in this volume was not warranted, but a selection of those that offered significant contributions in techniques and results has been made and presented in this chapter. Several of them have appeared as journal articles, and appreciation of permission to reproduce the most important parts of them is hereby expressed.

The first of the research reports by Heimann and Schenck appeared in the April, 1954, issue of *The School Review*. It presents some interesting findings on a subject about which there has been much controversy.

Relations of Social Class and Sex Differences to High School Achievement

Robert A. Heimann, Arizona State College, Tempe, Arizona, and Q. F. Schenck, University of Missouri

Academic performance and intelligence-test scores of high school youth are determined, in large measure, by the cultural milieu of which the student is a part. Several recent investigations[1] have shown that boys and girls of lower socioeconomic status do not attain as high scores on intelligence tests as do children in the higher positions. Earlier studies, among them that of Douglass and Olson,[2] have indicated that girls as a group often receive higher school marks than do boys. It was felt that investigation of school marks and test scores in relation to both social class and sex differences would throw new light on the relations of these factors to school achievement and would augment the findings of some of the recent social class studies which have not always included the variable of sex differences in their design.[3]

HYPOTHESES TESTED IN PRESENT STUDY

The study reported in this article is concerned with school achievement as measured by marks, and provides evidence to show that both social-class position and sex are positively related to the marks that students receive in high school as well as to their scores on intelligence tests. The hypotheses to be tested are: (1) There are no mean differences in the marks and test performances of students from higher and lower socioeconomic classes. (2) There are no mean differences in the marks and the test performances of boys and girls.

PROCEDURES

The data for this study were drawn from the larger study reported in this volume. For the present study a sample of 120 students was drawn by random sampling techniques from the parent population of all the sophomores. The number of students was reduced to 114 after the social class categorizations were

[1] a. Kenneth Eells, Allison Davis, Robert J. Havighurst, Virgil E. Herrick, and Ralph W. Tyler, *Intelligence and Cultural Differences: A Study of Cultural Learning and Problem Solving,* Chicago, University of Chicago Press, 1951.
b. August B. Hollingshead, *Elmtown's Youth,* New York: John Wiley & Sons, Inc., 1949.
c. W. N. Leonard, "Psychological Tests and the Educational System," *School and Society,* LXXV: 225–229 (April 12, 1955).

[2] Harl Douglass and Newman Olson, "Relation of High-School Marks to Sex in Four Minnesota High Schools," *School Review,* XLV: 283–288 (April, 1937).

[3] John G. Darley, "Special Review of Intelligence and Cultural Differences," *Journal of Applied Psychology,* XXXVI: 141–143 (April, 1952).

made, the six cases that were dropped being either in Class I or Class V. The study is concerned with differences between Classes III and IV, the only groups for which adequate numbers were found.

The primary criteria used in classifying the 120 individuals into social class categories were (1) father's occupation, (2) father's education, (3) mother's occupation, (4) mother's education, (5) number of siblings, (6) educational aspirations of family, (7) family participation in community affairs, (8) the type of curriculum followed by the student, and (9) the work experiences of the student. This information was obtained from the comprehensive guidance records that were compiled over a period of three years for each student in the study. The present authors arrived at independent classifications for each of the subjects of the present study and placed them in one of the five social classes. In 12 cases of disagreement in classification, the authors resolved them by joint conference and reinterpretation of all available information.

Social class categories as developed by Hollingshead in the *Elmtown's Youth* study were used as the criteria of classification, with two exceptions: father's income figures were not available; and since school marks were to be a variable under consideration in this investigation, they were not used in determination of social class status. The classifications are listed in Chapter III.

School marks [4] accumulated for the four years of high school attendance were averaged for each student. A standardizing and normalizing procedure was followed that took into account the shape and form of the distribution of marks for each school subject in the four schools. Marks in the major academic fields, such as English, social studies, science, mathematics, and languages, were used in addition to those for shop and commercial courses. Marks in art, home economics, physical education, and music were not included in determination of the overall averages. Mark dis-

[4] While school marks may be said to be unreliable, in current educational practice they play such an important part in most schools that the use of any other criterion would not be as meaningful in a study such as this. It was felt that any social class implications with respect to marks should have operational meaning for every teacher, counselor, and college admissions officer.

tributions for the school subjects used were carefully examined by subject and by separate school, and T-scores were calculated for each subject in each school.

The Henmon-Nelson Tests of Mental Maturity are given to almost all high school students in Wisconsin as part of a statewide testing program. Scores from this test were standardized, and a mean score of 50 was set for all students of this study.[5]

DISTRIBUTION OF SUBJECTS BY SOCIAL CLASS

As Table 91 indicates, the majority of the group of 120 high school students in this study were found to be in social Classes III and IV. Therefore, only the students in these two social class groups, a total of 114, are considered in the analysis to follow.

Approximately 37 percent of the students were classified in Class III, both in this study and in the Elmtown study, but the percentages of students in Classes I and V in the present investigation were low. The percentage of the Wisconsin students in this sample who were classified in Class IV (58.3) was somewhat higher than the percentage reported by Hollingshead (46.9). This

TABLE 91. Distribution by Social Class of Eleventh-Grade Students in Wisconsin Study and Elmtown Study

Class	Students in Wisconsin Study Number	Students in Wisconsin Study Percent	Students in Elmtown Study Number	Students in Elmtown Study Percent
I and II	4	3.3	35	9.0
III	44	36.7	146	37.4
IV	70	58.3	183	46.9
V	2	1.7	26	6.7
Total	120	100.0	390	100.0

difference may be attributable to the use of communities of other types than that represented by Elmtown, the influence of new legislation in Wisconsin making school attendance compulsory

[5] Robert Heimann, *Intra-Individual Consistency of Performance in Relation to the Counseling Process,* unpublished Ph.D. thesis, University of Wisconsin, 1952.

until the age of 16, or to the increasing emphasis given in recent years to the need for a high school education in current employment practices and in the armed services.

After normalizing procedures, no appreciable interschool differences were noted in comparing distributions of marks among the four schools. Because of the similarity and homogeneity in the school performances of the subjects of the four schools, they were treated together in the following comparisons.

DIFFERENCES BETWEEN SOCIAL CLASSES IN SCHOOL MARKS

Differences in school marks were examined both between students in social Classes III and IV and between boys and girls. A test of significance was applied, and the hypothesis of no mean difference in school marks was rejected at a probability level of .01 or less. The data are presented in Table 92.

TABLE 92. Performance Differences by Social Class and by Sex

		School Marks				Henmon-Nelson Test Scores			
Category	Number of Cases	Mean	Standard Deviation	Critical Ratio	Probability Level	Mean	Standard Deviation	Critical Ratio	Probability Level
Class III	44	53.69	6.35	5.38	.01	54.09	9.19	3.83	.01
Class IV	70	47.79	4.71			47.42	8.65		
Girls	61	51.97	5.93	3.76	.01	51.22	9.08	1.50	.10
Boys	53	47.89	5.61			48.58	8.65		

Greater-than-chance differences in school marks are noted both between students in social Classes III and IV and between the sexes. In general, the students in social Class III and the girls achieved significantly higher school marks.

MENTAL ABILITY

Scores on the Henmon-Nelson Test of Mental Ability were selected for analysis of test performance in relation to social-class and sex differences. No appreciable interschool differences in distribution of test scores were noted; therefore the data were treated as one unit. Comparisons of intelligence test scores were made between students in different social classes and of both sexes. They are also reported in Table 92.

Statistically significant differences were found between intelligence test performance of students in Classes III and IV, favoring Class III at the 1 percent level of probability. Differences somewhat short of significance were found in comparing Henmon-Nelson performances of boys and girls.

DIFFERENCES IN MARKS OF SEXES IN SAME SOCIAL CLASSES

Further investigation was carried out to determine the performance differences in school marks between sex groups within a given social class. As the data of Table 93 demonstrate, girls accumulated higher marks than boys in both social classes. These

TABLE 93. Within-Class Sex Differences in School Marks

ocial Class and Sex	Number of Cases	Mean Mark	Standard Deviation	*t*	Probability Level	*F*	Probability Level
Class III							
Girls	26	55.51	5.45	2.38	.01	1.45	Not significant
Boys	18	51.08	6.57				
Class IV							
Girls	35	49.35	4.77	2.74	.01	1.31	Not significant
Boys	35	46.22	4.16				

differences were significant at the 1 percent level and would seem to be in general agreement with the usual findings of sex differences in marks. It would also seem that social class differences on this measure are related to sex differences.

COMPARISON OF SCHOOL MARKS OF SEXES IN DIFFERENT SOCIAL CLASSES

Social class differences were compared within the same sex group to illustrate the general superiority of students in the higher social classes in accumulation of superior school marks. These data are found in Table 94.

Students in social Class III were found to obtain marks superior to those made by students in social Class IV, regardless of sex. These differences were greater than chance.

Comparison between the marks of Class III boys and those of Class IV girls (Table 94) yielded some differences in favor of the boys of higher social class, but these differences failed to be significantly greater than chance would allow.

TABLE 94. Within-Sex Social Class Differences in School Marks and Henmon-Nelson Test Scores

Sex and Class	Number	Mean	Standard Deviation	t[a]	Probability Level	F	Probability Level
			School Marks				
Girls							
Class III	26	55.51	5.45	4.62	.01	1.31	Not significant
Class IV	35	49.35	4.77				
Boys							
Class III	18	51.08	6.57	2.35	.02	2.49	.01
Class IV	35	46.22	4.16				
Boys							
Class III	18	51.08	6.57	1.07	.30 .20	1.90	Not significant
Girls							
Class IV	35	49.35	4.77				
			Henmon-Nelson Test Scores				
Girls							
Class III	26	55.15	7.66	3.08	.01	1.36	Not significant
Class IV	35	48.31	8.94				
Boys							
Class III	18	52.55	10.89	2.18	.02	1.75	Not significant
Class IV	35	46.54	8.23				
Boys							
Class III	18	52.55	10.89	1.49	.20 .10	1.48	Not significant
Girls							
Class IV	35	48.31	8.94				

[a] A special form of the "t" test was used in comparing the performance of Class III and Class IV boys as the F test indicated a heterogeneous variance. Edwards presents a special formula for t which allows some inference about mean differences when a significant F is found. (Allen Edwards, *Experimental Design in Psychological Research,* New York: Rinehart & Company, Inc., 1950, pp. 167–170.)

MENTAL ABILITY

Further differences between social classes were explored, following rejection of the hypothesis of no mean differences in level of test performances for social class groups. These data are presented in Table 94. They show differences, favoring Class III, significant at the .01 level of confidence for girls and at the .02 level for boys.

These contrasts in performance illustrate further the social class differences of high school pupils on the Henmon-Nelson test. Students in Class III, both boys and girls, received higher scores than did those in Class IV. Within-class sex differences failed to reach a significant level, but they were somewhat higher for girls.

When test scores of Class III boys were compared with scores of Class IV, no differences greater than chance were found, although the direction of the differences favored the Class III boys as a group.

ILLUSTRATIVE CASES

It was felt that a closer look at the performances of several individuals in this study, a "blue-ribbon sample," would bring out further the relation of social class and of sex to school achievement. Brief thumbnail sketches of selected students from this study follow.

Bert

Bert, a Class IV boy, was the first of his family to finish high school. Consistently high in performance on some twenty tests, including two Henmon-Nelson scores (his modal percentile rank was 90), Bert said, "I'll take 50 tests if it will help me get a scholarship . . . to college." Despite ridicule and his family's active opposition to his educational aspirations, Bert represents a potentially mobile Class IV youth, anxious to rise in social position through education. His school marks were low, however, and he graduated 169th in his class of 250. Much of his consistently low academic record may be laid to his habitual classroom behavior of exhibitionism, "wisecracking," and pranks. In their reports his teachers noted a general lack of cooperation. Bert is representative of a Class IV youth who in his desire for higher education must go against the pattern and expectations of his family and the social group to which he belongs. Part of this conflict of values seems to be reflected in the great disparity of his performances on tests and in his marks.

Diane

Diane, a Class IV girl, scored at the ninth percentile on the Henmon-Nelson test; yet she graduated with a rank of 133 in a class of 250 students. Although she was pleasant, agreeable, and a fluent conversationalist, Diane's impression upon teachers and counselors was that of a student anxious to please and almost too ready to accept every suggestion made to her. The counselor felt that, in Diane's readiness to accept any suggestion without discrimination, there lay a basic desire to identify with the value system of the teachers in the school. With her counselor Diane explored the vocational possibilities of factory work, teaching, governess, early marriage, and physical education in the three years of counseling. Following graduation she enrolled in a one-year course in practical nursing. Diane seems to be an average Class IV girl who in her aspirations to "get ahead" is a model student, obedient, coöperative, but suggestible to an extreme.

Jim

Jim, a Class II boy, was expected by his mother to follow the family pattern and go on to college. His early vocational choice of a hobby shop or a woodworking shop, where he could "tinker with tools," was dropped in his junior year when he announced that the family had definitely decided on further schooling for him. The most striking feature of Jim's postschool planning lay in his indecision and uncertainty. Eight times during the three years of counseling Jim was given an opportunity to express a vocational choice. In all but the first interview, when he told of his interest in the hobby shop, he failed to express any choice other than a strong feeling that he would not like a job involving manual labor but wanted to be a "whitecollar" worker. His Henmon-Nelson score was at the tenth percentile, but he managed to graduate 33d out of a class of 100. "The Boy Scout type," was the way one of his counselors described Jim. "A pleasant, nice chap . . . a model student anxious to please . . . a slightly built boy with a lack of aggressiveness and self-assurance" were descriptions of him given by several of his teachers. Jim enrolled as a freshman in the state university following high school graduation, but he "flunked out" before the year was up. Jim's in-school behavior followed family expectations although he entered college without reconciling his own aspirations with those of his family and his class.

John

John, a Class III boy, successfully resisted pressure by his banker father, who strongly wished that he would go on to college. John's main interest was in mechanics, and his consistent job choice while in high school was in this area. He scored at the 55th percentile on the Henmon-Nelson test, and generally scored above average in all his tests, but graduated with a rank of 236 out of a class of 353 students. His teachers and counselor reported that he seemed apathetic in his general attitude toward school but that he showed marked enthusiasm when the subject of mechanics was brought up. Following graduation he began working for an uncle who owned an automobile repair shop. This pattern—a case of a boy who does not come up to the expected occupational level of his family group—is one observed rather often.

Margaret

Margaret, a Class III girl, reluctantly agreed to her father's desire that she attend a teacher-training institution rather than go ahead with her plans for an early marriage. She made this decision in an effort to pacify her family who had definite plans for her higher education. Her mother, who had been a night club singer, encouraged her to try for the concert stage. Her father, who rose from employment as a machinist to the vice-presidency of a growing industrial firm, wished her to attend a private girls' college known as a "finishing school" to get the social polish he lacked.

Margaret's engagement and plans for marriage to a postal clerk were fought by her family who, according to Margaret, did not wish her to "marry below her class." Her Henmon-Nelson scores were near the 50th percentile, but her rank in a class of 100 was 39. Margaret's situation seems to be an example of the use of education to further a family's social ambitions through a child.

CONCLUSIONS

1. Both social class and sex factors operate as important differentials in the school performance for the individuals of this

study. Girls and Class III students, on the whole, received higher overall marks than did boys and Class IV students when compared group by group.

2. Performance differences on the Henmon-Nelson test were in favor of Class III students over Class IV students to a significant degree. Girls scored somewhat higher than boys, but not quite to a significant degree.

3. The across-class sex comparisons tend to stress the importance of recognizing the interrelation of sex differences to social class differences. Further, they would warn of the oversimplifications which might be made in a social class study that did not include analysis of sex differences in its design.

4. Clinical evidences of differences in individual performance warn of the danger of overgeneralization of group data in relation to social class and sex differences in achievement. Many variables operate to modify the relation between social class and achievement for a group. Some of the factors suggested by the brief sketches of selected students are level of aspiration, family educational expectations, and a behavioral pattern of compliancy or rebellion on the part of the individual students.

IMPLICATIONS

1. Knowledge of the relationship of social class and sex factors to school achievement should be stressed more in teacher training programs, so that teachers will be cognizant of the important differences in performance stemming from social class and sex factors regardless of causal inferences.

2. It is the observation of the writers that the value system and the educational aspirations of Class III students seem to be more in keeping with the value systems in operation in many high schools today than are those of students of the other classes. This hypothesis is more fully elaborated in much of recent educational writing dealing with social class concepts.[6] In the higher social

[6] W. B. Brookover, "The Implications of Social Class Analysis for a Theory of Education," *Educational Theory,* I: 97–105 (August, 1951).
Neal E. Miller and John Dollard, *Social Learning and Imitation,* New Haven, Yale University Press, 1941, p. 133.

classes the motivation for success within the framework of the school system has certain aspects of identification with the adult—the teacher. Students of higher social classes often are members of the same social group that creates and maintains the values taught in the classroom. Upper-class girls, especially, may have an advantage in their accumulation of higher marks, which influence the gaining of scholarships and awards and meeting college entrance requirements. This bias should be recognized in considering the relation of secondary schools to colleges.

3. Marks do not reflect an absolute quantity but are influenced by motivation, intelligence, and personality characteristics. Therefore, it should be recognized that marks are, in part, functions of the background that the student brings to school with him. School personnel should be aware that they may tend to identify with, and accept, those students whose backgrounds best permit their learning within the middle-class curriculums taught in many schools, and that these forces are often reflected in the marks awarded.

4. Educators should again recognize the phenomenon that girls often receive better marks than boys. Educators should also be aware of the factors that give rise to this differential in order that academic evaluations may become more individualized and less partial to the more compliant cultural characteristics of girls. Another variable, reported by Carter,[7] Swenson,[8] and others, seems to indicate that women high school teachers favor girls in their marking practices; and, since women teachers are in the majority, this factor must also be acknowledged in explaining the sex differential in marks.

Sex differences, while not constant in their impact among various cultural groups, nevertheless are apparent in all social groups.

W. Lloyd Warner, "Education Effects of Social Status," *Environment and Education,* Human Development Series, Vol. I, Supplementary Educational Monographs, No. 54. Chicago, University of Chicago Press, 1942, pp. 16–28.

W. Lloyd Warner, Robert J. Havighurst, and Martin B. Loeb, *Who Shall Be Educated?* New York, Harper & Brothers, 1944, pp. 58–109.

[7] Robert Scriven Carter, "How Invalid Are Marks Assigned by Teachers?" *Journal of Educational Psychology,* XLIII: 218–228 (April, 1952).

[8] Clifford Swenson, "The Girls Are Teachers' Pets," *Clearing House,* XVII: 537–540 (May, 1943).

Therefore, it seems important that school personnel evaluate academic performance, not only in terms of the socioeconomic level of their students, but also in terms of the sex of the individual and the role that sex differences play in the value system of the group of which the student is a part.

Discriminant Analysis in Evaluation of Counseling [9]

Henry R. Kaczkowski and John W. M. Rothney

Progress toward adequate evaluation of counseling programs has been limited by such factors as inadequate criteria, uncertainty about the best time of assessment, and unsatisfactory experimental design. The quality of criteria used is critical because the program of evaluation can be only as good as the criteria. Various proposals of proper criteria to be used in evaluating the counseling program have been made. Satisfaction with a job has been one of the most frequently used criteria of the effectiveness of counseling, but job satisfaction is a value judgment that varies with the individual, his situation, and his culture.

Recent developments in statistical theory have made it possible to reduce some of the difficulties of design in guidance evaluation studies. It will be shown in this paper that one of the newer techniques, discriminant analysis, facilitates the task of designing suitable procedures for the evaluation of counseling.

Comprehensive reviews pertaining to the background, theory, and utility of discriminant analysis have already been made (3, 7, 8, 9).[10] Though the theoretical aspects of the technique have been developed since the 1930's, it has had limited use in educational research.

APPLICATIONS OF DISCRIMINANT ANALYSIS

Generally speaking, discriminant analysis can be applied to any

[9] This article is condensed from part of Dr. Kaczkowski's thesis, *Discrimination Among Eight Groups of High School Students,* on file at the University of Wisconsin. It appeared originally in *The Personnel and Guidance Journal,* December, 1956.

[10] The numbers in the parentheses refer to the references at the end of the report.

problem where individuals are divided into groups. For example, a group of doctors and a group of mechanical engineers could be differentiated by a set of measures. A senior in high school who has the same set of measures could then be told whether he appears to be more like a doctor than an engineer. The common practice in doing so is to compare his profile of measurements point by point with those of doctors and engineers. This process does not indicate how much more important it is for him to be an eighth of an inch above the norm for doctors than engineers in, say, spelling. The advantage of the technique of discriminant analysis is that it permits the simultaneous analysis of differences among several groups in respect to several variables. Friedman (9) states:

> There are really two questions which can be asked of a set of data for several groups. One of these is "How can I best analyze these data so I may determine the group in which an individual will perform the best?" To answer this question multiple regression analysis is appropriate. The other question is "How can I analyze the data so I may determine the group which an individual is most like?" To answer this question discriminant analysis is proposed as the appropriate technique.

Multiple regression techniques are designed to study relationships between measurements of a single group and they usually require some criterion of excellence or goodness within it. When two or more groups are used the problem of comparable criteria arises, and even if they are obtained there is still the problem that the regression technique can only reveal within-group relationships. Discriminant analysis does not require a criterion of goodness, for the group to which an individual normally belongs is the criterion that orients the analysis of the data. The technique shows between-group relationships. It does require that all members of each group have the same set of data.

In a research problem discriminant analysis attempts to answer three questions: (1) Is the *a priori* basis for classifying individuals into groups mere labeling, a distinction without a difference, or does a real difference in terms of appropriate tests of significance exist? (2) What is the "reason" or "reasons" for the differences between groups? (3) With what accuracy is it possible to classify a new set of individuals into previously used *a priori* groups?

It has been pointed out that one of the major difficulties in evaluation studies is that of establishing appropriate criteria for studying the effects of counseling. If a counseling program is evaluated by the discriminant analysis technique, the difficulties of setting up suitable criteria are reduced, for the group to which an individual normally belongs is the criterion that orients the analysis of data. The study (4) reported in the following pages is not primarily concerned with the value of some technique of setting up criteria, but it is concerned with the effect of *a priori* grouping. In many studies groups are assumed to be different and one variable at a time is examined in order to find some factors that will discriminate between the groups, but the mere process of attaching a label does not make it distinct from another group not having the same name. The utility of simultaneous comparison of variables to determine whether groups were different was assessed by the procedures described below.

PROCEDURE FOLLOWED

Discriminant analysis was used in an attempt to distinguish among eight groups of high school students on the basis of measures commonly available at the time of high school attendance (6). The students were classified into eight groups on the following bases: (1) male or female; (2) counseled or not during high school; (3) satisfied or not with post-high school activity. The groups as shown in Figure 1 were male-counseled-satisfied; male-counseled-dissatisfied; etc. The students were drawn from a group of subjects who were "counseled" or "non-counseled" while they were subjects of the major study reported in this volume.

Follow-up data obtained from all 690 students, secured by postal card questionnaire six months after graduation, were used to determine satisfaction or dissatisfaction with their post-high school activities. Three judges rated the subjects' statements about their degrees of satisfaction. The responses were classified as above average satisfaction, and dissatisfaction. The middle classification was not used in this study because extreme groups seemed likely to yield more meaningful results and the addition of extra groups would have increased the numbers in the final classification to the point where a desk calculator could not be used. Three hundred and twenty-four subjects were classified as being either satisfied or dissatisfied with their post-high school activity.

One of the requirements of discriminant analysis is that all the same kinds of measurements be made on all the members of each of the groups. Without them there would be no basis for differentiating the groups. Because of differences in amounts of information for the "counseled" and "noncounseled" subjects, the selection of variables common to all was a difficult task. The data were obtained from the ACE cumulative record folder kept on all the subjects and from the Senior Report, an intensive report obtained from all graduating seniors one month before graduation. The specific variables used were: scores on two administrations of the Henmon-Nelson Test of Mental Ability; scores on the verbal, number, space, reasoning, and word fluency subjects of the Primary Mental Abilities test; Differential Aptitude Test scores of numerical ability; two consistency indices obtained by computing the standard deviation of each individual's array of psychological test scores and high school marks; rank in class; attendance; satisfaction with school; self-evaluation; social index of family; quest for occupational security.

ANALYSIS OF RESULTS

The first aspect of the analysis was an overall test of significance between groups using the methods of analysis developed by Block, Levine, and McNemar (*1*) (an analysis of variance scheme) and Rao's dispersion analysis (*5*). In the analysis of dispersion the chi-square test was significant at the 1 percent level.[11] This finding indicates that the students arranged into the eight groups vary significantly with respect to the variables. In the Block, Levine, and McNemar design the F ratio for the overall

[11] The writers are indebeted to Professor Chester W. Harris for his assistance with statistical procedures.

group difference was significant at the 5 percent level. This implies that the *a priori* grouping is meaningful. The F ratio for the variable pattern was significant at the 1 percent level. From this one can infer that the arrangement or pattern of variables within the group differentiates the groups.

The second aspect of the analysis was concerned with relative distance in space between each pair of the eight groups. Mahalanobis' D^2 statistic (*5*), a measure of the magnitude of divergence or distance between groups, was used. Two groups having the same type of measures can be differentiated by the degree of overlap between them. If the measures are identical, the overlap is at its maximum and the groups can be classified as homogeneous. As the overlap of the measurements decreases, the divergence between the two groups increases and the groups can be classified as dissimilar. The F ratios of 21 of 28 groupings as shown in Table 95 were significant beyond the 5 percent level. All the D^2 values comparing the divergence between the male and female groups were significant. The girls tend to group in respect to satisfaction and dissatisfaction, while the boys had no rigorous grouping. Nonsignificance does not mean that the groups are identical.

The third aspect of the analysis was concerned with variation in different dimensions on the basis of 16 variables and eight groups. Geometrically, the variables used in the study can be regarded as defining a space of 16 dimensions and an individual can be represented as a point in that space on the basis of his 16 measures. Individuals belonging to any group can be represented as a cluster of points around a point defined by the means of the 16 variables for that group. However, by means of discriminant analysis, the space occupied by the original variables and groups can be reduced. In this problem it was found that the two canonical variates named below were needed to exhaust the significant variation. In other words, all the significant variation between the groups is accounted for by two components or dimensions. This indicates that a two-dimensional representation gives a fairly accurate picture of the configuration of the groups in the 16-dimensional space. The two-dimensional representation with canonical

TABLE 95. The Variance Ratio of All Combinations of Groups

	MCS	MCD	MUS	MUD	FCS	FCD	FUS	FUD
MCS[a]								
MCD	.9096							
MUS	2.0368	2.1698[c]						
MUD	1.3978	.8368	1.5846					
FCS	6.4252[b]	8.7729[b]	8.8578[b]	11.7877[b]				
FCD	3.0236[b]	6.1833[b]	8.0564[b]	7.7304[b]	2.0610			
FUS	9.3153[b]	11.7708[b]	11.1395[b]	10.6182[b]	1.2443	2.9092[b]		
FUD	2.7147[c]	4.3907[b]	5.2255[b]	4.2548[b]	1.7982	1.2057	2.6414[c]	

[a] Explanation of code: *M*—male; *F*—female; *C*—counseled; *U*—uncounseled; *S*—satisfied; *D*—dissatisfied.
[b] Significant at 1 percent level.
[c] Significant at 5 percent level.

variates as coördinate axes is given in Figure 1. Comparison of the magnitude of divergence or distance between various groups shows that the variation in the first dimension is primarily the result of

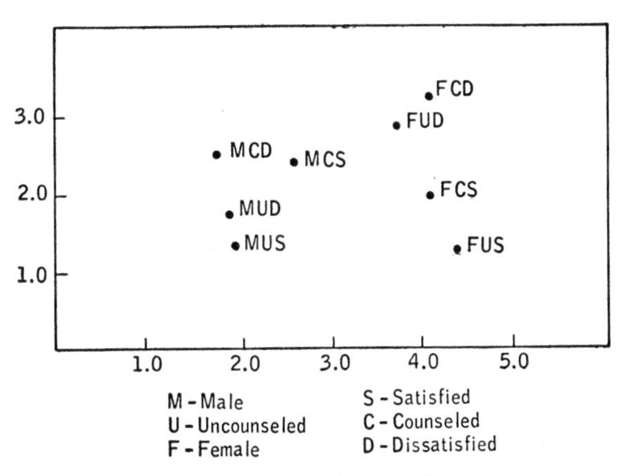

FIGURE 1. Configuration of the Groups

sex differences. This finding suggests that sex of counselees should be considered in any counseling situation. The variation in the second dimension cannot be attributed to any single factor. It appears to be a mixture of the degree of counseling and satisfaction or dissatisfaction with post-high school activity. Figure 1 indicates that the female groupings favor the latter and the male groupings the former.

The largest linear weights on the variables in the first dimension are: (1) quest for occupational security, (2) social class index, (3) rank in graduating class. An examination of the means of the groups shows that these weights aid in differentiating along sex lines. The largest linear weights on the variables in the second dimension are self-rating, school-satisfaction, and the score on the first administration of the Henmon-Nelson Test of Mental Ability. An examination of the means of the groups shows that these weights aid in differentiating the groups along lines of satisfaction or dissatisfaction. This finding suggests that students who know how well they can perform and who score above normal on an intelligence test tend to be satisfied with their post-high school activities.

The final aspect of the analysis was concerned with the establishment of criteria for determining to which group an individual belongs. These criteria were in the form of linear discriminant scores. A cross-validation study was used to determine the validity of the criteria. Follow-up data obtained from 67 subjects secured by a questionnaire two and a half years after graduation were used to determine satisfaction or dissatisfaction with post-high school activity at that time. Fifty of 67 students were correctly predicted as being satisfied or dissatisfied with their post-high school activity. The test of effectiveness of this classification was significant at the 8 percent level.

RESULTS

With the above findings in mind the answers to the three questions proposed earlier in the paper can now be given as follows.

1. The *a priori* basis for classifying individuals into groups was meaningful. The "distance" or divergence (D^2) among the groups was significant in 21 of 28 calculations.

2. Essentially the "reason" for the overall difference among groups is the arrangement or patterning of variables within groups. When the eight groups were plotted in the reduced space

of two dimensions, as in Figure 1, the groups were differentiated on the basis of sex and to a limited degree on satisfaction or dissatisfaction. In addition, variables that contributed most to this differentiation were located.

3. It was demonstrated that prediction of the kind of response an individual would make two and a half years after graduation is possible to a limited extent.

No clear-cut distinction between counseled and noncounseled groups was found. This finding suggests that the six-month interval between counseling and follow-up was not long enough to permit the effects of counseling to be demonstrated. It was shown, however, that answers to questionnaires can be used to classify students as satisfied or dissatisfied with their post-high school activities.

This study was an exploratory attempt in the use of a relatively new technique in evaluation of counseling. It has demonstrated that criteria need not be developed before evaluation is done. The practical results in this particular study are of less significance than the finding that the technique can be so utilized. Further exploratory attempts with this technique are recommended to those who seek to evaluate counseling practices.

REFERENCES

1. Block, J. Levine, and Q. McNemar, "Testing for the Existence of Psychological Pattern," *Journal of Abnormal and Social Psychology,* 1951, *32*:356–359.
2. Harris, C. W., "Note on Dispersion Analysis," *Journal of Experimental Education,* 1954, *22*:289–291.
3. Hodges, J. L., *Discriminatory Analysis: Survey of Discriminatory Analysis,* Randolph Field, Tex., U.S.A.F. School of Aviation Medicine.
4. Kaczkowski, H., *Discrimination Among Eight Groups of High School Students,* unpublished Doctor's dissertation, University of Wisconsin, 1954.
5. Rao, C. R., *Advanced Statistical Methods in Biometric Research,* New York, John Wiley & Sons, Inc., 1952.
6. Rothney, J. W. M., *The High School Student,* New York: The Dryden Press, Inc., 1954.

7. Rulon, P. J., "Distinctions Between Discriminant Analysis and Regression Analysis and a Geometric Interpretation of the Discriminant Function," *Harvard Educational Review,* 1951, *21*: 80–90.
8. Tatsuoka, M. and D. Tiedeman, "Discriminant Analysis," *Review of Educational Research,* 1954, *24*:402–417.
9. Tiedeman, D., "The Utility of Discriminant Function in Psychological and Guidance Investigations," *Harvard Educational Review,* 1951, *21*:71–81.

Test Scores and Postschool Performances

TEST SCORES AND PERFORMANCE IN COLLEGE

The reader will recall that the official transcripts of all the 164 subjects who went on to colleges and the 17 who attended nursing schools were obtained. Examination of those transcripts made it possible to determine the progress of all individuals during their training careers. The data in Table 96 show the extent to which the tests taken in high school, the grade-points earned during their last two years, and rank in graduating class differentiated the subjects who had performed at different levels in college. The 25 subjects who dropped from school for reasons other than poor grades were not used in the analysis which follows.

The figures in Table 96 are mean raw scores on the Henmon-Nelson Test of Mental Ability, the Primary Mental Abilities Test, and selected sections of the Differential Aptitude Test battery. These tests were described in Chapter III and procedures for computing the grade points are also described in that chapter. The high school rank was obtained directly from the school records and the reader should note that the lower the figure given the higher the students' standings in their classes. The categories for progress in college or nursing school at the left of the table were determined from the transcripts. The honors category was used for those cases where attainment of academic honors was indicated clearly on the official document. The usual progress category was reserved for those who were graduated in the usual number of years required to complete the course and who had not been on probation or won honors at any time. Subjects put in the third category were those for whom academic probation was indicated on the record, or where it was clear that the subject had required more than the usual time to complete the course because of academic difficulties. The last of the four categories contained those cases in which the transcript indicated that official action had been taken to drop the student because he had failed to meet minimum academic requirements.

TABLE 96. Mean Raw Test Scores, High School Ranks and Grade Points of Subjects Who Achieved at Indicated Levels in College and Nursing Schools

Tests, Grades, and Ranks	Honor Students (N=21)	Made Usual Progress (N=83)	On Probation or Delayed Graduation (N=34)	Dropped for Low Grades (N=18)	Total Groups (N=156)	Chi-Square (See Text)	Levels of Significance
Henmon-Nelson Mental Ability	67.4	60.3	57.9	56.3	60.3	10.79	.001
Primary Mental Abilities							
Verbal	33.6	27.8	25.8	22.8	27.6	10.09	.01
Space	19.2	19.2	23.3	19.4	20.5	0.81	NS
Reasoning	21.1	18.2	16.2	14.6	17.7	7.38	.01
Number	25.2	20.5	19.1	18.9	20.6	2.89	NS
Word fluency	47.3	39.0	36.5	36.6	39.3	3.28	.05
Differential Aptitude Test							
Verbal reasoning	36.7	30.6	29.8	29.1	31.1	1.17	NS
Number	30.4	27.1	22.0	22.7	25.9	4.67	.05
Spelling	76.3	67.6	50.9	55.3	63.7	13.83	.001
Sentences	53.2	42.6	36.9	33.8	41.8	8.09	.01
Grade points in 11th and 12th grades	73.7	64.3	57.6	53.0	62.8	10.87	.001
High school rank	9.4	27.2	39.0	49.1	29.9	19.13	.001

The reader will note that the figures in the table offer evidence of the relationship of scores achieved in high school with the performance of the subjects (except for the 18 students who were dropped) over the whole training period. The value offered by the length of the period covered is offset somewhat by the fact that many different training institutions and courses with varying standards were represented. It would be highly desirable for each institution to carry on long-term studies of the relationship of various high school measuring devices to performances of its own students, but since the numbers of our subjects in many colleges was very small, it was not possible to do so with these data.

Study of Table 96 indicates a regular progression downward of means of test scores for the various college achievement groups in eight of the 12 high school measures. In two of four deviations from regularity there is only a fraction of a raw score point and in the other two the variation is less than four points. Since three of the four are in the last category in which there were only 18 cases, the fluctuations are probably the result of chance. The greatest departure from regularity was found for the PMA space test. It had been discovered during administration of this test that the directions were not clear to many of the subjects.

In order to determine whether the tests, ranks, and grade points had differentiated between those who had made usual progress or better and those who had difficulty as evidenced by probation, delayed graduation, or being dropped for low grades, the following procedures were used. Fourfold tables were set up in which test scores above and below the average were used for two cells, and success in college (usual progress and honors) or lack of it (probation, delay, dropped) were used as the others. The chi-squares and the significance of the differences between the test scores of the two achievement groups are indicated in the last two columns of Table 96. The factors that discriminated between achievers and nonachievers in college and nursing schools in order of their effectiveness were high school rank, DAT spelling score, grade points, Henmon-Nelson score, PMA verbal score, DAT sentence score, PMA reasoning score, DAT number score, and PMA word fluency. The DAT verbal reasoning and the PMA tests of space and number did not discriminate significantly between the achievers and nonachievers in college.

The reader is reminded that these findings refer only to the use of tests for groups of subjects. Since counselors must deal with just one subject at a time, such results as those reported above provide general background material. They do not indicate that high scores on one or even all of the tests guarantee successful work in college by any particular counselee.

TEST SCORES AND POST-HIGH SCHOOL OCCUPATIONAL PROGRESS

It was noted in Chapter III that all the subjects of the study had taken the Henmon-Nelson Test of Mental Ability, and all sections of the Primary Mental Abilities Test while they were in the tenth grade. In the eleventh grade those subjects who had indicated that they did not plan to go on to post-high school training were given selected sections of the Differential Aptitude Test. Girls who had indicated that they were planning to go into commercial work were given the clerical, number, sentence, and spelling sections of the DAT, and boys who did not plan to go to college were given the mechanical number and space sections of the same test. Intensive study of the relationship of such test scores to performances in related fields are in progress. Since only the DAT number was given to all the subjects, it is the only test in that battery reported upon at this time.

The classifications at the left of Table 97 were obtained from analysis of the subjects' questionnaire and supplemented by a sample of reports from their employers in the manner described in Chapter IV. These supplementary reports indicated that the employment progress reported by the subjects was verifiable by their employers. The 396 cases for whom dependable employment progress records were available constitute the population whose mean test scores are reported in the table.

The averages of the test scores and measures of academic performance in high school do not show as regular variation by occupational progress groups as was revealed in the study of progress through college. Perhaps they should not be expected to do so since a wide variety of jobs (see Appendix I) are represented. Chi-squares were computed from fourfold tables that were made up from the first and last two categories of employment progress and from scores above or below the mean for the total groups of employed subjects. The results of the computations and their levels of significance are reported in Table 97. Only the scores

TABLE 97. Mean Raw Test Scores, High School Grade Points and Ranks in Graduating Classes of Subjects Who Had Made the Progress Indicated in Employment Five Years After Graduation

Tests, Grades, and Ranks	Occupational Progress: Owned Business, Fast Promotion, Better Jobs (N=86)	Promoted on Schedule (N=54)	Remained Same Job Level (N=217)	Reduced Job Level (N=39)	Total Group (N=396)	Chi-Square (See Text)	Levels of Significance
Henmon-Nelson Mental Ability	52.9	56.9	50.5	50.1	51.4	8.96	.01
Primary Mental Abilities							
Verbal	23.4	24.4	22.6	22.7	22.8	1.56	NS
Space	20.1	19.8	17.9	21.1	18.9	0.65	NS
Reasoning	15.7	17.6	15.3	15.2	15.7	2.18	NS
Number	18.9	20.3	19.8	19.7	19.7	0.05	NS
Word fluency	34.2	36.1	35.0	33.1	34.8	0.53	NS
Differential Aptitude Tests							
Number	18.8	20.8	17.3	17.1	18.1	6.64	.01
Grade points in 11th and 12th grades	49.3	50.1	48.8	43.4	48.6	2.23	NS
High school rank	57.7	47.0	59.0	70.8	58.2	1.82	NS

from the Henmon-Nelson Test of Mental Ability and the DAT number test discriminated significantly between those who had made better than usual progress in employment and those who had not.[12] Marks in school as summed up in rank in graduating class did not do so.

It appears that when the progress in post-high school jobs of men and women is considered in general, the tests that attempt to measure rather general mental performances (and the DAT number test seems to do so, despite its title) discriminate most effectively between those who progress faster than usual and those who do not. They are more efficient in doing so than their teachers' marks indicate. More detailed studies of the relationship between specific tests and performance on specific jobs are in progress.

[12] See the correlation coefficients reported in a later section on prediction studies.

RELATIONSHIP OF SCORES ON THE KUDER PREFERENCE RECORD TO POST-HIGH SCHOOL ACTIVITIES

Members of the school staff of one of the cities administered the Kuder Preference Record [13] to some of the subjects of this study while they were in the ninth grade and during their senior year. The scores derived from the administration of the Record made it possible to determine the extent to which the subjects were employed, or in training for employment, in the fields in which their strongest preferences had supposedly been measured.

The relationships between expressed preferences in the ninth and twelfth grades and occupational or training activity five years after high school are presented in Tables 98 and 99. It should be noted that comparisons are made between the field (as defined by the Kuder) in which his percentile was highest and the actual field of work, again as defined in the Kuder manual, in which he was employed. Unfortunately, many of the occupations in which the subjects were working were not covered in the Kuder manual so no comparisons could be made for them.

One may read Tables 98 and 99 in several ways. It may be seen by reading the figures in the diagonals that only 21.9 and 27.9 percent respectively were in the fields for which they had expressed strongest preference while they were in the ninth and twelfth grades. One may also note the percentages of subjects employed in particular fields who had scored highest in those fields in the column at the right of the tables. Percentages of those who expressed highest preference for a field and who were in that field are at the bottom of the tables. Although the actual numbers are too small to permit comparison in all cases, it does appear that the highest relationships are between mechanical preferences and mechanical employment. This seeming high relationship appears to be attributable, however, to the large numbers of occupations that have to be classified as mechanical even though they vary greatly. Laundrymen and butchers, for example, are grouped in the mechanical field, although they require quite

[13] Published by Science Research Associates, Chicago, Ill. Note that this is not an interest *test*. It is a questionnaire about preferences.

TABLE 98. Relationship of Occupational Field in Which Highest Ninth Grade Kuder Preference Record Percentile Was Obtained to Occupational Field in Which Subjects Were Employed Five Years After High School

Actual Occupational Field	Numbers with Highest Score on Kuder Preference Record in Field Indicated										Percent with Highest Score in Field Employed in It
	Mechanical	Computational	Scientific	Persuasive	Artistic	Literary	Musical	Social Service	Clerical	Total	
Mechanical	11	5	5	0	9	2	4	2	3	41	26.8
Computational	2	0	0	2	1	0	4	0	0	9	0.0
Scientific	2	1	3	0	0	1	1	1	0	9	33.3
Persuasive	1	1	1	2	1	0	1	0	1	8	25.0
Artistic	1	1	1	0	2	0	0	0	2	7	28.6
Literary	0	0	0	0	1	0	0	0	0	1	0.0
Musical	0	0	0	0	0	0	0	0	0	0	0.0
Social service	1	0	0	0	2	1	5	5	1	15	33.3
Clerical	2	1	1	0	3	3	5	0	0	15	0.0
Total	20	9	11	4	19	7	20	8	7	105	21.9
Percent in field indicated by Kuder score	55.0	0.0	27.3	50.0	10.5	0.0	0.0	62.5	0.0	21.9	

TABLE 99. Relationship of Occupational Field in Which Highest Twelfth Grade Kuder Preference Record Percentile Was Obtained to Occupational Field in Which Subjects Were Employed Five Years After High School

Actual Occupational Field	Numbers with Highest Score on Kuder Preference Record in Field Indicated										Percent with Highest Score in Field Employed in It
	Mechanical	Computational	Scientific	Persuasive	Artistic	Literary	Musical	Social Service	Clerical	Total	
Mechanical	22	1	2	5	7	2	1	11	3	54	40.7
Computational	3	0	3	3	0	0	1	2	0	12	0.0
Scientific	2	1	2	1	3	0	1	1	0	11	18.2
Persuasive	2	0	1	1	0	0	1	3	0	8	12.5
Artistic	1	2	0	1	3	0	1	0	0	8	37.5
Literary	0	0	0	0	2	0	0	0	0	2	0.0
Musical	0	0	0	0	0	0	0	0	0	0	0.0
Social service	1	2	3	2	0	1	2	10	2	23	43.5
Clerical	0	0	3	2	3	1	6	3	0	18	0.0
Total	31	6	14	15	18	4	13	30	5	136	27.9
Percent in field indicated by Kuder score	71.0	0.0	14.3	6.7	16.7	0.0	0.0	33.3	0.0	27.9	

different kinds of performances. In the twelfth grade table, the artistic preferences and artistic occupations match in three out of eight cases, but two of the three, whose occupations according to the Kuder manual should be classified as artistic, were barbers. Perhaps they do give artistic haircuts and shaves! Cooks and bakers are also artists, but the Milwaukee brewmasters are in the scientific category! Most of the subjects in the social service diagonals are teachers, but others are nurses. The length and kind of training required and the actual duties performed in teaching and nursing are so different that many go into one because they vigorously reject the other. Yet both are classified under social service.

The extent to which the subjects gave the same choice of occupational *area* while they were interviewed in the twelfth grade as had been indicated by their highest percentile on the Kuder Preference Record taken during their senior year may be observed in Table 100. As indicated above, the placing of twelfth grade occupational choices into the Kuder areas, which requires the classification of barbers, chefs and cooks as artistic, and laundrymen and butchers as mechanical, makes the whole matter of Kuder preference groups ludicrous. Even if such classifications are used, however, it will be seen that there is little relationship between the scores made and the interview choices indicated except in those areas where the scores simply elaborate the obvious. Of the 32 subjects whose highest Kuder percentiles were in the clerical area 71.9 percent chose occupations in that area. They were all girls who had been enrolled in the commercial curriculum for the past three years and no administration of an expensive and time-consuming instrument for obtaining records of their preferences was necessary. (Eighty-one subjects had chosen to work in the clerical area, but only 23 of them had scored their highest Kuder percentile in it. From the figures given the reader may want to set up a table in which the computations are in terms of percents of twelfth grade choices that are the same as those indicated by highest Kuder percentile.) The second highest percentage in the table is the 59.3 for mechanical, but this is attributable to the fact that so many occupations of such different kinds are

TABLE 100. Percentages of Subjects Whose Highest Kuder Occupational Area Score Was Similar to Twelfth Grade Occupational Choice

Kuder Occupational Area	Number with Highest Score in Kuder Area	Percentages of Highest Kuder Scores Same as Twelfth Grade Choice								
		Cler. (N=81)	S. Serv. (N=62)	Mus. (N=1)	Lit. (N=4)	Art (N=14)	Pers. (N=6)	Sci. (N=17)	Comp. (N=12)	Mech. (N=54)
Mechanical	32	12.5	0	0	0	12.5	3.1	6.3	6.3	*59.3*
Computational	19	15.8	36.8	5.3	0	10.5	0	5.3	*21.0*	5.3
Scientific	17	5.9	23.5			5.9		*41.2*	0	23.5
Persuasive	32	25.0	28.1	0	3.2	0	*12.5*	0	3.1	28.1
Artistic	30	30.0	20.0	0	0	*20.0*	0	6.7	0	23.3
Literary	9	33.3	33.3	0	*22.3*	0	0	0	0	11.1
Musical	25	60.0	16.0	*0*	4.0	4.0	4.0	4.0	4.0	4.0
Social Service	55	27.3	*41.8*	0	0	0	0	7.3	5.4	18.2
Clerical	32	71.9	18.7	0	0	0	0	0	3.1	6.3
Total	251									

put in the Kuder Mechanical occupations area. The social service area has the next highest percentage, made up largely of teachers and nurses, but it has been shown that these were among the subjects who had been most consistent in their expressions of vocational choice, and no standardized instrument was necessary to determine their preferences. In the other areas the numbers are small, as they must be because of the Kuder classification system of occupations, and generalization would be difficult. In general, however, the administration of this instrument would seem to offer little assistance to the counselor who has become well acquainted with his counselees.

The results reported in this section are, in a sense, evidence of the lack of concurrent or predictive validity of the Kuder Preference Record during high school years and over the five-year period after high school graduation. When such results from use of an instrument are combined with the theoretical limitations described by Rothney and Schmidt,[14] one can find little justification for its widespread use.

Since the work described above was done a new form of the Kuder has appeared. Its inadequacies have been pointed out by Siegel,[15] who ended his review of the new form of the instrument with these words, "Much remains to be done with this instrument, however, before its worth becomes clearly established . . . if rectified it will be used by a large number of counseling and perhaps even personnel services." It appears that this last sentence was incomplete. In view of past experience it seems he might have added that, *whether or not* the shortcomings are rectified, it will be used by a large number of counseling and personnel services.

A Comparison of Methods of Classifying Occupations

Robert Remstad
Research Assistant, University of Wisconsin

Among the major tasks facing a school counselor today are

[14] John W. M. Rothney and Louis G. Schmidt, "Some Limitations of Interest Inventories," *The Personnel and Guidance Journal,* 109–204, December, 1954.

[15] Laurence Siegel, "Review of Preference Record, Occupational," *Journal of Counseling Psychology,* Vol. 4, No. 2, 169–171, 1957.

those of directing the student in an effective exploration of the world of work, of helping him to understand those personal traits and characteristics that are pertinent to the choice of an occupation, and finally, of assisting him with the synthesis of this exploration and increased self-understanding into an appropriate occupational choice.

Some indication of the magnitude of the exploratory task can be gleaned from the fact that between the years 1939 and 1949 the number of separate job titles listed in *The Dictionary of Occupational Titles* (*5*) [16] increased from 29,744 to over 40,000 and, with the rapid growth in the past eight years of such new industries as television and atomic power, this number is certainly far larger today. Furthermore, a thorough investigation of any one occupation must necessarily include such varied factors as a description of what is actually done on the job, the amount and nature of the training required, the sources of this training, the physical and mental demands of the job, the income to be expected, the number and geographical location of employment opportunities, and the chances for advancement. Thus, it is clearly impossible to expect any high school youth to have an adequate picture of all the occupational possibilities open to him.

In the area of reaching increased self-understanding of one's capabilities and limitations, the problem is not so much one of magnitude. Rather, it lies in the lack of knowledge and understanding we possess about the contribution that various personal traits and characteristics make toward a satisfactory vocational adjustment. Indeed, do we even know what constitutes a satisfactory vocational adjustment? While many studies have been carried on in attempts to determine the role of factors such as intelligence (*11*), physical strength and agility (*19*), interests (*2*), parental attitudes (*2*), socioeconomic home background (*9*), and personality abnormalities (*8*) in determining satisfactory adjustment to a job, not much has definitely been established. Studies that are well designed and executed are apt to be inconclusive (*12*), while those that do arrive at definite conclusions suffer from the inadequacies of the instruments used (*23*), from

[16] The numbers in the parentheses refer to the entries in the bibliography.

small or very select populations (*7*), inadequate study design (*13*), and from lack of longitudinal data.

Trends of recent years seem to have shifted the emphasis, temporarily at least, away from studies designed to discover and define the role of a particular factor in determining an individual's choice toward attempts to formulate a broad comprehensive theory of occupational choice. However, much of what goes under the guise of knowledge about the process of occupational choice is just theory and conjecture. Only sound research can give us any definite answers and there has not been enough sound research on this subject.

One of the tools that the researcher in the area of occupational choice must have at his disposal is that of an adequate occupational classification system. As will be discussed at greater length later, the number of occupations that a particular group of persons will consider as possible choices or, at one time or another, actually enter, rapidly climbs into the hundreds. Classification thus becomes a necessity in keeping the number of variables within manageable limits.

The purpose of this paper is to describe the more commonly used classification systems, to discuss the difficulties in classification that arise in a practical situation, and to examine different classifications by actually applying them to the occupations which, over an eight-year period, were considered as possibilities or entered into by a group of 685 young men and women.

What are some of the difficulties that arise in the use of some of the common classification systems? What problems confront one in attempting to devise a new classification system? What effect does cataloguing the same set of data by various classifications have on results obtained? These are questions that will be explored.

NATURE OF OCCUPATIONAL CLASSIFICATIONS

The most widely used occupational classification systems in use today are the ones devised by the United States Department of Labor, the nine category division made by Kuder (*10*), the *Min-*

nesota Occupational Rating Scales (*15*), and a two-dimensional classification suggested by Roe (*16*). In addition, occupations and occupational materials have been grouped in a multitude of ways for the purposes of specific studies. But, with the exception of the Department of Labor's *Dictionary of Occupational Titles* (*5*), there is no system of classification into which more than a fraction of the thousands of different jobs have been placed. Either the occupational system has been developed to deal solely with relatively few jobs or else interest has been merely in developing what appears to be a logical system. No one has followed up with the painstaking task of deciding where large numbers of jobs fit within the system.

The Dictionary of Occupational Titles, compiled by the United States Department of Labor, is the only really comprehensive classification pertinent to the United States. First published in 1939, and later revised in 1949, *The Dictionary of Occupational Titles* does a thorough job of naming, defining, and classifying some forty thousand jobs. The classification system sets up seven major occupational groups:

1. Professional and Managerial Occupations (Examples: physician, school superintendent, banker, factory superintendent).
2. Clerical and Sales Occupations (Examples: typist, retail clerk, bank teller, door-to-door salesman).
3. Service Occupations (Examples: policeman, waitress, chef, male nurse).
4. Agricultural, Fishery, Forestry, and Kindred Occupations (Examples: farmer, lumberjack, fishing guide, tuna fisherman).
5. Skilled Occupations (Examples: carpenter, tool and die maker, foreman in factory, radio repairman).
6. Semiskilled Occupations (Examples: railroad brakeman, milk smeller, lathe operator, truck driver).
7. Unskilled Occupations (Examples: hod carrier, railroad section hand, warehouseman).

This system uses two criteria for grouping. The focus in the first four groups is in similarity in types of activities performed on the job and in the environment in which the job takes place. The last three groups are organized as to level of skill, training, or experience. Within these seven groups there is further subdivision by industry, similarity of materials worked with, and similarities of the operations performed.

This *D.O.T.* classification is primarily a job-orientated one, and therein lies its greatest fault from the viewpoint of a counselor. By job-orientated we mean that it is constructed so that a particular occupation can be located and defined quickly. Its primary use is in finding the right man for a particular job. However, the counselor needs a man-orientated classification system since his approach is that of finding the right job for a particular man.

Among those recognizing the shortcomings of the present *D.O.T.* classification system have been the personnel of the Department of Labor and the United States Employment Service who were responsible for compiling the original *D.O.T.* As far back as 1950, research was under way by these organizations to draft a more functional approach to the problem of classifying occupational information. Studdiford (*20*) describes eight classification components, or criteria, which were being studied. They are:

1. *Work done.* (The integrated pattern of activity performed by the worker involving such variables as the variety of tasks occurring, the tools and equipment used, and the materials worked upon.)
2. *Knowledge and abilities.* (The possession of information involved in the performance of a job and the capacity to apply it in achieving a specific result.)
3. *Aptitudes.* (Those capacities or abilities required to facilitate the learning of a new job.)
4. *Physical demands.* (Such as lifting, climbing, kneeling, talking, color vision, etc.)
5. *Temperament demands.* (Personality qualities such as adaptability to routine, emotional control, gregariousness, objectivity, etc.)
6. *Working conditions.* (External conditions in which the job is performed.)
7. *Industry.* (Product manufactured or type of activity carried on.)
8. *Training time.* (From less than sixth grade education to over four years of college or varying numbers of years spent on the job.)

Results of a pilot study on 4000 occupations that were classified according to the above criteria have been published by the Department of Labor (*4*) and complete classification of all titles in the *D.O.T.* is now in process. Completion of this will provide counselors with a tool long needed.

Another of the common systems of occupational classification is that of the *Kuder Preference Record.* The *Kuder Preference Record* is not usually thought of as an occupational classification system, but, if inventoried interests are to be used in guiding counselors into particular fields of work, then jobs must be grouped into interest categories. The widespread use of the *Kuder* is attested to by the results of a poll of guidance centers by Berkshire (*3*) about their test preferences. He found the *Kuder* to be the most widely used psychological instrument among a sample of 290 centers. This widespread popularity demands that it be given considerable critical attention.

The Kuder classification has nine separate categories: Mechanical, Computational, Scientific, Persuasive, Literary, Artistic, Musical, Social Service, and Clerical. The combinations of these nine, taken two at a time, make 36 intermediate groups or a total of 45. Aside from the weaknesses of the *Preference Record* itself (*18*), the classification system presents difficulties that seem formidable. Here is a classification system at the opposite extreme from the *D.O.T.* system—a system that is individual-orientated to the point where one has a great deal of difficulty in deciding in which group a particular occupation belongs. Kuder has placed only a small fraction of the thousands of jobs into his classification and, not only is it sometimes impossible to classify jobs not mentioned in the *Preference Record* manual, but occasionally one finds it difficult to understand the rationale which, for example, prompted the placing of "barber" in the artistic classification. Perhaps this is attributable to the fact that inventoried interests are neither predominantly nor exclusively vocational characteristics, and one often has difficulty in differentiating between an interest which is to be considered as a vocational future as distinct from one which will be satisfied avocationally.

The system used by the Minnesota Occupational Rating Scales

(*15*), commonly abbreviated MORS, is probably the third most commonly used classification system. While there is no evidence about the extent of its use, its prominence in occupational and guidance literature suggests that it is considerable, at least for research purposes. Designed as a tool to aid the vocational counselor, it is, essentially, a list of 430 occupations rated in terms of four levels or degrees of proficiency in six different ability areas. These ability areas are: (1) academic ability, (2) mechanical ability, (3) social intelligence, (4) clerical ability, (5) musical talent, and (6) artistic ability. The levels of ability needed are defined by a percentile range and by a description of activity or behavior typical of the particular level. Difficulties in its application are at once apparent. For example, how does one determine percentile rank in social intelligence? Also, while the authors claim that approximately three-fourths of the working population of the United States is included in the 430 occupations listed in the MORS,[17] the list of occupations in Appendix I of this volume, which represents the job preferences and actual jobs of only 685 people, contains dozens of jobs not included in the MORS. The *Minnesota Occupational Rating Scales* seems to be used because of lack of availability of anything else to use, and because of the attractive mechanical profile gadget.

In 1954 Roe (*16*) introduced a classification system that has received considerable attention. In contrast to the three previously discussed classifications, Roe's system was designed as a research tool rather than a counseling aid. It is two-dimensional, with occupations being grouped both by primary focus of activity and by level of functioning within that activity. The eight divisions of primary focus of activity are: (1) physical activities, (2) social and personal welfare, (3) persuasive business contacts, (4) government and industry, (5) math and physical sciences, (6) biological sciences, (7) humanities, and (8) arts. The levels of functioning range from the "creators" at the top to the "unskilled" at the bottom.

The only reported application of this system in a practical re-

[17] Donald G. Paterson, Clayton d'A. Gerken, and Milton E. Hahn, *The Minnesota Occupational Rating Scales,* Chicago, Science Research Associates, 1941, p. 12.

search situation has been in connection with Super's Career Pattern Study (*21*). Mosier (*14*) reported on some of the difficulties encountered when, as a part of the Career Pattern Study, it was used to classify the occupational preferences of ninth grade boys. It is a well thought out and seemingly practical system, yet it needed revision to meet the demands of the very first practical use to which it was put. This is, of course, a difficulty that arises with all the present classification systems. It points up the need for a stable classification system that will permit comparison of the results of one research project with others.

Undoubtedly many other classification systems have been devised for local use or for a particular research project, but only the four described above have had anything approaching nation-wide use. The Roe classification has been included because of the considerable literature that has appeared with reference to it. A system of classification adequate in breadth of coverage and depth of detail, functional from the point of view of researcher and counselor alike, and orientated toward both the job and the individual who is seeking that job is needed so that isolated bits of research can be meaningfully tied together and the results of research can be put to the counselor's use efficiently. Perhaps the revision of the *Dictionary of Occupational Titles* now in progress will meet this need. No system now does.

A STUDY IN OCCUPATIONAL CLASSIFICATION

The data used in this study were obtained in the Wisconsin Counseling Study. They have been described previously in this volume. The occupational information, which had been collected and needed to be classified and coded, included the following:

1. Father's occupation.
2. A tenth grade occupational preference, obtained during counseling interviews from all the subjects.
3. An eleventh grade occupational preference, obtained by interview from the experimental subjects only.
4. A twelfth grade preference given during an interview with each experimental subject.

5. A twelfth grade occupational preference, obtained from all the subjects by a questionnaire that asked, "What do you expect to be doing six months from now?"
6. The actual occupations worked at by all the subjects, reported in six-month intervals, from the time of graduation until the receipt of the third follow-up approximately five and one-half years later.
7. Occupational preferences made by all the subjects two and one-half and five years after high school graduation in response to the questions, "What would you like to be doing five years from now?" and "Ten years from now?"
8. The occupations of the husbands of female subjects who had married.

Thus, the number of occupations and occupational preferences that had to be coded exceeded 12,000. Classification of some kind was necessary if this mass of information was to be interpreted meaningfully.

SPECIFIC DIFFICULTIES IN CLASSIFYING OCCUPATIONS

The occupational data, which had been collected as part of the study previous to the mailing of the five-year follow-up questionnaires in the fall of 1956, had been classified according to a code with the following divisions: (1) attending colleges and universities, (2) attending other schools, (3) unskilled labor, (4) skilled labor, (5) clerical workers, (6) farmers, (7) members of the armed forces, (8) married (girls only), (9) telephone operators, (10) store sales clerks, (11) apprentices, and (12) miscellaneous. Since the occupations that a student usually considers while in high school are, for the most part, general in scope, and since the entry occupations for more persons just out of high school are ones requiring little skill, experience, or specialization, this classification had been set up mainly to differentiate among various types of training and among the lower less skilled levels of work.

However, the period between the second and fifth years after high school brought great changes in the skill levels of the occupations at which the subjects were working. Many had been graduated from colleges and other types of post-high school training, others had completed apprenticeships or worked up on the job to fairly skilled positions. With this increased skill and training there was a tendency toward specialization, and, with this specialization, a great increase in the number and variety of occupations entered. Another factor contributing to increased specialization was the training received in the various branches of the armed forces. At one point, during the height of the Korean conflict, nearly half of the men in the study were serving in one branch or another.

Before many of the five-year questionnaires had been received it became obvious that the classification set up to handle the previously collected data would not suffice for this new data. Large groups, such as the telephone operators who had comprised 6 percent of the girls in 1951, had almost completely disappeared by 1956. On the other hand, the "skilled labor" category, which had included only a handful of subjects in 1953, by 1956 took in such varied occupations as airport control tower operator, tile setter, butcher, tool and die maker, milk smeller, stator winder, and electronics technician.

Since the data were to be coded and placed on I.B.M. cards to facilitate statistical analysis, it at first appeared that grouping of occupations would be necessary to keep the number of digits to be punched within manageable limits. Investigation showed, however, that even with as many as 12,000 occupational entries to be made, the total number of different occupations was not likely to exceed a thousand. Thus, by expanding the code to three digits, it was possible to give each different job a separate code number and, in that way, to permit grouping the occupations into any number of classifications after the occupations had been collected, coded, and transferred to the I.B.M. cards.

The final total of occupational titles was 401. Additional code numbers, needed to differentiate between a person in training for a particular occupation and a person actually working at it and to indicate conditions such as being unemployed, in the armed forces, or married, brought the number of titles to approximately six hundred.[18] The number would probably have been slightly

[18] See Appendix I for a complete list of the occupational titles.

higher but for the vagueness with which some people described their jobs. This forced some grouping into fairly general categories such as "laborer, factory" and "clerical, general."

The greatest difficulty in coding the occupations was caused by the wording of responses on the questionnaire. This resulted from subjects' misinterpretations of the questions, from the filling in of the name and product made by the employer, from inability to title and describe their jobs accurately, and from attempts to glamorize or upgrade the job by giving it a fancy name. For a job title to have meaning it must be defined. The *D.O.T.* was used as the authority in titling the jobs and the job title given by the questionnaire was always cross-checked against the job description and other occupational material asked for on the questionnaire.

The distinction between secretarial and stenographic, and low-level filing and typing clerical jobs was the most difficult to make. Most of the girls referred to themselves as secretaries or stenographers, but these terms seemed to have no clear-cut meaning from one girl to the next. As a result, it was necessary to ignore the job title given by the girl and rely exclusively on the job description. This same upgrading of job titles was noted among the men. Typical of this type of response were the two draftsmen who referred to themselves as "plant engineer" and "estimating engineer" and the laborer from the state conservation department who was in "forestry work."

In summing up the problem of organizing, classifying, and coding occupational materials for research purposes there are two points that should be stressed. One is that occupational titles, as supplied by the individual subjects, cannot be relied upon to give an accurate picture of the job. A description of the actual tasks performed should be requested. Secondly, even a fairly large sample of persons will enter a relatively small number of occupations. Coding each job separately is not a very time-consuming job and it should be done. Then, after all the material has been collected, it can be classified and grouped in a multitude of ways.

A COMPARISON OF THREE CLASSIFICATION SYSTEMS

To study the effect of different classifications on the results of analyses of occupational material, specifically in regard to the degree that father's occupation influences one's eventual occupation, and the degree of realism present in tenth and twelfth grade vocational preferences, three different classification systems were used.

One system was the basic *Dictionary of Occupational Titles* classification. The "Professional" category was divided into "Professional," "Semiprofessional," and "Managerial" groups, which, with the remaining six categories, made a total of nine major divisions. All occupations were classified into their particular group by use of the *D.O.T.* In the few cases where the *D.O.T.* did not list the particular title in question, it was classified on the basis of the coder's judgment of the job description found in the questionnaire. An example of this was the young man who responded that he was a stator winder, a title not listed in the *D.O.T.* Knowledge that a stator is part of an electric motor, and that the subject had just completed four years in the air force, combined with his statement of average weekly earnings of $150, resulted in the job being classified as skilled.

The second system used was the nine-category Kuder classification. This presented many more difficulties than the first. The manual for the *Kuder Preference Record* [19] classifies approximately twelve hundred occupations. Approximately a third of the occupations to be used were not found on the list. The manual suggests that the user refer to either the *D.O.T.* or the *Minnesota Rating Scales* for help in expanding the lists. It does not, however, explain exactly how these references are to be used. No criteria for placing a particular occupation in a particular category are given. Furthermore, the *D.O.T.* does not classify by interest and the MORS lists fewer occupations than does the Kuder manual. Eventual placement of a nonlisted occupation in a particular classification became, in the absence of any criterion, solely a matter of the coder's judgment.

The third system used was one devised by this writer. It was decided to construct the classification system around a single

[19] Frederic G. Kuder, *Revised Manual for the Kuder Preference Record,* Chicago, Science Research Associates, 1946, pp. 5–8.

variable. Among those considered were such factors as amount of physical activity involved, degree of freedom that the job allows, amount of training usually needed, whether the job is indoor or outdoor, and the pay and prestige connected with the position. The criterion finally decided upon was that of the amount of training necessary to hold a particular job. The following ten categories were set up and defined as below.

1. *Graduate school.* Includes the type of position that usually involves work beyond the bachelor's degree. Examples: lawyer, dentist, school administrator.
2. *College degree.* Examples: Girl Scout executive, city planner, high school teacher, mechanical engineer.
3. *Some college.* Positions which, while often held by persons with degrees, do not require it. Examples: radio announcer, reporter, salesmen of technical equipment.
4. *Extensive on-the-job training plus some schooling.* The apprenticeship type of training. Examples: plumber, electrician, carpenter.
5. *School other than college.* Examples: beautician, air conditioning technician, radio repairman.
6. *Long years of experience.* Fairly skilled jobs, usually requiring long experience to attain proficiency. Examples: some foreman jobs, politician, bank cashier, brewmaster, This category also included the farmers. For this reason many young boys who had grown up on farms were coded in this category their first year out of high school.
7. *Short period of on-the-job training.* Examples: dance instructor, airline stewardess, stator windor, lathe operator, bus driver.
8. *High school.* Includes those jobs which, while not highly skilled, usually require a high school diploma. Examples: forest ranger, many clerical jobs, mail carrier, teacher's assistant.
9. *Less than high school.* Relatively unskilled jobs that can be learned in a few hours. No educational requirement. Examples: railroad section hand, boxcar loader, construction laborer, taxi driver.
10. *Special talent in addition to long training.* Examples: professional athlete, movie star, concert singer.

Occupational material classified for each subject included the father's occupation, occupational preferences expressed in tenth and twelfth grades, and on the two-and-one-half and five-year questionnaires, and the occupational status six months, one and a half, two and a half, four, and five and a half years after graduation from high school. All of the males were classified by each of the three systems. The factor of marriage had such a distorting effect on the data for the female subjects that they were classified only by the *D.O.T.* method.

RESULTS OF THE COMPARISONS

As mentioned previously, the two factors to be studied were the degree of realism present in tenth and twelfth grade vocational preferences and the extent to which occupational choice was associated with the father's occupation. Again, the purpose of this experiment was not to determine the extent to which either factor was operating, but rather to see what differences and distortions might appear when the same set of data was studied, using various classification systems. To be more specific, the questions are raised as to how constant the relationship of father to child's occupation was and how realistic the choices were when various classifications of occupations were used. Does the apparent influence of the father's occupation change when one classification is used rather than another? Does one classification system present occupational preferences in a more realistic light than another would? Which classification system does show greater relationships?

The realism of occupational preferences is a difficult factor to define, let alone measure. Certainly, however, if a person indicates a certain preference in tenth grade for a skilled mechanical type of work and then, four years later, is found working as an auto mechanic, this should be an indication that the original preference was realistic. This was the criterion of realism used. Did the subject actually enter the work area indicated by his stated preference? The results are summarized in Tables 101, 102, 103, and 104.

Table 101 presents the percentages of males who manifested

tenth and twelfth grade preferences in the categories listed and also the percentages of those in each classification who later went to work at jobs in that same area. This does not mean that they stayed in that category, but only that they spent at least six months

TABLE 101. Percentages of Male Subjects' Tenth and Twelfth Grade Occupational Preferences Classified by a Modified *D.O.T.* Classification and Percentages of Those Who Actually Entered Their Choices

Occupational Category	Tenth Grade Preference Percent	N	Percent Entering Area of Preference	Twelfth Grade Preference Percent	N	Percent Entering Area of Preference
Professional	29.2	94	69.1	20.5	66	81.8
Semiprofessional	12.0	39	10.3	8.1	26	34.6
Managerial	2.2	7	42.9	9.3	30	30.0
Clerical	2.5	8	37.5	2.2	7	71.4
Sales	1.9	6	16.7	2.8	9	11.1
Service	2.2	7	28.6	0.9	3	0.0
Agriculture	20.5	66	65.2	15.5	50	78.0
Skilled	17.0	55	34.5	11.5	37	35.1
Semiskilled	1.9	6	100.0	5.3	17	82.4
Unskilled	1.6	5	80.0	0.9	3	100.0
Armed forces (enlisted)	2.8	9	44.4	2.8	9	44.4
No choice indicated	6.2	20				
Totals	100.0	322	47.8	100.0	322	46.9

at a job, or in training for a job, that belonged in the same classification. At both the tenth and twelfth grade levels, the percentage in the Professional, Semiprofessional, and Managerial groups were far above those found in the entire male working population of these communities. This bears out what has been found elsewhere (*22*). The lack of correspondence between the occupational preferences of high school students and the proportions of people actually working in the various occupational areas has often been cited as evidence that high school students are not realistic in selecting vocational goals. The total percentage of subjects who entered the area of their tenth grade choice was 47.8 percent. For the twelfth grade preference the percentage of those in each classification who later went to work in it was 46.9. It had been expected that, since occupational choice supposedly becomes more realistic as the adolescent approaches graduation from high school, the relationship between the twelfth grade choice and later jobs would be considerably greater than between tenth grade choice and later jobs.

This difference does not appear to exist. The same result was obtained when classification was done by means of the Kuder and Amount of Training codes (see Tables 102 and 104). Under none

TABLE 102. Percentages of Male Subjects' Tenth and Twelfth Grade Occupational Preferences Classified by the Kuder Classification [a] and Percentages of Those Who Actually Entered Their Choices

Category	Tenth Grade Preference Percent	N	Percent Entering Area of Preference	Twelfth Grade Preference Percent	N	Percent Entering Area of Preference
Mechanical	43.8	141	87.2	35.0	113	92.0
Computational	1.9	6	50.0	2.5	8	62.5
Scientific	12.4	40	42.5	7.8	25	76.0
Persuasive	6.2	20	35.0	12.4	40	35.0
Artistic	8.7	28	39.3	6.6	21	66.7
Literary	1.6	5	20.0	1.6	5	40.0
Musical	3.3	11	18.2	1.6	5	40.0
Social Service	8.7	28	25.0	5.9	19	21.1
Clerical	1.9	6	16.7	1.6	5	80.0
Nonclassifiable	2.5	8		2.2	7	
Armed forces (enlisted)	2.8	9	44.4	2.8	9	44.4
No choice indicated	6.2	20		20.0	65	
Total	100.0	322	54.7	100.0	322	53.4

[a] Note that this does not refer to scores on the Kuder Preference Record. It refers only to the system of classifying occupations described in the Kuder manual.

of the three classifications was the difference between the percentage of subjects entering the area of their tenth grade choice and the total entering their twelfth grade choice more than 1.3 percent. This is not significant. For the women, coded by the *D.O.T.* classification (see Table 103), a difference of 14.1 percent

TABLE 103. Percentages of Female Subjects' Tenth and Twelfth Grade Occupational Preferences Classified by a Modified *D.O.T.* Classification and Percentages of Those Who Actually Entered Their Choices

Occupational Category	Tenth Grade Preference Percent	N	Percent Entering Area of Preference	Twelfth Grade Preference Percent	N	Percent Entering Area of Preference
Professional	44.6	162	50.6	25.4	92	81.5
Semiprofessional	5.0	18	11.1	3.9	14	28.6
Managerial	0.0	0	0.0	0.8	3	0.0
Clerical	34.7	126	81.7	13.2	48	68.8
Sales	1.4	5	0.0	0.3	1	0.0
Service	4.1	15	13.3	3.4	13	15.4
Agriculture	1.1	4	0.0	0.3	1	0.0
Skilled	0.8	3	0.0	0.6	2	50.0
Unskilled	0.6	2	0.0	0.0	0	0.0
Married	0.6	2	50.0	39.1	142	88.7
No choice indicated	7.1	26		12.1	47	
Total	100.0	363	52.3	100.0	363	66.4

was found, but this was attributable to the factor of marriage which, almost totally absent from the tenth grade preferences, accounted for 39.1 percent of the twelfth grade choices.

The data within these tables are, of course, noncomparable. There are, however, two large groups of subjects who contribute most to the relationships between tenth and twelfth grade preferences and later occupations. These are the farm boys and those who were headed for college long before tenth grade. The farm group is consistent on all three tables, in the Agriculture, Long years of experience, and Mechanical classifications respectively. The Kuder classification (not Kuder scores), however, breaks the college-bound group into seven different categories. This is more than balanced by the fact that such a large proportion of all the occupations had to be coded as Mechanical.

Here are three different tables. Each was based on the same raw data. The headings on the tables and relationship that they are intended to support are the same. Yet one, because of a difference in the method of classification, implies a greater relationship

TABLE 104. Percentages of Male Subjects' Tenth and Twelfth Grade Occupational Preferences Classified by Training Required and Percentages of Those Who Actually Entered Their Choices

Amount of Training Needed	Tenth Grade Preference Percent	N	Percent Entering Area of Preference	Twelfth Grade Preference Percent	N	Percent Entering Area of Preference
Graduate school	4.7	15	26.7	3.4	11	63.6
Bachelor's degree	20.8	67	68.7	17.1	55	78.2
Some college	2.2	7	0.0	1.6	5	20.0
Extensive training plus some schooling	18.3	59	16.9	11.5	37	29.7
Schooling other than college	6.5	21	9.5	3.1	10	30.0
Long years of experience	20.2	65	63.1	25.2	81	59.3
Short period of on-the-job training	1.2	4	25.0	2.5	8	62.5
High school	5.3	17	29.4	2.2	7	85.7
Less than high school	4.3	14	100.0	5.0	16	93.8
Requiring special talent in addition to long training	7.5	24	8.3	5.6	18	16.7
Armed forces (enlisted)	2.8	9	44.4	2.8	9	44.4
No choice indicated	6.2	20		20.0	65	
Total	100.0	322		100.0	322	

than the other two. The Kuder classification (Table 102) shows that 54.7 percent of the subjects entered the area of their tenth grade choice and 53.4 percent entered the area of their twelfth grade choice. These figures are both at least 6.5 percent higher than the highest corresponding figure on either of the other two tables.

Now let us turn to the other factor to be studied, that of the influence of father's occupation on occupational choice. Two methods of indicating this relationship would be to determine the number of subjects who, at one time or another, entered the same occupational area as their father, or the number of subjects who not only entered this same area, but stayed in it. Tables 105, 106

TABLE 105. Percentages of Male Subjects Who Entered the Same Occupational Areas as Their Fathers and Percentages of Subjects Still in That Area Five Years After High School (Grouped by Modified *D.O.T.* Classification)

Category	Father's Occupation N	Father's Occupation Percent	Percent Who Entered Same Area as Father	Percent in Same Area 5 Years After High School
Professional	20	6.2	85.0	75.0
Semiprofessional	5	1.6	0.0	0.0
Managerial	40	12.4	7.5	7.5
Clerical	12	3.7	8.3	8.3
Sales	19	5.9	10.5	10.5
Service	28	8.7	7.2	7.2
Agriculture	51	15.8	76.5	41.2
Skilled	82	25.5	31.7	26.8
Semiskilled	25	7.8	44.0	20.0
Unskilled	40	12.4	45.0	22.5
Total	322	100.0	36.9	24.8

TABLE 106. Percentages of Male Subjects Who Entered the Same Occupational Areas as Their Fathers and Percentages of Subjects Still in That Area Five Years After High School (Grouped by Kuder Classification)

Kuder Category	Father's Occupation N	Father's Occupation Percent	Percent Who Entered Same Area as Father	Percent in Same Area 5 Years After High School
Mechanical	210	65.1	76.1	53.8
Computational	17	5.3	29.3	23.5
Scientific	4	1.2	0.0	0.0
Persuasive	51	16.0	33.3	25.5
Artistic	3	0.9	0.0	0.0
Literary	0	0.0	0.0	0.0
Musical	0	0.0	0.0	0.0
Social Service	28	8.7	7.1	7.1
Clerical	9	2.8	11.1	11.1
Total	322	100.0	57.2	41.3

and 107 show both these factors. The subjects were first divided as to their fathers' occupations and then the percentages of subjects within each division who had entered it and who had stayed in it were found. Again, it is the total that interests us more than the figures for each category. The range of total percentages is even greater on these three tables than it was on the first three. Classified by the *D.O.T.* system, 36.9 percent of the subjects entered the same areas as their fathers, by the Amount of Train-

TABLE 107. Percentages of Male Subjects Who Entered the Same Occupational Areas as Their Fathers and Percentages of Subjects Still in That Area Five Years After High School (Grouped by Amount of Training Classification)

Amount of Training Needed	Father's Occupation N	Father's Occupation Percent	Percent Who Entered Same Area as Father	Percent in Same Area 5 Years After High School
Graduate school	6	1.8	33.3	33.3
Bachelor's degree	16	5.0	87.5	68.7
Some college	5	1.6	80.0	20.0
Extensive training plus some schooling	58	18.0	20.7	17.2
School other than college	6	1.8	0.0	0.0
Long years of experience	108	33.6	44.3	25.8
Short period of on-the-job training	36	11.2	25.0	22.2
High school	16	5.0	12.5	6.3
Less than high school	71	22.0	73.3	28.2
Total	322	100.0	45.1	25.2

ing classification 45.1 percent and by the Kuder 57.2 percent. For those who remained in this area five years after high school, the corresponding figures are 24.8 percent, 25.2 percent, and 41.3 percent. The Kuder system again implies a greater correlation than the other two. This time the percentages from the Kuder table are at least 12.1 percent higher than any on the other two tables.

Admittedly, the *D.O.T.* and Amount of Training classifications are much more similar than either is to the Kuder grouping. On the first table the difference between the two is so slight that one wonders if any changes have been made at all, but on this second factor, that of influence of father's occupation, a sizable difference also occurs between the 36.9 percent who entered the area of fathers' occupations when coded by the *D.O.T.* system and the 45.1 percent who entered this area when coded by the Amount of Training classification. But the Kuder classification on both sets of tables clearly demonstrates a greater apparent relationship between the variables than does the *D.O.T.* classifications.

CONCLUSIONS

One obvious conclusion which must be reached is that the problem of occupational classification is an extremely complex and difficult one. Yet, in perusing the vocational guidance literature, one is struck by the paucity of attention paid this factor. It would appear that many researchers in this area, bent on establishing a variety of relationships, have used any convenient occupational classification apparently without appreciating the difficulties involved or, at least, without recognizing such difficulties in their writings.

The type of classification system used can definitely alter the results of any study using occupation of the subject as one of the variables. With a little experimentation, one could easily find a classification that did a better job of "proving" the relationship (if one were trying to establish one) than would other classifications. However, what should be looked for is the classification system that would do the best job of presenting the data to be studied. For this purpose present knowledge is both sketchy and incomplete.

Increased attention to the problems presented by the need to classify occupations for research purposes will eventually lead to more meaningful research. More meaningful research, through its contributions to our knowledge of the multitude of factors involved in the process of occupational choice, will eventually lead to better counseling with regard to such choices.

REFERENCES

1. Bell, Daniel, "Notes on Work," *Encounter,* June, 1954, *9*:3–15.
2. Berdie, R. F., "Factors Associated with Vocational Interest," *Journal of Educational Psychology,* 1943, *34*:257–277.
3. Berkshire, J. R., "Test Preferences in Guidance Center," *Occupations,* 1948, *26*:337–343.
4. Department of Labor, Bureau of Employment Security, *Estimates of Worker Trait Requirements for 4,000 Jobs as Defined in the Dictionary of Occupational Titles,* 1956.
5. Federal Security Agency, *Dictionary of Occupational Titles,* Washington, D.C., Government Printing Office, 1949.
6. Ginzberg, Eli, Sol W. Ginsberg, S. Axelrod, and J. L. Herma, *Occupational Choice: An Approach to a General Theory,* New York, Columbia University Press, 1951.
7. Harrison, E. C., "A Study of Occupational Attitudes," *Journal of Negro Education,* 1953, *22*:471–475.
8. Hendrick, Ives, "Work and the Pleasure Principle," *Psychoanalytic Quarterly,* 1943, *12*:311–324.
9. Korner, A. F., "Origin of Impractical or Unrealistic Vocational Goals," *Journal of Consulting Psychology,* 1946, *10*:328–334.
10. Kuder, G. Frederic, *Revised Manual for the Kuder Preference Record,* Chicago, Science Research Associates, 1946.
11. Lehman, H. C. and P. A. Witty, "A Study of Vocational Attitudes and Intelligence," *The Elementary School Journal,* 1931, *31*:735–746.
12. Lehman, H. C. and P. A. Witty, "Vocational Guidance: Some Basic Considerations," *Journal of Educational Sociology,* 1934, *8*:174–184.
13. Moser, W. E., "The Influence of Certain Cultural Factors Upon the Selection of Vocational Preferences by High School Students," *Journal of Educational Research,* 1952, *45*:523–526.
14. Mosier, Helen P., William Dublin, and I. M. Shelsky, "A Proposed Modification of the Roe Occupational Classification," *Journal of Counseling Psychology,* 1956, *3*:27–31.
15. Paterson, Donald G., *The Minnesota Occupational Rating Scales,* Chicago, Science Research Associates, 1941.
16. Roe, Anne, "A New Classification of Occupations," *Journal of Counseling Psychology,* 1954, *1*:215–220.
17. Roe, Anne, *The Psychology of Occupations,* New York, John Wiley & Sons, Inc., 1956.

18. Rothney, John W. M. and Louis G. Schmidt, "Some Limitations of Interest Inventories," *The Personnel and Guidance Journal,* 1954, *33*:199–204.
19. Seashore, R. H., C. E. Buxton, and I. N. McCollum, "Multiple Factorial Analysis of Five Motor Skills," *American Journal of Psychology,* 1940, *53*:251–259.
20. Studdiford, Walter S., "A Functional System of Occupational Classification," *Occupations,* 1951, *30*:37–42.
21. Super, Donald E., "Career Patterns as a Basis for Vocational Counseling," *Journal of Counseling Psychology,* 1954, *1*:12–20.
22. Trow, W. C., "Phantasy and Vocational Choice," *Occupations,* 1941, *20*:89–93.
23. Wilkinson, M. A., "A Brief Study of the Relationships Between Personality Adjustment and Vocational Interests as Measured by the Multiple Choice Rorschach and the Strong Vocational Interest Blank," *Journal of Educational Research,* 1954, *48*:269–278.

Prediction Studies [20]

The procedures and the difficulties involved in making clinical predictions of postschool performances of youth have been described in Chapter III. In this section evidence about the effectiveness of the method is presented.

FORECASTING PERFORMANCES IN COLLEGE

At the time that the subjects began college in 1951, clinical predictions of their academic achievement throughout the whole training period were made. They were done independently by the counselor after study of the subjects' high school records supplemented by his personal knowledge of the subjects and by a graduate student in guidance (a counselor-in-training), who worked only with the records. They used the categories described in detail in Chapter III and presented in abbreviated form in the tables on the following pages.

Evidence of the academic performances of the subjects was available in official transcripts obtained from the 65 colleges and universities they had attended. No attempt was made to equate

[20] Most of the work for this section was done by Perry Rockwell, Jr.

the marks from these institutions because it was impossible to obtain course-by-course distributions of grades given in all the divisions of all the colleges over the four-year period. If a student had achieved Phi Beta Kappa status, for example, he was classified in the high honor category, but if his transcript contained only the notation of honors, or honors could be figured from grade points, he was listed in the honors group. If he was graduated in the usual time and his record contained no evidence that he had been put on probation, he was placed in the category for those who had completed their training in the usual time but had neither won honors nor been put on probation. Those subjects who were required to take an extra summer session or semester to complete the usual four-year course, even though they had never been on probation, were placed in the fourth category. Those whose records indicated that they had been on academic probation at any time during their college careers were put in the marginal class. Subjects who were dropped officially by the college for academic failures and those who left school while in good academic standing for such reasons as marriage or poor health were placed in the last two groups.

Attempts to predict performances in this manner and in such categories may seem foolhardy, but they do reflect, in a sense, what counselors do when they work with high school students who plan to go on to college. Counselors, in one sense, predict honors when they encourage and assist students to apply for scholarships. In the same sense, they predict satisfactory accomplishment in college when they do not attempt to dissuade a student from going on; and they do, in effect, predict that a student will have difficulties when they suggest that a counselee's previous performances may fall short of those required by the college that he plans to attend. These actions are not commonly called predictions but they do have the same effect, and it seemed desirable to determine how effectively such forecasting could be done.

The percentages of correct predictions made by the counselor are presented in Table 108. From them the reader will note that the counselor was right in half of his predictions about high honors and right approximately one-third of the time in predict-

TABLE 108. Accuracy of a Counselor's Prediction of Performances of the Experimental Subjects Who Entered College

Academic Achievement in College	Number Predicted at Each Level	Percent of Number Predicted Who Actually Achieved at Level Indicated						
		Left for Other Reasons	Dropped for Low Grades	Probation Student	Delayed Graduation	Completed in Usual Time	Minor Honors	High Honors
High honors	6	0	0	0	0	34	16	*50*
Minor honors	18	0	0	0	0	44	*34*	11
Completed training in usual time	53	13	4	15	2	*64*	2	0
Delayed graduation	3	33	67	0	*0*	0	0	0
On probation at some time	9	11	0	*22*	11	56	0	0
Dropped for low grades	1	0	*100*	0	0	0	0	0
Left in good standing for other reasons	17	30	5	5	11	36	11	0

ing minor honors. In the prediction that 53 of the students would complete college without difficulty in the usual time he was right in 64 percent of the cases, but he was too optimistic as shown by the fact that 34 percent of them did much less than expected. His prediction of performance at less than the usual level and of the numbers who would leave college for other than academic reasons were (with the exception of the one case whom he predicted would be dropped for low grades) well below the 50 percent level. In general it appears that the counselor tended to be over-optimistic about the prediction of honors and completion of college without minor difficulties. He was too pessimistic in his prediction that 17 subjects would leave college for reasons other than low academic performances since only 30 percent of those for whom that forecast was made did so. He had expected that some of the girls would leave college to marry, but many of those who married remained to graduate.

The percentage of correct predictions made by the counselor-in-training are presented in Table 109. Examination of the table shows that the counselor-in-training had a perfect score in predicting high honors and the number who would be dropped for low grades. He was right 64 percent of the time in predicting the completion of training in the usual time for 58 cases. His percentages of correct predictions of performances for the categories of minor honors, probationary status, and leaving for reasons other than grades are less than 25 percent. The counselor-in-training had no success in predicting two cases of delayed graduation.

Of the 16 students who dropped from college training for reasons other than grades the counselor-in-training predicted correctly in only two cases. He predicted that two of these students would be marginal students, that nine would complete their college training in the usual time, and that three would achieve minor honors.

Still another way to look at the performance of the predictors is to indicate the total number of subjects who achieved in each of the categories and to compute the percentage of them predicted correctly by each of the forecasters. When that is done the following tabulation is obtained.

TABLE 109. Accuracy of a Counselor-in-Training's Prediction of Performances of the Experimental Subjects Who Entered College

Academic Achievement in College	Number Predicted at Each Level	Percent of Number Predicted Who Actually Achieved at Level Indicated						
		Left for Other Reasons	Dropped for Low Grades	Probation Student	Delayed Graduation	Completed in Usual Time	Minor Honors	High Honors
High honors	2	0	0	0	0	0	0	*100*
Minor honors	25	12	0	0	0	52	*24*	12
Completed training in usual time	58	16	2	10	2	*64*	6	0
Delayed graduation	2	0	50	0	*0*	50	0	0
On probation at some time	9	22	11	*22*	11	34	0	0
Dropped for low grades	3	0	*100*	0	0	0	0	0
Left in good standing for other reasons	8	24	0	39	24	13	0	0
Total	107							

TABLE 110. Effectiveness of Prediction of College Achievement

Achievement Level	N	Correct Predictions by Counselor		Correct Predictions by Counselor-in-Training	
		N	Percent	N	Percent
Achieved high honors	5	3	60	2	40
Achieved minor honors	10	6	60	6	60
Completed college in usual time (no honors or probation)	55	34	62	37	67
Required longer than usual time to complete	4	0	0	0	0
On probation at some time	11	2	18	2	18
Dropped for low grades	6	1	17	3	50
Left in good standing for other reasons	16	5	31	7	44
Total	107	51	44	57	53

The figures suggest that the counselor-in-training was slightly more successful in his predictions than the counselor, but that neither was a highly effective forecaster. In general it seems that the personalities of the subjects caused the counselor to be too optimistic. It should be noted that these are much more difficult predictions than are usually attempted. Most previous studies have been concerned with forecasts for such shorter periods of time as first year or even first semester performances in which the many factors that may influence achievement in post-high school training have not yet been in operation. It should also be observed that there are many more categories than are commonly used. The results obtained when coarser groupings are used are reported in the following pages.

In the tables that follow, the seven categories used previously have been reduced to five by combining the honors groups, and the probation and delayed graduation categories. In study of the tables the reader will note that the first figure in each row indicates the *numbers* that were predicted to achieve in the category, and the following figures are the *percentages* of those numbers who actually achieved at the level indicated. Thus in the first row of the first table, 24 students were predicted to achieve honors. Of those 24 subjects, 8 percent left for reasons other than low grades, none were dropped, put on probation, or took longer than usual time to graduate, 42 percent graduated at the usual time without honors, and 50 percent did win honors. The diagonal figure in each intersection of row and column gives the percentage of correct predictions for each achievement category.

Examination of Table 111 reveals that the counselor's "hits"

TABLE 111. Accuracy of Counselor's Clinical Prediction of Performances of Experimental Subjects Who Entered College

Academic Achievement in College	Number of Predictions in Category	Percent of Number Predicted Who Actually Achieved at the Level Indicated				
		Left for Other Reasons	Dropped for Low Grades	Probation or Delayed Graduation	Usual Progress	Honors
Won honors	24	8	0	0	42	50
Usual progress, no probation or delay	53	13	4	17	64	2
On probation or took longer than usual time to complete	12	17	17	25	41	0
Dropped for low grades	1	0	100	0	0	0
Left in good standing for other reasons	17	30	6	17	35	12
Total	107					

ranged from 25 to 64 percent correct when the one case for which perfect prediction of being dropped for low grades is excluded. Only half of those for whom he had predicted honors achieved them, but the others had no academic difficulties. Approximately two out of three or 64 percent of those for whom he had predicted usual progress through college made usual progress, but 17 percent were on probation at some time or did not make the usual progress toward graduation. Four percent were dropped for low grades and 17 percent left for other reasons while they were in good standing. Two percent of them achieved honor status. Only one-quarter for whom the counselor predicted trouble in the form of probation or delayed graduation experienced it, while 41 percent made a better record than had been predicted. Thirty-four percent were dropped or left college for other reasons. Of those for whom leaving had been predicted before graduation, only 30 percent did so. Thirty-seven percent went on to graduate and 12 percent of the group reached the honors category.

Evaluation of the counselor's clinical prediction performance will depend on the point of view of the reader. Of the 89 cases that the counselor predicted would finish college, 74 actually did so. Since the dropout rate from colleges is known to be nearly 50 percent, it appears that the score of 74 out of 89 (approximately 83 percent) correctly predicted to finish is a good record.[21] Of the 18 who he predicted would not finish college, only seven, or 39 percent, left without graduating at the usual time or later. The counselor seems to have been slightly optimistic about the achievement of the first group and unduly pessimistic about the chances of success of members of the second one.

The accuracy of the counselor-in-training's predictions of college success is shown in Table 112. A study of this table reveals that the counselor-in-training forecasted correctly in 25 to 100 percent of the cases. He achieved 100 percent accuracy in predicting the three cases who were dropped for low grades. Only 38 percent of those for whom he had predicted honors achieved them but none of those predicted for honors had academic difficulties.

[21] It was not possible to get exact antecedent probabilities of completion of college for each of the colleges that these students attended. It is known that when 74 out of the 89 of the experimental subjects finished college, this is well beyond the usual rate for colleges in general and for the one university that most of our subjects attended. For a discussion of antecedent probability see P. E. Meehl and A. Rosen, "Antecedent Probability and the Efficiency of Psychometric Signs, Patterns, or Cutting Scores," *Psychological Bulletin,* May, 1955, pp. 194–216.

Half completed their studies in the usual time and 12 percent left for reasons other than grades.

Excluding the three cases dropped because of low grades, the counselor-in-training's best percentage of accuracy was achieved in the category of "usual progress." Sixty-three percent of those whom he predicted would be graduated in the usual time without

TABLE 112. Accuracy of Counselor-in-Training's Clinical Prediction of Performances of Experimental Subjects Who Entered College

Academic Achievement in College	Number Predicted in Category	Percent of Number Predicted Who Actually Achieved at the Level Indicated				
		Left for Other Reasons	Dropped for Low Grades	Probation or Delayed Graduation	Usual Progress	Honors
Won honors	26	12	0	0	50	*38*
Usual progress, no probation or delay	59	15	2	12	*63*	8
On probation or took longer than usual time to complete	11	18	18	*27*	37	0
Dropped for low grades	3	0	*100*	0	0	0
Left in good standing for other reasons	8	25	0	62	13	0
Total	107					

academic difficulties did so. Eight percent were able to win honors, 12 percent were on probation at some time during their college careers, and 2 percent were dropped because of low grades. Fifteen percent of this category left school for reasons other than grades. Twenty-seven percent of those predicted to be on probation or to delay their graduation actually did so. Thirty-seven percent did better than he predicted, and equal percentages were dropped or left for other reasons. Only a fourth of those predicted by the counselor-in-training to leave school for reasons other than grades did so. Thirteen percent were able to be graduated in the usual time, while 62 percent took longer than the usual time to be graduated or were on probation. It is interesting to note that *none* of the cases predicted by the counselor-in-training to be on probation, to take longer than usual to graduate, to be dropped for low grades, or to leave for other reasons were able to achieve honor status.

The counselor-in-training seems to have shared the counselor's optimism when he predicted that 85 of the cases would complete college. He was correct in 70 of his predictions for a percentage of about 82. It appears that the counselor-in-training predicted academic success or failure from the available records almost as well as the counselor who had known the individuals personally.

The figures are presented by sex groups to see if the male counselor and counselor-in-training were more successful in the prediction of boys' than girls' achievements in college. The tabulation indicates that the counselor was more successful in the prediction of honors, usual progress, and leaving for other than scholastic reasons for girls. He was much more successful in predicting pro-

TABLE 113. Effectiveness of Counselor's Prediction of College Achievement of Males and Females

Achievement	Number of Girls Predicted by Counselor	Percent of Correct Prediction for Girls	Number of Boys Predicted by Counselor	Percent of Correct Prediction for Boys
Honors	16	57	8	37
Usual Progress	29	69	24	59
Probation or delayed	3	0	9	33
Dropped for grades	0	0	1	100
Left for other reasons	8	50	9	12
Total	56	57	51	43

bation or delayed graduation for boys. The one case of success in forecasting that a boy would be dropped for low grades may have been a fortunate accident. There seems to be good reason to believe that the counselor was a better predictor for girls than for boys.

The counselor-in-training who used only the cumulative records in making his predictions, and who may have been less influenced

TABLE 114. Effectiveness of Prediction of College Achievement of Males an Females by a Counselor-in-Training

Achievement	Number of Girls Predicted by Counselor-in-Training	Percent of Correct Predictions for Girls	Number of Boys Predicted by Counselor-in-Training	Percent of Correct Predic tion for Boys
Honors	16	44	10	30
Usual progress	36	64	23	30
Probation or delayed	2	0	9	33
Dropped for low grades	0	0	3	100
Left for other reasons	2	100	6	0
Total	56	32	51	31

by the "personalities" of the girls, did not show the difference in successful prediction of boys and girls displayed by the counselor. It appears that the sex factor in prediction is more important when the subjects are well known by the forecaster.

Those counselors and others who are called upon to write statements to admissions officers about the probable success of high school students who are applying for entrance to college might examine the findings reported in this section with considerable interest. Impressed by the records and personalities of high school students, one may be tempted to assume that their performances in college will continue to be at the level at which they performed in secondary school.[22] During the years in the college situation, changes within and without the individual may be such that the consistency in performance that is often implied in letters to ad-

[22] Agatha Townsend, *College Freshmen Speak Out,* New York, Harper & Brothers, 1956.

missions officers may not be realized.[23] Four years is a long period ahead in the life of a youth.

FORECASTING PERFORMANCE IN EMPLOYMENT

The categories used in the employment predictions were described in Chapter III. The success of the counselor in prediction may be summarized briefly as follows.

Of the two cases predicted to develop their own business, one did so.

Of the 11 cases predicted to be promoted faster than usual, five did so.

Of the 37 cases predicted to change to better jobs, 12 did so.

Of the 59 cases predicted to be promoted on schedule, 16 did so.

Of the 50 cases predicted to remain at same job level as begun, 30 did so.

Of the ten cases predicted to drift from jobs to poorer jobs, three did so.

Of the one case predicted to be dismissed from a job 0 did so.

From the record it appeared that the counselor predicted correctly in only 37 of the 170 cases for a record of only 21.8 percent. The counselor-in-training, working only from the records, concentrated 160 of his 170 predictions in the three middle categories and was correct in 44.1 percent of the cases. It appears that the counselor who knew the subjects well was much too optimistic about their chances of progress. The counselor-in-training who worked only from the records and who was not influenced by personal contacts with the subjects played it safely and fared much better.

Both forecasters' effectiveness may have been reduced by the fact that it was difficult to determine the exact category in which the subject should be placed at the time of the follow-up, on the basis of the descriptions provided by the subjects and their employers. In order to reduce that difficulty the prediction categories

[23] Arthur Traxler and Agatha Townsend, *Improving Transition from School to College,* New York, Harper & Brothers, 1953; Dean Chamberlin, *Did They Succeed in College?* New York, Harper & Brothers, 1942.

and the actual records of progress in employment were grouped into the five categories described below.

Category 5. Owned his own business, was promoted faster than usual, or moved on to better jobs. An example in this category was the boy who worked as a farm hand, worked for a boat company, bought it, and now operates it. A girl who, rated 5, began as a filing clerk, was raised to merchandising, and then became an assistant buyer for the same company.

Category 4. Promoted on schedule. A girl who moved from filing clerk to clerk-typist to stenographer was placed in this category. Boys who completed apprenticeship and became journeymen were placed in category 4. One who worked in a warehouse and then began ordering for it was also put in this group.

Category 3. Remained at same job level. Those subjects who remained at the same job for the five years or who returned to the same one after returning from service were classified as 3.

Category 2. Dismissal or reduction to lesser job. When definite information on dismissal from a job or reduction to a lesser job was available the subject was placed in this category.

Category 1. Drifted from jobs to poorer jobs. Persons in this category may be generally described by the boy who wrote, "Since the fall of 1951 I have had a number of jobs that I was not really interested in or liked. Had two factory jobs, installed TV antennas and have had two smaller jobs since."

With these descriptions of the categories in mind the reader may turn to the figures in Table 115. It is apparent from the percentages reported there that the counselor had been generally too optimistic. Seventy of the 160 cases (or approximately 44 percent) predicted to progress at levels above the lowest category actually performed at a lower level than he had expected. Only 39 percent of the predictions were direct hits.

To determine whether the counselor had been more effective in forecasting the employment progress of girls than boys, the figures in Table 116 were tabulated. Comparisons of the figures in the diagonals of the tables indicated that there are enough differences to indicate better prediction for women than for men when the top three classifications are grouped. The small numbers in the other categories preclude any generalization about the dif-

TABLE 115. Accuracy of Counselor's Clinical Prediction of Performances of 170 Experimental Subjects Who Entered Employment

Occupational Progress	Number Predicted in Category	Percent of Number Predicted Who Made the Progress in Employment Indicated				
		Drifts From Job to Job, Poorer Jobs	Reduced Job Level or Dismissed	Remained at Same Job Level	Promoted on Schedule	Fast Promotion, Better Jobs, Has Own Business
Has own business, moved to better jobs, promoted rapidly	50	10	0	34	18	*38*
Promoted on schedule	59	3	0	50	*28*	19
Remained at same job level	50	14	0	*60*	12	14
Reduced job level or was dismissed	1	0	*0*	100	0	0
Drifted, moved to poorer jobs	10	*30*	0	50	0	20
Total	170					

ferences. There was a general tendency to be overoptimistic about the performances of both boys and girls except in the middle category where two-thirds of the girls and almost half of the boys were predicted correctly.

The effectiveness in prediction of the counselor-in-training is indicated by the figures which appear in Table 117. Although he used the rather safe middle category much more frequently than the counselor, he scored correct hits in only 75 of the 170 cases for a percentage of 44. He, too, was overoptimistic about the persons he put in the top categories.

Analysis of his predictions for the sex groups, similar to the one described previously for the counselor, indicated that he was very slightly more successful in forecasting the progress of boys

TABLE 116. Accuracy of Counselor's Prediction of Performance of 103 Experimental Girls and 67 Boys Who Entered Employment

Progress in Employment	Number Predicted at Each Level		Percent of Numbers Predicted Who Actually Achieved at Levels Indicated 5 Years After High School Graduation: Drifted Job to Job		Reduced in Pay, etc.		Remained at Same Job Level		Promoted on Schedule		Had Own Business, etc.	
	Girls	Boys	Girls	Boys	Girls	Boys	Girls	Boys	Girls	Boys	Girls	Boys
Had own business, promoted faster than usual, or changed to better jobs	21	29	9	10	0	0	43	28	9	24	*39*	*38*
Promoted in pay and responsibility on schedule	42	17	3	6	0	0	55	35	*32*	*24*	10	35
Remained at same job level at which begun	35	15	11	20	0	0	*66*	*47*	14	7	9	26
Reduced in pay and responsibility	1	0	0	0	*100*	*0*	0	0	0	0	0	0
Drifted from job to job, not to better jobs	4	6	*0*	*50*	0	0	50	50	0	0	50	0
Total	103	67										

TABLE 117. Accuracy of Counselor-in-Training's Prediction of Performance of 170 Experimental Subjects Who Entered Employment

Progress in Employment	Number Predicted at Each Level	Percent of Numbers Predicted Who Actually Achieved at Levels Indicated 5 Years After High School				
		Drifted Job to Job	Reduced in Pay, etc.	Remained at Same Job Level	Promoted on Schedule	Had Own Business, etc.
Had own business, promoted faster than usual, or changed to better jobs	27	11	0	33	23	*33*
Promoted in pay and responsibility on schedule	49	4	0	40	*33*	23
Remained at same job level at which begun	86	13	0	*57*	10	20
Reduced in pay and responsibility	0	0	*0*	0	0	0
Drifted from job to job, not to better jobs	8	*13*	0	50	12	25
Total	170					

than girls. The small differences do not indicate that the sex factor was significant in the forecasting procedures.

In general the results indicate that the personnel of this study were not highly effective in forecasting the progress in employment that would be made by the subjects within the five-year period after high school. Perhaps it was foolhardy to attempt it, but if it was so with all the information available to this counselor and counselor-in-training it would seem to be much more so for those who do not have it. It may be that the interval between forecast and performance was too great and that time had permitted too many factors within and without the individual to influence performances. It does seem to be true that characteristics of high school students observed by the counselors of this study and reported on cumulative records are not closely related to work progress after the students graduate. Counselors who predict confidently that students will or will not make progress might well take heed. The data presented here suggest that they are not likely to make correct predictions in more than two out of five cases.

PREDICTION OF PROGRESS IN MARRIAGE, ARMED FORCES, AND FARMING

The numbers of cases who entered categories of marriage, farming, and the armed forces were much smaller than had been anticipated at the time the categories were set up. The small numbers prevent generalization about the results of attempts to forecast performance in the three areas. The general summary given below gives only a hint of what might have been accomplished with larger numbers.

In the marriage classification the counselor predicted 12, or 80 percent of the total of 15 cases correctly. In those for whom he had predicted happy marriages he was 86 percent accurate. The counselor-in-training was successful in 73 percent of his total predictions and correct in 79 percent of his predictions of happy marriages. The classification, "Husband will end marriage by desertion, separation, or divorce," was not used. None of the subjects was predicted to fall into this category and none did so.

In predicting performance in the armed forces the counselor was correct in 7 of 16 cases. He was most accurate in predicting those who would be promoted on the usual schedule with a record of 64 percent accuracy. In the category of those who would not rise above the level of automatic promotions, only 25 percent of the cases were accurately predicted. The counselor-in-training concentrated his predictions in the automatic promotions and promoted-on-schedule categories only. He achieved his best record of 70 percent in the latter classification, but his overall record of accuracy was 50 percent. None of the subjects was predicted to fall into the dishonorably discharged or desertion categories and none did so.

The counselor and counselor-in-training made very similar scores in their predictions of performance of 18 subjects in farming. Each was 44 percent accurate in his overall predictions and each was 42 percent successful in forecasting those who would receive increased responsibility on the farm as the result of good work.

COMPARISON OF CLINICAL AND STATISTICAL PREDICTIONS OF COLLEGE ACHIEVEMENT

Now that the reader has seen the relationships between "clinical" predictions of achievement and actual achievement, he may now compare them with the relationships between actual achievements and "statistical" predictions made from data that were copied directly from the cumulative records. The relationships are shown by the coefficients that appear in Tables 118 and 119.

Data for computations of the coefficients were obtained from the record of grade points earned during the eleventh and twelfth grades, from the school's record of number of days absent during the last three years of high school, from the measure of socioeconomic status described in Chapter III (the higher the status the lower the figure used to describe it), from a count of the subjects' extracurricular activities obtained from school records, from self-ratings on the Senior Report (again the higher the rating the lower the score), and from test scores. The last two items in the tables are the "clinical" predictions from the records by the counselor-in-training and the counselor's forecasts.

The coefficients in the table indicate that the relationships between the various factors and college achievement may be listed in these rank orders for men and women.

49 MEN	COEFFICIENTS	54 WOMEN	COEFFICIENTS
Henmon-Nelson score	.321	Counselor's prediction	.420
DAT number score	.281	Grade points	.350
Grade points	.231	Counselor-in-training prediction	.344
Counselor's prediction	.174	DAT number score	.286
PMA space score	.163	Extracurricular activities	.266
Counselor-in-training prediction	.157	PMA space	.242

TABLE 118. Correlation Among Variables Used in the Prediction of Achievement in College for 54 Women

	0	1	2	3	4	5	6	7	8	9	10
	College Achievement	Grade Points Grades, 11, 12	Attendance (Days absent)	Socioeconomic Status	Extracurricular Activities	Henmon-Nelson	PMA Space	PMA Fluency	DAT Number	Self-Rating	Prediction from Records
Grade points	.350										
Attendance	.136	–.017									
Socioeconomic status	.037	.013	–.198								
Extracurricular activity	.266	.273	–.030	.175							
Henmon-Nelson	.220	.317	–.098	.086	.375						
PMA space	.242	.176	–.116	.313	.052	.195					
PMA fluency	.152	–.001	–.051	–.236	.280	.399	.098				
DAT number	.286	.267	–.126	.101	.280	.553	.164	.285			
Self-rating	–.228	–.403	–.213	–.003	–.365	.484	.059	–.138	–.305		
Prediction from records (counselor-in-training)	.344	.411	–.071	–.084	.287	.389	.230	.167	.452	–.129	
Counselor prediction	.420	.322	–.194	–.101	.263	.374	.243	.181	.434	–.369	.587

TABLE 119. Correlation Among Variables Used in the Prediction of Achievement in College for 49 Men

	0 College Achievement	1 Grade Points Grade, 11, 12	2 Attendance (Days absent)	3 Socioeconomic Status	4 Extracurricular Activities	5 Henmon-Nelson	6 PMA space	7 PMA fluency	8 DAT number	9 Self-rating	10 Prediction from Records
Grade points	.231										
Attendance	–.045	–.018									
Socioeconomic status	.029	.022	–.218								
Extracurricular activity	.117	.173	–.011	.120							
Henmon-Nelson	.321	.166	.101	.184	.238						
PMA space	.163	.143	–.129	.095	.112	.287					
PMA fluency	.110	–.307	–.010	.068	.006	.261	.101				
DAT number	.281	.145	.331	–.164	.237	.617	.235	.096			
Self-rating	.034	.130	.252	.153	.005	–.106	–.067	.137	–.194		
Prediction from records (counselor-in-training)	.157	.284	.119	.066	.331	.524	.424	.302	.314	–.102	
Counselor prediction	.174	.162	.225	–.036	.170	.571	.234	–.006	.362	–.298	.560

49 MEN	COEFFICIENTS	54 WOMEN	COEFFICIENTS
Extracurricular activities	.117	Self-rating	.228
PMA word fluency	.110	Henmon-Nelson score	.220
Attendance	.045	PMA word fluency	.152
Self-rating	.034	Attendance	.136
Socioeconomic status	.029	Socioeconomic status	.037

Only the first two of the 11 coefficients with the criterion for men and the first five of the 11 for women differed significantly from zero. It will be observed that the counselor's prediction for women correlated higher with the criterion than any of the other measures and that the counselor-in-training's forecasts correlated as highly with the criterion as grade points earned in the eleventh and twelfth grades. For men, however, the Henmon-Nelson test scores, grade points, and DAT number scores all correlate higher with the criterion than the counselor's and counselor-in-training's predictions although all four coefficients fell within the very narrow range of .157 to .321.

In view of the size of the correlation coefficients with the criterion and the relative size of the intercorrelations, it did not seem worth while to compute all the multiple correlation coefficients that the data made possible. The multiple R for college women computed from all the coefficients in Table 118, except the predictions of the counselor and counselor-in-training and the PMA space score, was .456. Thus the combining of attendance records, measures of socioeconomic status, extracurricular activities, self-ratings, the Henmon-Nelson, DAT number scores, and PMA word fluency scores added only .106 to the coefficient of .350 obtained from grade points alone. The time and labor required to procure and process the additional data would hardly seem justified for counselors unless very large numbers were involved. Even in that case they would not be particularly helpful to the counselor in dealing with particular cases.

It is worth noting that, for the college females, the combining of the counselor's and counselor-in-training's forecasts produced a multiple R of .437. Thus, the R of .456 obtained from the combination of the eight variables noted in the previous paragraph is only slightly and not significantly higher than the .437 obtained by combining the counselor's and counselor-in-training's forecasts. In the case of college-going girls, then, it appears that the clinical predictions, for all practical purposes, were as effective as the statistical forecasts.

The multiple R obtained by combining counselor and counselor-in-training's judgments, grade points, DAT number score, and number of extracurricular activities was .497. This is the highest of all the multiple correlation coefficients obtained in any of the attempts. It suggests that the counselors, by using their judgment and combining it with the kind of data used in this study, could do, at their best, only a fair job of forecasting the post-high school performances of their counselees in the five-year period following graduation from high school.

With college males the combined forecasts of the counselor and counselor-in-training produced a multiple R of only .187. Since this is smaller than such single coefficients as the .321 for the Henmon-Nelson, the .281 for the DAT number score, and the .231 for grade points, there can be no doubt that the statistical prediction measures were more efficient than the clinical judgments in forecasting the progress of college-going males. In view of the size of the criterion and intercorrelation coefficients and the amount of labor involved, it did not appear worth while to pursue further studies of the coefficients for the college males.

CLINICAL AND STATISTICAL PREDICTIONS OF PROGRESS IN EMPLOYMENT

Relationships between various scores or records obtained while the subjects were in high school, predictions made immediately after graduation and employment progress for 67 men and 103 women are indicated by the correlation coefficients which appear in Tables 120 and 121.

The arrangement of the coefficients in the first column of the tables in rank order produces the following lists.

MEN (N-67)	COEFFICIENTS	WOMEN (N-102)	COEFFICIENTS
Attendance	.281	DAT number score	.182
Grade points	.245	Grade points	.147

TABLE 120. Correlation Among Variables Used in Prediction of Post-High School Employment for 102 Women

	0 Employment Achievement	1 Grade Points	2 Attendance (Days absent)	3 Socioeconomic status	4 Extracurricular activities	5 Henmon-Nelson	6 PMA space	7 PMA Fluency	8 DAT Number	9 Self-Rating	10 Prediction from Records
Grade points	.147										
Attendance	.065	.275									
Socioeconomic status	.014	–.268	.145								
Extracurricular activity	.049	.112	–.144	.229							
Henmon-Nelson	.146	.319	–.079	.312	.346						
PMA space	.016	.152	–.055	.280	.149	.375					
PMA fluency	–.047	–.170	–.237	.041	.142	.363	.192				
DAT number	.182	.283	.157	.260	.090	.594	.087	.132			
Self-rating	–.098	–.296	–.044	–.184	–.150	–.192	–.036	.108	–.134		
Prediction from records (counselor-in-training)	.135	.186	.168	.142	.040	.226	.056	–.223	.290	–.042	
Counselor prediction	.058	.280	.093	.023	.112	.415	.240	–.060	.416	.095	.461

TABLE 121. Correlation Among Variables Used in Prediction of Progress in Post-High School Employment for 67 Men

	0 Employment Achievement	1 Grade Points	2 Attendance (Days absent)	3 Socio-economic status	4 Extra-curricular Activities	5 Henmon-Nelson	6 PMA Space	7 PMA Fluency	8 DAT Number	9 Self-Rating	10 Prediction from Records
Grade points	.245										
Attendance	.281	.173									
Socioeconomic status	.020	.123	.095								
Extracurricular activity	.032	.320	.143	.094							
Henmon-Nelson	.133	.044	.111	.060	.183						
PMA space	.012	.013	–.024	–.174	–.048	.152					
PMA fluency	.062	–.170	.023	–.054	.151	.383	.064				
DAT number	–.028	.166	–.073	.107	.186	.622	.241	.128			
Self-rating	–.178	–.180	–.189	–.182	–.139	.173	.013	–.032	–.272		
Prediction from records (counselor-in-training)	.063	–.054	–.011	.108	–.176	.104	–.064	.071	.293	–.150	
Counselor prediction	.213	.148	–.086	.105	–.133	.314	.086	.078	.343	–.056	.341

MEN (N-67)	COEFFICIENTS	WOMEN (N-102)	COEFFICIENTS
Counselor's predictions	.213	Henmon-Nelson score	.146
Self-rating	.178	Counselor-in-training's prediction	.135
Henmon-Nelson score	.133	Self-rating	.098
Counselor-in-training's prediction	.063	Attendance	.065
PMA word fluency	.062	Counselor's prediction	.058
Extracurricular activities	.032	Extracurricular activities	.049
DAT number score	.028	PMA word fluency	.047
Socioeconomic status	.020	PMA space	.016
PMA space	.012	Socioeconomic status	.014

None of the 11 coefficients with the criterion for women differed significantly from zero. By combining the three highest criterion coefficients (DAT scores, Henmon-Nelson scores, and grade points) the multiple R was only .208. Combination of predictions for the counselor and counselor-in-training produced an R of .135. Comparison of the two R's suggests that the statistical method was slightly superior to the clinical method in the forecasting of progress in women's employment. When the three statistical items given above were combined with the two clinical forecasts, the multiple R was raised to only .236. It appears that the combination of statistical and clinical forecasts of the performances in employment of the women was not high enough to suggest that either method could be used meaningfully by counselors who work with individual cases.

In view of the insignificant criterion coefficients, the size of the intercorrelation coefficients, and the results obtained by use of the five variables noted above, the labor of computing a multiple R for all the items in Table 120 for women did not seem to be warranted.

Only the first two of the 11 criterion coefficients for men differed significantly from zero. When the two were combined the multiple R was .314. This figure can be contrasted with the .213

obtained when the counselor and counselor-in-training's forecasts were combined. When the two statistical items and the two clinical judgments were combined, the multiple R rose to .402. In view of the size of the remaining criterion and intercorrelation coefficients, it appeared likely that the .402 would not be raised any meaningful amount so further computation with the items in the table was omitted.

It appears that prediction of employment progress of the men could be done more successfully than for women. For both sexes the statistical method appeared to be slightly superior to the clinical method but neither, separately or combined, produced evidence to suggest that methods of the kind used here were likely to be very helpful to the counselor.

Those who predict confidently that young men and women will or will not make progress in post-high school employment on the basis of observation of their behavior and measurement of their performances in high school should be warned by the figures presented above that their predictions are not likely to be accurate.

SUMMARY OF THE PREDICTION STUDIES

It was suggested at the beginning of this section that prediction of post-high school performances of his counselees is implied if not explicitly stated in many of a counselor's activities. The limited accuracy of forecasts of students' performances over such periods as the first semester or year of college or on first jobs has been indicated in many previous studies, but the accuracy of such forecasts for a five-year period has not previously been determined because of lack of such data as have been obtained in this study.

The results reported in this section indicate that the forecasts (clinical judgments) of a counselor and counselor-in-training made on the basis of data usually obtained by counselors were frequently in error. They tended to be overoptimistic about the persons they placed in top categories and unduly pessimistic about those placed in the lower ones. Their success in predicting which subjects would remain to be graduated, with or without difficulties in the process, was high despite the fact that they had predicted higher percentages of college graduation than usually occur. The forecasts of a counselor-in-training who worked only from the records and who did not know the subjects personally were markedly similar to those of the counselor. Both predicted college success more accurately for women than for men.

In general the forecasts of progress in employment were less accurate than those for progress through college. The counselor was again overly optimistic about those he placed in the top categories. The counselor-in-training used the extremes of the scale less frequently and was slightly more accurate in his forecasts. Both were right in approximately two out of five cases.

Comparison of the accuracy of clinical (counselor judgment) and statistical forecasts revealed that the statistical method was slightly superior except in the case of the women who went to college. Neither the clinical nor statistical methods proved accurate enough to suggest that forecasting of post-high school performances of youth in college or employment could be done with a high degree of accuracy. The common practice of forecasting the post-high school performances of secondary school graduates with a high degree of confidence seems not to be warranted.

Discriminant Analysis of Longitudinal Data in Evaluation of Counseling

Peter F. Merenda
Research Assistant, University of Wisconsin

A special study to evaluate the outcomes of counseling given to the experimental students was conducted with 676 of the 685 subjects who were still alive five years after high school graduation and whose records were complete enough for the purposes of this study. The relative effectiveness of counseling and noncounseling was studied separately for the experimental and control subjects whose post-high school activities placed them in one of the following five categories:

1. Men who had attended, for at least one full year, a post-secondary level school of higher education or training and/or were in full-

time residence at such an institution five years after high school graduation.

2. Unmarried women in the above status.
3. Men whose most significant post-high school experiences were in the field of employment and/or whose academic post-high school training was limited to less than one full year. All apprenticeships were classified in this category.
4. Unmarried women in the above status.
5. Married women who were married within the first five years after high school graduation and who were still married at the time of the third (1956) follow-up study.

The evaluative criteria of this study were developed from responses made by these subjects on the three follow-up questionnaires. They were classified on the basis of their cumulative responses into the following four areas of personal attitudes and feelings: (1) satisfaction-adjustment; (2) optimism; (3) reflection on high school training; and (4) persistency in post-high school endeavors.

The method of statistical analysis used in this evaluation study was the discriminatory analysis developed by Fisher.[24] The essential property of the Fisher linear discriminant function is that it will distinguish better than any other linear function between specified groups on which common measurements are available.

The linear discriminant function yields the relative optimal weights on the individual variables that will provide maximum separation of the groups. The technique also provides a test of the overall statistical significance of the difference between the two groups on a set of measurements common to both. In terms of the specific design of this study, the two groups of persons were: (1) counseled and (2) uncounseled subjects. The common sets of measurements were the four criterion variables given above.

If a statistically-significant difference between the two groups could be found on this set of measurements, and if the mean differences on the criterion variables were substantially in the same direction, then that group showing the higher individual means

[24] R. A. Fisher, "The Use of Multiple Measurements in Taxonomic Problems," *Annals of Eugenics,* 7:179–188, 1936.

would be judged to have been superior on the basis of the evaluative criteria. In this case one might conclude that the treatments applied to the group showing the higher means produced the more desirable outcomes. It is true, of course, that the discriminant function is a linear composite of *all* the variables. If it is desirable to determine more precisely the nature of the group differences, the means of the individual variables may be inspected. This procedure was followed in this study.

When discriminant analysis was applied to the set of normalized scale values for these criterion measures, the following results were obtained. They applied to all except those subjects of category 4 (unmarried women) for whom no significant differences were noted.

In general, the counseled subjects tended to give responses that indicated a higher degree of satisfaction with their post-high school experiences and more satisfactory adjustments in their activities after high school. In their outlook toward the future, the counseled subjects tended to give slightly more optimistic responses, although both groups appeared to express a highly optimistic view. With respect to their attitude on how they felt high school training either helped or failed to prepare them for post-high school life, there was a tendency on the part of both the counseled and uncounseled subjects to point out the failings as well as the values of the training received. In general, they indicated that high school helped more than it failed. The counseled subjects expressed a more favorable attitude. In terms of persistency in educational and vocational choice, as well as in carrying such plans through to fulfillment, greater stability was indicated by the counseled subjects.

In this study one discriminant function was derived for each category of subjects described above. They are presented in Table 122. All but one of these proved either to border on statistical significance at the 5 percent level of confidence or exceeded this standard. The mean differences between the control and experimental subjects on this set of evaluative criteria were practically all in favor of the latter subjects.

TABLE 122. Differences in Means, Discriminant Weights, and Tests of Significance

Sample	N	Differences in Means (Exp.—Con.)	Discriminant Weights	F	P
chool males	NE = 63	d_1 = 1.0355	v_1 = 0.00278	2.24	.07
	NC = 47	d_2 = 0.2280	v_2 = 0.00012		
	N = 110	d_3 = 0.2753	v_3 = 0.00018		
		d_4 = 0.3455	v_4 = 0.00077		
chool females (unmarried)	NE = 23	d_1 = 1.0732	v_1 = 0.00322	2.36	.07
		d_2 = −0.5927	v_2 = −0.00617		
	NC = 19	d_3 = 0.5927	v_3 = 0.00529		
	N = 42	d_4 = 0.9634	v_4 = 0.01527		
Nonschool males	NE = 97	d_1 = 0.6741	v_1 = 0.00067	2.91	<.05
	NC = 109	d_2 = 0.5113	v_2 = 0.00046		
	N = 206	d_3 = 0.6515	v_3 = 0.00069		
		d_4 = 0.0444	v_4 = −0.00020		
Nonschool females (unmarried)	NE = 14	d_1 = −0.4023	v_1 = −0.00400	0.49	—
		d_2 = 0.2744	v_2 = 0.00046		
	NC = 19	d_3 = −0.2820	v_3 = −0.00439		
	N = 33	d_4 = −0.6015	v_4 = −0.00937		
Married females	NE = 144	d_1 = 0.6850	v_1 = 0.00067	4.99	<.01
	NC = 141	d_2 = 0.5322	v_2 = 0.00056		
	N = 285	d_3 = 0.4950	v_3 = 0.00048		
		d_4 = −0.0217	v_4 = −0.00028		

NE = Number experimentals.
NC = Number controls.

The data of this study strongly suggest that desirable outcomes, as measured by the set of evaluative criteria used, may be enhanced by providing intensive counseling services to high school students. The fact that the counseled subjects of this study tended to show a pattern of more favorable early adult behavior and attitudes is an indication that special counseling is related to certain significant and desirable results, which are achieved to a lesser degree by the usual informal-type counseling that is typically offered in the majority of our high schools today.

Intra-Individual Consistency

Robert A. Heimann
Arizona State College

Counselors and others who work with students in school have generally assumed the fact of consistency of performance on the part of the individuals with whom they work and have used this construct as a basis for their attempts at predictions of subsequent successful performance in the postschool world. Little direct evidence has been presented to substantiate this assumption, although most theories of personality organization postulate consistency or continuity of behavior as one of their basic hypotheses. This study was undertaken to examine the assumption of intra-individual consistency of performance by examining the academic and test records of a group of students from the major study described in this volume in an effort to determine to what extent their performance records bore out the hypothesis of a consistent intra-individual pattern.

The study was designed to examine the concept of intra-individual consistency of performance with particular reference to its use by school counselors in their work with individual high school students. The counselor is often confronted with the problem of how much weight to attach to a particular performance of a given individual. He may be better able to assess the relative importance of various data about an individual if he has some knowledge of that individual's previous performances and some estimate of how consistent they have been. If he has some evidence that the individual under concern has a stable and consistent record of past performances, he may be able to make his predictions with more assurance than if the past pattern has been erratic and variable.

For the purposes of this study 120 high school students were selected at random from the total population of the Wisconsin Counseling Study and an analysis was made of their individual school records. These records included scores from tests administered over a period of three years and school marks obtained during the four years of high school. In addition, evidence of behavioral consistency was sought in reports of the behaviors of these subjects described by their teachers over a three-year period of time.

Consistency was measured by use of an *Index of Consistency* determined by equating and averaging the individuals' gross test scores and gross school marks with a standard score technique and deriving their respective standard deviations. In this manner the individual with a small index of consistency score (a small standard deviation of his intra-individual array of such scores) was classed as more consistent in his total performance than an individual with a large index of consistency score (a large standard deviation of his intra-individual arrays of scores). Thus each individual in the study became a distribution in himself and the analysis of the relative consistency of performances of each subject was made possible.

The group statistical findings seem to imply that the construct of consistency is fairly independent of the level of achievement of the individual (r .06 to —.31). In general, the more consistent performers received higher scores on their tests (C.R. .23, P .80); accumulated higher overall school grades (C.R. 1.44; P <.10> .20;) and scored higher on intelligence tests. Girls were generally more consistent than boys when consistency was determined by test scores (C.R. 1.85, P >.05<.10) and received higher scores on both tests and marks (Tests C.R. 1.82, P <.01>.05; Marks C.R. 3.72, P .01).

When further analysis was made of the consistency scores of the 40 percent of the subjects judged to be the most consistent and the least consistent, more marked differences were observed. The more consistent subjects were superior school achievers when compared to the nonconsistent subjects (t 2.88, P = .01) and had slightly higher overall test scores. The group of subjects rated the most nonconsistent as determined by their distribution of school marks were the lowest school achievers and the lowest test performers.

Coefficients of correlation between test scores and school marks for the more consistent subjects were somewhat higher than coefficients usually found (r .59 to .73) and an unusually low coefficient was determined for the subgroup rated least consistent (r .22). This differentiation should prove of interest to the counselor in prediction attempts, and may explain the usual moderate group relationships found between test scores and school marks in groups undifferentiated as to consistency as a generalized trait.

Consistency scores for a subgroup of 80 students in one school were obtained by use of the behavior description method described in Chapter III.[25] Subjects who were found to be consistent in behavior were found to be consistent in terms of their overall test and school mark performances. They were also found to be higher achievers than the nonconsistent subjects in terms of test scores and school achievement as well as higher in their scores on intelligence tests. Sixty-four percent of the consistent subjects of this subgroup were girls and only 36 percent were boys. The nonconsistent group was composed of 28 percent girls and 72 percent boys. The nonconsistent subjects as determined by behavior descriptions were also more nonconsistent than the rest when their overall index of consistency scores was examined, they were lower scorers on intelligence tests, lower school achievers, and lower scorers in tests in general than the consistent group.

These findings may be reflections of a systematic bias of the teachers who described their behavior, and the more consistent pattern of the girls may reflect the somewhat stereotyped, superior reputation of girls in a behavioral classroom situation. The similarity of consistency classifications by such different techniques as tests, marks, and behavioral descriptions, seems, however, to give additional weight to the concept of consistency of performance as a high-level, generalized trait present in the several aspects of this study.

The investigation of consistency of performance was followed by case study analysis of the case records of ten subjects in great detail. In this individual analysis, consistency as a trait appeared to be closely related to the motivation and intensity of drive of the

[25] Robert A. Heimann, *Intra-Individual Consistency of Performance in Relation to the Counseling Process,* unpublished Ph.D. thesis, University of Wisconsin, 1952.

persons whose consistency classifications seemed to hold up in the study of their life histories. Through this investigation the concept of consistency was broadened to include the consistently variable performer whose record when examined as a whole appeared as a very consistent unity despite its pattern of specific variability or nonconsistency. For this type of individual a patterned variability in performance was as consistent in its unevenness as the regular pattern of performance of the nominally consistent person.

From this evidence there appears some justification for regarding consistency as a configurational trait present in the performance record of 40 percent of the high school students of this study. This consistent pattern may appear in a marked evenness in the overall record of these subjects, or it may be reflected in a markedly erratic, uneven pattern in the record. Each of these patterns would seem to be an illustration of a certain unity in the performances of these particular individuals in their trait-to-trait behaviors over a period of time.

This unity of performance would not seem unrelated to several factors in the cultural background in which these subjects function. The passivity, docility, and compliant behavior demanded of most adolescent girls in our culture may account for some of the consistent performances of these girls, particularly when it comes to school marks and behavior. The general superiority and the greater pattern of consistency in the testing situation evidenced by the girls may be explained by their acknowledged superiority as a group in linguistic and verbal tasks that are called for in the items in many of the commonly used testing instruments. In several of the cases of consistent persons, very strong motivation for success in the academic situation was indicated as a factor in explanation of their markedly consistent patterns of attainment. The home backgrounds and the field situation in which these young people were functioning were also regarded as major contributing factors in their motivational patterns and, in turn, in their development of a consistent performance record.

The following educational and psychological implications would seem to stem from these conclusions. Consistency of performance is a concept that includes both generally even performances of individuals and generally uneven, erratic patterns of performance. The counselor can use these concepts to give him some indication of the weight to be attached to past performances of a given individual in helping him plan for the future.

Many consistent performers are high in their achievement level and many nonconsistent performers are apt to be low in their general attainment level in school. However, among both the high and low achievers are found both consistent and nonconsistent subjects. For the counselor, then, consistency or its absence becomes an independent variable or trait useful in evaluation of the records of individual students. Since girls are both higher achievers and more consistent performers than boys, a markedly nonconsistent record of a given girl would be more significant and would merit more study in the counseling situation.

Intensive case study of individuals-in-particular revealed patterns of strong motivation for success in the academic situation for the consistent subjects. This suggests that any study of the whole individual must involve more than perusal of the actuarial record. The counselor should become more sensitive to the strong motivational patterns of the consistent persons, and can gain some understanding of the nonconsistent subject by consideration of his relatively weaker drives for success in the academic situation.

Further, consistency of performance seems to be positively related to compliant behavior of the individual under study. For the counselor's appraisal, a consistent pattern of performance can be helpful in order to gain some insight into some of the usual behaviors of the individual concerned in his role of adjusting and being molded by the institutional pressures of school and family. The nonconsistent subject is more apt to be less influenced by the pressures to conform demanded by school and society, and the counselor can help such a person prepare for the resultant consequences of such habitual behavior.

These conclusions and implications seem to point out further that the study of individuals by the counselor should be implemented by careful accumulation of records of varied performances over a period of several years, that the inclusion of personal documents and all evidence concerning the total behavior of the individual should be included in this record, and that generalizations based on group data often lack depth of understanding of the behavorial patterns of individuals under study. Finally, by utilization of clinical procedures that pay attention to the background, motivations, the subject's picture of self, and the field situation in which the individual functions, the counselor can make a meaningful study of the individual-in-particular.

CHAPTER VIII

Summary and Conclusions

A study such as the one reported in this volume is never quite completed. Contact with the subjects who have been followed for five years after graduation from high school will be maintained and the data added to those collected during the past eight years. All the information will be analyzed by methods in the process of development so that greater utilization of their longitudinal aspects can be made. The time must come, however, when a halt must be called to the data-collecting process so that the findings may be summarized and reported. As the reader reviews the report of the study in this volume he may regret that a halt has been made at a period only five years beyond high school graduation. It may lessen his feelings of regret somewhat if he notes that this study is the first of its kind to carry so many subjects over as long a period of time.

It is not necessary to make a detailed summary of the materials in the first four chapters at this time since they were described fully at the time they were presented. In general the reader will have noted that some concerns of a good cross section of high school students were outlined, some principles of counseling to deal with them enunciated, the implementation of the principles in typical secondary school situations described, and methods for follow-up appraisal to get maximum returns were detailed. The techniques for collecting and collating data and putting them to use in the service of youth that have been described could be employed in public high schools if members of their faculties were willing to do so.

Before a summary of the general findings is presented, the reader should be reminded about some of the limitations noted several times throughout this volume. Those who are familiar with only those short-term, small-population, and precisely formulated studies that emphasize the symbol-manipulative aspects of educational research will recognize that the study reported here does not fit into the classic textbook illustration. It does not do so because an attempt was made to duplicate conditions that counselors find on the "firing line" rather than in the situations an experimenter can create in the laboratory. The investigators had to work in the situations they found and these situations could not be changed quickly. The subjects all had parents, teachers, friends, relatives, employers, other adults, and, later, husbands and wives who influenced their choices. Health, religion, location, financial circumstances, economic changes, and many other factors influenced their behavior. They were free subjects in a free society after they left school and coercion and supervision would not have been possible even if that had seemed desirable. These are some of the conditions that counselors meet and it was under such conditions that the researchers of this study worked. Some of the limitations might have been avoided by setting up a precise laboratory situation, but it would never have been known whether the results from it could have been translated meaningfully to conditions as they exist outside of laboratories.

The budget for this study limited the size of the experimental population and this was particularly unfortunate when the researcher was concerned with vocational choices. Only three subjects of this study, for example, may yet become physicians, so there can be no generalization about persons who choose that profession. And lumping of several occupations into a professional category results in distortions due to differences in training requirements and work performed. Personal limitations and biases of particular individuals who counsel cannot be eliminated and one can only hope that they were minimized. Economic circumstances, military demands, and even changes in customs (more marriage among the greater numbers going to college, for example) have changed significantly in the eight-year period of the study, which encompassed the Korean War. Perhaps one would like to do a longitudinal study of development of youth in a more normal period but this author despairs of accomplishing it. The first one on which he worked was completed during a period of economic depression,[1] the second [2] and third [3] were completed during World War II, and during this study a war and period of economic prosperity developed. Those who do only cross-sectional studies can never really know the problems that directors of longitudinal studies meet, but they should recognize that many insuperable obstacles develop. Such obstacles must be considered in the interpretation of results.

It should be noted that the author of this volume, in setting up the design for this study, recognized that he could never get a control group of subjects who had not received or would not receive *any* counseling. One cannot, or should not, prevent teachers, counselors, ministers, physicians, friends, and relatives from advising young persons. This study is not one, then, of the difference between youth who had absolutely no counseling (an impossible situation) and those who had some even though the terms "counseled" and "uncounseled" have been used for convenience. It is a study of some youth who were given special counseling by the workers in this study *over and above* that which they might ordinarily have obtained, and of another similar group of young people who did not have such special attention. In effect, it attempts to answer the question about whether the addition of special counselors where there had been none before under the stated conditions influences the behavior of youth during and following their period of senior high school attendance.

One final and serious limitation must be considered in the interpretation of the findings given below. It was caused by the

[1] Walter F. Dearborn and John W. M. Rothney, *Scholastic, Social and Economic Backgrounds of Unemployed Youth,* Cambridge, Harvard University Press, 1938.

[2] W. Aiken, *The Story of the Eight-Year Study,* New York, Harper & Brothers, 1942.

[3] John W. M. Rothney and B. A. Roens, *Guidance of American Youth,* Cambridge, Harvard University Press, 1950.

difficulty of reporting, in statistical terms, a study that was primarily concerned with individuals. As developments occur in the relatively new field of social statistics, a method that is accepted almost to the point of a fad today becomes passé tomorrow. Any of the procedures recommended by one statistician seem to be subject to criticism by another, and a researcher must recognize that any method he uses will be considered inadequate by some persons. The feelings of statisticians about the inadequacy of the methods used here will probably not be as great as those felt by the writer when he was forced to put these counselees who seemed unique into distributions in which their similarity to others was assumed. If it were possible to give all the details about all the characteristics and conditions of the subjects of this study in complete case histories and to evaluate their development from such records, it is quite possible that the results might have been different from those reported in this volume.

GENERAL FINDINGS

The reader may have observed additional limitations to those given above. With all of them in mind, he may now turn to the following general conclusions, which seem to be indicated by statistically significant differences (or by strong directional trends of many small differences) between the members of the control and experimental groups. General summarizing statements of comparisons of the two groups follow. They suggest that the experimentals

1. achieved slightly higher academic records in high school and post-high school education;
2. indicated more realism about their own strengths and weaknesses at the time they were graduated from high school;
3. were less dissatisfied with their high school experiences;
4. had different vocational aspirations;
5. were more consistent in expression of, entering into, and remaining in their vocational choices, classified by areas;
6. made more progress in employment during the five-year period following high school graduation;

7. were more likely to go on to higher education, to remain to graduate, and to plan for continuation of higher education;
8. were more satisfied with their post-high school education;
9. expressed greater satisfaction with their status five years after high school and were more satisfied in retrospect with their post-high school experiences;
10. participated in more self-improvement activities after completing high school;
11. looked back more favorably on the counseling they had obtained.

Among the many differences noted between the male and female subjects of this study, regardless of their control or experimental status, the following seem to have special significance for counselors.

1. Girls tended to get better marks than boys in high school and in college.
2. Almost twice as many girls as boys were married within five years after graduation.
3. Girls were less mobile occupationally but more mobile geographically than boys.
4. Girls expressed greater satisfaction than boys with their post-high school status.
5. Girls looked more optimistically than boys toward their futures.
6. Boys gave different priorities from those of girls for choosing jobs.
7. Boys were much less active in community and self-improvement activities than girls during the five years after high school graduation.

The following general statements about the total population of this study during the five years following high school graduation provide some interesting data about the period of youth and early adulthood.

1. Attitudes toward the future were generally optimistic and confident.
2. When looking back at their high school experiences they reported that high school had helped them more in preparing

for vocations and post-high school training than in the development of personal and social skills and values.

3. Variability rather than consistency was the rule in the making of vocational choices and in carrying them through into action.
4. The great enthusiasm about first jobs or training after high school waned steadily throughout the following five years.
5. Satisfactions associated with post-high school activities were expressed in terms of personal rather than financial and social values.
6. Approximately half of the subjects said that they had voted in political elections although all were of age to do so.

The following findings about procedures and instruments have been selected for presentation here because they may be helpful to those who plan to do research in guidance. The specifics upon which these general statements are based will be found throughout the text.

1. Unless replies to follow-up questionnaires are obtained from all the subjects, distortion of results will occur. Such distortion cannot be avoided by making comparisons of the pre-follow-up characteristics of responders and nonresponders.
2. Agreement among raters or classifiers of *factual* questionnaire responses is sufficiently high, and the consistency of individual raters stable enough, to warrant use of such items in evaluation of counseling. Items that require responders to give reasons or express attitudes are not likely to be classified or rated with enough interperson or intraperson consistency to justify analysis of questionnaire returns by one person. (This finding resulted in the use of committee discussion methods in the analyses of the follow-up questionnaire responses obtained in this study.)
3. Checks of questionnaire responses by securing reports of employers and by obtaining official records of post-high school training indicated that high school graduates reported their employment and training progress accurately.
4. There is currently no satisfactory method of classifying the occupations that youth choose and enter. Research results in this area may vary with the use of different classifications.

5. Scores on tests of the kind commonly employed in counseling do provide crude indications of success in post-high school academic training but do not do so for progress in employment. There was no meaningful relationship between preference record scores and post-high school activities.
6. Academic achievement in high school was a fair predictor of achievement in college but not of progress in post-high school employment.
7. The counselor of the subjects of this study and a counselor-in-training who used the cumulative records of the subjects in predicting performances in college or employment after high school graduation tended to be overoptimistic in their predictions.
8. Clinical (counselor) forecasts of employment and training progress for the five-year period after high school were slightly less accurate than those made from statistical data. Neither produced highly accurate forecasts.
9. An exploratory investigation with methods of discriminant analysis indicated that criteria need not always be developed before evaluation of guidance is done.

CONCLUDING STATEMENT

It seems clear that the differences between the counseled and comparison subjects of this study after they had been graduated from high school were less than one would hypothesize in view of the claims frequently made by guidance workers. The size of the differences may be attributable to the failure of the counselors to make the most of their opportunities or inadequacies in the evaluation procedures and instruments. They may, however, indicate that counseling as it is commonly done with the heterogeneous populations in secondary schools has little relationship to the post-high school activities of youth and young adults.

There can be no doubt, however, that some important differences between the counseled and comparison groups did appear and that they could not be attributed to chance alone. When so many small and a few large differences in the directions hypothesized by guidance workers can be obtained under representative high school counseling conditions, it seems likely that greater differences would appear if counseling were done under more ideal circumstances. Such circumstances would seem to require more acceptance of counseling as a regular part of secondary school experience, more enthusiastic support by parents and school personnel, and better techniques of evaluation.

High school counselors cannot work toward objectives that continue to differ significantly from those of other workers in secondary schools. They can probably work most effectively as members of a team which is striving toward objectives that have been developed coöperatively. It has been shown previously that *intensive* counseling of youth during their high school years and close collaboration of the counselors with members of a high school staff do assist materially in the accomplishment of the objectives of the American secondary school.[4] In this study less intensive counseling representative of what is offered in the usual high school situation has been shown to contribute less than intensive counseling to the accomplishment of such objectives, but both studies offer some justification for the provision of counseling programs in high schools.

It is hoped that this study may offer suggestions to others who are attempting to determine whether counseling should or should not be offered and who are willing to base their decisions on evidence rather than on hope and faith.

[4] John W. M. Rothney and Bert A. Roens, *Guidance of American Youth,* Cambridge, Harvard University Press, 1950.

APPENDIX I

Occupations Mentioned by Subjects During and After High School

The list of occupations given in the following pages may be helpful to those who are attempting to provide occupational library materials for high school students. The titles comprise the complete tabulation of occupations named by the subjects of this study as

1. their own stated vocational choices;
2. their own stated vocational activities;
3. occupations for which they were in training;
4. occupations of fathers or mothers;
5. occupations of husbands or wives.

The frequency with which they were mentioned in all the above circumstances follows each title. If at least one of the subjects actually entered or began training for an occupation, it is marked with an asterisk.

Those counselors who wish to set up an occupational file for a high school may find the list particularly helpful. Although there will usually be differences in local situations, the list provided should indicate the relative frequency of occupations that high school counselors meet in their work.

*Accountant	78
*Actor	13
*Air conditioning technician	7
*Ambulance attendant	2
*Animal caretaker	5
*Animal husbandry	22
*Announcer, radio and TV	7
Archeologist	1
*Architect	33
*Artist	76

Occupation	Number
*Asbestos installer	2
*Assembler, factory	70
*Assembler, steel windows	3
Athlete, professional	19
*Athletic coach	27
Bacteriologist	1
Baker	3
*Bank messenger	3
Bank teller	6
*Barber	21
*Bartender	3
Beautician	19
Blacksmith	1
Bobbin winder	1
*Body shop helper	2
*Bookkeeper	79
Bottle washer	1
Brewmaster	1
Brickmason	21
Brushmaker	1
*Bus driver	14
Business agent, union	1
*Butcher	26
*Butcher's assistant	13
*Buyer	9
Cabinetmaker	6
*Calf skinner	2
*Canvas cutter	1
Caretaker	1
*Carpenter	39
Cartographer	3
*Cashier, office	11
*Cashier, retail store	9
*Casketmaker	2
*Caster, plumbing fixtures	3
*Cement finisher	3
*Chemist	16
Chiropractor	3
Church worker	1
*City planner	3
*Civil Service (nothing specified)	6
*Clerical, general	473
*Clerk, account	16
*Clerk, assistant traffic	1
*Clerk, billing	10
*Clerk, cost	7
*Clerk, file	8
*Clerk, mail	6
*Clerk, order	10
*Clerk, payroll	17
*Clerk, reservation	7
*Clerk, shipping and receiving	22
*Clerk, stock	29
Clerk, toolroom	1
Coilmaker	1
*Communications technician	5
*Comptometer operator	25
*Conservation worker	30
Contractor, construction	21
Contractor, painting	3
*Cook (chef)	13
*Cook, short order	3
Core dipper	1
*Core maker	14
*Counselor, employment	1
Counselor, school	2
County agent	1
Crane operator	3
*Dancer	2
*Dental assistant	28
*Dental hygienist	8
*Dentist	22
*Design engineer	1
Designer, general	6
Designer, mechanical	3
Diesel engineer (stationary)	1
Diplomat	1
*Dispatcher	3

Occupation	Number
*Doctor's assistant	8
*Domestic servant	13
Doormaker	1
*Draftsman	164
Dressmaker	1
*Drill press operator	6
Drop forge operator	1
*Druggist (pharmacist)	31
*Dry cleaning helper	6
*Economist	11
*Editorial writer	4
Electrical technician	2
*Electrician	30
*Electrician, diesel locomotive	2
*Electrician's helper	9
*Electronics technician	31
*Engineer, agricultural	9
*Engineer, chemical	9
*Engineer, civil	26
*Engineer, electrical	27
*Engineer, mechanical	60
Engineer, metallurgical	7
*Engineer, mining	20
*Estimating engineer	5
Executive, commercial	14
Executive, industrial	12
Expediter	1
*Factory repairman	4
*Farmer *Farm laborer	690
*Field man, building company	5
Fireman, city	6
Fireman, stationary boiler	1
Flight engineer	2
Floor finisher	1
*Florist	17
Foreman, brewery	2
Foreman, construction	1
Foreman, electrical	1
Foreman, factory	28
Foreman, farm	1
Foreman, garage	6
Foreman, heating plant installation	2
Foreman, plumbing	1
Foreman, telephone company	3
*Foreman, warehouse	6
*Forester (college trained)	17
Forest ranger	5
*Foundry layout man	6
Fruitgrower	1
Furniture finisher	1
*Garage laborer (mechanic's helper)	26
*Garage parts man	11
Gas company worker	4
Gasoline power plant engineer	1
*Gas station serviceman	26
Glazier	1
Governess	1
Greenhouse worker	1
*Grinder	13
Guard, hospital	1
Guide, hunting and fishing	3
Heat treater	1
Heavy machinery operator (construction)	10
*Home economist (specializing in clothing and textiles)	22
*Home economist (specializing in foods)	27
Horse raiser	2
Horse trainer	1
Hospital attendant	3
Inspector, brewery	1
Inspector, dairy	1
*Inspector, factory	17

Inspector, laundry	1
Inspector, sewer	1
*Installer, heating plant	1
*Instructor, baton twirling	3
*Instructor, dance	15
*Insulator, heating plants	11
Interior decorator	8
Interpreter	2
Investigator, FBI and tax	2
Janitor	8
Jeweler	2
*Jeweler's assistant	1
*Laboratory assistant	4
*Laborer (not specified)	43
*Laborer, city and county	8
*Laborer, construction	74
*Laborer, dairy plant	64
*Laborer, factory	155
*Laborer, foundry	26
*Laborer, highway department	3
*Laborer, laundry	7
Laborer, retail store	2
*Laborer, telephone company	3
*Laborer, water department	7
Lathe operator	27
Lather	4
*Lawyer	62
Librarian	2
*Lineman, telephone company	17
*Loader, boxcars, trucks, etc.	22
Machine operator	48
*Machine setup man	5
*Machine tender	28
Machinist, railroad	1
*Machinist, regular	146
*Mail carrier	14
Maintenance and repair mechanic	2
Manager, bowling alley	3
Manager, bus line	2
Manager, hospital	1
Manager, milk plant	2
*Manager, office	8
*Manager, restaurant	3
*Manager, retail store	25
Manager, theater	1
*Management trainee	8
Marketing	3
Masseur	1
Mechanic, auto	24
*Mechanic, auto body	6
Mechanic, aviation	4
*Medical technician	21
*Milk checker	3
*Milk smeller	2
Milling machine operator	2
Millwright	2
*Minister	5
Mink farmer	1
Missionary	3
Model	6
Molder	6
Mover	1
Movie projectionist	2
Musical arranger	1
*Musical director	17
Musical director, church	5
*Musician	22
*Nurse	202
*Nurse, practical	25
*Nurse's aide	20
Nursing teacher	1
*Occupational therapist	17
*Office machine operator	55
*Oil distributor's helper	2
Oiler	1
*Optometrist	5
*Outdoor advertising display man	7

Occupation	Number
Oven tender	1
*Packer	17
*Painter	24
*Painter, stained glass	11
*Painter's helper	1
*Paint sprayer	1
*Pattern gater	4
*Patternmaker	20
*Personnel worker	6
Photographer	1
*Photographer's assistant	4
*Physician	108
Physiotherapist	4
Piano tuner	1
Pilot (airplane)	16
Pipe layer	2
Plant engineer	2
*Plasterer	13
*Plumber	22
Policeman	20
*Police trainee	1
Polisher	2
Politician	1
*Post office clerk	10
Power brake operator	1
*Printer	9
*Printer's assistant	1
*Process man (sign company)	2
Proprietor, bakery	1
Proprietor, barber shop	3
*Proprietor, boat building company	3
Proprietor, brush company	1
Proprietor, dairy	1
Proprietor, drug business	2
Proprietor, electrical company	8
Proprietor, feed mill	1
Proprietor, garage	6
Proprietor, gas station	12
Proprietor, laundry	1
Proprietor, lumber company	1
Proprietor, machine shop	4
Proprietor, meat packing company	1
Proprietor, monument shop	1
Proprietor, music store	1
*Proprietor, oil distribution	3
Proprietor, print shop	1
Proprietor, resort	6
Proprietor, restaurant	5
Proprietor, retail store	21
Proprietor, roofing company	1
Proprietor, shoe repair shop	11
Proprietor, tavern	6
Proprietor, textile business	1
*Proprietor, trucking company	18
Proprietor, welding shop	3
Psychiatrist	5
*Psychologist	37
Public relations worker	2
*Purchasing agent	13
*Quality control worker	6
Radio and TV engineer	8
Radio operator	3
Railroad baggage man	1
Railroad brakeman	2
Railroad car inspector	1
Railroad conductor	3
Railroad engineer	1
Railroad fire builder	1
*Railroad fireman	8
Railroad section hand	1
*Railroad shop laborer	7
Railroad switchman	1
Rancher	1
Realtor	2
*Receptionist	17
*Recreation worker	13

*Refrigeration mechanic	1
*Repairman, appliance	4
Repairman, electronics	2
*Repairman, ignition and electrical systems	1
*Repairman, radio and TV	21
*Repairman, shoe	3
*Repairman, typewriter	3
*Reporter	27
*Roofer	3
*Routeman, milk	19
Routeman, newspaper	1
*Routeman, soft water	3
*Salesclerk, retail	104
*Sales management and promotion	19
*Salesman, auto	7
Salesman, auto parts	1
Salesman, farm machinery	1
*Salesman, furniture and appliances	9
*Salesman, house-to-house	7
Salesman, insurance	7
Salesman, oil burners	1
Salesman, real estate	8
Salesman, technical	3
Salesman, wholesale	9
*Sandblaster	3
Sand mixer	1
School administrator	3
Scientist	12
*Scout executive	15
*Seaman	5
Seamstress	2
*Seamstress, factory	10
*Secretary	128
*Secretary, medical	11
Service representative	1
Shear operator	2
*Sheet metal worker	18
*Singer	26
*Social worker	35
*Soda dispenser	1
*Sorter, factory	9
*Spot welder	10
*Stator winder	2
*Stenographer	97
*Stewardess	13
Stonecutter	2
Stonemason	1
*Store display man	2
Supervisor, city laborers	1
*Supervisor, commercial	37
*Supervisor, construction	11
Supervisor, county shop	1
Supervisor, industrial	2
*Supervisor, telephone operators	4
Tailor	2
Tank tester	1
Tanner	4
Tannery limer	1
*Taxi driver	3
*Teacher, college	42
*Teacher, elementary	332
*Teacher's asssitant	3
*Teacher, secondary	393
Telegrapher	3
*Telephone operator	96
*Telephone technician	9
*Teletypesetter	5
*Ticket agent	1
Tile setter	1
*Timekeeper	12
*Time study man	3
Tool designer	2
*Toolmaker	19
*Tower operator, airport	7
Town clerk	1

Occupation	Number
Trapper	2
Truck driver	128
*Typist	107
*Undertaker	9
V.A. service officer	1
Veterinarian	2
*Waiter	3
*Waitress	34
*Warehouseman	10
Washer, auto	1
Water tester	1
*Welder	44
Window trimmer	1
Wood carver	1
*Writer	17
*X-ray technician	2

APPENDIX II

Vocational or Training Choices and Activities of Individual Subjects from Tenth Grade to Ten Years After High School Graduation

Problems in vocational choice continue to be a subject of concern to guidance workers. Much of the data collected in this area has been cross-sectional and very little information has been collected about the choices of the same individuals over a period of years. In order to provide such data for other researchers to examine (as well as to indicate the amount of variability in our subjects' preferences), the vocational choices and activities of the experimental and control subjects of this study are given in detail in the following pages. In the data for the experimentals, the items range from the choices given in the last interview while they were in the tenth grade (in 1948) to the choices that they made five years after high school (in 1956) for the year 1961. Similar data for the controls are given except that there are no interview choices in the eleventh and twelfth grades.

The following symbols and abbreviations are used. The line (———) indicates no answer or irrelevant response.

AC—accounting
Acct.—accountant
Adm.—administration
AF—armed forces
Agr.—agriculture
Aly.—alley
Appr.—apprentice
Arch.—architecture
Asst.—assistant
Att.—attendant
Avn.—aviation
Bact.—bacteriologist

Bookkpr.—bookkeeper
Brbr.—Barber
Bus.—business
Bwl.—bowling
Carptr.—carpenter
Carptr.rgh.—carpenter rough
Chem.—chemistry
Clk.—clerk
Cln.help.—dry cleaner's helper
Co.—company
Coll.—college
Comm.—communications
Condit.—conditioning
Conserv.—conservation
Constr.—construction
Contr.—contractor
Coun.—counselor
Del.—delivery
Dir.—director
Drill prs.—drill press
Drv.—driver
Econ.—economics
Edit.—editorial
El.ed.—elementary education
Elec.—electrical
Electron.tech.—electronics technician
Eng.—engineer
Exec.—executive
Fac.lab.—factory laborer
For.rngr.—forest ranger
Funl.dir.—funeral director
Gas sta.att.—gas station attendant
Greenhse.wkr.—greenhouse worker
Home ec.—home economics
Hwy.dept.—highway department
Husb.—husbandry
Hyg.—hygiene
Ind.—industrial
Instl.htg.plt.—installer heating plant
Insp.—inspector
Instr.—instructor
Inter.dec.—interior decorator
Jour.—journalism
L&S—letters and science
Lab.—laborer
Lab.tech.—laboratory technician
Laun.—laundry
M—married
Mach.—machinist
Mach.appr.—machinist apprentice
Manag.tr.—management trainee
Mech.—mechanic
Med.—medical
Med.tech.—medical technology
Mgr.—manager
Mkr.—maker
Mus.—music
Norm.sch.—normal school
Occ.ther.—occupational therapy
Off.mach.opr.—office machine operator
Opr.—operator
Pharm.—pharmacy
Phot.—photographer
Phys.ther.—physical therapy
PO—post office
PR—public relations
Prac.nurse—practical nurse
Premed—premedical
Pro.ath.—professional athlete
Promo.—promotion
Prop.—proprietor
Psych.—psychology
Pts.—parts
Purch.—purchasing

Qual.—quality
Rdo.—radio
Recreat.—recreation
Rep.—repair
Rest.—restaurant
Reserv.clk.—reservation clerk
Ret.str.—Retail store
RR—railroad
Rte.—route
Sec.—secondary
Sec.ed.—secondary education
Secy.—secretary
Sht.met.—sheet metal
Ship.—shipping
Sm.bus.—small business
Stu.—student
Sch.—school
Social wk.—social work
Sta.—station
Steno.—stenographer
Str.—store
Super.—supervisor
Supt.—superintendent
Tech.—technician
Tel.—telephone
Teletypestr.—teletypesetter
Text.co.—textile company
Tndr.—tender
Trk.drv.—truck driver
U—undecided
Voc.sch.—vocational school
Weld.shop—welding shop
Wkr.—worker

Case No.	Grade 10 Interview	Grade 11 Interview	5-Year Future Choice at Grade 11 Interview	Grade 12 Interview Choice	Choice 1 Month Before Graduation	5-Year Futu Choice at MonthBefo Graduatio
004	Reporter	Reporter	Reporter	Trk.drv.del.	Trk.drv.del.	Prop.trk.co.
006	Farmer	Farmer	U	Farmer	Farmer	Farmer
008	Farmer	U	U	U	Mach.	U
010	Mech.avn.	Mech.avn.	Flight eng.	AF	———	———
011	U	U	Fac.lab.	Fac.lab.	Timekeeper	Prop.sm.bu
013	Farmer	Farmer	———	Farmer	Farmer	Farmer
016	Lawyer	AF	Prop.sm.bus.	AF	Foundry lab.	U
017	Eng.	Scientist	Stu.L&S	Stu.L&S	Stu.bus.adm.	Acct.
022	Teacher	Teacher	Interpreter	Teacher	Stu.sec.ed.	Teacher
028	Bookkpr.	AF	U	AF	Stu.sec.ed.	Teacher
044	Farmer	Farmer	Farmer	Farmer	AF	Farmer
046	Eng.	Eng.	Eng.	Eng.	Stu.L&S	Eng.
061	Teacher	Teacher	Writer	Teacher	Stu.sec.ed.	Actor
071	U	AF	Brickmason	Brickmason	U	Brickmason
072	Mach.	Gas sta.att.	Prop.gas sta.	Mach.	Mail carrier	Mach.
089	Farmer	Farmer	Farmer	Farmer	Farmer	Farmer
094	AF	AF	Pilot	Mech.	Mech.	Mech.
103	Physician	Pharmacist	Stu.	Pharmacist	Stu.premed.	Stu.premed.
112	Chef	Chef	Prop.rest.	Trk.drv.del.	Trk.drv.del.	Rte.man mil
118	Farmer	Farmer	Eng.	Farmer	Constr.lab.	Farmer
120	Cabinet mkr.	Cabinet mkr.	Cabinet mkr.	Cabinet mkr.	Constr.lab.	Contr.constr.
123	Salesman	Salesman	Bus.exec.	Salesman	Stu.bus.adm.	Salesman
140	Teacher	Mach.	Mach.	Carptr.	Cabinet mkr.	Cabinet mkr.
141	Draftsman	Mech.auto	Mech.auto	Mach.	Mech.	———
144	Reporter	Reporter	Reporter	Ath.coach	Stu.jour.	Writer
150	Musical dir.	Inter.dec.	Artist	Artist	Stu.sec.ed.	U
162	Shoe repair	Acct.	Shoe repair	Prp.shoe rep.	Shoe repair	Shoe repair
165	Policeman	AF	U	AF	Fac.lab.	Prop.sm.bus.
169	Teacher	U	U	U	U	Prop.sm.bus.
175	Bus drv.	Lab.hwy.dpt.	U	U	Roofer	U
182	Cln.help	Cln.help.	Prop.laun.	Cln.help.	Cln.help.	Cln.help.
206	Farmer	Farmer	Farmer	Farmer	Butcher	Farmer
209	Chemist	Instl.htg.plt.	Instl.help.	AF	AF	AF
213	Trk.drv.	Trk.drv.	Eng.	Trk.drv.	Trk.drv.	Contr.constr.
218	Farmer	Farmer	Farmer	Farmer	Farmer	Farmer
223	Physician	Crane opr.	Teacher	Mech.auto	U	Teacher
224	Teacher	Teacher	Teacher	Teacher	Stu.sec.ed.	Teacher
234	Farmer	Farmer	Farmer	Farmer	Farmer	Farmer
236	Singer	Singer	Singer	Singer	Stu.music	Singer
239	Mgr.bwl.aly.	Mgr.bwl.aly.	Prop.bwl.aly.	Constr.lab.	U	U
245	Pilot	Pilot	Sht.met.wkr.	Sht.met.wkr.	AF	Farmer

erimental Boys Tenth Grade to Ten Years After High School

ctivity 6 nths After aduation	Activity 2½ Years After Graduation	5-Year Future Choice 2½ Years After Graduation	Activity 5 Years After Graduation	5-Year Future Choice 5 Years After Graduation
.drv.del.	AF	Stu.L&S	Stu.bus.adm.	PR
mer	AF	Farmer	Farmer	U
	AF	Machine opr.	Mach.appr.	Mach.
	Seaman	Stu.	Repair mech.	Designer
.lab.	AF	———	Stu.L&S	U
mer	Stu.	U	Stu.agr.	U
k.drv.del.	AF	Teacher	Fac.lab.	Fac.lab.
.acct.	Stu.acct.	Acct.	Acct.	Acct.
.bus.adm.	Stu.bus.adm.	Bus.exec.	Coach	Coach
.sec.ed.	AF	Stu.sec.ed.	AF	Cartographer
rmer	AF	———	Tool/die appr.	Tool/die mkr.
.prep.sch.	Stu.bus.adm.	Bus.exec.	Stu.bus.adm.	U
u.L&S	Stu.L&S	Teacher coll.	Stu.grad.	Teacher coll.
ip.clerk	AF	———	Machine opr.	PO clerk
ail carrier	AF	Mail carrier	Lathe opr.	———
rmer	Farmer	Farmer	Farmer	Farmer
ac.lab.	AF	———	AF	AF
u.premed.	Stu.premed.	Stu.premed.	Med.stu.	Physician
F	AF	U	Trk.drv.del.	Policeman
rk.drv.	Trk.drv.	Trk.drv.	AF	Prop.trk.co.
onstr.lab.	AF	U	Trk.drv.del.	Prop.trk.co.
tu.bus.adm.	Stu.bus.adm.	Bus.exec.	AF	Bus.exec.
tock clerk	AF	Mech.auto	Trk.drv.	Salesman
arage lab.	Mech.auto	———	Constr.lab.	Carptr.rgh.
tu.jour.	AF	———	Assembler	Elec.tech.
tu.sec.ed.	Stu.sec.ed.	U	Stu.grad.	Teacher coll.
hoe repair	AF	Prop.shoe rep.	Shoe repair	Prop.shoe rep.
Machine opr.	AF	———	Unemployed	Teacher coll.
armer	AF	Clerical	Foundry	Prop.sm.bus.
Trk.drv.	AF	———	Drill prs.opr.	———
Cln.help.	Elec.help.	Electrician	Elec.help.	Elec.help.
Butcher asst.	Butcher	Butcher	Butcher	Mgr.ret.str.
Foundry lab.	AF	———	Stu.pre-law	Lawyer
Trk.drv.	Trk.drv.	Prop.trk.co.	Trk.drv.	Prop.trk.co.
Farmer	AF	Farmer	Stu.L&S	Prop.sm.bus.
Stu.sec.ed.	Stu.sec.ed.	Teacher	Unemployed	U
Stu.sec.ed.	Stu.sec.ed.	Teacher	AF	Salesman
Fac.lab.	Fac.lab.	Farmer	Farmer	Farmer
Stu. music	Stu.music	Singer	Stu.music	Chur.mus.dir.
Fac.lab.	Unemployed	U	Carptr.rgh.	Carpenter
Welder	Mgr.ret.str.	Sht.met.help.	Instl.help.	Sht.met.help.

Case No.	Grade 10 Interview	Grade 11 Interview	5-Year Future Choice at Grade 11 Interview	Grade 12 Interview Choice	Choice 1 Month Before Graduation	5-Year Fu Choice a Month Bef Graduati
249	Draftsman	Draftsman	Fac.lab.	Fac.lab.	U	U
251	Actor	Actor	U	Actor	Stu.bus.adm.	———
258	Farmer	Farmer	Farmer	Farmer	Farmer	Farmer
259	Mach.	Mach.	Mach.	Mach.	Tool/die mk.	U
260	Mech.	Mech.	Mach.	Mech.	Constr.lab.	———
263	Pilot	Announcer	Announcer	Salesman	Stu.L&S	AF
267	Farmer	Farmer	Farmer	Farmer	AF	Farmer
280	Artist	Artist	Artist	Artist	Stu.artist	Artist
283	For.rngr.	U	U	Draftsman	Draftsman	Draftsman
285	Farmer	Teacher	U	Farmer	Farmer	Farmer
299	U	Mech.	Prop.gas sta.	Gas sta.att.	Fac.lab.	Gas sta.att.
305	Scientist	U	U	Dentist	Stu.premed.	Dentist
311	Trk.drv.	Trk.drv.	Trk.drv.	Trk.drv.	Trk.drv.	Trk.drv.
313	Mus.arranger	Salesman	U	Salesman	Fac.lab.	Salesman
314	Pro.ath.	U	Trk.drv.	Mach.	Me.autobdy	Mach.
318	U	U	Acct.	Acct.	Stu.L&S	U
324	Bus.exec.	Scientist	Stu.	Physician	Stu.psych.	Physician
327	Trk.drv.del.	Trk.drv.	Trk.drv.	Trk.drv.	Trk.drv.	Trk.drv.
331	U	U	U	U	AF	Acct.
333	Rdo.rep.man	Rdo.opr.	Rdo.opr.	Rdo.opr.	AF	Rdo.opr.
335	Farmer	Farmer	Farmer	Farmer	Farmer	Farmer
351	Eng.	Eng.	Eng.	Eng.	Stu.me.eng.	Eng.
353	Pilot	Pilot	AF	Pilot	U	Pilot
354	Trapper	AF	Cabinet mkr.	AF	AF	U
356	Forester	Conserv.wkr.	Conserv.wkr.	Forester	Stu.forestry	Conserv.wk
363	Farmer	Farmer	Farmer	Farmer	Farmer	Farmer
368	Draftsman	Draftsman	U	Mech.	AF	Mach.
370	Physician	Physician	Stu.grad.	Physician	Stu.premed.	Stu.L&S
371	Farmer	Farmer	Farmer	Farmer	U	Farmer
375	Dentist	U	Mgr.ret.str.	Bus.exec.	Stu.bus.adm.	Prop.sm.bus.
383	Artist	Eng.	Eng.	Eng.	Stu.me.eng.	———
387	Acct.	Acct.	Acct.	Acct.	U	Stu.L&S
393	AF	AF	Pilot	AF	Lab.	U
394	Architect	Architect	Architect	Architect	U	U
396	Mach.	Mach.	Mach.	Mach.	Mach.appr.	Mach.
402	Draftsman	U	Minister	U	Stu.L&S	Prop.sm.bus.
418	Journalist	Teacher	Teacher	Journalist	Stu.L&S	Writer
424	Teacher	Teacher	———	Eng.	Stu.agr.eng.	———
427	Mech.	Draftsman	U	Mech.	Foundry lab.	Draftsman
441	Rdo.rep.man	Fac.lab.	Fac.lab.	Machine opr.	U	Fac.lab.
445	Farmer	Farmer	———	Farmer	Farmer	Farmer

ɔerimental Boys Tenth Grade to Ten Years After High School (*Continued*)

ctivity 6 nths After raduation	Activity 2½ Years After Graduation	5-Year Future Choice 2½ Years After Graduation	Activity 5 Years After Graduation	5-Year Future Choice 5 Years After Graduation
c.lab.	AF	———	Coremaker	———
ı.bus.adm.	AF	Stu.	AF	Stu.
rmer	Farmer	U	Tel.lineman	Tel.lineman
F	AF	Mech.avn.	AF	Prop.weld.shp.
ıs sta.att.	AF	Elec.tech.	Unemployed	Prop.elec.co.
u.L&S	Stu.L&S	AF	Stu.bus.adm.	———
rmer	AF	Stu.	Fac.assembler	Farmer
u.artist	Stu.artist	Artist	Artist	U
raftsman	AF	Stu.	Stu.mech.eng.	Elec.eng.
u.agr.	Stu.agr.	Teacher sec.	Teacher sec.	County agent
íachine tndr.	Loader	U	Foundry lab.	Mach.
:u.premed.	Stu.premed.	U	Stu.med.	Physician
ac.lab.	AF	Prop.sm.bus.	Trk.drv.	Trk.drv.
'rk.drv.del.	Unemployed	Stu.L&S	Butcher asst.	Salesman
andblaster	Stu.brbr.sch.	Brbr.	Brbr.	Brbr.
tu.L&S	Ship.clerk	———	AF	———
tu.psych.	Stu.psych.	Psychologist	Stu.L&S	Psychologist
'rk.drv.	AF	———	Loader	———
AF	AF	———	Lab.	U
AF	Fac.lab.	Rdo.rep.man	Lab.	Rdo.eng.
'armer	Farmer	Prop.sm.bus.	Prop.sm.bus.	———
Stu.mech.eng.	Manag.tr.	Salesman	Sales mgr.	Sales promo.
Stu.chem.	Stu.chem.	———	AF	AF
AF	AF	———	Trk.drv.del.	Salesman
AF	AF	Stu.	Stu.sec.ed.	Teacher
Farmer	Farmer	Farmer	Farmer	Farmer
Fac.lab.	U	———	PO clerk	City fireman
Stu.premed.	Stu.premed.	Physician	Stu.med.	Physician
Farmer	AF	Stu.	AF	Person'l man
Stu.bus.adm.	Stu.bus.adm.	Person'l man	Sales promo.	Marketing
Stu.mech.eng.	AF	Stu.	Stu.mech.eng.	Mech.eng.
Trk.drv.	AF	Eng.	Draftsman	Supt.constr.
Welder	Fac.lab.	———	AF	Civil service
Constr.lab.	AF	Contr.wkr.	Lather	Contr.wkr.
Mach.tndr.	Mach.	Tool/die mkr.	Machine opr.	Machine opr.
AF	AF	Stu.	Unemployed	———
Stu.L&S	Stu.L&S	Teacher coll.	Stu.sec.ed.	Teach.sec.sch.
Stu.agr.eng.	Stu.agr.eng.	Agr.eng.	Stu.agr.eng.	Supt.constr.
Sandblaster	AF	Prop.sm.bus.	Wareh'sman	U
AF	AF	Rdo.rep.man	Stu.elec.eng.	Elec.tech.
Farmer	Farmer	Farmer	Farmer	Farmer

Case No.	Grade 10 Interview	Grade 11 Interview	5-Year Future Choice at Grade 11 Interview	Grade 12 Interview Choice	Choice 1 Month Before Graduation	5-Year Futu[re] Choice at Month Befo[re] Graduatio[n]
453	Electrician	Electrician	Electrician	Electrician	AF	Prop.elec.co
458	Scientist	Scientist	———	Teacher	Stu.L&S	Teacher
459	Rdo.eng.	Rdo.eng.	Mach.	Mach.	Tel.co.lab.	Electrician
467	Rdo.rep.man	Elec.eng.	Rdo.eng.	Elec.tech.	Stu.me.eng.	Rdo.eng.
476	Bus drv.	Mech.auto	U	Mech.auto	Mech.auto	Garage lab.
478	Pharmacist	Jeweler	U	U	Salesman	Jeweler
484	———	Archeologist	Archeologist	U	U	Rancher
490	AF	Mech.auto	Mech.auto	Mech.auto	Mech.auto	Mech.auto
491	Teacher	Teacher	Electrician	Teacher	Stu.el.ed.	Teacher
497	Mach.	Prop.ret.str.	Prop.ret.str.	Prop.ret.str.	Salesman	Mgr.ret.str.
504	Eng.	Draftsman	Eng.	Pattern mkr.	Constr.lab.	Pattern mkr.
507	Contr.constr.	Draftsman	Contr.constr.	Eng.	Draftsman	Architect
514	Mach.	U	Edit.wkr.	Sht.met.wkr.	Sht.met.asst.	U
516	Artist	Artist	Artist	Artist	Stu.art	Artist
519	Realtor	Artist	Artist	U	Stu.art	Artist
525	Lawyer	U	U	Diplomat	Stu.L&S	Diplomat
534	U	AF	AF	U	Dairy lab.	———
536	Conserv.wkr.	Conserv.wkr.	Forester	Photogrphr.	U	Forester
537	Architect	Architect	Architect	Architect	Stu.arch.	Architect
554	Eng.	Eng.	Eng.	Eng.	Stu.civil eng.	Eng.
556	Minister	Minister	U	Cook	AF	Prop.rest.
558	Musician	U	U	U	U	U
572	Mach.	Mach.	Mach.	Mach.	Farmer	Mach.
576	Mech.auto	Mech.auto	Mech.	Mech.auto	Constr.lab.	Mech.
584	Pro.ath.	Pro.ath.	Pro.ath.	Jeweler	Jeweler	Pro.ath.
585	Carpenter	Carpenter	U	Brickmason	Gas sta.att.	Brickmason
590	Pilot	Pilot	U	U	Fac.lab.	U
591	Coach	Salesman	Sales	Salesman	Stu.L&S	Sales
593	Carpenter	Carpenter	Prop.garage	Mech.auto	Carpenter	Prop.garage
598	Accountant	Accountant	Accountant	Accountant	Stu.account.	Accountant
603	Actor	Actor	Actor	Actor	Stu.sec.ed.	Actor
607	U	Pro.ath.	Pro.ath.	Carpenter	U	AF
609	Telegrapher	Telegrapher	Rancher	Mech.auto	Fac.lab.	Prop.garage
621	Farmer	Farmer	Farmer	Farmer	Farmer	Farmer
627	Draftsman	Draftsman	Draftsman	Engineer	Draftsman	Pattern wkr.
634	Draftsman	Bus.exec.	U	Cook	Stu.bus.sch.	Prop.rest.
640	U	U	———	Tel.lineman	Constr.lab.	Tel.lineman
641	U	Farmer	Farmer	Farmer	Farmer	Farmer
648	Engineer	Mach.	U	Mach.	AF	U
651	Farmer	Farmer	Pro.ath.	Farmer	Farmer	Farmer
652	Eng.	Roofer	U	Constr.lab.	Roofer	Constr.lab.

ctivity 6 nths After aduation	Activity 2½ Years After Graduation	5-Year Future Choice 2½ Years After Graduation	Activity 5 Years After Graduation	5-Year Future Choice 5 Years After Graduation
	AF	Electrician	Salesman	Mgr.ret.str.
L&S	AF	Electron.tech.	Stu.elec.eng.	Elec.eng.
.rep.man	AF	Policeman	Electrician	Tel.tech.
.mech.eng.	Stu.bus.adm.	Artist	AF	Tech.salesman
	AF	U	Mach.appr.	Mach.appr.
.reh'sman	Salesman	Prop.sm.bus.	Purch.agent	Prop.drug bus.
ok	AF	U	Unemployed	U
rage lab.	AF	Garage lab.	Garage lab.	Prop.sm.bus.
.el.ed.	Stu.el.ed.	Teacher sec.	Teacher el.	Teacher
rage lab.	Mach.appr.	Mach.	Mach.	Mach.
splay man	Display man	Mech.auto	Bookkpr.	Draftsman
aftsman	Draftsman	Pilot	AF	AF
t.met.asst.	AF	———	Sht.met.wkr.	U
ito washer	AF	———	Tel.lineman	Tel.lineman
1.art.	Stu.L&S	U	Stu.L&S	Teacher
1.pre-law	Stu.pre-law	AF	AF	Lawyer
.c.lab.	AF	U	Butcher asst.	———
'elder	AF	Elec.eng.	AF	Elec.eng.
u.arch.	AF	Stu.L&S	Stu.arch.	Architect
u.civil eng.	Constr.lab.	Stu.eng.	Tel.tech.	Elec.tech.
F	AF	U	Welder	U
iip.clerk	AF	———	Tel.co.lab.	Tel.co.lab.
ırmer	Farmer	Farmer	Lab.	Lab.
Iason appr.	AF	Brickmason	Mason appr.	Brickmason
weler asst.	AF	———	Buyer	———
aint sprayer	AF	———	AF	———
tu.L&S	Stu.pre-law	Lawyer	AF	U
Inemployed	AF	Stu.L&S	AF	Elec.tech.
Velder	AF	Welder	Welder	Welder
tu.AC.	Stu.account.	Accountant	AF	Accountant
tu.sec.ed.	Stu.sec.ed.	Teacher sec.	Teacher sec.	Teacher sec.
'ac.lab.	AF	U	Stu.sec.ed.	Coach
'oundry lab.	AF	Writer	Laborer	Engineer
'armer	Lather	U	Lather	Lather
Stu.mech.eng.	Stu.mech.eng.	U	Draftsman	Draftsman
Stu.radio	Mgr.rest.	———	Cook	Mgr.rest.
AF	AF	Policeman	Assembler	Assembler
Farmer	AF	———	AF	AF
AF	AF	Stu.bus.adm.	Tel.lineman	Tel.lineman
Farmer	Farmer	Farmer	Farmer	Farmer
Roofer	AF	Brickmason	Stu.eng.	Eng.

Vocational or Training Preferences, Choices and Activitie

Case No.	Grade 10 Interview	Grade 11 Interview	5-Year Future Choice at Grade 11 Interview	Grade 12 Interview Choice	Choice 1 Month Before Graduation	5-Year Fu Choice a Month Be Graduati
664	Pro.ath.	Pro.ath.	Pro.ath.	Pro.ath.	Constr.lab.	U
667	Architect	Coach	Bus.ex.	Bus.exec.	Stu.bus.adm.	U
687	Mach.	U	U	U	Sht.met.wkr.	Sht.met.w
691	Dentist	Plasterer	Plasterer	Plasterer	Plasterer ap.	Plasterer
703	Farmer	Farmer	Farmer	Farmer	Farmer	Farmer
706	Lawyer	Teacher	Teacher	Eng.	Foundry lab.	Stu.L&S
717	U	Trk.drv.	U	Fac.lab.	Mach. tndr.	U
735	Bact.	U	U	U	Stu.L&S	U
744	Gas sta.att.	Pro.ath.	Mech.	Mech.eng.	Stu.me.eng.	Mech.eng.
745	Coach	Announcer	Stu.	Lawyer	Stu.L&S	Lawyer
746	Pro.ath.	Eng.	Designer	U	Stu.L&S	Lawyer
750	Musician	U	U	Elec.eng.	Stu.elec.eng.	Elec.eng.
754	Fac.lab.	Fac.lab.	Laborer	U	Fac.lab.	AF
758	Eng.	Mech.auto	Mech.	U	U	Draftsman
773	Eng.	U	U	AF	Stu.pharm.	U
774	U	Forester	U	U	U	Minister
778	Farmer	Farmer	Farmer	Farmer	Farmer	Farmer
779	Coach	U	Salesman	Salesman	Stu.jour.	Salesman
789	Salesman	Salesman	Salesman	Prop.sm.bus.	Farmer	Prop.sm.bu
791	Farmer	Farmer	Farmer	Farmer	Farmer	Farmer
794	Dancer	U	Forester	Dancer	Bus.exec.	Dancer
795	Draftsman	Draftsman	U	Prop.ret.str.	U	Prop.ret.str.
796	Butcher	Butcher	Butcher	Butcher	Butcher	Trapper
798	Coach	Coach	Coach	Coach	Salesm'n auto	Coach
802	Pro.ath.	Pro.ath.	Printer	Teacher	Stu.sec.ed.	Teacher sec.
808	Mach.	U	Architect	U	———	Bus.exec.
812	Farmer	Farmer	Farmer	Farmer	Farmer	Farmer
814	Singer	Singer	Musician	Singer	Salesman	Singer
824	Pro.ath.	Butcher	Pro.ath.	Carptr.	Carptr.	Contr.constr
833	Farmer	Farmer	Farmer	Farmer	Farmer	Farmer
836	Bus.exec.	Bus.exec.	Prop.rest.	Bus.exec.	Mach.tndr.	Salesman
840	Bus.exec.	Mach.	Mach.	Mach.	Lab.fac.	Mach.
843	Physician	Prop.trk.co.	Pro.ath.	Acct.	Stu.bus.adm.	———
845	Conserv.wkr.	Salesman	Salesman	Salesman	Stu.bus.adm.	Salesman
846	Rdo.rep.man	Mech.auto	Mech.	Mech.eng.	Roofer	Mech.
850	Musician	Musician	Musician	Musician	Stu.L&S	Musician
855	Forester	Forester	For.rngr.	U	Stu.bus.adm.	Bus.exec.
862	Scientist	Scientist	Scientist	U	Stu.L&S	Stu.L&S
867	Coach	U	U	U	Stu.sec.ed.	U

:tivity 6 ıths After ıduation	Activity 2½ Years After Graduation	5-Year Future Choice 2½ Years After Graduation	Activity 5 Years After Graduation	5-Year Future Choice 5 Years After Graduation
:sman	AF	Stu.L&S	Unemployed	———
bus.adm.	Unemployed	Stu.L&S	Stu.bus.adm.	Bus.adm.
met.wkr.	Unemployed	Coremaker	Coremaker	Coremaker
;terer	Plasterer	Plasterer	Plasterer	Plasterer
mer	Farmer	Farmer	AF	Farmer
:sman	Salesman	Mgr.ret.str.	Mgr.tr.	Mgr.ret.str.
.lab.	AF	———	Fac.lab.	Trk.drv.
.L&S	Stu.art	Artist	Stu.art	Teacher coll.
ıstr.lab.	Constr.lab.	Flight eng.	Gas sta.att.	Pilot
.L&S	Stu.L&S	Lawyer	Stu.law	Lawyer
.L&S	AF	Lawyer	Stu.law	Lawyer
ı.elec.eng.	Mech.auto	———	Garage lab.	Elec.tech.
c.insp.	AF	Prop.sm.bus.	———	Fac.foreman
k.drv.	AF	Draftsman	Draftsman	Draftsman
ı.pharm.	Stu.pharm.	Pharmacist	Pharmacist	Pharmacist
:ceiving clk	AF	———	RR Fireman	RR Fireman
k.drv.	Farmer	———	City lab.	City lab.
u.jour.	Stu.bus.adm.	Prop.sm.bus.	Lab.	Salesman
.rmer	Sm.bus.wkr.	———	Sm.bus.wkr.	Prop.motel
.c.lab.	AF	Farmer	AF	Cabinet mkr.
ance instr.	AF	Dance instr.	Dance instr.	Dance instr.
ırmer	Lab.dairy	Prop.gas sta.	Mach.tndr.	Mach.tndr.
utcher asst.	AF	Butcher	Calf skinner	Butcher
ac.sorter	Draftsman	Engineer	Draftsman	Draftsman
.F	AF	———	Spot welder	Printer
Vareh'sman	AF	Stu.L&S	Stu.bus.adm.	Bus.adm.
armer	Farmer	Farmer	Farmer	Farmer
alesman	Draftsman	Draftsman	Draftsman	Draftsman
Constr.wkr.	Constr.wkr.	Foreman fac.	Insulator	———
'armer	Farmer	Farmer	Farmer	Farmer
tu.L&S	AF	Prop.sm.bus.	Bookkpr.	———
Welder	AF	U	AF	U
Stu.bus.adm.	AF	Stu.bus adm.	Stu.sec.ed.	Teacher sec.
Stu.bus.adm.	AF	Salesman	Clk.order	U
Fac.sorter	AF	Mach.tndr.	Fac.assembler	Eng.
Stu.L&S	Clerk office	Salesman	Office supt.	Office supt.
Stu.bus.adm.	Stu.bus.adm.	Sales promo.	Stu.bus.adm.	Personnel mgr.
Stu.L&S	Stu.L&S	Teacher	Stu.ed.	Writer
Stu.sec.ed.	Stu.sec.ed.	Teacher sec.	Teacher sec.	Teacher sec.

Vocational or Training Preferences, Choices and Activities of Control Boys From the Tenth Grade to Ten Years After High School

Case No.	Grade 10 Interview	Quest. Choice 1 Month Before Graduation	5 Year Future Choice at 1 Month Before Graduation	Activity 6 Months After Graduation	Activity 2½ Years After Graduation Choice 2½	5 Year Future Choice 2½ Years After Graduation	Activity 5 Years After Graduation	5 Year Future Choice 5 Years After Graduation
009	Coach	Stu.coach	Prop.sm. bus.	Salesman	AF	U	Mach.	———
019	Nurse	AF	AF	Receiving clk.	Ambulance att.	Ambu.att.	AF	———
021	U	AF	———	Machine opr.	AF	Mach.	Stu.diesel sch.	Eng.
024	Musician	U	Musician	Stu.mus.ed.	Constr.lab.	Teacher	Stu.eng.	Eng.
026	Coach	Stu.coach	Coach	Stu.bus.adm.	Stu.bus.adm.	Bus.exec.	Constr.mgr.	Constr.mgr.
031	Trk.drv.	U	Constr.lab.	Trk.drv.	AF	U	Fac.rep.man	U
035	Mach.	U	U	AF	AF	U	Stock clk.	Stu.rdo/tv
040	Mach.	Floor finisher	RR shop lab.	Doormaker	AF	———	Prison inmate	Plumber appr.
042	Farmer	Farmer	Farmer	Farmer	Farmer	Farmer	AF	Farmer
045	Architect	Stu.arch.	Artist	Artist appr.	Artist appr.	U	Artist	Artist
049	Rancher	AF	Draftsman	Instl.sht.met.	Instl.sht.met.	Instl.sht.met.	Instl.sht.met.	Instl.sht.met.
058	Mach.	Mach.appr.	Mach.	Mach.appr.	AF	Tool/die mkr.	Tool/die mkr.	Tool/die mkr.
063	Farmer	Machine opr.	———	Rte.man	Unemployed	Tool/die mkr.	Carptr. appr.	Constr.contr.
073	AF	Carptr.rgh.	Carptr.	Roofer help.	AF	U	Carptr. appr.	Carptr.
080	U	U	U	Wareh'sman	AF	———	Unemployed	Bus.exec.
081	Banker	Draftsman Ap.	Draftsman	Draftsm'n Ap.	Draftsm'n Ap.	Draftsman	Draftsman	Mech.auto.
102	Auto mech.	AF	U	Stock clk.	AF	———	Gas sta.att.	Prop.sm.bus.
104	Rdo.rep.man	U	———	Unemployed	Unemployed	———	Animal ctkr.	Animal ctkr.
107	Farmer	Farmer	Farmer	Farmer	Creamery lab.	Creamery lab.	Creamery lab.	Creamery lab.
117	AF	Mach.appr.	———	AF	AF	U	Spot welder	Electrician
119	U	Constr.lab.	U	Trk.drv.	AF	U	Assembler	Assembler
122	Eng.	Elec.appr.	Electrician	Elec. appr.	AF	Electrician	Electrician	Electrician
124	Farmer	Stu.agr.	Mgr.milk.plt.	Smeller, milk	AF	———	Stu.air condit.	Air cond.tech

129	Teacher	Fac.lab.	———	AF	AF	———	Stu.sec.ed.	U
131	Salesman	AF	U	Dairy lab.	AF	U	Police trainee	Policeman
135	Salesman	AF	Eng.	AF	AF	Stu.L&S	Bus.wkr.	Teacher
138	Teacher	Stu.premed.	U	Stu.premed.	Stu.premed.	Physician	Med.stu.	Physician
149	Mech.	Mech.	Mech.	Me.auto hlp.	AF	Prop.sm.bus.	Salesman str.	Salesman str.
177	Eng.	Stu.elec.eng.	Eng.	Stu.elec.eng.	Dairy lab.	———	Dairy lab.	———
184	Grocer	Stu.sec.ed.	Teacher	Stu.L&S	Grocer	———	Grocer	———
187	Farmer	Farmer	Farmer	Farmer	Farmer	Farmer	Farmer	Farmer
191	Farmer	U	Brickmason	Lab.	AF	———	Trk.drv.	U
196	Optometrist	Stu.premed.	Stu.L&S	Stu.premed.	Stu.premed.	Physician	Med. stu.	Physician
199	Mach.	Pattern mkr.	Pattern mkr.	Pattern mkr.	Pattern mkr.	Pattern mkr.	Pattern mkr.	Pattern mkr.
205	Trapper	Farmer	Farmer	Constr.lab.	AF	Farmer	Farmer	Farmer
207	Draftsman	Mech.	U	Stu.eng.	Stu.eng.	Eng.	AF	Eng.
225	Artist	Draftsm'n Ap.	Architect	Casket mkr.	Rte.man milk	Prop.trk.co.	Salesman	———
230	Pilot	Lab.	———	Coremaker	AF	Hvy.mach.opr.	Fac.assembler	Draftsman
232	Pilot	U	Draftsman	AF	AF	Rdo.opr.	Stu.bus.adm.	Acct.
233	Musician	Salesman auto	Salesman auto	Welder	Welder	U	Welder	Welder
235	Mech.	Farmer	U	Carptr.rgh.	Farmer	Farmer	AF	Printer
237	Carptr.	Farmer	U	Farmer	Farmer	U	AF	Farmer
238	Farmer	Farmer	———	Elec.tech.	Dairy lab.	U	Dairy lab.	U
240	Mach.	AF	U	Salesman auto	AF	U	Trk.drv.	Prop.trk.co.
243	Butcher	Stock clk.	U	Salesman	AF	Salesman	Mgr.ret.str.	Mgr.ret.str.
246	Eng.	Stu.bus.adm.	Salesman	Gas sta.att.	AF	Stu.	Draftsman	Designer
253	Teacher	U	U	Bank messgr.	Stu.el.ed.	Teacher el.	Teacher el.	Teacher el.
254	Salesman	U	Salesman ins.	Trk.drv.	Shipping clk.	Salesman	Shipping clk.	Salesman
270	Bookkpr.	Foundry lab.	U	Fac.lab.	AF	U	Grinder	———
276	Baker	Baker	Fac.lab.	Baker help.	AF	———	Lather	Lather
278	Mach.	Pro.ath.	Pro.ath.	Mach.appr.	Mach.appr.	U	AF	Mach.
281	Plumber	Draftsm'n Ap.	Draftsman	Draftsm'n Ap.	Draftsm'n app.	Eng.	Draftsman	Draftsman
284	U	U	Coach	AF	AF	Stu.L&S	Mach. appr.	U
287	Bus.exec.	Lab.	———	Dairy lab.	AF	———	Time stdy.man	———

Vocational or Training Preferences, Choices and Activities of Control Boys From the Tenth Grade to Ten Years After High School (*Continued*)

Case No.	Grade 10 Interview	Quest. Choice 1 Month Before Graduation	5-Year Future Choice at 1 Month Before Graduation	Activity 6 Months After Graduation	Activity 2½ Years After Graduation	5 Year Future Choice 2½ Years After Graduation	Activity 5 Years After Graduation	5 Year Future Choice 5 Years After Graduation
290	Mach.	U	Prop.rest.	Gas sta.att.	Bus.adm.	Stu.bus.adm.	Stu.bus.adm.	U
291	Pro.ath.	U	Pro.ath.	Mach.appr.	Mach.appr.	Mach.	AF	Mach.
295	Mach.	Machine tndr.	———	Mach. set up	AF	———	AF	Mach.
297	Farmer	Constr. lab.	Farmer	Roofer	AF	U	Sht.met.wkr.	Sht.met.wkr.
298	Conserv.wkr.	U	Prop.resort	Fac.lab.	Conserv.wkr.	Conserv.wkr.	Lineman	U
300	U	Hwy.dept.lab.	U	Unemployed	Constr.lab.	U	Tel.tech.	Tel.tech.
309	Farmer	Farmer	Farmer	Farmer	Farmer	Farmer	Farmer	Farmer
310	Electrician	Stu.elec.eng.	Rdo.eng.	AF	AF	———	Inspector	TV tech.
320	For.rngr.	Stu.econ.	Stu.L&S	Stu.sec.ed.	Stu.sec.ed.	Coach	Teacher sec.	Teacher sec.
321	Draftsman	Stu.rdo./tv	Rdo.announcer	Spot welder	AF	Elec. tech.	Draftsman	Draftsman
326	U	Stu.AC	Acct.	Stu.commerce	Unemployed	Acct.	Bookkpr.	Prop.sm.bus.
329	AF	U	Mech.avn.	AF	AF	Stu.bus.adm.	Stu.L&S	Bus.adm.
332	Farmer	Stu.agr.	Farmer	Stu.agr.	Stu.agr.	Farmer	Farmer	Farmer
343	Farmer	Farmer	Farmer	Farmer	Stu.econ.	Economist	AF	Wareh'se f'rm
364	Lawyer	Stu.bus.adm.	Bus.exec.	Stu.L&S	Stu.bus.adm.	Sales promo.	Salesman auto	Sales promo.
367	Draftsman	AF	Draftsman	Stu.rdo.sch.	AF	Rep.man tv	Rep.man tv	Rep.man tv
369	Electrician	Bus drv.	Prop.sm.bus.	Bus drv.	Bus drv.	Prop.sm.bus.	Grinder	Grinder
376	Mgr.ret.str.	AF	Mech.	AF	AF	Stu.elec.eng.	Rep.man ap.	Prop.sm.bus.
378	Farmer	Farmer	Farmer	Farmer	Farmer	Farmer	Farmer	Farmer
380	Eng.	Mech.	———	Mech. auto	Draftsman	Draftsman	Estimat'g.eng.	Estimat'g eng.
381	Singer	Stu. mus.	Singer	Fac.inspector	Unemployed	Singer	AF	Rdo/tv ancr.
390	Clerical	Stu.bus.coll.	Acct.	Stu.bus.coll.	Unemployed	Clerical	Stu.bus.adm.	Teacher
392	Farmer	U	Farmer	Farmer	Farmer	Farmer	Farmer	Farmer

409	Architect	Stu.arch.	Architect	Stu.arch.	Stu.visual arts	Designer	Stu.art	Artist
422	Eng.	Stu.bus.adm.	Bus.exec.	Stu.bus.adm.	AF	Stu.bus.adm.	Stu.bus.adm.	Sell insurance
428	Farmer	Farmer	Farmer	Farmer	Farmer	Farmer	Machine opr.	Farmer
429	Farmer	Farmer	Farmer	Farmer	Farmer	Farmer	Farmer	Farmer
433	AF	Caretaker	Farmer	Pipe layer	AF	Prop.garage	Gas sta.att.	Prop.garage
434	Eng.	Stu.bus.adm.	Prop.ret.str.	Salesman	Stu.rdo.sch.	Elec.tech.	Comm.tech.	Stu.
439	Eng.	Stu.eng.	Eng.	Stu.mech.eng.	Stu.mech.eng.	Mech.eng.	AF	Mech.eng.
448	Trapper	U	For.rngr.	Fac.lab.	AF	For.rngr.	AF	———
450	Mach.	U	———	AF	AF	Tower opr.	Prop.tavern	Prop.tavern
452	Fac.lab.	Fac.lab.	U	Fac.lab.	AF	———	Loader	U
454	Draftsman	Drftsm'n Ap.	Draftsman	Draftsman	Draftsman	Civil service	Draftsman	Draftsman
455	Carptr.	Lab.	Carptr.	Brewery insp.	AF	U	Loader	Loader
461	Acct.	Stu.bus.adm.	U	Stu.bus.adm.	AF	Stu.bus.adm.	Stu.bus.adm.	Bus.adm.
466	U	U	Prop.garage	AF	AF	———	AF	AF
474	Forester	Farmer	For.rngr.	Constr.lab.	AF	Prop.resort	AF	Prop.resort
477	Pro.ath.	Coach	Teacher sec.	Stock clk.	AF	Stu.bus.adm.	Stu.bus.adm.	Bus.adm.
488	AF	Scout exec.	U	AF	Unemployed	———	Unemployed	———
492	Farmer	Welder	U	Welder	AF	U	Assembler	Assembler
493	Farmer	U	U	Fac.lab.	Machine set up	U	AF	Machine set up
499	Physician	AF	AF	AF	AF	Physician	Bus.exec.	Bus.adm.
506	Farmer	Farmer	Farmer	Farmer	Farmer	Farmer	AF	Farmer
522	Eng.	Stu.chem.eng.	Eng.	Stu.chem.eng.	Stu.bus.adm.	Bus.exec.	Manag.tr.	———
530	Architect	Stu.arch.	Architect	Stu.arch.	Stu.arch.	Architect	City planner	City planner
531	For.rngr.	Farmer	Animal husb.	AF	AF	Farmer	Farmer	Farmer
532	Acct.	Stu. AC	Civil service	Stu.AC	Stu.AC	Acct.	Acct.	Acct.
533	Teacher	U	U	Stu.L&S	AF	U	Undertaker ap.	Undertaker
538	Florist	Stu.bus.adm.	Stu.bus.adm.	Stu.L&S	AF	Civil service	Stu.bus.coll.	———
544	Lab.	U	U	Trk.drv.help.	Trk.drv.	Trk.drv.	Trk.drv.	PO clk.
553	Electrician	Mech.auto	Mech.auto	Gas sta.att.	AF	U	Machine opr.	Machine opr.
559	Farmer	Farmer	Mech.auto	Gas sta.att.	Fac.lab.	Trk.drv.	Assembler	Policeman
560	Prop.ret.str.	AF	Mgr.ret.str.	Canvas cutter	AF	U	Qual.cont.wkr.	———

Vocational or Training Preferences, Choices and Activities of Control Boys From the Tenth Grade to Ten Years After High School (*Continued*)

Case No.	Grade 10 Interview	Quest. Choice 1 Month Before Graduation	5-Year Future Choice at 1 Month Before Graduation	Activity 6 Months After Graduation	Activity 2½ Years After Graduation	5 Year Future Choice 2½ Years After Graduation	Activity 5 Years After Graduation	5 Year Future Choice 5 Years After Graduation
566	Farmer	Farmer	Farmer	Farmer	Farmer	Farmer	Stu.agr.	Farmer
578	AF	AF	AF	Billing clk.	AF	Purch.agent	Stator winder	Prop.sm.bus.
581	Farmer	Farmer	Guide	Farmer	AF	Elec.tech.	Fac.insp.	Elec.tech.
583	Eng.	Stu.bus.coll.	Prop.sm.bus.	Clk.	Timekeeper	Clk.	Mail clk.	U
586	Coach	Garage lab.	U	Gas sta.att.	Salesman	Salesman auto	Gas sta.att.	Gas sta.att.
592	Farmer	Farmer	Farmer	AF	AF	Farmer	AF	AF
595	Farmer	Farmer	Farmer	Farmer	Farmer	Farmer	Farmer	Farmer
601	Clk.	Salesman	Salesman	Instl.help.	AF	Buyer	Off.mach.op.	Elec.rep.man
604	Contr.constr.	Foundry lab.	———	Fac.insp.	AF	Prop.sm.bus.	Trk.drv.	U
605	Dentist	Stu.eng.	———	Stu.mech.eng.	Drftsm'n Ap.	Design eng.	Draftsman	———
610	Mach.	AF	Garage lab.	Machine tndr.	Constr.lab.	Machine opr.	Cement fnshr.	Contr.constr.
614	Coach	Farmer	Farmer	Farmer	Farmer	U	Stu.L&S	Forester
630	Tool/die man	———	———	Tool/die help.	Mach.	Machine opr.	Machine opr.	U
633	Farmer	Farmer	Farmer	Bartender	Unemployed	U	Assembler	———
638	Physician	Stu.premed.	Physician	Stu.premed.	Stu.premed.	Prop.sm.bus.	Stu.optometry	Optometrist
644	Eng.	AF	AF	AF	AF	Chemist	Stu.L&S	———
647	Policeman	U	Policeman	Stu.L&S	Farmer	Garage lab.	File clk.	File clk.
650	Bus.exec.	Stu.bus.adm.	Salesman	AF	AF	Prop.sm.bus.	Stu.sec.ed.	U
669	Welder	———	———	Mech.	Trk.drv.	Cabinet mkr.	Carptr.rgh.	Carptr.rgh.
677	Farmer	Farmer	Farmer	Farmer	AF	Rdo.rep.man	Carptr.	Elec.tech.
681	AF	AF	Pilot	Stu.rdo.sch.	AF	Elec.tech.	Stu.elec.eng.	Elec.eng.
690	Eng.	Eng.	Eng.	Stu.eng.	Stu.eng.	Eng.	AF	U
695	Lab.	Window trmr.	U	Salesman	AF	Stu.L&S	Salesman	Civil service

708	Clk.	Stu.bus.coll.	Acct.	Wind'w.trim.	Stu.brbr.sch.	Brbr.	Brbr.	Brbr.
710	Eng.	Trk.drv.	Trk.drv.	Stu.high school	Fac.sorter	Mach.	Machine opr.	—
711	Announcer	Lab.	Pro.ath.	Salesman	Stock clk.	Pro.ath.	Shipping clk.	U
712	Draftsman	Fac.lab.	AF	Receiving clk.	AF	AF	AF	Teacher
718	Farmer	Farmer	Farmer	Farmer	Farmer	Farmer	Farmer	Farmer
724	Conserv.wkr.	Stu.forestry	Stu.L&S	Stu.forestry	Stu.forestry	Forester	Cook	Cook
726	Guide	Farmer	Prop.resort	Farmer	Farmer	U	AF	Prop.sm.bus.
728	Mach.	Lab.	Machine opr.	Lab.	Fac.lab.	U	Welder	—
741	Farmer	Farmer	Farmer	Farmer	Farmer	Farmer	Farmer	Farmer
747	Eng.	Machine opr.	Prop.sm.bus.	Conserv.wkr.	AF	—	Contr.painter	Contr.painter
760	Farmer	U	Carptr.	Dairy lab.	AF	—	Dairy lab.	U
764	U	Fac.lab.	U	Spot welder	AF	Trk.drv.	Dairy lab.	—
768	Draftsman	Stu.chem.	—	Stu.pre-dent.	Stu.pre-dent.	Dentist	Stu.dentist	Dentist
770	Farmer	Gas co.wkr.	U	Gas co.wkr.	AF	Plumber	Plumber appr.	Plumber
772	Mech.	Stu.AC	Acct.	Stu.bus.adm.	Stu.bus.adm.	Prop.sm.bus.	Office mgr.	Teacher
784	Musician	Musician	—	Fac.lab.	Draftsman	Draftsman	Draftsman	Draftsman
797	Draftsman	Pattern mkr.	Pattern mkr.	Pattern mkr.	AF	Pattern mkr.	Draftsman	Mech.eng.
799	Coach	Stu.sec.ed.	Coach	Stu.psych.	Stu.psych.	Person'el man	Salesman	Salesman
805	Tanner	Stu.agr.	Dairy lab.	Dairy lab.	AF	Prop.sm.bus.	Unemployed	—
811	Rdo.rep.man	AF	Inter.dec.	Painter appr.	Painter appr.	Prop.sm.bus.	Painter	Inter.dec.
817	Fac.lab.	U	U	RR Sec.hand	AF	U	Roofer	—
828	Farmer	Farmer	Farmer	Farmer	AF	Farmer	PO clk.	Farmer
830	Mech.auto	AF	Electrician	AF	AF	U	Constr.lab.	Artist
835	Draftsman	RR shop lab.	Seaman	Machine tndr.	AF	Civil service	Garage lab.	Garage lab.
838	Baker	Fac.lab.	Baker	Machine tndr.	Conserv.wkr.	Conservat'n'st	AF	Forester
842	Pilot	U	Prop.sm.bus.	Tool mkr.	Lather	Prop.sm.bus.	Lab.	Prop.sm.bus.
857	Farmer	Fac.lab.	U	Farmer	Farmer	Farmer	Farmer	U
858	Lawyer	Stu.pre-law	Res'ch. chem.	Stu.pre-law	Stu.pre-law	Lawyer	AF	Lawyer
868	Mach.	Carptr.appr.	Carptr.	Trk.drv.	AF	U	Lather	Lather

Case No.	Grade 10 Interview	Grade 11 Interview	5-Year Future Choice at Grade 11 Interview	Grade 12 Interview Choice	Choice 1 Month Before Graduation	5-Year Fu Choice a Month Be Graduati
002	Phys.ther.	Nurse	Phys.ther.	Nurse	Nurse	Nurse
027	Author	Author	U	AF	U	U
029	Nurse	Sales	———	Sales	Sales	M
032	Clerical	Stewardess	Stewardess	Steno.	———	Prop.bus.
036	Dressmaker	Designer	Prop.bus.	Artist	Stu.voc.sch.	M
037	Musician	Musician	Singer	Singer	U	Singer
039	Clerical	Clerical	M	Steno.	Clerical	M
053	M	U	M	Steno.	Steno.	M
057	Artist	Artist	Artist	Teacher	Fac.lab.	El. teache
060	Nurse	U	M	U	U	M
064	Nurse	Nurse	Nurse	Nurse	Nurse	Nurse
069	Bookkpr.	Steno.	M	Clerical	Steno.	M
076	Teacher	Teacher	Teacher	Teacher	Stu.ed.	Teacher
077	Teacher	Nurse	Nurse	Nurse	Stu.nurse	Nurse
079	Danc'g inst.	U	———	Dancer	Clerical	Dancer
084	Writer	Writer	Writer	Clerical	Clerical	M
086	Teacher	Teacher	———	Clerical	Clerical	Steno.
091	Clerical	Clerical	———	Steno.	Steno.	Clerical
093	Beautician	Clerical	Clerical	Clerical	Clerical	M
097	Singer	Singer	Singer	Teacher	Stu.med.tech.	M
099	Musical dir.	Musical dir.	Teacher sec.	Musical dir.	Stu.mus.ed.	Teacher sec
106	U	Missionary	Missionary	Missionary	Tel.opr.	Church wk
114	Clerical	Beautician	U	Clerical	Clerical	M
121	Teacher	Teacher	M	Teacher	Stu.el.ed.	M
125	Teacher	Teacher	Teacher	Teacher	Stu.el.ed.	Teacher
127	U	U	U	Teacher	Stu.sec.ed.	Teacher
130	Lawyer	Lawyer	Stu.L&S	Radio writer	Stu.L&S	Radio write
134	Social wkr.	Teacher	U	Teacher	Steno.	Teacher
137	Nurse	Clerical	Nurse	Nurse	Stu.nurse	Nurse
145	U	U	M	Tel.opr.	Tel.opr.	M
154	Designer	Designer	Designer	Occ.ther.	Stu.occ.ther.	Occ.ther.
157	Clerical	Clerical	U	U	Stu.bus.coll.	M
159	Clerical	U	M	M	M	M
160	Clerical	Clerical	M	Clerical	Clerical	M
171	Lab.tech.	Lab.tech.	M	Lab.tech.	Nurses aid	M
176	Psych.	Psych.	Psych.	Psych.	Stu.psych.	M
179	Writer	Edit.work	———	Writer	Stu.jour.	Edit.work
180	Stewardess	Nurse	Teacher el.	Nurse	Stu.ed.	Teacher el.
185	Nurse	U	U	Church wkr.	Stu.sec.ed.	Teacher
189	Clerical	Clerical	M	U	Fac.lab.	M
192	Sales	Sales	Seamstress	Sales	M	M

Activity 6 Ionths After Graduation	Activity 2½ Years After Graduation	5-Year Future Choice 2½ Years After Graduation	Activity 5 Years After Graduation	5-Year Future Choice 5 Years After Graduation
.nurse	Stu.nurse	Nurse	Nurse	M
l.opr.	Clerical	M	M	M
c.lab.	M	M	M	M
no.	Steno.	———	M	M
.es	Clerical	M	Clerical	M
erical	M	M	M	M
okkpr.	M	M	M	M
amstress	Seamstress	M	Seamstress	M
l.opr.	M	M	M	M
l.opr.	Tel.opr.	M	M	M
u.	Dental asst.	M	Dental asst.	M
okkpr.	M	M	M	M
u.ed.	Waitress	M	M	M
u.nurse	Stu.nurse	Nurse	M	M
ancing instr.	M	M	M	———
lerical	M	———	M	———
lerical	Stu.ed.	Teacher	Teacher el.	Teacher el.
lerical	Stu.ed.	Teacher	M	M
ookkpr.	M	M	M	M
tu.med.tech.	M	M	Divorced	———
tu.mus.ed.	Stu.mus.ed.	M	Mus.Teacher	M
Off.mach.opr.	Stu.nurse	M	Stu.sec.ed.	M
Clerical	Clerical	M	M	M
tu.el.ed.	Stu.el.ed.	M	M	M
tu.sec.ed.	Stu.el.ed.	Teacher	Teacher el.	M
Stu.sec.ed.	Stu.sec.ed.	Teacher	M	M
tu.sec.ed.	Stu.sec.ed.	M	M	M
Clerical	Steno.	M	M	M
Stu.nurse	Clerical	M	M	M
Mach.opr.	Clerical	M	M	M
Nurses aide	M	M	M	M
Clerical	Clerical	M	M	M
Sales	M	M	M	M
Off.mach.opr.	M	M	M	M
Waitress	M	M	M	M
Stu.psych.	Stu.psych.	M	Stu.social wkr.	M
Stu.jour.	Stu.sec.ed.	Writer	Teacher	M
Fac.lab.	M	M	M	M
Stu.sec.ed.	Stu.sec.ed.	M	M	M
Receptionist	Dental asst.	M	M	M
M	M	M	M	M

Case No.	Grade 10 Interview	Grade 11 Interview	5-Year Future Choice at Grade 11 Interview	Grade 12 Interview Choice	Choice 1 Month Before Graduation	5-Year Fu Choice 1 Mont Before Graduat
193	Governess	M	M	U	Nurses aide	M
200	Nurse	Nurse	Nurse	Nurse	Stu.nurse	Nurse
211	Clerical	Clerical	M	U	M	M
216	Clerical	Clerical	Clerical	Steno.	Clerical	M
222	Teacher	Teacher	U	Nurse	Stu.nurse	Nurse
227	U	U	M	M	M	M
229	Clerical	Teacher	Clerical	Beautician	Tel.opr.	Tel.opr.
244	Nurse	Nurse	Nurse	Teacher	Stu.el.ed.	M
255	Horse raiser	Horse raiser	Horse raiser	Horse raiser	Fac.lab.	Horse rais
256	Clerical	U	Clerical	U	Clerical	M
264	Steno.	Steno.	M	Steno.	Steno.	M
269	U	U	U	U	U	U
273	Clerical	U	M	Clerical	Clerical	U
279	Veterinarian	Writer	Writer	Teacher	Stu.home ec.	Teacher
286	Clerical	Clerical	M	Steno.	Clerical	M
293	Teacher	U	M	U	Stu.L&S	Psych.
296	Teacher	Psych.	Stu.L&S	Teacher	Stu.sec.ed.	Teacher
308	Clerical	Beautician	Beautician	Beautician	Domestic	Beautician
316	Clerical	Clerical	Clerical	Steno.	Steno.	Steno.
319	Clerical	Teacher	M	Teacher	Stu.sec.ed.	Teacher
325	Physician	Med.tech.	M	Phys.ther.	Stu.sec.ed.	Social wkr.
330	Social wkr.	Beautician	Social wkr.	Clerical	Clerical	M
337	Clerical	Clerical	M	Nurse	Nurses aide	M
338	Clerical	Clerical	U	Prac. nurse	Nurses aide	M
341	U	Nurse	———	Nurse	Stu.sec.ed.	Teacher
344	Clerical	Clerical	Steno.	Model	Stu.mod.sch.	Model
345	Nurse	Stewardess	Bus.exec.	U	Waitress	Stewardess
350	Teacher	Teacher	M	M	M	M
358	Clerical	Teacher	U	Teacher	Stu.nurse	Nurse
359	Teacher	Of.mach.opr.	Singer	Teacher	Off.mach.op.	M
361	Teacher	Clerical	M	Sales	Sales	Mgr.ret.str.
365	Teacher	U	M	M	M	M
373	Teacher	Teacher	Teacher	Teacher	Stu.el.ed.	Teacher
377	Greenh's wk.	Forest ranger	Rancher	Greenh's wk.	Clerical	U
379	Clerical	Clerical	M	Steno.	Clerical	M
382	Clerical	Nurse	Clerical	Nurse	Stu.nurse	M
384	Clerical	Clerical	Clerical	Tel.opr.	Tel.opr.	Tel.opr.
385	Stewardess	Teacher	M	U	M	M
406	Chemist	Teacher	Nurse	Teacher	Tel.opr.	Teacher el.
407	Clerical	Model	Model	Model	Sales	Model
411	Nurse	Nurse	Med.tech.	Nurse	U	Nurse

Activity 6 onths After raduation	Activity 2½ Years After Graduation	5-Year Future Choice 2½ Years After Graduation	Activity 5 Years After Graduation	5-Year Future Choice 5 Years After Graduation
	M	M	M	M
ırses aide	Prac.nurse	M	Prac.nurse	M
erical	M	M	M	M
f.mach.opr.	M	M	M	M
ı.nurse	Stu.nurse	M	M	M
	M	M	M	M
:l.opr.	M	M	M	M
u.el.ed.	Stu.el.ed.	M	M	M
ıc.lab.	Fac.lab.	M	Clerical	U
el.opr.	Tel.opr.	M	Tel.opr.	M
lerical	M	M	M	M
:u.L&S	Stu.L&S	Teacher	M	M
'nemployed	M	M	M	M
tu.home ec.	Stu.home ec.	Dietician	Dietician	M
.lerical	M	M	M	M
tu.L&S.	Stu.bus.adm.	M	M	M
tu.sec.ed.	Stu.sec.ed.	M	Teacher sec.	M
ales	M	M	M	M
Clerical	Clerical	M	Clerical	M
ѕtu.sec.ed.	M	M	M	M
ѕtu.sec.ed.	Stu.sec.ed.	M	M	M
Clerical	M	M	M	M
Clerical	M	M	M	M
Clerical	Stewardess	M	———	M
Stu.sec.ed.	Mach.tender	U	Fac.assembler	Fac.assembler
Clerical	Clerical	Model	M	M
Waitress	Stu.nurse	Nurse	M	M
M	M	M	M	M
Stu.nurse	Stu.nurse	M	M	M
Phot.asst.	M	M	M	M
Clerical	Clerical	M	M	M
Off.mach.opr.	M	M	M	M
Stu.el.ed.	Stu.el.ed.	M	M	M
Insp.laundry	Sales	———	Sales	Mgr.ret.str.
Clerical	Clerical	M	M	M
Stu.nurse	Stu.nurse	M	Unemployed	M
Tel.opr.	M	M	M	M
M	M	M	M	M
Tel.opr.	Tel.opr.	U	M	M
Waitress	M	M	M	M
Clerical	Clerical	———	Clerical	M

Case No.	Grade 10 Interview	Grade 11 Interview	5-Year Future Choice at Grade 11 Interview	Grade 12 Interview Choice	Choice 1 Month Before Graduation	5-Year Fu Choice 1 Mont Before Graduati
413	Teacher	Teacher	Med.tech.	Med.tech.	Stu.med.tech.	Med.tech.
416	Steno.	Steno.	Steno.	Steno.	Steno.	M
419	Singer	Singer	Singer	U	Beautician	Singer
426	Teacher	Teacher	Teacher	Teacher	Stu.sec.ed.	Teacher
430	Beautician	Dietician	Dietician	Dietician	Stu. home ec.	M
431	Nurse	Nurse	Nurse	Nurse	Stu.nurse	Nurse
435	Nurse	U	U	Teacher	Stu.el.ed.	Teacher
436	Clerical	Clerical	M	Steno.	——	M
437	Clerical	Clerical	Clerical	Steno.	M	Clerical
438	Clerical	Scout exec.	Scout exec.	U	Stu.L&S	M
446	AF	Clerical	M	Stewardess	Waitress	Stewardess
449	Model	M	M	M	M	M
451	Stu.agr.	Animal husb.	Farmer	Farmer	Stu.mod.sch.	M
456	Clerical	Clerical	Receptionist	Steno.	Steno.	Receptionis
462	Nurse	Nurse	M	Nurse	Stu.nurse	Nurse
468	Reporter	Reporter	Reporter	Reporter	Stu.L&S	M
473	Musician	Musician	Musician	Social wkr.	Stu.el.ed.	U
483	Clerical	Teacher	Teacher	M	U	M
487	Sales	Clerical	Pro.ath.	Clerical	Pro.ath.	U
494	Clerical	Clerical	Stu.	Cook	M	M
500	Teacher	Teacher	Teacher sec.	Teacher	Bookkpr.	Teacher sec.
508	Nurse	Nurse	Nurse	Stewardess	Clerical	Stewardess
511	Reporter	Reporter	M	U	Receptionist	M
521	Teacher	Writer	Writer	Writer	Stu.jour.	Writer
524	Clerical	Clerical	Clerical	Clerical	Clerical	M
526	Nurse	Nurse	Nurse	Nurse	Stu.nurse	Nurse
528	Clerical	Clerical	Clerical	Clerical	Clerical	Steno.
529	Clerical	Clerical	Clerical	Clerical	Clerical	Clerical
535	Clerical	Clerical	M	Clerical	Clerical	M
540	Teacher	Teacher	Teacher	Teacher	Stu.el.ed.	Teacher
543	Teacher	Teacher	Teacher	Teacher	Stu.ed.	M
547	Teacher	Writer	Writer	U	Stu.sec.ed.	Stewardess
550	Teacher	Teacher	Bus.exec.	Teacher	AF	M
551	Florist	Florist	M	Florist	Bookkpr.	M
562	Artist	Clerical	U	Clerical	Clerical	M
564	Teacher	Recreat.wkr.	Recreat.wkr.	Teacher	Stu.el.ed.	Recreat.wkr.
565	Farmer	Clerical	M	Clerical	Clerical	M
567	Teacher	Teacher	Teacher	U	U	M
568	Nurse	Nurse	Nurse	Nurse	M	Nurse
574	Clerical	Clerical	U	Clerical	Clerical	M
577	Nurse	Phys.ther.	M	Social wkr.	Stu.psych.	Social wkr.

tivity 6 ths After duation	Activity 2½ Years After Graduation	5-Year Future Choice 2½ Years After Graduation	Activity 5 Years After Graduation	5-Year Future Choice 5 Years After Graduation
ned.tech.	Stu.med.tech.	M	M	M
mployed	Timekeeper	M	M	M
lab.	Unemployed	Waitress	Fac.assembler	M
sec.ed.	Stu.sec.ed.	Teacher sec.	Teacher sec.	Teacher sec.
ier	Stu.home ec.	M	M	M
nurse	Stu.nurse	M	M	M
el.ed.	Stu.el.ed.	M	M	M
ical	M	M	M	M
	M	M	M	M
.mach.opr.	M	M	M	M
rical	Clerical	M	M	M
	M	M	M	M
mer	Farmer	Farmer	M	M
rical	Clerical	M	M	M
.nurse	Stu.nurse	M	M	M
.L&S	M	M	M	M
.el.ed.	Stu.el.ed.	Teacher el.	Teacher el.	M
.opr.	M	M	M	M
ck clerk	M	M	M	U
f.mach.opr.	M	M	M	M
nk teller	M	M	M	M
ceptionist	M	M	M	M
erical	M	M	M	M
1.sec.ed.	Stu.sec.ed.	Teacher sec.	Teacher sec.	M
	M	M	M	M
1.nurse	M	M	M	M
ff.mach.opr.	Timekeeper	M	M	M
nemployed	Clerical	M	M	M
lerical	M	M	M	M
u.el.ed.	Stu.el.ed.	M	Teacher el.	M
u.ed.	Teacher	M	M	M
u.sec.ed.	Stu.sec.ed.	M	M	M
F	M	M	M	M
ookkpr.	M	M	M	M
lerical	Bank teller	Bank teller	M	M
tu.el.ed.	Stu.el.ed.	M	Teacher el.	M
lerical	M	M	M	M
tu.el.ed.	Stu.el.ed.	M	M	M
ɅI	M	M	M	M
Clerical	Clerical	U	Clerical	M
tu.psych.	Stu. psych.	———	M	M

Case No.	Grade 10 Interview	Grade 11 Interview	5-Year Future Choice at Grade 11 Interview	Grade 12 Interview Choice	Choice 1 Month Before Graduation	5-Year Fu[t] Choice a[t] 1 Mont[h] Before Graduati[on]
580	Clerical	Beautician	Beautician	Clerical	M	M
582	Clerical	Clerical	Clerical	Clerical	Clerical	M
587	Clerical	Clerical	M	Clerical	Clerical	M
597	Clerical	U	U	Clerical	U	Steno.
599	Teacher	Clerical	Steno.	Clerical	Clerical	Teacher
602	Clerical	Clerical	Clerical	Teltypestr.	Teltypestr.	Teltypest
606	U	Scientist	Stu.L&S	U	Stu.recreat.	U
611	Funl.dir.	Funl.dir.	Clerical	Clerical	Clerical	Clerical
613	Artist	Artist	Artist	Artist	Clerical	M
619	Artist	Artist	Artist	Artist	Stu.art	M
623	Pro.ath.	Pro.ath.	Pro.ath.	Clerical	Receptionist	———
625	Teacher	Teacher	Teacher	Teacher	Stu.el.ed.	M
629	Nurse	Psych.	U	Clerical	Stu.bus.coll.	M
635	Teacher	Teacher	Teacher	Artist	Stu.art	Artist
637	Nurse	U	Singer	M	M	M
643	Teacher	U	Med.tech.	U	Stu.med.tech.	U
645	Teacher	Clerical	Artist	Clerical	M	Clerical
646	Clerical	Clerical	M	Clerical	Clerical	M
654	Clerical	Clerical	M	Clerical	Clerical	M
660	Clerical	Clerical	———	Clerical	Clerical	———
661	Teacher	Teacher	Home ec.	U	Stu.el.ed.	Teacher
666	Teacher	Med.tech.	Med.tech.	M	Med.tech.	M
673	Artist	Artist	Artist	Artist	Stu.sec.ed.	Teacher
674	U	Clerical	M	Clerical	Clerical	Nurse
675	U	U	Singer	U	Sales	M
679	Receptionist	Receptionist	Clerical	Clerical	Clerical	Clerical
682	Domestic	M	M	Governess	U	M
683	Teacher	Teacher	Teacher	Teacher	Stu.el.ed.	Teacher el
689	Nurse	Stewardess	Stewardess	Tel.opr.	Clerical	M
692	Clerical	Clerical	M	Clerical	Tel.opr.	M
707	Clerical	Inter.dec.	M	Clerical	Clerical	M
709	U	U	U	Teacher	Stu.home ec.	U
721	Clerical	Clerical	M	Clerical	Clerical	M
723	Florist	Florist	Florist	Clerical	Clerical	M
725	Nurse	Nurse	Nurse	Nurse	Stu.bus.coll.	Nurse
734	Clerical	Clerical	M	Clerical	Clerical	M
737	Beautician	Beautician	Beautician	Clerical	Clerical	M
751	Teacher	U	Bus.exec.	U	Stu.sec.ed.	M
757	Beautician	Beautician	M	M	M	M
762	Designer	Writer	Writer	Waitress	Waitress	Waitress
766	Missionary	Missionary	M	U	Stu.sec.ed.	U

tivity 6 iths After duation	Activity 2½ Years After Graduation	5-Year Future Choice 2½ Years After Graduation	Activity 5 Years After Graduation	5-Year Future Choice 5 Years After Graduation
	M	M	M	M
ical	M	———	M	M
ical	M	M	M	M
ical	M	M	M	M
mach.opr.	Off.mach.opr.	M	Off.mach.opr.	M
ypestr.	M	U	M	M
recreat.	Stu.recreat.	Teacher	M	M
rical	Clerical	M	Med.secy.	M
rical	M	M	M	M
s	M	M	M	M
eptionist	Receptionist	M	M	M
el.ed.	M	M	M	M
rical	Clerical	M	Med.secy.	M
art.	Stu.art	Artist	Teacher sec.	Teacher coll.
	M	M	M	M
.med.tech.	Stu.occ.ther.	M	M	M
	M	M	M	M
rical	M	M	M	M
rical	Off.mach.opr.	M	Packer	M
erical	Clerical	M	M	M
.el.ed.	Stu.el.ed.	Teacher el.	Teacher el.	M
eno.	Stu.med.tech.	M	M	M
ı.sec.ed.	Sales	M	M	M
erical	Clerical	M	M	M
erical	M	M	M	M
ceptionist	M	M	M	M
u.prac.nurse	M	M	M	M
u.el.ed.	Stu.el.ed.	U	Teacher el.	M
les	M	M	M	M
el.opr.	Tel.opr.	M	M	M
lerical	M	M	M	M
u.home ec.	Stu.home ec.	M	M	M
lerical	Clerical	M	Steno.	M
lerical	M	M	M	M
tu.nurse	Stu.nurse	M	M	M
lerical	M	M	M	M
ashier	Cashier	M	M	M
tock clerk	Clerical	M	M	M
M	M	M	M	M
Waitress	M	M	M	M
Stu.sec.ed.	Stu.sec.ed.	Teacher sec.	Teacher sec.	M

Vocational or Training Choices and Activities

Case No.	Grade 10 Interview	Grade 11 Interview	5-Year Future Choice at Grade 11 Interview	Grade 12 Interview Choice	Choice 1 Month Before Graduation	5-Year Future Choice at 1 Month Before Graduation
776	Singer	U	Singer	Clerical	Clerical	Clerical
782	Clerical	Clerical	Teacher	Clerical	Clerical	Teacher
785	U	U	M	U	Stu.L&S	M
790	Nurse	Sales	M	Sales	Sales	M
801	Clerical	Clerical	Clerical	Clerical	———	———
804	Teacher	Clerical	M	U	Clerical	U
806	Nurse	Nurse	Nurse	Nurse	Stu.nurse	Nurse
810	Writer	U	Interpreter	Singer	Stu.music	M
818	U	Clerical	M	M	M	M
820	Clerical	U	M	U	Clerical	M
822	Clerical	Clerical	Clerical	Clerical	M	M
827	Clerical	Clerical	Receptionist	Clerical	M	M
829	U	U	M	U	Clerical	———
841	Nurse	Nurse	Nurse	Nurse	Stu.nurse	M
853	Teacher	Teacher	Teacher	Clerical	U	M
859	Nurse	Stewardess	Stewardess	U	Stu.nurse	U
864	Stewardess	U	M	U	Clerical	M

xperimental Girls Tenth Grade to Ten Years After High School (*Continued*)

Activity 6 Months After Graduation	Activity 2½ Years After Graduation	5-Year Future Choice 2½ Years After Graduation	Activity 5 Years After Graduation	5-Year Future Choice 5 Years After Graduation
aker	M	M	M	M
lerical	Unemployed	M	M	M
tu.sec.ed.	Stu.sec.ed.	M	M	M
ales	M	M	M	M
lerical	M	M	M	M
lerical	M	M	M	M
lerical	Clerical	M	M	M
tu.music	Stu.sec.ed.	M	Edit.work	M
M	M	M	M	M
lerical	Acct. clerk	M	M	M
M	M	M	M	M
M	M	M	M	M
Clerical	Clerical	M	M	M
Stu.prac.nrs.	Prac.nurse	M	M	M
Off.mach.opr.	Off.mach.opr.	Clerical	M	M
Tel.opr.	M	M	M	M
Receptionist	Receptionist	M	M	M

Vocational or Training Preferences, Choices and Activities of Control Girls from the Tenth Grade to Ten Years After High School

Case No.	Grade 10 Interview	Choice 1 Month Before Graduation	5-Year Future Choice at 1 Month Before Graduation	Activity 6 Months After Graduation	Activity 2½ Years After Graduation	5 Year Future Choice 2½ Years After Graduation	Activity 5 Years After Graduation	5 Year Future Choice 5 Years After Graduation
001	Nurse	Stu.nurse	Nurse	Stu.nurse	Med.tech.	M	M	M
007	U	Fac.lab.	———	Laundry lab.	Sorter	Fac.lab.	M	M
012	Clerical	Model	Model	Receptionist	Clerical	M	M	M
014	Clerical	Stu.nurse	Nurse	Waitress	Clerical	U	Stewardess	Stewardess
015	Clerical	AF	M	M	M	———	M	M
025	U	Stu.	Teacher	Stu.sec.ed.	M	M	M	M
030	Saleswork	Clerical	M	M	M	M	M	M
034	Clerical	U	Beautician	Mail clk.	Clerical	M	Clerical	M
041	Clerical	———	———	Bobbin winder	M	M	M	M
047	Saleswork	Clerical	Clerical	Clerical	Clerical	M	M	M
051	Clerical	Steno.	M	Teltypestr.	M	M	M	M
062	Clerical	Tel.opr.	M	Clerical	Reserv.clk.	M	Ticket agent	M
066	Physician	Beautician	M	Off.mach.opr.	M	M	M	M
067	Scientist	Stu.sec.ed.	Teacher sec.	Stu.sec.ed.	Stu.sec.ed.	Counselor	Teacher sec.	———
068	Scientist	Stu.med.tech.	Teacher	Stu.sec.ed.	Stu.sec.ed.	M	M	M
070	Clerical	Beautician	Beautician	Clerical	Clerical	Beautician	Clerical	M
074	Teacher	Clerical	M	Clerical	Clerical	M	Clerical	M
078	Teacher	Stu.el.ed.	Teacher	Stu.el.ed.	Stu.el.ed.	M	M	M
085	Clerical	Clerical	M	M	M	———	M	M
087	Nurse	AF	AF	Tel.opr.	M	M	M	M
088	Inter.dec.	M	M	M	M	M	M	M
090	Social wkr.	Stu.nurse	M	Stu.L&S	M	M	M	M
092	Clerical	Clerical	Dancer	Stu.off.mach.	Off.mach.opr.	U	M	M

098	Artist	Tel.opr.	Med.tech.	Tel.opr.	Tel.opr.	M	Super.tel.opr.	———
105	Clerical	M	M	M	M	M	M	M
109	Physician	Stu.dental hyg.	M	Stu.dental hyg.	M	M	M	M
116	Physician	Stu.sec.ed.	Teacher	Stu.sec.ed.	Stu.sec.ed.	Actress	Teacher sec.	M
128	Social wkr.	Stu.soc.wkr.	Social wkr.	Stu.soc.wk.	Stu.soc.wk.	Social wkr.	Employ.coun.	M
136	Clerical	Clerical	Prop.sm.bus.	Clerical	Clerical	M	M	M
139	Nurse	Stu.el.ed.	U	Stu.home ec.	Stu.home ec.	Prop.text.co.	M	M
143	Clerical	Clerical	M	Clerical	Clerical	M	M	M
148	Teacher	Receptionist	M	M	M	M	M	M
155	Clerical	Clerical	M	Clerical	M	M	M	M
163	Clerical	Clerical	———	Clerical	M	M	M	M
167	Designer	Saleswork	Model	Receptionist	M	M	M	M
168	Clerical	Clerical	M	Clerical	M	M	M	M
170	Artist	Clerical	———	Clerical	Clerical	M	M	M
172	Clerical	Tel.opr.	U	Tel.opr.	M	M	M	M
174	Nurse	Stu.nurse	Nurse	Stu.nurse	M	M	M	M
178	U	Stu.nurse	Nurse	Stu.nurse	Stu.nurse	M	Nurse	M
181	Clerical	Clerical	Clerical	Clerical	M	M	M	M
188	Scientist	Stu.L&S	Lab.tecs.	Stu.L&S	Stu.recreat.	Recreat.wkr.	Scout exec.	Scout exec.
194	Teacher	Stu.el.ed.	Home ec.	Stu.home ec.	Seamstress	M	M	M
197	U	Stu.sec.ed.	Teacher sec.	Stu.sec.ed.	Stu.sec.ed.	M	M	M
208	Phys.ther.	Stu.secy.	M	Stu.secy.	M	M	M	M
210	Missionary	Stu.L&S	Missionary	Stu.L&S	Stu.L&S	Stu.sec.ed.	M	M
212	Clerical	U	M	Tel.opr.	M	M	M	M
214	Physician	Stu.el.ed.	U	Stu.L&S	Stu.L&S	M	Stu.soc.wk.	M
217	Dietician	Stu.el.ed.	Teacher	Stu.el.ed.	Stu.el.ed.	M	M	M
220	Prac.nurse	Med.secy.	———	Nurse's aide	M	M	M	M
221	Farmer	Stu.agr.sch.	Physician	Stu.agr.	Stu.agr.	Rancher	Stu.agr.	M
226	Designer	M	Model	Bookkpr.	M	M	M	M
241	Occ.ther.	Stu.occ.ther.	Occ.ther.	Stu.occ.ther.	Stu.occ.ther.	M	M	M

Vocational or Training Preferences, Choices and Activities of Control Girls from the Tenth Grade to Ten Years After High School (*Continued*)

Case No.	Grade 10 Interview	Choice 1 Month Before Graduation	5-Year Future Choice at 1 Month Before Graduation	Activity 6 Months After Graduation	Activity 2½ Years After Graduation	5 Year Future Choice 2½ Years After Graduation	Activity 5 Years After Graduation	5 Year Future Choice 5 Years After Graduation
248	Teacher	Stu.sec.ed.	Interpreter	Stu.sec.ed.	Stu.sec.ed.	M	Unemployed	M
257	Beautician	Clerical	M	Clerical	M	M	M	M
261	Clerical	Clerical	M	Clerical	Clerical	M	Clerical	M
262	Nurse	Stu.nurse	Nurse	Stu.med.tech.	Off.mach. opr.	M	M	M
265	Teacher	Tel.opr.	M	Tel.opr.	Tel.opr.	———	M	M
272	Teacher	Stu.el.ed.	M	Stu.el.ed.	Stu.el.ed.	M	M	M
274	Clerical	Soda dispenser	M	Soda dispenser	M	M	M	M
275	U	M	———	M	M	M	M	M
277	Clerical	Clerical	M	Clerical	M	M	M	M
288	Florist	Steno.	Clerical	U	Clerical	M	M	M
306	Writer	Stu.el.ed.	Teacher	Stu.el.ed.	Stu.el.ed.	M	M	M
307	Artist	Stu.art	Artist	Stu.art	Stu.bus.sch.	M	M	M
312	Clerical	Clerical	M	Tel.opr.	M	M	M	M
315	Clerical	Receptionist	M	Clerical	Off.mach.opr.	M	M	M
317	Singer	Clerical	Clerical	Clerical	Machine opr.	M	M	M
323	Artist	Clerical	Stu.L&S	Clerical	Stu.L&S	M	Stu.L&S	Teacher el.
328	Clerical	Clerical	M	Clerical	M	M	M	M
334	Inter.dec.	Saleswork	U	Machine tndr.	M	M	M	M
336	Civil service	Steno.	M	Clerical	Clerical	M	M	M
339	Clerical	Clerical	M	Clerical	Clerical	M	M	M
340	Clerical	Clerical	M	Clerical	Payroll clk.	M	M	M
342	Clerical	Clerical	M	Clerical	Clerical	M	M	M
346	Nurse	AF	Nurse	Unemployed	M	———	M	M

347	Social wkr.	Stu.psych.	Stu.L&S	Stu.L&S	Reserv.clk.	M	Personnel wkr.	Bus.adm.
348	Nurse	Clerical	U	Clerical	Cost clk.	M	M	M
349	Nurse	Stu.nurse	Nurse	Cashier	Clerical	M	M	M
352	Clerical	Stu.floral wk.	Florist	Florist	Florist	Florist	M	M
357	Saleswork	M	M	Tel.opr.	M	M	M	M
362	U	Stu.bus.adm.	M	Stu.bus.adm.	M	———	M	M
366	Clerical	Steno.	M	Clerical	M	M	M	M
372	Bookkpr.	Bookkpr.	Bookkpr.	Bookkpr.	Bookkpr.	Bookkpr.	M	M
374	Nurse	Waitress	Saleswork	Waitress	Clerical	———	M	M
397	Clerical	U	Steno.	Packer	Clerical	M	M	M
399	Clerical	Clerical	Clerical	Clerical	Clerical	M	M	M
400	Clerical	Clerical	Clerical	Clerical	Bookkpr.	M	M	M
410	Clerical	Clerical	Clerical	Clerical	Clerical	U	Clerical	M
415	Fac.lab.	Steno.	Steno.	Clerical	Clerical	M	Steno.	M
425	Nurse	Stu.nurse	Nurse	Stu.nurse	Stu.nurse	Nurse	M	M
432	Nurse	Stu.nurse	Nurse	Stu.nurse	Stu.nurse	M	M	M
442	Clerical	Clerical	M	Clerical	M	M	M	M
443	Scout exec.	Receptionist	Clerical	Clerical	Clerical	Clerical	Clerical	M
444	Clerical	Clerical	Dancer	Receptionist	Receptionist	M	M	M
447	Clerical	Stu.	Teacher el.	Stu.el.ed.	M	M	M	M
457	U	Clerical	Clerical	Clerical	Clerical	M	Clerical	M
463	Clerical	M	M	M	M	M	M	M
465	Clerical	Clerical	M	Clerical	Payroll clk.	M	M	———
470	Clerical	Tel.opr.	AF	Clerical	M	M	M	M
472	Teacher	Clerical	Clerical	M	M	M	M	M
480	Beautician	U	M	Stu.nurse	Stu.nurse	Nurse	Nurse	Nurse
481	Clerical	Clerical	M	Off.mach. opr.	M	M	M	M
485	Clerical	Clerical	Clerical	Clerical	Clerical	M	Clerical	M
489	Civil service	Clerical	M	Clerical	Clerical	M	M	M
495	Clerical	Stu.bus.coll.	———	Mail clk.	M	M	M	M

Vocational or Training Preferences, Choices and Activities of Control Girls from the Tenth Grade to Ten Years After High School (*Continued*)

Case No.	Grade 10 Interview	Choice 1 Month Before Graduation	5-Year Future Choice at 1 Month Before Graduation	Activity 6 Months After Graduation	Activity 2½ Years After Graduation	5 Year Future Choice 2½ Years After Graduation	Activity 5 Years After Graduation	5 Year Future Choice 5 Years After Graduation
496	Clerical	Stu.sec.ed.	M	Clerical	Clerical	M	Clerical	M
501	Clerical	Stu.nurse	M	Nurse's aide	M	M	M	M
505	Clerical	U	Model	Packer	M	M	M	M
512	Musician	Clerical	M	Clerical	M	M	M	M
513	Clerical	Clerical	M	M	M	M	M	M
517	Clerical	Clerical	M	Clerical	Clerical	M	M	M
520	Writer	Stu.	Soc.wkr.	Stu.	Stu.	M	M	M
527	Teacher	Drill prs.opr.	Clerical	Tel.opr.	M	M	M	M
539	M	Clerical	M	Clerical	M	M	M	M
548	Nurse	U	U	Fac.seamstress	Clerical	U	M	M
549	Clerical	Clerical	U	Clerical	Unemployed	———	M	———
552	Clerical	Stu.secy.sch.	Med.secy.	Stu.secy.sch.	Clerical	M	M	M
557	Teacher	———	———	Stu.off.mach.	M	M	M	M
561	Teacher	Stu.el.ed.	Teacher	Stu.el.ed.	Teacher	Teacher	Teacher	Teacher
563	Clerical	———	———	Clerical	M	M	M	M
570	Phot.	Saleswork	M	Saleswork	M	M	M	M
575	Clerical	Tel.opr.	M	Tel.opr.	M	M	M	M
589	Teacher	U	U	Off.mach.opr.	M	M	Divorced	———
594	Teacher	Clerical	M	Clerical	Dental asst.	M	M	M
600	U	Steno.	M	Clerical	Clerical	M	M	M
608	Teacher	M	M	M	M	M	M	M
618	Clerical	Steno.	M	Clerical	Stu.nurse	Nurse	Stu.nurse	M
626	Teacher	Waitress	M	Waitress	M	M	M	M

628	Nurse	Stu.nurse	Nurse	Clerical	Stu.nurse	M	M	M
632	Artist	Stu.L&S	U	Stu.L&S	Stu.jour.	U	M	M
636	Nurse	AF	Prop.sm.bus.	Waitress	Unemployed	M	Cook	Prop.rest.
653	Clerical	Clerical	M	Clerical	Clerical	M	Clerical	M
655	Teacher	Stu.norm.sch.	Waitress	M	M	M	M	M
656	Nurse	Stu.nurse	Nurse	Stu.nurse	Stu.nurse	M	M	M
662	Teacher	Stu.el.ed.	Teacher	Stu.el.ed.	Stu.el.ed.	Teacher el.	Teacher el.	M
665	Dietician	Stu.home ec.	Dietician	Bookkpr.	AF	M	Cashier	M
668	Clerical	Stu.el.ed.	Teacher	Stu.norm.sch.	M	M	Divorced	M
670	Teacher	Fac.lab.	M	Expediter	M	M	M	M
678	Nurse	Stu.nurse	M	Stu.nurse	Stu.nurse	M	M	M
684	Seamstress	Seamstress	M	Bank msgr.	Clerical	M	M	M
685	AF	U	M	Unemployed	M	M	M	M
686	Clerical	Clerical	U	Clerical	Clerical	M	Clerical	M
688	Lab.tech.	Stu.pharm.	U	Stu.pharm.	Stu.pharm.	M	Pharmacist	M
696	Inter.dec.	Stu.occ.ther.	Occ.ther.	Stu.L&S	Manag. tr.	———	Mgr.ret.str.	Mgr.ret.str.
697	Clerical	Clerical	Clerical	Sales work	Clerical	M	M	M
701	Nurse	Stu.nurse	Nurse	Stu.L&S	M	M	M	M
702	Clerical	Clerical	M	Clerical	M	M	M	M
704	Clerical	Clerical	M	Clerical	Clerical	M	M	M
719	Teacher	Stu.el.ed.	Teacher	Stu.L&S	Clerical	———	Cashier	M
720	Clerical	Clerical	U	Clerical	Clerical	U	Clerical	Clerical
722	Clerical	Tel.opr.	M	Tel.opr.	Drill prs.opr.	———	M	M
730	Nurse	Stu.nurse	Missionary	Stu.nurse	M	M	M	M
731	Social wkr.	Clerical	Steno.	Clerical	M	M	M	M
733	Clerical	Tel.opr.	M	Tel.opr.	M	M	M	M
742	Nurse	Stu.el.ed.	Med.secy.	Stu.el.ed.	Stu.el.ed.	M	M	M
748	AF	U	AF	Teacher asst.	M	M	M	M
749	Beautician	M	M	M	M	M	M	M
753	Nurse	Stu.nurse	M	Stu.nurse	Stu.nurse	M	M	M

Vocational or Training Preferences, Choices and Activities of Control Girls from the Tenth Grade to Ten Years After High School (*Continued*)

Case No.	Grade 10 Interview	Choice 1 Month Before Graduation	5-Year Future Choice at 1 Month Before Graduation	Activity 6 Months After Graduation	Activity 2½ Years After Graduation	5 Year Future Choice 2½ Years After Graduation	Activity 5 Years After Graduation	5 Year Future Choice 5 Years After Graduation
755	Clerical	Clerical	———	Clerical	M	M	M	M
763	Nurse	Stu.nurse	M	M	M	M	M	M
765	U	U	Artist	Packer	Packer	Packer	M	M
767	Clerical	Clerical	M	Off.mach.opr.	M	M	M	M
775	Beautician	Sales work	———	Sales work	M	M	M	M
780	Musician	M	M	M	M	M	M	M
783	U	Stu.nurse	Bus.exec.	Fac.lab.	Stu.prac.nurse	U	M	M
786	Teacher	Clerical	M	M	M	M	M	M
787	Teacher	U	U	Clerical	Clerical	M	Clerical	M
788	Artist	AF	Nurse	M	M	M	M	M
792	Teacher	Stu.secy.sch.	———	Stu.secy.sch.	Buyer	Buyer	M	M
809	Tel.opr.	Waitress	———	Unemployed	Unemployed	———	———	U
813	Clerical	Clerical	Clerical	Unemployed	M	———	M	M
816	Teacher	Nurse's aide	Teacher	Sales work	M	M	M	M
821	Beautician	Receptionist	Receptionist	Clerical	M	M	M	M
825	Clerical	Clerical	M	Clerical	M	M	M	M
831	Architect	Stu.home ec.	Inter.dec.	Stu.L&S	Clerical	Prop.sm.bus.	M	M
837	Social wkr.	U	Librarian	Sales	M	M	M	M
839	Clerical	Clerical	M	M	M	M	M	M
844	Teacher	Stu.sec.ed.	Teacher sec.	Stu.sec.ed.	M	M	M	M
847	Musician	Stu.mus.	Singer	Stu.mus.	M	M	M	M
849	Teacher	Stu.el.ed.	Teacher	Stu.el.ed.	Stu.	Teacher el.	Teacher el.	M
866	Nurse	Dairy lab.	M	Machine tndr.	Cook	M	M	M

APPENDIX III

First Pages of Senior Reports for Employment, Armed Forces, Married Within One Year, Farming, and Uncertain

The first pages of the Senior Report described in Chapter III which were filled out by all the subjects one month before graduation varied according to the vocational or training choices of the subject. The first page of the *education* form was given on pages 123 and 124. Those for students who chose *employment, armed forces, farming, married within one year* (girls only), and for those who were *uncertain* are presented below. They are given here so that others may use the Senior Report which, despite the limitations noted in the text, seems to have enough merit to justify its use. The actual responses of one subject in each area are given with only minor editing to prevent identification.

EMPLOYMENT SENIOR REPORT Your Name *Joseph*

City *Jonesville*

Date *May 10, 1951*

Give the name and address of someone who will always know where you will be so that they can send mail on to you.

NAME *Mrs. Mabel* ADDRESS *Box 100 Smithtown* CITY ______

1. What kind of work do you plan to do when you finish high school? Name the job and tell what you will be doing.
I plan on working in some kind of store business. Grocery store as clerk, and produce man.

2. Why did you choose this kind of work? *Because I find it very interesting and I like to meet people.*

3. When did you decide on this kind of work? Year *1949* Month *March*

4. Who, if anyone, helped you to make up your mind about the work you plan to do? *No body I made up my own mind.*

5. If more than one person helped you, who was most helpful?
______

6. If you have a promise of a definite job give the name and address of the person or company you will work for. Be sure to give the name of the city.
Company name, Smithtown

7. Is the employer a relative of yours? *No* What relation? *None*

8. Will you have an apprenticeship? *no*

9. If you do not have a job promised, name some places where they hire people to do the work you want to do. *Army-Navy*

10. If you do not get the job you want, what is your *second* choice?
Machinist or Inlist in the armed forces
Your third choice? *to be a cook*

Turn to the next page

Your Name Joseph

11. What kinds of jobs do *beginners* get in the kind of work you plan to do? clerking, check produce, read invoices, and take intfintory.

12. How much *per week* do most beginners get in this kind of work? $35.00

13. How much per week will *you* get? $ 50.00

14. What is the best job you ever expect to get in this line of work? Being a produce man. Just fruit + vegetables

15. What is there about *you* that might keep you from being successful at this work?

16. What is there about you that will make you successful at this work? I like to meet people and they say I have a very good personality.

17. If you know exactly where you are going to work, tell what you know about the place by answering these questions. If you don't know, write "don't know" on the lines.

A. Are there vacations with pay? No How much vacation per year? 1 week

B. Do they have a pension plan? ______ What do you know about it? Don't know

C. Is there a union? No If there is, do all workers belong to it? No

D. Do workers get raises for very good work? Yes

E. Do workers get regular pay raises? No How often? Don't know

F. Can a worker move up to better jobs? Yes How does a worker rise to a better job with the company? By doing good work and always finding things to do.

What is the best job a worker can reach in this type of work? Ownership

18. What, if anything, would make you change your mind about *wanting* to do this kind of work next year? The armed Forces

ARMED FORCES SENIOR REPORT Your Name *Jim*
City *Jonesville*
Date *5-4-51*

Give name and address of someone who will always know where you will be so that they can send on mail to you.

NAME *Mr. George* ADDRESS *119 Elm St.* CITY *Jonesville*

1. Check the branch of the armed services you expect to enter.
   Army_____ Navy *✓* Air Corps_____ Marines_____
2. When do you expect to enter? Year *1951* Month *September*
3. Why did you choose that branch of the service? *I thought it would be the one I would like best. Most of the fellows that I talked to that are in it, like it.*
4. Do you plan to enlist before you are drafted? *Yes*
   Why? *So that I can get in the Navy.*
5. Who, if anyone, helped you make up your mind about enlisting?
   Nobody
6. If more than one person helped you, who helped you most?
   —
7. Have you talked with enlistment officers about your plans? *No*
   Which ones?_____ When?_____
8. What are the advantages of the service you have chosen?
   Chances of learning a trade or choosing it as a career.
9. What are the disadvantages? *4 years enlistment*
10. If you have a choice of special training in the *Armed Forces* by going to their special training schools, which *one* will you choose? *Machine*
    Why? *I like that kind of work*

Turn to the next page

Name *Jim*

11. If you can't get your first choice of a special training school, what will your second and third choices be?
Second Choice *Drafting* Third *Carpenter*

12. What is there about *you* that will make you successful in the Armed Forces?
The fact that I would like it, if I would.

13. What is there about *you* that might keep you from being successful in the Armed Forces?
Don't like to take orders from everyone

14. What plans for employment or training did you have *before* you knew you were going into the Armed Forces?
Machine or Drafting

15. How has your plan about the Armed Forces changed the plans you had before?
I'm too young to get a good job. Most places won't take you as an apprentice because of the draft.

16. What, *if anything,* would make you change your mind about *wanting* to serve in the Armed Forces?
Probly, the change of the draft.

WORK ON PARENT'S FARM

SENIOR REPORT Your Name *James*

City *Jonesville*

Date *May 10, 1951*

Give the name and address of someone who will always know where you are so that they can send mail on to you.

NAME *Mr. A. B.* ADDRESS *R. 14 Box 555 Jonesville*

1. When did you definitely make up your mind that farming would be your occupation?
   Year *1951* Month *April*
2. Why did you decide you wanted this kind of work? *I like farming & I am started in farming now.*
3. Who, if anyone, helped you make up your mind about this kind of work?
   Mother & Dad & agr. teacher Mr. Carry
4. If more than one person helped you, who helped you most?
   Dad.
5. Have you made *definite arrangements* about getting paid for your share of work? *Yes* What are they? *Partnership*
6. How much *cash* would you expect to earn your first year? *$1000*
7. What other things would you expect to get in that first year? (Include such things as room and board and shares of livestock, land, and machinery.) *Room & board livestock increase by 2 shares*
8. What is there about you that will make you successful at this work? *I like farming & have had schooling & should success already*

Turn to next page

9. **What is there about you that might keep you from being successful on the farm?**

____

____

10. Do you expect to take over the farm yourself? *Yes* When? *after father retires*

11. Do you plan to attend the university short course in agriculture? *Yes* When? *1951*

12. In case we may want to visit you on the farm tell us exactly how to get there. If a map will help draw it at the bottom of this page.
4 miles east of Jonesville Hy 49

____

____

13. What, if anything, would make you change your mind about wanting to do this kind of work next year? *army*

____

____

____

SENIOR REPORT

MARRIED WITHIN
ONE YEAR
(Girls only)

Your Name *Mary*
City *Jonesboro*
Date *May 10, 1951*

Give the name and exact address of someone who will always know where you will be so that they can send mail on to you.

NAME *Mrs. Jack Olson* ADDRESS *Box 1234* CITY *Jonesboro*

1. What will your married name be? *Mrs. Jack Brown*
2. What will your address be? (If you don't know the exact address give the place, city or town, or rural route where you will get mail.) *Box 84 Jonesboro*
3. Do you plan to work at a regular job outside your home while you are married? *yes, but he doesn't really want me to.*
4. If so, what kind of work are you planning to do? *clerical work in an office*
5. How are you prepared for the kind of outside work you want to do? *yes*
6. If, for any reason, you are forced to earn your own living, how are you prepared to do so? *by getting a job in an office*
7. If you plan to work for a short period *before* your marriage, what kind of work will you do? *clerical work*
8. What kind of training do you expect to take in the future? *none*
9. When did you make up your mind to get married? *May 9, 1951*
   Month Year
   Before this but this is really when he asked me. We had talked about it before.
   What, if anything, would make you change your mind about *wanting* to be married within a year after leaving high school? *nothing*

UNCERTAIN SENIOR REPORT Your Name *Bill*
City *Smithville*
Date *May 10, 1951*

Give the name and address of someone who will always know where you are so that they can send mail on to you.

NAME *Delmar* ADDRESS *RR 4 Box 699* CITY *Smithville*

1. If you do not know what you want to do after you finish high school why are you still uncertain? *I plan to work on farm for a year or two then get a job at a filling station.*
2. What, if anything, could change you from not knowing to knowing what you will do next year? *If I am drafted in the armed forces.*
3. If you did have a definite plan before what was it? *I planning on taking up something in the armed forces.*
4. Why was it changed? *Because of the war.*
5. Who has tried to help you in planning what to do after high school? *My family*
6. If more than one person has tried to help you to make your plans, who has helped you most? *My older brother*
7. Does it bother you to feel uncertain about your future? *No*
8. In what way? *Because I know of a few different places where I could work to make a decent living.*
9. If you do not have a plan by the time you finish high school what will you do? *I will work on farm for a few years then join the service if I have not already been drafted.*

INDEXES

INDEX OF NAMES

INDEX OF SUBJECTS

Set in Intertype Garamond
Format by James T. Parker
Manufactured by Kingsport Press, Inc.
Published by HARPER & BROTHERS, *New York*